Broadband Cable
Access Networks

Broadband Cable
Access Networks
The HFC Plant

David Large
James Farmer

ELSEVIER

AMSTERDAM • BOSTON • HEIDELBERG • LONDON
NEW YORK • OXFORD • PARIS • SAN DIEGO
SAN FRANCISCO • SINGAPORE • SYDNEY • TOKYO

Morgan Kaufmann Publishers is an imprint of Elsevier

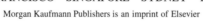

Morgan Kaufmann Publishers is an imprint of Elsevier.
30 Corporate Drive, Suite 400
Burlington, MA 01803

This book is printed on acid-free paper.

Library of Congress Cataloging-in-Publication Data

Large, David, 1940-
   Broadband cable access networks : the HFC plant / David Large,
James Farmer.—3rd ed.
      p. cm. — (Morgan Kaufmann series in networking)
   Includes bibliographical references and index.
   ISBN 978-0-12-374401-2 (alk. paper)
   1. Cable television.   2. Broadband communication systems.   3. Optical
fiber communication.   I. Farmer, James.   II. Title.   III. Title: Broadband
cable access networks, the hybrid fiber/coax plant.   IV. Title: Broadband
cable access networks, the hybrid fibre/coaxial plant.
   TK6675.L37 2008
   621.388'57–dc22   2008034236

For information on all Morgan Kaufmann publications, visit
our Web site at *www.mkp.com or www.books.elsevier.com.*

Printed in the United States

08   09   10   11   12   10 9 8 7 6 5 4 3 2 1

Contents

Acknowledgments

Much of the material in this book is based on the transmission system portion of our previous book, *Modern Cable Television Technology*, Second Edition. The material has been updated and expanded to reflect changes that have taken place in the broadband industry in the intervening four years. As with our previous works, we freely acknowledge that we stand on the shoulders of our associates, our mentors, and those who have developed and documented cable television technology.

We owe a continuing debt of gratitude to those who contributed to previous books and, additionally, to those who agreed to review the proposal and scope of this current work, including Michael Adams, Vice President of System Architecture, Tandberg TV/Ericsson Group; Dan Pike, Chief Technology Officer of GCI Cable; Joseph Van Loan, Consultant and Chair of the Xtend Networks Advisory Board; and Ray Thomas, Principal Engineer, Advanced Technology Group, Time Warner Cable; Dr. John Kenny, Wave7 Optics, an Enablence Technologies Company; and Dr. Lamar West, Cisco Systems.

We are particularly indebted to Ron Hranac, who currently works at Cisco and is Senior Technology Editor of *Communications Technology*, for his careful review of the entire book prior to publication.

Additionally, specific recognition is due to many whose work is reflected in these pages more directly. In most cases, the endnotes for each chapter document where the work of other authors and researchers has been quoted or characterized. Additionally, we acknowledge the following:

- Figure 2.12 is based on data furnished by Howard Carnes of Antec Corporation.

- Figure 4.6 is based on a figure in Ronald C. Cotten, *Lightwave Transmission Applications*, September 15, 1993 (p. 108). The graph is used with permission of CommScope, Inc., and Cable Television Laboratories Inc., Louisville, CO.

- Figures 4.10 and 4.11 are based on figures in Dogan A. Atlas, "Fiber-Induced Distortion and Phase Noise to Intensity Noise Conversion in Externally-Modulated CATV Systems," *1996 National Cable Television Association Technical Papers*, April 1996 (pp. 291–292). Washington, DC: National Cable Television Association.

- Tables 6.1 and 6.2 are adapted from material furnished by CableAML, Inc., Torrance, CA, September 5, 1997.

Finally, we are indebted to the staff at Morgan Kaufmann/Elsevier for their support and encouragement, including Rick Adams, senior acquisitions editor, who identified the need for a book aimed specifically at those who work with linear distribution systems; Maria Alonso, assistant editor; and Marilyn Rash, project manager.

About the Authors

David Large is an independent consultant whose career has included building and operating cable systems; designing products for the industry; and advising a wide variety of firms, governments, and organizations. He is a Fellow Member and Hall of Fame Honoree of the STCE, a Senior Member of the IEEE, an NCTA Science and Technology Vanguard Award Winner, and an SCTE-certified Broadband Communication Engineer.

James Farmer is Chief Technical Officer at Wave7 Optics, an Enablence Technologies Company. He has previously been with Scientific-Atlantic, ESP, and ANTEC. Jim is a Fellow of the IEEE and a Senior Member the SCTE and has served on administrative boards with both organizations. He is the recipient of the NCTA Vanguard Award in Technology and a member of the SCTE Hall of Fame.

Broadband Cable
Access Networks

Linear Broadband Distribution Systems

1.1 INTRODUCTION

Cable television systems have moved far beyond simple delivery of television programming to include high-speed data services, voice telephony, networking, transactional delivery of digital video under the interactive control of customers, and targeted advertising delivery, to name a few. To manage this complex business, what was formerly known simply as the "headend" has also evolved into a hierarchy of national, regional, and local signal processing centers. Similarly, the subscriber's premise has evolved to often include local distribution networks that allow communication among devices as well as with the external network. In the near future, communications will be provided by operators to multiple, diverse end terminals, including wireless devices. Our previous book, *Modern Cable Television Technology: Voice, Video and Data Communications*, 2nd ed. (Morgan Kaufmann, 2004) covered the entire range of technologies involved in a cable system and should be consulted for topics lying outside the scope of this volume.

At some point in this network, the modulated radio frequency (RF) signals that are to be transported to customer homes are delivered to a linear distribution network whose purpose is to deliver those same signals with no further per-signal processing and with as little degradation as economically possible. This book is devoted to that portion of the system, which we have referred to generically as the "hybrid fiber/coax (HFC) plant," although it need not always include both fiber optics and coaxial transport and may occasionally include microwave links.

The HFC plant is designed to be as transparent as possible and is characterized by its bidirectional RF bandwidth, the maximum level of various impairments to the transported signals, the number of homes or customers who share common signals, its reliability and availability, and its ability to scale to provide greater per-subscriber bandwidth as needed.

It is this portion of a cable television system that distinguishes it from, for instance, a direct-to-home satellite system; that is, a satellite provider is limited to **1** a one-way broadband path that, because of the characteristics of satellite antennas, delivers signals in common to millions of homes and, because of the characteristics of those signals, requires signal processing for every in-home television receiver. Because of the limitations of its networks, direct broadcast satellite (DBS) systems are practically limited to video distribution as their primary business.

By contrast, cable operators have the luxury of a two-way path with the ability to deliver a unique spectrum of signals to each small group of homes with a quality that is sufficiently high to support both analog video- and bandwidth-efficient digital modulation schemes. The HFC plant thus supports both broadcast and high-usage-rate transactional and two-way services.

New fiber-based telephone networks have many of the same advantages as cable, although with a different network architecture. In particular, some telephone carriers use a combination of linear and digital optical transport on different wavelengths sharing a single fiber. These emerging fiber-deep (including fiber to the home) networks are also covered in this volume.

1.2 ORGANIZATION OF THIS BOOK

We begin with the fundamentals of coaxial technology in Chapter 2, including all of the elements that make up the coaxial portion of the HFC network. In Chapter 3 we move on to coaxial distribution networks, how they are designed and powered, and the nature of signal degradation through such networks. Linear, single-wavelength fiber optics are introduced in Chapter 4, along with the signal degradation mechanisms that are unique to fiber optics. That chapter begins with some fundamental properties of light and ends with the calculated performance of complete transmitter–fiber–receiver links. Chapter 5 expands the optical topic to include multiwavelength systems and discusses at length the various ways in which the signals modulating various wavelengths in shared fibers interact to create crosstalk. Because physical plant construction is not always economically possible, linear microwave technology is still used in selected locations as an alternate interconnecting technology. Chapter 6 includes full step-by-step instructions for designing and calculating the performance of such links, including availability under predicted rainfall conditions.

In Chapter 7, we treat the entire HFC network as a system and discuss both performance requirements and typical performance of the cascaded elements. The upstream (subscriber-to-headend) direction of communications has unique characteristics, design, and alignment issues, which are treated in Chapter 8. In Chapter 9, we move to overall HFC architecture, with a look at service-specific requirements and architectural options that can address those requirements. Then Chapter 10 looks first at architectural elements and concludes with various examples of end-to-end HFC architectures. Chapter 11 complements that with a treatment of emerging fiber-deep systems, including hybrid analog/digital transport. Finally, Chapter 12 is devoted to reliability and availability, including a methodology for predicting these factors for any architecture.

Each chapter stands alone and can be referred to independently without reviewing the material leading up to it (for those who are already familiar with the subjects covered in preceding chapters), and a glossary is included to assist in identifying terms that may have been introduced earlier in the book. For those for whom broadband distribution systems are relatively new, we recommend starting with the fundamentals chapters. Because it is referred to throughout, we have included the full channelization plan for cable (CEA-542-B) as this book's appendix.

1.3 THE SOFTWARE APPLICATIONS

In a major change from previous publications, we have included with this book access to programs that allow the reader to readily duplicate some of the more complex calculations associated with predicting various aspects of the performance of HFC distribution systems. Any or all of these can be accessed through the following website: *www.elsevierdirect.com/companions/9780123744012*. The included applications and their functions are as follows:

Cascaded Noise-Distortion Calculator.xls—This Excel spreadsheet, referred to primarily in Chapter 3, allows the user to do two types of calculations: the cascaded C/N, C/CTB, and C/CSO of a system when the performance of its constituent elements are known, and the characteristics of an unknown element when the cascaded performance and the performance of other elements are known.

Single-Wavelength Performance Calculator.xls—This Excel spreadsheet, referred to in Chapter 4, predicts the C/N and C/CSO performance of a single-wavelength fiber-optic link, including contributions from transmitter RIN and chirp, shot noise, postamplifier noise, interferometric intensity noise, and phase noise.

Optical Crosstalk-Individual Mechanisms.xls—This Excel spreadsheet, referred to in Chapter 5, calculates and plots the magnitude of various individual crosstalk mechanisms as they cause interactions between two optical signals. Crosstalk mechanisms include those due to cross-polarization modulation, stimulated Raman scattering, crossphase modulation, and optical Kerr effect.

Optical Crosstalk Summary.xls—This Excel spreadsheet, also referred to in Chapter 5, is an extension of the individual mechanisms sheet that calculates the total crosstalk affecting the top, middle, and bottom optical signal when 16 DWDM optical signals share a single fiber. Total crosstalk is both calculated and plotted as a function of RF modulating frequency.

Micro.xls—This Excel spreadsheet, referred to in Chapter 6, includes all calculations required to design and calculate the performance of a linear amplitude-modulated microwave link, including path design, nominal performance, and predicted availability.

ReturnLevelCalculator-Ex2.xls—This Excel spreadsheet accompanies Chapter 8, the return path. It allows you to input parameters of your upstream transmitter, and the signals you wish to carry in the upstream direction. It then calculates the optimum signal level for each signal based on modulation type and bandwidth, and gives you the carrier-to-noise ratio to expect *for the optical portion of the upstream*. The numbers in the spreadsheet are those used to generate the second example near the end of the chapter. Instructions appear on the first page of the spreadsheet.

Soar Manual.doc and SOAR.xls—These companion applications, which are related to the material in Chapter 12, include the System Outage and Reliability Calculator Excel workbook and its companion instruction manual, a Word document. Between them they document how to analyze the reliability and availability of most HFC architectures, including those that include redundant elements, given a user-input table of component reliabilities, repair times, and how the components are interconnected. Extensive plotting of results is included.

1.4 WHY THIS BOOK

When the first edition of *Modern Cable Television Technology*, published in 1999, was about four years old, we determined that the industry had evolved sufficiently that a revision was required, leading to the second edition in 2004. Four years later, we have again reviewed the state of the industry and the need for an updated volume. The authors and publisher were concerned that a single-volume revision would simply be too large to be practical (it grew from 873 to 1053 pages between the first and second editions and a third edition would be larger still), and that there is a significant segment of the cable technical community whose job responsibilities do not extend beyond the distribution plant and for whom a comprehensive book is simply too expensive—hence the current work. We also saw an opportunity to provide distribution plant specialists with the calculation tools necessary to understand, design, and maintain linear distribution networks, and thus decided to provide online access to download application programs for the most complex calculations required in that effort.

Owners of the second edition of *Modern Cable Television Technology* will recognize that this book covers that same range of topics as Parts 4 and 5 of that work (11 of its 25 chapters). That material has been revised and updated as required to reflect changes in the intervening years. Major plant-related trends since the second edition was written include FCC standards for delivery of digital video signals, negotiated standards for digital "cable-ready" receivers, wide availability of 1-GHz equipment, an imminent change from analog over-air broadcasting to digital (and, increasingly, high-definition) video, and major deployments of wavelength multiplexing equipment as operators split existing nodes in fiber-sparse environments. On the competitive front, two of the largest telephone companies have moved aggressively into video transport, while DBS operators are rolling out large numbers of HDTV channels. It is an interesting time to be working with cable systems. We hope you find this book useful and relevant.

Coaxial RF Technology

2.1 INTRODUCTION

Cable television's technical roots are the distribution of analog television signals to the antenna terminals of customers' receivers. The least expensive way to accomplish that was to avoid the need for in-home equipment by carrying each video stream on a different, standard television channel so that subscribers could use their existing TV sets to select and view programs. Although cable systems have evolved since then into sophisticated bidirectional, multiservice networks using combinations of linear fiber optics and coaxial cable for transmission, the essential characteristics of the "last-mile" distribution networks have remained unchanged. In particular, the final link is still a linear, broadband coaxial network that simultaneously carries many modulated RF signals, each occupying a different band within the spectrum—frequency division multiplexing (FDM). Today, many of the modulating signals are digital rather than analog; however, the network must still be linear to avoid generation of unwanted distortion products.

This chapter will treat coaxial network technology in detail, including cable, amplifiers, passive components, and powering systems. Basic linear network concepts will be introduced that will also apply to the linear fiber-optic links whose unique characteristics are discussed in Chapter 4 and to the microwave links covered in Chapter 6. Chapter 3 will discuss coaxial design practices and cascaded performance.

2.2 COAXIAL CABLE

Coaxial cable is not the only option for transmitting broadband RF signals. Indeed, many early systems were built using open, parallel-wire balanced transmission lines, and a few even used an ingenious single-wire cable known as G-line, which had only a center conductor and dielectric. Coaxial cable, however, offers the advantages of a high degree of shielding, coupled with relatively low-cost and easy connectorization.   **5**

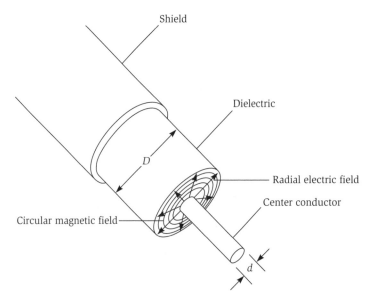

FIGURE 2.1

Coaxial cable basics.

2.2.1 Definition

Coaxial cable is constructed with a center conductor surrounded by a dielectric of circular cross-section and by an outer conductor (shield), also of circular cross-section. Signals within the normal operating bandwidth of coaxial cable have a field configuration known as transverse electric and magnetic (TEM). In the TEM mode, the electric field lines go radially between the center and outer conductor and are of uniform strength around a cross section of the cable, whereas the magnetic field lines are circular and perpendicular to the length of the cable (see Figure 2.1). In a cable with a continuous, perfectly conducting shield, no electric or magnetic fields extend beyond the outer conductor, preventing both signal leakage and ingress.

2.2.2 Characteristic Impedance

Coaxial cables have a property known as surge impedance or, more commonly, characteristic impedance, which is related to the capacitance and inductance, per unit length, of the cable. The characteristic impedance is most easily thought of in terms of the effect on signals being transported: if a cable is connected to an ideal pure resistor whose value is equal to its characteristic impedance, a signal transmitted toward the resistor will be entirely absorbed by the resistor and converted to heat. In other words, no energy will be reflected back up the cable.

The characteristic impedance, Z_0 (in ohms), is a function of the relative diameters of the center conductor and the inner surface of the outer conductor and of the dielectric constant of the dielectric:

$$Z_0 = \frac{138}{\sqrt{\varepsilon}} \log\left(\frac{D}{d}\right) \qquad (2.1)$$

where

$\quad D =$ the inner diameter of the shield
$\quad d \; =$ the outer diameter of the center conductor
$\quad \varepsilon \; =$ the dielectric constant

2.2.3 Attenuation as a Function of Frequency

Signal loss (attenuation) through coaxial cable can occur through any of four means:

- Radiation out of the cable due to imperfect shielding
- Resistive losses in the cable conductors
- Signal absorption in the dielectric of the cable
- Signal reflection due to mismatches between the cable and terminations or along the cable due to nonuniform impedance

Even when cables have perfect shields, exact impedance matches, and uniform construction, imperfect dielectrics and resistive conductors will cause loss. The general equation for this residual cable loss is

$$\alpha = 4.344\left(\frac{R}{Z_0}\right) + 2.774\,F_p\sqrt{\varepsilon}f \qquad (2.2)$$

where

$\quad \alpha =$ the attenuation of the cable in dB/100 feet*
$\quad R =$ the effective ohmic resistance of the sum of the center and outer
$\qquad$ conductors per 100 feet of cable length at f
$\quad F_p =$ the power factor of the dielectric used
$\quad f =$ the frequency in MHz

The currents in the conductors are proportional to the strength of the magnetic fields at the conductor surface. If the conductors had no resistance, the RF currents would travel only on the surface. In real conductors, however, the current extends into the conductor, decreasing exponentially with depth. This property is known as *skin effect*, and the distance from the surface to where the current has decreased

---

*In accordance with common North American practice, all attenuation values will be given in decibels per 100 feet of length. This has the advantage that signal loss becomes a linear function of length and of simple conversion to metric units of length.

to $1/e$ (36.8%) of the surface amount is known as the *skin depth* at that frequency. It is related to frequency by the formula

$$\delta = \frac{1}{\sqrt{f}} 2.60 \sqrt{\frac{\rho}{\rho_C}} \qquad (2.3)$$

where

δ = the skin depth in mils (thousandths of an inch)
ρ/ρ_C = the resistivity of the conductor relative to copper
f = the frequency in MHz[1]

The formula is valid only for nonferrous materials such as aluminum or copper.

Over a typical downstream frequency range of 54 to 750 MHz, the skin depth in copper will vary from 0.00035 to 0.00009 inch and will increase to 0.0012 inch at 5 MHz (the lower end of the upstream frequency range).

The effective resistance of the conductor is the same as if it were a tube of material whose thickness is equal to the skin depth with the current distributed equally throughout its volume. The resistance of this tube will be

$$R = 0.0996 \frac{\sqrt{f}}{d} \sqrt{\frac{\rho}{\rho_C}} \qquad (2.4)$$

where

R = the resistance per 100 feet of the conductor
ρ/ρ_C = the resistivity of the conductor relative to copper
f = the frequency in MHz
d = the conductor diameter in inches

Taking into account the resistance of both center and outer conductors, Equation 2.2 can be rewritten as

$$\alpha = \frac{0.433}{Z_0} \left(\frac{\sqrt{\rho_d/\rho_c}}{d} + \frac{\sqrt{\rho_D/\rho_c}}{D} \right) \sqrt{f} + 2.774(F_P\sqrt{\varepsilon})f \qquad (2.5)$$

where

ρ_d/ρ_c = the resistivity of the center conductor material relative to copper
ρ_D/ρ_c = the resistivity of the shield material relative to copper

This has one term that increases as the square root of frequency and one that increases linearly with frequency. For most cable constructions (discussed later), the conductor loss will dominate the dielectric loss so that the overall cable attenuation will increase approximately as the square root of frequency. Figure 2.2 shows the specified variation in loss for several cables in comparison to an ideal square-root relationship (with the curves matched at 100 MHz). Note that the agreement is excellent for cables ranging from drop sizes to the largest trunk cables, indicating the relatively small contribution from dielectric losses.

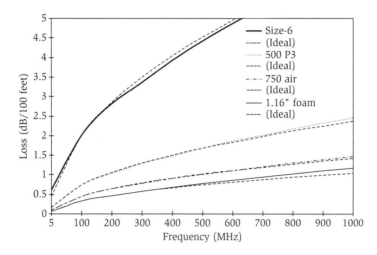

FIGURE 2.2

Cable loss: specified versus ideal.

A common cable construction, known as P3, uses a solid aluminum outer conductor, a foamed dielectric ($\sqrt{\varepsilon} = 1.15$), and a copper-coated aluminum center conductor. It is available in a number of nominal sizes (referenced to the *outer* diameter of the aluminum shield in inches). For this family of cables, the attenuation can be approximated using

$$\alpha = \left[\frac{0.036}{D_{\text{nom}}}\right]\sqrt{f} + 0.0002f \qquad (2.6)$$

where

α = the attenuation in dB/100 feet
D_{nom} = the nominal shield outer diameter in inches
f = the frequency in MHz

Other cable types using thinner shields and/or air dielectrics will have slightly lower losses for the same outer diameter, whereas solid dielectric cables will have higher losses.

2.2.4 Attenuation as a Function of Temperature

As Equation 2.2 shows, the attenuation of a coaxial cable, in decibels, is a linear function of its conductor resistance, provided that conductor losses are much larger than dielectric losses. As previously mentioned, the most common trunk/feeder cable construction uses an aluminum shield and copper-coated aluminum center conductor. Copper has a resistivity at 68°F of about 0.68×10^{-6} ohm-inches, whereas aluminum has a resistivity of about 1.03×10^{-6} ohm-inches, and each has a temperature coefficient of resistivity of 0.22%/°F. Since conductor resistance varies as the square root of resistivity, the resistance of both conductors, and therefore the attenuation, would be expected to change by about 0.11%/°F—consistent with typical commercial cable specifications of 0.1%/°F.

2.2.5 Attenuation as a Function of Characteristic Impedance

For a given outer diameter (the primary determinant of the amount of materials used and, therefore, cost and weight), different impedance cables will be optimized for different characteristics. If the dielectric loss is assumed to be of only secondary importance and typical copper/aluminum construction is assumed, then Equations 2.1 and 2.5 can be combined to find cable attenuation as a function of characteristic impedance:

$$\alpha = \frac{0.433\sqrt{f}}{D} \left[\frac{1.23 + 10^{\left(\frac{Z_0\sqrt{\varepsilon}}{138}\right)}}{Z_0} \right] \tag{2.7}$$

As Figure 2.3 shows, the loss minimum is at about 80 ohms for air dielectric (dielectric constant = 1.0) and decreases as the dielectric constant increases. Cables with air dielectric also have lower overall loss since the center conductors are larger, and therefore have less resistance, for the same impedance. Although the choice of impedances near the minimum of the curve was not important, 75 ohms may have been chosen because it is also close to the feedpoint impedance of a half-wave

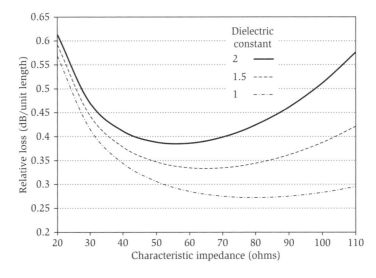

FIGURE 2.3

Coaxial cable loss versus characteristic impedance for various values of dielectric constant.

dipole antenna. In order to minimize the need for repeaters, wide area distribution systems universally use 75-ohm cables. They are also used for local interconnection of baseband video signals within headends and broadcast facilities in order to minimize the differential loss across the video baseband spectrum.

Although the losses are higher, 50-ohm cables are generally used by the broadcast and radio communications industries because the power-handling capability is higher, the cables are less fragile, and they are a close match to the feedpoint impedance of a vertical quarter-wave antenna.

2.2.6 Wavelength

Along the length of the cable, at any one instant in time, the electric fields vary sinusoidally in strength. At some point, the center conductor will be at its most positive with respect to the shield. Moving along the cable, the voltage will decrease to zero, become negative, move to zero, and then return to its positive maximum again. The distance between the maximum points of one polarity is known as the wavelength at the frequency being transmitted and is equal to the distance the signal traverses during one period of its frequency.

In free space, signals travel at the rate of 3×10^8 meters per second or, in more convenient terms, about 984 feet per microsecond. Signals in cable, however, travel more slowly due to the higher dielectric constant of the dielectric material. The ratio between velocity in cable and free-space velocity is the *relative propagation velocity*, V_P, and varies from about 0.85 to 0.95 for common cable types. V_P is related to the dielectric constant by

$$V_P = \frac{1}{\sqrt{\varepsilon}} \qquad (2.8)$$

The wavelength of a signal in a coaxial cable is thus

$$\lambda(\text{feet}) = \frac{984 V_p}{f(\text{MHz})} = \frac{984}{f\sqrt{\varepsilon}} \qquad (2.9)$$

2.2.7 Theoretical Size Limitation

If the size of a coaxial cable is sufficiently large, it will support modes other than TEM. In particular, if the mean diameter exceeds one wavelength in the cable, it will support a mode in which the electric and magnetic fields are not uniform around the cable. This *cutoff wavelength* can be expressed as[2]

$$\lambda_C = \pi(D + d)/2 \qquad (2.10)$$

where

    D = the inner diameter of the shield
    d = the outer diameter of the center conductor

Non-TEM-mode generation is a problem since higher-order modes may not propagate at the same velocity and because coaxial components may not react the same to the higher-order mode. Standard practice is to limit cable sizes to those that do not support modes higher than TEM at the maximum operating frequency. The maximum-size cable that will support a given frequency in TEM mode can only be found by substituting Equation 2.9 for λ in Equation 2.10, then solving Equation 2.1 for d, substituting in Equation 2.10, and solving the resultant expression for D:

$$D_{max} = \frac{1968}{\pi f \sqrt{\varepsilon}\left[1 + 10^{-\left(\frac{Z_0 \sqrt{\varepsilon}}{138}\right)}\right]} \tag{2.11}$$

Alternatively, we can solve for the maximum frequency that can be transmitted in only in TEM mode through a given cable:

$$f_{max} = \frac{1968}{\pi D \sqrt{\varepsilon}\left[1 + 10^{-\left(\frac{Z_0 \sqrt{\varepsilon}}{138}\right)}\right]} \tag{2.12}$$

For example, 75-ohm cables with foamed dielectrics (ε about 1.3) will support 1-GHz signals at up to about 5.2 inches inside shield diameter. Since this is more than four times the largest cable used by network operators, higher-order mode suppression is not an issue with current operating bandwidths.

2.2.8 Precision of Match: Structural Return Loss

One measure of cable quality is how closely it adheres to its nominal impedance. This has two aspects: the precision with which its *average* characteristic impedance matches the ideal value, and the *variations* of impedance along the length of a cable. As an alternative to attempting to measure the physical structure of the cable along its length, the most frequent measure of quality used is the percentage of incident power from a source that is reflected at the input of a cable being tested when the cable's output is connected to a precision termination. If the source is calibrated using a precision, resistive terminator, then the result of the measurement is *return loss*.

Often, however, the frequency variation of the reflection is of more interest than the absolute match. In order to measure the variation, a variable bridge is used to match, as precisely as possible, the average surge impedance of the cable being tested. Then the reflection is measured over the full frequency range of desired operation, and the result is known as *structural return loss* (SRL). Its numeric value is the smallest measured ratio of incident to reflected power as the frequency is varied, expressed in decibels. Recommended worst-case SRL is 26 to 30 dB for trunk and feeder cable, whereas 20 dB is considered adequate for drop cable. The absolute impedance should be within ±2 to 3 ohms for trunk and distribution cables and ±5 ohms for drop cables.[3]

SRL is a compromise measurement, as the reflected power is a measure, at each frequency, of the composite effect of discontinuities at all distances. Because of the attenuation of the cable, signals traveling toward more distant discontinuities will be reduced in amplitude, and the reflections from those discontinuities will be further attenuated so that imperfections farther from the end of the cable being measured will have less effect than those closer. At higher frequencies, this effect will be increased. On the other hand, most cable imperfections cause a greater reflection at higher frequencies.

Where multiple reflections are spaced along a transmission line, the effects can add, cancel, or do anything in between, depending on the length of line between them and the frequency. (Chapter 8 includes a more complete discussion of multiple reflections in coaxial transmission systems.) Absent line losses, small, identical discontinuities will approximately cancel when spaced odd multiples of a quarter wavelength, whereas they will reinforce when spaced multiples of one-half wavelength. This is especially important when considering multiple, equally spaced discontinuities arising, for instance, from an imperfection in a roller over which a cable passes during the manufacturing process. Each revolution of the roller produces an identical fault, spaced along the cable by a distance equal to the circumference of the roller. Testing such a cable over the full frequency range will show maximums and minimums of return loss as the effects of the discontinuities interact. This is why it is important to test cable over its full expected frequency range with sufficient frequency resolution to detect sharply resonant discontinuities.

Though structural return loss measurements accurately assess the composite reflection from a cable, it is a poor method of determining the location of major defects. If a cable includes only a single major defect, its location can be estimated from the change in test frequency between successive maxima or minima of return loss; however, in most cases, cable loss plus a multiplicity of reflections will prevent accurate determination.

2.2.9 Precision of Match: Time Domain Reflectometry

An alternative measurement method—also a compromise—is used to more accurately determine discontinuity location but averages the magnitude of the discontinuity as a function of frequency. In this test, a pulse is transmitted down the cable, and the distance is determined from the time required for the energy reflected from a discontinuity to return to the transmitter. The magnitude of the discontinuity is related to the amplitude of the returned signal. Secondary information about the frequency "signature" of the fault can be determined by comparing the shape of the returning pulse with the original.

Although time domain reflectometry (TDR) testing of short, low-loss cables is an accurate process, there are many compromises in testing the relatively long cables used in typical cable system construction. With very short cables, the classic pulse waveform is a very fast rise-time step function. A Fourier transform of this voltage waveform reveals that its frequency content is inversely proportional to rise time and frequency, and therefore the power spectrum falls inversely as the square of frequency (see Figure 2.4a). When such a pulse is used to test long cables, it suffers from two problems: (1) most of the energy is concentrated at low frequencies, whereas most discontinuities primarily affect higher frequencies, and (2) the relatively higher cable loss at high frequencies further masks the reflections.

For that reason, long cables are most frequently tested using a narrow "impulse" (see Figure 2.4b). This waveform has a spectrum that extends more uniformly to a frequency equal to approximately $1/P_W$, where P_W is the pulse width (the exact shape of the curve in the frequency domain depends on the shape of the voltage pulse). The trade-off is that the distance resolution is limited to approximately $cP_W V_P$, or about 1 foot per nanosecond of pulse width for typical foam dielectric cables. By increasing P_W, it is possible to increase the total energy (and therefore sensitivity) at the expense of frequency and distance resolution. As with step-function pulses, impulse-function testing suffers in accuracy because of the variation of cable loss with frequency. Because of the compromises, TDR testing of CATV-type cables is primarily limited to field operations such as measuring the cable remaining on a reel or locating an underground cut so that the cable can be repaired.

An instrument that is able to simultaneously resolve both frequency and time (distance) domain information is a network analyzer with gated TDR and Fourier

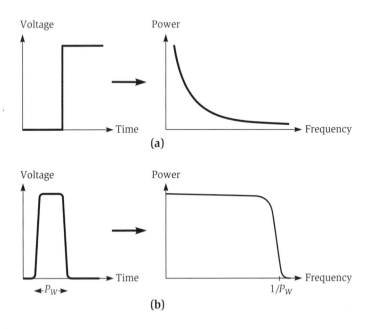

FIGURE 2.4

Frequency spectra of step and pulse TDR waveforms. (a) Step function. (b) Pulse.

transform capability. This instrument measures the reflection coefficient, but "gates" the measurement so as to measure only reflections from a narrow range of distances at a time. A Fourier transform is then used to convert the waveform of the reflected signal into its frequency domain, resulting in a reasonably accurate measurement of the reflection coefficient of an individual discontinuity, even in the presence of other discontinuities at other distances. It is still, of course, affected by the cable loss and loss variation with frequency. As of the writing of this book, this technology has not been extensively used in field work in cable systems.

2.2.10 Practical Factors in Cable Selection

From an electrical standpoint, the ideal cable would have conductors with the highest possible conductivity, the largest diameter consistent with higher-order mode suppression, and a vacuum separating the conductors. Practical cables, however, are a compromise among several characteristics:

- Manufacturing cost (which will vary somewhere between being a linear function of diameter and being the square of the diameter)

- Weight (which affects the cost of the supporting structure for overhead lines)

- Diameter (which affects required conduit size for underground lines, minimum bend radii, visibility of overhead lines, and cost of connectors)

- Loss (which limits the distance between repeater amplifiers)

- Mechanical expansion coefficient (which affects the amount of sag that must be used with overhead lines)

- Connector cost (related to cable size)

- Shielding (although solid outer conductors provide nearly perfect isolation, braided shields may provide adequate shielding for some applications and afford greater flexibility)

- Environmental protection (mechanical protection layers, compounds used to retard water ingress, integral support members, and so on)

- Handling characteristics (reforming ability, crush resistance, pulling force resistance, and so on)

- Electrical resistance and current-carrying capacity at low frequencies (since the cables typically carry system power as well as RF signals)

In oversimplified terms, the selection of optimum cable size for a distribution network design consists of comparing the cost of cable (and associated components) per decibel of loss with the cost per decibel of amplification to overcome that loss, and choosing the least expensive combination. Of course, practical system design includes many additional factors that may affect the ultimate decision.

Trunk and Feeder Cable

Design optimization has resulted in several typical cable designs that are widely used. The most common distribution cable design in most of the world uses a solid aluminum shield, foamed polyethylene dielectric, and a copper-clad aluminum center conductor. The use of aluminum offers the best combination of cost, handling characteristics, weight, and strength, whereas the foamed dielectric offers a good compromise among loss, moisture ingress protection, and mechanical strength for the center conductor. Because of its rigidity, compared with cables that use braided wire shields, trunk and feeder cables using this basic structure are sometimes known as *hard-line* cable. The use of an aluminum core for the center conductor provides a match for the expansion coefficient of the shield, whereas the copper cladding provides a lower resistance to RF. Since the conducting area of the center conductor is much smaller than the shield, the total resistive losses are dominated by it. Thus, copper cladding the center conductor is cost efficient, though coating the inner side of the shield is not.

The need to provide low resistance to the multiplexed power, as well as low RF loss, has led to the use of cables with outer shield diameters ranging from 0.412 to 1.125 inches, with larger cables being used where distance of coverage is paramount (trunk or express feeders) and smaller cables being used for shorter distances and cases where a substantial amount of the loss is due to tap losses rather than cable losses (tapped feeder cables). This family of cables is generically labeled by the outer shield diameter in thousands of an inch; for example, "500 cable" refers to a hardline cable with an outer shield diameter of 0.500 inch. Common diameters include 0.500, 0.625, 0.750, 0.825, and 1.000 inch, although others are also used.

Versions of these same cables are available with solid copper center conductors, for use where 60-Hz power losses must be reduced. Protection options include combinations of none (bare aluminum), polyethylene jackets of various designs and degrees of sun and fire resistance, flooding compounds (a substance inserted between the shield and jacket to retard the ingress of water), and additional steel shields for crush resistance. Since the added environmental protection layers can considerably increase the cost and weight, builders generally use several designs in a single system, optimized by application.

A variation of this design uses air dielectric with periodic center conductor supports. This design has slightly smaller diameter for the same loss per foot because of the lower dielectric loss and lower ratio of shield to center conductor diameter. Special design features are required to prevent water, which may enter the cable owing to a fault, from traveling down the center conductor/shield space. Other features are required to maintain the required concentricity and crush or bending resistance.

Drop Cable

In a typical cable system, well over half the total cable footage is taken up by drop cables. For that reason, cost is an important parameter for that application, as well as weight and appearance. In North America, four common sizes of drop cable have

Table 2.1 Common Drop Cable Designations and Sizes

Size designation	59	6	7	11
Approximate diameter over jacket in inches	0.24	0.27	0.34	0.40

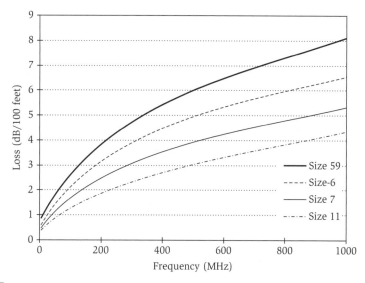

FIGURE 2.5

Drop cable loss versus frequency.

evolved, as shown in Table 2.1. The approximate loss for each size, as a function of frequency, is shown in Figure 2.5.[4]

Drop cables are constructed using a copper-plated steel center conductor, foamed dielectric, a shield made up of at least one layer of an aluminum foil and one layer of an aluminum braid, and a plastic jacket. Additional layers of foil and braid are available as options for greater shielding effectiveness. Although size 59 cable was the historical choice of the cable television industry, size-6 cable is most frequently used in modern systems due to the use of increasingly higher frequencies. The larger sizes are generally reserved for occasional longer drop cables.

The jacket material for general use is usually PVC or polyethylene. Cables used for overhead drops often also include a separate steel strength member (the *messenger*) enclosed in the same plastic sheath structure. See Figure 2.6 for a composite drop cable structure that includes a messenger.

An array of drop cable variations are available for special purposes, including those with *flooding compounds* to retard water ingress in case the plastic coating is damaged, multiple cables within a common jacket, those with varying degrees

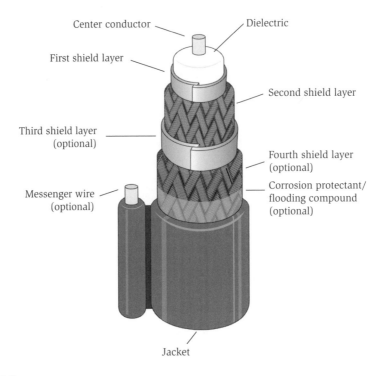

FIGURE 2.6

Typical drop cable construction.

of fire resistance for use inside buildings, silver-plated center conductors, copper braids, solid dielectric cables, and so on.

As with distribution cables, North American practice has been adopted by some countries, whereas others (e.g., Germany) have chosen to use semirigid drop cables with solid copper shields and center conductors for their underground drops.

2.2.11 Shielding Effectiveness in Drop Cables

Although distribution cables constructed with solid aluminum tube shields offer nearly perfect signal isolation from external fields, drop cables depend on the overlap in the aluminum wrap and the interaction between the aluminum braid and wrap for shielding integrity. It is a compromise that is justified on the basis of cost and cable-handling characteristics. The cable industry has long struggled to find unambiguous testing methodology for evaluating shielding integrity. Although these are beyond the scope of this book, readers may wish to refer to industry standard test procedures developed by the Society of Cable Telecommunications Engineers (SCTE) for this purpose.[5]

2.3 AMPLIFIERS

In order to overcome the loss of the distribution cables and to provide power to drive end terminals, signal boosting amplifiers are used throughout the coaxial distribution system. These must be designed to add as little signal degradation as possible, particularly noise and distortion, consistent with providing the required gain and total power output.

2.3.1 Broadband Random Noise

Because of the random motion of electrons in conductors, all electronic systems generate an irreducible amount of noise power. This noise is a function of the absolute temperature and the bandwidth in which the noise is measured. The minimum thermal noise power (the *noise floor*) can be calculated using

$$n_p = kTB \qquad (2.13)$$

where

n_p = the noise power in watts
k = Boltzmann's constant (1.374×10^{-23} joules/°K)
T = the absolute temperature in °K
B = the bandwidth of the measurement in Hz

Signal power in cable television systems is commonly expressed in decibels relative to 1 mV[†] across 75 ohms (dBmV), so the thermal noise power at 62°F is approximately

$$N_p(\text{dBmV}) = -125.2 + 10 \log B \qquad (2.14)$$

Finally, although the allocated channel bandwidth for analog NTSC signals is 6 MHz, the effective noise bandwidth of receivers is less. For a variety of reasons, a 4-MHz bandwidth is used as the standard for noise measurements and has been codified in the FCC's rules.[6] At that bandwidth, Equation 2.14 becomes

$$N_p = -59.2 \text{ dBmV} \qquad (2.15)$$

This value will vary by a few tenths of a decibel across the temperature range normally of interest to cable operators.

For QAM receivers, whose noise susceptibility bandwidth is, estimating conservatively, the full 6-MHz bandwidth, the noise floor is 10 log (6/4) = 1.8 dB higher, or −57.4 dBmV.

[†]In some countries, the reference is 1 μV rather than 1 mV. Levels in dBμV are therefore numerically greater by 60 than levels in dBmV. In either case, however, the reference is power, not voltage. Finally, for the convenience of those accustomed to working in systems referenced to 1 mW (dBm), 0 dBmV = −48.75 dBm. For consistency, this book uses dBmV as the units for RF power unless otherwise specified.

2.3.2 Amplifier Noise

Amplifiers generate added noise at various points in their circuitry. For convenience, however, the added noise is treated as if it were coming from an independent generator and summed into the input port (although it cannot be measured there, of course). The ratio of total effective input noise power to the thermal noise floor, expressed in decibels, is known as the *noise figure* of the amplifier. Thus, an amplifier with a noise figure of F_A dB will have a total equivalent input noise power of N_A, where

$$N_A(\text{dBmV}) = N_p(\text{dBmV}) + F_A(\text{dB}) \tag{2.16}$$

And the output noise power will be the input, increased by the gain, G, of the amplifier in decibels:

$$N_{\text{out}}(\text{dBmV}) = N_P + F_A + G \tag{2.17}$$

Similarly, a desired (noise-free) input signal, C_i, will be amplified by the same amount so that the desired signal output level $C_{\text{out}} = C_i\,(\text{dBmV}) + G(\text{dB})$, and the carrier-to-noise[‡] ratio will be

$$\begin{aligned}C/N\,(\text{dB}) &= (C_i + G) - (N_P - F_A + G)\\ &= C_i - N_P - F_A\end{aligned} \tag{2.18}$$

When evaluated relative to the 4-MHz bandwidth commonly used for NTSC C/N measurements, this becomes

$$C/N\,(\text{dB}) = C_i\,(\text{dBmV}) + 59.2 - F_A(\text{dB}) \tag{2.19}$$

(Substitute 57.4 for 59.2 for QAM signals.) Note that, in an FDM system, C/N is evaluated on each signal independently, with the level of individual carriers compared with the noise in the bandwidth that affects that signal. As will be seen, the C/N may vary considerably among different signals in the spectrum. (The design of systems with cascaded amplifiers will be treated in Chapter 3.)

2.3.3 Distortion

Amplifiers are not perfectly linear. That is, if the instantaneous output voltage is plotted against the instantaneous input voltage, the graph will not be a perfectly straight line. There are two causes of this nonlinearity: the inevitable minor small-signal nonlinearities of the semiconductor devices used and the compression that takes place as the amplifier nears its saturation voltage. Though the small variations define a distortion "floor," most of the distortion is due to saturation effects. They can take any of three related forms: even-order distortion, odd-order distortion, and cross-modulation.

[‡]The term C/N (carrier-to-noise ratio) is used in this book for RF-modulated signals, whereas S/N (signal-to–noise ratio) is used for measurements of the noise level on baseband (unmodulated) signals. This is consistent with both regulatory terminology and common industry practice.

Even-Order Distortion (Composite Second Order)

A perfectly linear amplifier has a transfer function that is a constant; that is, the output voltage is a linear function of the input voltage. If the transfer function is not linear, in general it can be expressed as a power series; that is,

$$e_o = Ae_i + Be_i^2 + Ce_i^3 + De_i^4 + \dots \tag{2.20}$$

where

e_o = the output voltage
e_i = the input voltage
$A, B, C, D, \dots$ = the gains at the various powers of the input voltage[7]

Those terms with even-numbered powers are called even-order distortion, and those with odd-numbered powers are called odd-order distortion. They act in very different ways in cable systems using the most common channelization plans.

If a single sine wave signal $[e_i = E_i \sin(\omega t)]$ is transported through an amplifier with second- and fourth-order distortion, the output voltage will be

$$e_o = A[E_i \sin(\omega t)] + B[E_i \sin(\omega t)]^2 + D[E_i \sin(\omega t)]^4 \tag{2.21}$$

where

ω = the angular frequency
A = the linear component of gain
B = the amplitude of the squared nonlinear component
D = the amplitude of the fourth-power component
E_i = the peak input voltage

Using standard trigonometric identities, this is equivalent to

$$e_o = \frac{BE_i^2}{2} + \frac{3DE_i^4}{8} + AE_i \sin(\omega t) - \frac{(BE_i^2 + DE_i^4)}{2}\cos(2\omega t) + \frac{DE_i^4}{8}\cos(4\omega t) \tag{2.22}$$

Analyzing this expression, we find that

- The first two terms represent a change in the average dc voltage that may correspond to a change in the power dissipation of the active device, but is not transmitted into the ac-coupled transmission system.
- The third term represents the desired output signal. Note that this amplitude does not change as the result of the even-order distortion.
- The fourth term represents an additional signal at twice the frequency of the input signal, and in phase with it at $\omega = \pi/2$. In real amplifiers, B is substantially greater than D. Thus, for small values of E_i the amplitude of this factor will increase as the square of the input voltage. At some input level, the fourth power term will begin to dominate, and the second harmonic level will increase more quickly. Since the level of the fundamental increases linearly with input signal level, the *ratio* of the fundamental to the second harmonic, at low levels, is a linear function of input level. Expressed in logarithmic terms, the ratio of carrier to composite second-order beats (C/CSO) degrades by 1 dB for every decibel increase in operating level so long as the

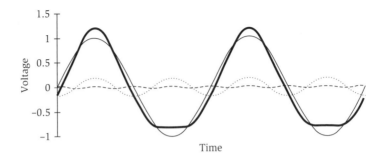

FIGURE 2.7

Even-order distortion.

amplifier is "well behaved" (meaning the fourth-power terms are insignificant relative to the second-power terms).

- The final term is the fourth harmonic of the fundamental. Like the fourth-power term of the second harmonic, this product is generally small at normal operating levels and at all levels is at least 12 dB (one-fourth the voltage) below the second harmonic term. Note that this term is also in phase with the fundamental at $\omega = \pi/2$.

If we plot the fundamental and first two even harmonics on a time scale (Figure 2.7), we see an interesting relationship: the distortion-caused products are *antisymmetrical* with respect to the fundamental; that is, whatever voltage they have at the positive peak of the fundamental, they have exactly the opposite during the negative peak. The usual case of the combined composite signal is shown in the bold line in the figure, which shows one peak of the composite waveform flattened relative to the fundamental, whereas the other peak is sharpened.

The North American Standard channel plan (CEA-542-B), whose frequency assignments are included in this book as the Appendix, places most analog television visual carriers approximately 6 MHz apart and offset approximately 1.25 MHz upward from harmonics of 6 MHz.[§] Each such carrier can be expressed as

$$\sin[2\pi(6n + 1.25)t] \tag{2.23}$$

where the angle is expressed in radians and

n = the closest harmonic of 6 MHz
t = the time in microseconds

When two such signals (on different channels) are transported through an amplifier with second-order distortion (for simplicity, and because the effects are often small, the fourth-order term has been dropped), output is

---

[§]Variations from exact spacing are due to equipment frequency tolerances, broadcast station offsets of 10 or 20 kHz, aeronautical band offsets of 12.5 or 25 kHz, and the nominal broadcast assignments for channels 5 and 6 (which are not close to harmonics of 6 MHz).

$$e_o = AE_i(\sin[2\pi(6n + 1.25)t] + \sin[2\pi(6m + 1.25)t])$$
$$+ BE_i^2(\sin[2\pi(6n + 1.25)t] + \sin[2\pi(6m + 1.25)t])^2 \tag{2.24}$$

where the first term is the linear amplification of the input signals and

> n and m = the multiples of 6 MHz closest to the two visual carriers
> E_i = the peak voltage of either of the input signals (they are assumed to have equal amplitudes)

The last term has a dc component plus the following intermodulation products:

$$- BE_i^2 \cos[2\pi(6[m + n] + 2.5)t]$$
$$+ BE_i^2 \cos[2\pi(6[m - n])t]$$
$$- (BE_i^2/2) \cos[2\pi(12n + 2.5)t]$$
$$- (BE_i^2/2) \cos[2\pi(12m - 2.5)t]$$

The first product falls 1.25 MHz above the visual carrier nearest the $(m + n)^{\text{th}}$ harmonic of 6 MHz, whereas the second product falls 1.25 MHz below the visual carrier nearest the $(m - n)^{\text{th}}$ harmonic of 6 MHz.

The third and fourth products will be half the voltage (-6 dB in power) and will each lie 1.25 MHz above another visual carrier (provided, in all cases, that the products fall within the occupied bandwidth of the distribution system). Note that these last products are identical in amplitude to those analyzed with a single carried signal and are, in fact, just the second harmonics of the two original signals.

The amplitude of each of these four distortion products, as with the single channel analysis, depends on the square of the input voltage so that the *ratio* of fundamental to second-order products varies linearly with input level. A similar analysis for fourth-order distortion, the next even power, will show low-amplitude components at four times the original frequencies and additional components at twice the original frequencies.

When many similarly spaced carriers in the Standard channel plan are subjected to second-order distortion, each of the individual carriers and each of the carrier pairs will mix as analyzed earlier. This will result in clusters of products 1.25 MHz above and below each of the original carriers.** As a general rule, the number of beats falling closest to a specific carrier can be calculated using the expression

$$N_L = n - m - x + 1 \tag{2.25a}$$

where x varies from 1 to $n - m$

$$N_U = INT\left[\frac{x - 2m + 1}{2}\right] \tag{2.25b}$$

where x varies from $2m + 1$ to $m + n$

**Actually, there are also some products spaced ±750 kHz from the visual carriers because two of the channels (5 and 6) are offset from the comb in the Standard channel plan.

$$N_U = INT\left[\frac{2n - x - 1}{2}\right] \qquad\qquad (2.25c)$$

where x varies from $m + n + 1$ to $2n - 1$, INT indicates that the expression is to be rounded down to the nearest integer, and

N_L = the number of lower $(A - B)$ beats
N_U = the number of upper $(A + B)$ beats
n = harmonic number of highest carrier
m = harmonic number of lowest carrier
x = harmonic number of carrier being evaluated

Since, in the CEA-542-B Standard channel plan, the analog video carriers are not exactly spaced, the second-order products are not frequency coherent, but rather are clustered around the nominal product frequencies.

The usual measurement technique when evaluating this type of distortion is to use a filter bandwidth of 30 kHz, which is wide enough to contain all the significant products in a group and to measure the total apparent power within the filter bandwidth. The power level of the upper composite beat cluster, relative to the sync peak power of the visual carrier, is known as composite second order (CSO) and is sometimes expressed in units of dBc (meaning decibels relative to the carrier power level of the affected channel, which is always a negative number). Some engineers prefer the notation C/CSO, the ratio of the carrier to beats in decibels (a positive number). This book will use this notation. The absolute values are the same in either case. Although the lower CSO cluster will generally have greater magnitude than the upper cluster on lower-frequency channels, it falls at the edge of the video channel and is often ignored since it has a minor effect on video quality compared with the in-band upper cluster. Similarly, in systems carrying a hybrid load of analog video and QAM signals, those second-order discrete products that fall at the lower band edge of QAM signals will cause fewer problems than those in the middle of the band, since the band-edge products will be partially attenuated by the QAM filter rolloff.

Since analog video carrier modulation results in average signal levels that vary with program content, equipment is specified and evaluated when loaded with unmodulated carriers of a defined level in order to achieve repeatable measurements. When loaded with video carriers whose peak level is the same as the unmodulated levels used for the test, the average carrier power will be about 6 dB lower, resulting in an improvement of about 6 dB in C/CSO.

When the IRC channel plan is used, the visual carrier frequencies are derived from a common source so that all channels are phase coherent and offset from harmonics of 6 MHz by exactly the same amount. The result is that the second-order beats are also coherent. When the HRC channel plan is used, the visual carrier frequencies are derived from a common source and *not* offset. Under those circumstances, the upper and lower second-order beats fall exactly on the visual carrier frequencies, and the difference frequency beats cannot be ignored.

The individual products' amplitudes and the number in each cluster are a function of the amplifier's nonlinearity, the levels of the carriers generating the beat, and the number of test signals used. Although the preceding analysis assumes a uniform carrier level, standard operating practice is to vary carrier power in a controlled way as a function of frequency. This will result in varying individual beat levels.

When a comb of signals is subject to second-order distortion, the greatest number of products will fall on the highest and lowest channels of that comb. Figure 2.8, as an example, gives the total number of upper and lower 1.25-MHz second-order products in a system carrying 77 analog video signals between 54 and 550 MHz and using the Standard channel plan (in which channels 5 and 6 are offset by 2 MHz); channels 95 to 97 were assumed to be unoccupied.

Note that the lower-side composite beat energy continues to increase below the lowest occupied channel, with the strongest beat being at 6 MHz in the upstream band. Amplifier diplex filters normally prevent these lower-side products from appearing in the upstream spectrum; however, the presence of any nonlinear elements in the signal path shared by upstream and downstream signals creates common path distortion (CPD) products at these frequencies, as discussed in Chapter 8. Note, however, that for channels 4 and 5, the lower second-order beats are not at the band edge but rather in band at 750 kHz above the visual carrier.

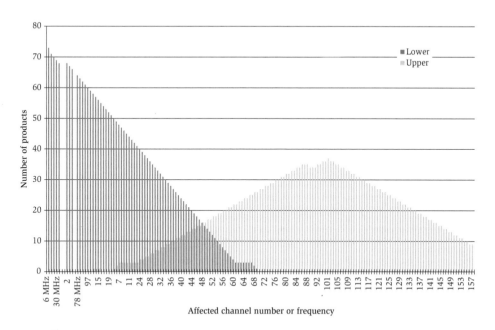

FIGURE 2.8

Number of 1.25-MHz CSO beats: 77 analog signals, Standard channel plan.

Note also that the number of upper-side (in-band) products increases linearly, peaking at channel 101 (well above the analog spectrum), then declines linearly but with a significant number of products even at 1 GHz.

If amplifiers were operated with all output levels equal, the power in each beat cluster could be calculated to be $10 \log(n)$, where n is the number of beats. With tilted amplifier outputs, however, it would be necessary to calculate the power of each beat, and then calculate the power sum of the beats falling in each cluster. In general, however, the low-side beats will tend to be more uniform in power (the 6-MHz beat, for instance, is generated by pairs of adjacent signals throughout the spectrum, while the highest beat is generated by the mixture of the highest and lowest carrier), and thus the ratio of beat power to desired channel power at the lowest channels is maximum, as the result of combining the greatest number of beats with the lowest desired signal power. By contrast, the upper-side, in-channel individual beats increase with increasing frequency because the highest-frequency beats are the product of the highest signals. On the other hand, the desired signal power also increases, so that the variation of desired signal to beat power ratio (C/CSO) with frequency is more complex.

The visual effect of the upper-side second-order products on analog NTSC television pictures is similar to that of a discrete interfering carrier—that is, closely spaced diagonal lines. As discussed earlier, the lower CSO beats have relatively little effect on visual quality (except on channels 4 and 5). The effect of discrete beats from analog video signals on QAM signals sharing the same transmission system is a lowering of the operating margin.

Many simple broadband RF amplifiers are single-ended class-A devices, meaning that their output stages consist of a single active device that is biased to the approximate middle of its dynamic range. Such a device typically exhibits an asymmetrical compression behavior so that second-order distortion products dominate. In recognition of this problem, the North American VHF off-air frequency plan designated channel boundaries such that neither second harmonic nor second-order beats from any combination of channels affect any other channels even if the drive levels to television receivers are high enough to result in compression.

Early cable television amplifiers used single-ended designs for reasons of economy. However, as the industry began using non–off-air channels, CSO quickly became the primary performance-limiting parameter, leading to use of "push–pull" amplification, as discussed later. As will be seen in Chapters 4 and 5, however, the dominant distortion mechanism in linear optical links is second order, to which the preceding analysis is relevant.

Odd-Order Distortion (Composite Triple Beat)

All modern cable RF line amplifiers are "push–pull," meaning that their output stages contain two devices in a balanced circuit that ensures symmetrical, or nearly symmetrical, compression. As will be seen, this will result in primarily odd-order distortion products.

If a single sine wave is transmitted through a circuit that has only third-order distortion, the output can be described by the following equation (derived from Equation 2.20):

$$e_o = Ae_i + Ce_i^3 \qquad (2.26)$$

where A and C are the coefficients of the linear and cubed products, respectively, and

$$e_i = E_i \sin(\omega t)$$

Using a standard trigonometric identity, this reduces to

$$e_o = \left[AE_i + \frac{3CE_i^3}{4}\right][\sin(\omega t)] - \left[\frac{CE_i^3}{4}\right][\sin(3\omega t)] \qquad (2.27)$$

C may be either positive or negative. In the case where the nonlinearity is due to compression, it is negative so that the third-order distortion results in a reduction in the amplitude of the fundamental (unlike second-order distortion, which does not affect the amplitude of the fundamental).

Additionally, there will be a product at three times the original frequency whose peaks are in opposition to those of the fundamental. The level of the third-order products rises as the cube of the input voltage (e.g., the rise is 3 dB for every 1-dB rise in input level) so that the *ratio* of fundamental to third harmonic at the output decreases by 2 dB for every 1-dB rise in the input level *so long as the ratio between them is high.* When the reduction in the amplitude of the fundamental becomes material, the ratio will decrease more quickly. At some point, fifth harmonic products also become significant.

Figure 2.9 shows visually the fundamental, the third harmonic, and the sum of the two. As can be seen, third-order distortion is equivalent to a reduced-amplitude, symmetrically flattened waveform. If higher odd multiples of the original frequency are also plotted on the graph, it will be seen that all such harmonics will have exactly the same effect on both peaks of the original waveform.

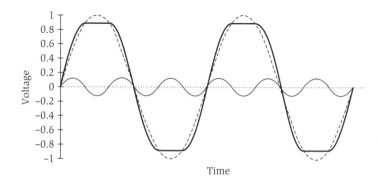

FIGURE 2.9

Effect of third-order distortion.

If multiple signals are transmitted through a system exhibiting this type of distortion, the input can be described by the following general formula:

$$e_i = E_1 \sin[(\omega_1 t)] + E_2 \sin[(\omega_2 t)] + \ldots + E_n \sin[\omega_n t] \qquad (2.28)$$

where

$\omega_{1,2,\,\ldots,\,n}$ = the angular frequencies of the input signals
$E_{1,2,\,\ldots,\,n}$ = the levels of each subcarrier (peak voltage)

If we insert this definition of e_i into Equation 2.26, it can be shown that the output spectrum will have signals at the fundamental frequencies of the input signals and all combinations of $3\omega_x$, $2\omega_x \pm \omega_y$, and $\omega_x \pm \omega_y \pm \omega_z$, where ω_x ω_y, and ω_z are any of the input frequencies. In particular, products with contributions from one, two, and three signals will be present, as follows:

Terms arising from a single input signal:

$$\left[AE_x + \frac{3CE_x^3}{4} \right] [\sin(\omega_x t)] - \left[\frac{CE_x^3}{4} \right] [\sin(3\omega_x t)] \qquad (2.29)$$

Just as with a single sine wave, this indicates that the output contains, in addition to the linearly amplified input signals, two terms proportional to the cube of the input voltage level of each of the carriers, one at the fundamental carrier frequency and one at three times the carrier frequency. When the input consists of carriers corresponding to the CEA Standard or IRC channel schemes (offset 1.25 MHz from harmonics of 6 MHz), the third harmonic term will fall 3.75 MHz above a harmonic of the root frequency (2.5 MHz above a carrier if one is present). With carriers that fall exactly on harmonics of a common root (HRC), the distortion products will also fall on harmonics of the root. The number of single-frequency terms will be the same as the number of FDM carriers.

Terms arising from the mixture of two input signals:

$$\left[\frac{3CE_x^2 E_y}{2} \right] \sin(\omega_y t) - \left[\frac{3CE_x^2 E_y}{4} \right] \sin([2\omega_x + \omega_y]t) + \left[\frac{3CE_x^2 E_y}{4} \right] \sin([2\omega_x - \omega_y]t) \qquad (2.30)$$

Each unique ordered pair of input signals mixes to produce a product at the fundamental of the input signal at frequency ω_y plus products at $2\omega_x \pm \omega_y$. The amplitude of the fundamental component is twice that produced by the single-signal term analyzed earlier (assuming equal amplitude input signals). The voltage amplitudes of the other two terms are three times that of the single-frequency third harmonic terms (+9.5 dB). When the input consists of carriers corresponding to the CEA Standard or IRC channel schemes, the $2\omega_x + \omega_y$ term will fall 2.5 MHz above a carrier assignment, while the $2\omega_x - \omega_y$ term will fall on a carrier assignment. With an HRC channel assignment scheme, all products will fall directly on channel frequencies.

When the input signals consist of an FDM spectrum of q input carriers, the number of ordered pairs is $q(q - 1)$. Since each ordered pair results in the generation of products at two new frequencies, the number of new products will be $2q(q - 1)$. Thus, when the number of carriers is large, the total number of products will increase approximately as the square of the channel count.

Terms arising from the mixture of three input signals:

$$\left[\frac{3E_xE_yE_z}{2}\right] [\sin([\omega_x + \omega_y - \omega_z]t) + \sin([\omega_x - \omega_y+\omega_z]t)$$

$$-\sin([\omega_x + \omega_y+\omega_z]t) - \sin([\omega_x - \omega_y - \omega_z]t)] \qquad (2.31)$$

Each unique combination of three input signals mixes to produce terms at $\omega_x \pm \omega_y \pm \omega_z$. When the input signal amplitudes are equal, the voltage amplitudes of these terms are six times that of the single-input-frequency terms (+15.6 dB). When the input consists of carriers corresponding to the CEA Standard or IRC channel schemes, the $\omega_x + \omega_y - \omega_z$ and $\omega_x - \omega_y + \omega_z$ terms will fall on a carrier frequency, the $\omega_x + \omega_y + \omega_z$ term will fall 2.5 MHz above a carrier frequency, and the $\omega_x - \omega_y - \omega_z$ term will fall 2.5 MHz below a carrier frequency. Note that although $\omega_x \pm \omega_y \pm \omega_z$ is sometimes negative, the only effect is the polarity of the magnitude since $\sin(-x) = -\sin(x)$.

When the input signals consist of an FDM spectrum of q input carriers, the number of unique three-signal combinations is $q(q - 1)(q - 2)/6$. Since each of these combinations results in the generation of four new products, the total number of new third-order products caused by three-signal mixing will be $4q(q - 1)(q - 2)/6$. Thus, when the number of carriers is large, the total number of products will increase approximately as the cube of the channel count.

In summary, when an FDM spectrum of q signals is transmitted through an amplifier exhibiting third-order distortion, the original signals will be amplified and a number of new products will be generated:

- Some that affect the output amplitude of each original carrier.

- q new signals, one at the third harmonic of each of the original signals. With the CEA-542-B Standard or IRC frequency plan, these fall 2.5 MHz above visual carrier frequencies.

- $2q(q - 1)$ new signals at frequencies $2\omega_x \pm \omega_y$, where ω_x and ω_y are any two input carrier frequencies. Each of these signals is about 9.5 dB higher in level than the third-harmonic frequencies. With the Standard or IRC frequency plan, half of these fall 2.5 MHz above, and half nominally on, visual carrier frequencies.

- $4q(q - 1)(q - 2)/6$ new signals at frequencies $\omega_x \pm \omega_y \pm \omega_z$, where ω_x, ω_y, and ω_z are any three different carrier frequencies. Each of these products will be about 15.6 dB higher in level than the third-harmonic frequencies. With the Standard or IRC frequency plan, half of these will fall nominally on visual carrier frequencies, whereas one-quarter will be 2.5 MHz below and one-quarter will be 2.5 MHz above visual carrier frequencies.

The level of each of these products increases by 3 dB for every 1-dB increase in the levels of the input signals so that the ratio between the desired output signals and third-order products decreases by 2 dB.

Since the three-signal products ("triple beats") are the greatest in both number and magnitude, they quickly dominate other third-order effects. Since half of them fall nominally on visual carrier frequencies, those product groups are always the largest. Thus, composite triple beat (CTB) distortion is defined as the total power in a 30-kHz bandwidth centered on the visual carrier frequency (without the visual signal present), relative to the peak level of the visual carrier in dBc (decibels relative to a reference carrier level). As with CSO, it can also be expressed as the ratio of visual carrier level to apparent beat power, or C/CTB, in decibels.

For a contiguous set of equally spaced carriers, the number of third-order beats falling in any given channel is approximately[8]

$$N_{CTB} = \frac{(a-1)^2}{4} + \frac{(a-b)(b-1)}{2} - \frac{a}{2} \qquad (2.32)$$

where

N_{CTB} = the number of third-order beat products whose frequencies are nominally the same as the carrier being evaluated

a = the total number of contiguous, equally spaced carriers

b = the index number of the carrier being evaluated; that is, the bth carrier from the bottom or top

For the center channel, which receives the greatest number of beats, this reduces to

$$N_{CTB} = \frac{3a^2 - 10a + 2}{8} \approx \frac{3a^2}{8} \quad \text{for } n \gg 1 \qquad (2.33)$$

At the end channels, which receive the fewest number of beats, it becomes

$$N_{CTB} = \frac{a^2 - 4a + 1}{4} \approx \frac{a^2}{4} \quad \text{for } n \gg 1 \qquad (2.34)$$

Actual cable systems using the CEA Standard channel plan, however, do not conform exactly to this model, with channels 4 and 5 being offset and some or all of the channels falling in the FM broadcast plan seldom used for video. Thus, "beat quantity tables" published for the industry show several percent fewer beats.

Figure 2.10 is a plot of the number of beats for some common, fully loaded system bandwidths.[9] As can be seen, channels slightly above the middle of the spectrum are affected by the greatest number of beats. As with CSO, however, it does not follow that the channel with the greatest number of beats is necessarily the channel most affected by third-order interference. Amplifiers are not typically operated with equal power carriers, but rather with a uniform upward "slope" of levels with frequency (for reasons explained later in this chapter), causing some beats to be stronger than others. Moreover, signal quality is affected by the *ratio* between

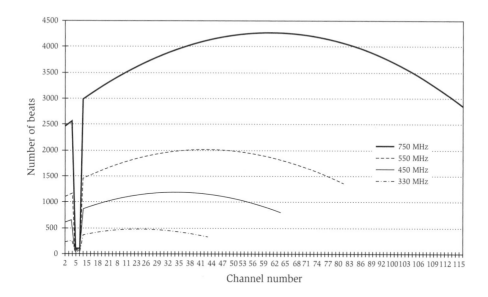

FIGURE 2.10

Number of triple beats per channel versus system bandwidth.

visual carrier level and interference level and thus to the logarithmic difference between the upward sloping desired signal levels with frequency and the unequal amplitudes of individual beats.

Although not plotted in the figure, the number of third-order beats continues to decrease above and below the analog signal spectrum. For instance, in a system with analog video signals occupying 54 to 550 MHz, the highest beat will occur at 1033.25 MHz, just above the top of the graph.

Since the third-order products are phase incoherent in most systems, their powers will add on a power, rather than a voltage, basis, and the measured CTB level will theoretically be proportional to $10 \log(n)$, where n is the number of beats in a channel if the levels of all carriers are equal. In actuality, owing to the unequal carrier levels and beat amplitudes, and possibly differences in distortion across the spectrum, CTB may increase as slowly as $5 \log(n)$ to $7 \log(n)$.[10]

The visual effect of CTB on an analog television picture depends on whether the signals are harmonically related or not. With unlocked carriers, the differences in frequency between the desired carrier and the various beats produces low-frequency interference that has been described as "streakiness" in the picture. With locked carriers, the various products will be frequency coherent with the carrier and, like the fundamental frequency products, will alter the amplitude and phase of the original signals. The visual effects depend on many factors, including the amount of phase noise on each of the signals. As with second-order products, the effect on QAM signals is a reduction in operating margin.

Since analog video carrier modulation results in an average signal level that varies with program content, equipment is specified and evaluated when loaded with unmodulated carriers of a defined level on each of the nominal visual carrier frequencies. This results in more repeatable measurements. When loaded with video carriers whose peak level is the same as the unmodulated levels used for the test, the average carrier power will be about 6 dB lower, resulting in an improvement of about 12 dB in CTB (although the improvement will vary over time depending on video modulation levels and timing and carrier phase relationships). Typical amplifiers provide a C/CTB of 70 to 90 dB when loaded with unmodulated carriers at recommended operating levels, depending on design.

Cross-Modulation

Another form of distortion occurs when amplifiers exhibiting third-order distortion are loaded with multiple amplitude-modulated signals.

Although second-order distortion has no products that affect the gain of the primary FDM carrier amplitudes, as Equations 2.22 and 2.24 demonstrate, two classes of third-order products affecting every channel cause effective gain variations of the fundamental signal. In particular, Equations 2.30 and 2.31 show that the effective amplifier gain affecting each FDM subcarrier is modified by a series of terms that include the amplitude of every other signal in the spectrum carried. Thus, when the average levels of any other signals are varied because of modulation, the output level of the desired channel will also vary slightly. This effect is known as cross-modulation (XMOD).

If the modulation of the other signals were truly independent of each other and random, the effects of cross-modulation from various channels could be expected to be noiselike (as is the case for QAM signals, discussed later). Unfortunately, analog video modulation is not random. The change in amplitude from synchronizing peak to black level is identical for every channel and, furthermore, occurs at nearly identical and quite precise modulation frequencies. Thus, if the video signals carried on multiple channels are synchronized (which happens when they are locked to a common timing reference in a multichannel generation facility), or if they drift into alignment occasionally, the level of cross-modulation can become significant.

The standard test for cross-modulation is to load the amplifier with a comb of simultaneously 100% modulated carriers plus one unmodulated carrier on the frequency to be tested. The level of modulation is measured on the nominally unmodulated carrier. Cross-modulation is defined as the difference between the cross-modulation sideband level and the sideband level that corresponds to 100% modulation, expressed in decibels.

Since it is caused by third-order distortion, the level of cross-modulation varies in the same way as CTB; that is, the relative level varies 2dB for every 1-dB change in operating levels. Because of the difficulty in making the test and demonstrated inconsistency in the results, cross-modulation has become less important than CTB as a means of characterizing third-order distortion. The inconsistency may be due to the many terms, whose effects may reinforce or cancel, affecting the cross-modulation on any channel.

When the desired signal is an analog television program and the major cross-modulating signals are also analog television programs, the first visible indication of cross-modulation takes the form of a single faint, broad horizontal line and another broad vertical line that may slowly move through the desired picture. These are caused by the horizontal and vertical synchronizing pulses (the highest carrier levels) of another television signal. In an improperly operated system, cross-modulation can also be caused by a single very-high-amplitude channel that causes cross-modulation onto other channels. In extreme cases, not only synchronizing bars but video modulation may be visible. The visual appearance of cross-modulation is similar to that which results from direct pickup interference where an undesired signal "leaks" into the system and interferes with a cable signal on some channel.

Composite Intermodulation Noise

The preceding analysis was based on the carriage of a spectrum of signals, each of which has a carrier that represents most of the energy in the channel. Though that is a valid model for analog television signals and many conventional AM and narrow-band FM signals, digital signals differ significantly. A QAM signal, for instance, has a suppressed carrier and, when viewed on a spectrum analyzer, looks like a flat block of noise occupying the entire communications channel.

When such signals are subject to second- and third-order distortion, they do not produce single-frequency products but rather noiselike bands of energy whose amplitude *versus* frequency signature depends on the distortion mechanism. The products of this type of distortion are alternatively known as composite intermodulation noise (CIN), composite intermodulation distortion (CID), and intermodulation noise (IMN). This is an exception to our use of the term *noise* to refer only to thermal noise since CIN is actually a distortion product.

IM products involving digital carriers will be of three types:

- Products formed from the mixture of one or two analog carriers and one digital signal will appear as blocks of flat noise with a bandwidth equal to that of the digital signal.

- Products formed from the mixture of two digital signals (with or without an analog signal) will appear to have a symmetrical triangular-shaped amplitude-versus-frequency spectrum, where the triangle will have a spectral width equal to the sum of the widths of the two individual digital signals.

- Products formed from the mixture of three digital signals will appear to have a band-limited Gaussian shape with a spectral width equal to the sum of the widths of the three mixing signals.

Since digital signals are carried lower in level than analog signals, the preceding product types are listed in decreasing order of individual amplitude. On the other hand, as cable systems use an increasing percentage of available bandwidth for QAM signals, there will be a greater number of the third product type.

The calculated performance (partially based on laboratory measurements) of a cascade consisting of an optical link driving five amplifiers showed that a 750-MHz plant, operating with a signal load of 77 modulated analog television signals (54–550 MHz) and 33 QAM digital signals (550–750 MHz) and typical operating conditions and levels, suffered about 1 dB of effective analog video C/N degradation on the most affected (highest) analog channel due to CIN, with the digital signal levels suppressed 5 dB relative to analog signals.[11] With a thermal C/N of 49 dB, that implies a CIN level of −50.6 dB relative to the analog signals. At that operating level an adjacent 256 QAM signal would have a thermal C/N of 42.2 dB due to level and bandwidth differences, and suffer a 0.6-dB C/N degradation to 41.6 dB due to CIN. As discussed before, that might or might not be the most affected QAM channel.

2.3.4 Group Delay Variation and Amplifier Stability

Group delay is a measure of the rate of change of phase shift through a device as a function of frequency. In equation form,

$$\text{group delay (sec)} = \frac{1}{2\pi}\frac{d\gamma}{df} \tag{2.35}$$

where

γ = the phase shift through the device in radians
f = the frequency in Hz

In an ideal RF system, the transmission time is the same at all frequencies and the group delay is therefore a frequency-independent constant; if it is not, the various frequency components of a signal will not arrive simultaneously at a receiver.

Signal types have differing tolerances to group delay variation. For example, chroma delay is a measure of the arrival time of the chroma signal relative to an analog video luminance signal. To avoid visible artifacts in the viewed picture, the difference should not exceed 170 ns.

High-speed digital signals are also affected by group delay. For example, fast-rise-time waveforms will broaden if the higher-frequency components are delayed relative to the lower-frequency components. Systems are required to deliver QAM video channels with a group delay variation of no more than 0.25 μs/MHz across the entire 6-MHz RF channel.

The principal contributors to group delay variation are the characteristics of modulators and demodulators for individual channels and the diplex filters used at each of the signal ports of broadband amplifiers and nodes to separate upstream and downstream spectra. Figure 2.11 illustrates the key components of a two-way amplifier. The input and output diplex filters each consist of a high-pass section connecting the forward gain block to the external ports and a low-pass section feeding the reverse gain block. Each of the filter sections, as well as the amplifier modules, will have a gain (negative in the case of the filters) that is a function of frequency.

To ensure absolute stability, the sum of the gains around the loop shown in the heavy arrow must be less than zero at all frequencies. This condition must be met not only for matched loads on the external ports but for any mismatch encountered

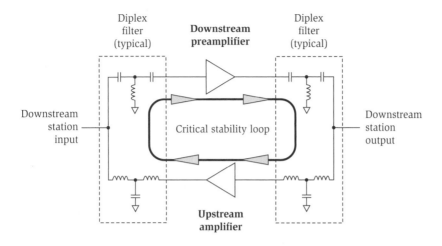

FIGURE 2.11

Bidirectional amplifier.

in an actual field installation. With simple filter designs, this is most easily achieved by having the cutoff frequencies of the filters as far apart as possible and thus close to the edge of well-separated forward and reverse passband edges. Since group delay variation gets worse as the cutoff frequency is approached, there is an inherent conflict among (1) the separation between the top of the upstream spectrum and the bottom of the downstream spectrum, (2) the cost of the diplex filter, (3) the group delay variation at the extremes of the spectra, and (4) the stability margin of the amplifier.

Ensuring a nonoscillatory condition may not be adequate. Even if the loop gain is less than zero, frequency response variations may result unless there is adequate isolation. As a practical test, adequate performance may be deduced by observing the swept frequency response of an amplifier at all frequencies, including the diplexer crossover region. Peaking of the response indicates the possibility of a loop gain problem.

Figure 2.12 illustrates the downstream group delay performance of a typical commercially available amplifier having a "42/52 split" (upper edge of the upstream spectrum is at 42 MHz, whereas the lower edge of the downstream spectrum is at 52 MHz). The curve illustrates the group delay, with the shaded regions indicating the frequencies and chroma/luma delay difference for the four lowest NTSC television channels in the CEA-542-B Standard frequency plan. The direction of the chroma delay is to advance the chroma with respect to the luminance. Serendipitously, this is the opposite delay sense (luminance is delayed with respect to chrominance) to that which is commonly encountered in the modulation–demodulation process, but any delay is not good.

End-to-end group delay requirements and typical network performance are discussed in Chapter 7, and upstream group delay is discussed in Chapter 8.

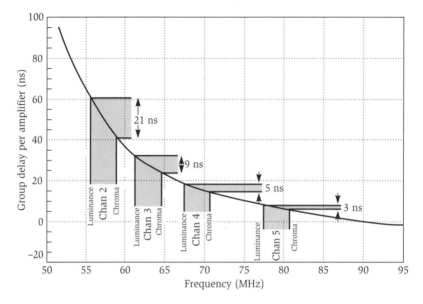

FIGURE 2.12

Downstream group delay due to diplex filters.

2.3.5 Hum Modulation

Although amplifiers that plug into conventional wall outlets are available (and used in headend and apartment house applications where convenient), most distribution amplifiers are powered via ac voltage that is multiplexed with the signals on the common coaxial distribution cable. Along with their signal-processing circuits, amplifier stations include circuitry for separating the power and signal voltages and for connecting the power to local power circuits that convert it to direct current to power the various electronic modules used.

Amplitude modulation of the transmitted signals at the power-line frequency (hum) can occur in two ways: excessive ac voltage at the output of an amplifier's local power pack and parametric modulation of magnetic component properties. Power pack "ripple" can modulate amplifier gain or be coupled into other circuits such as the automatic gain control (AGC). This ripple can result from faults in the power pack or loss of voltage regulation due to excessive voltage drop between the power supply and the amplifier's power pack.[††]

[††]In accordance with standard industry terminology, the term *power supply* is used to designate the device that generates the system power for multiplexing on the coaxial cable, whereas the term *power pack* is used to designate the device within each amplifier that converts the multiplexed power to the appropriate regulated dc levels for the circuitry.

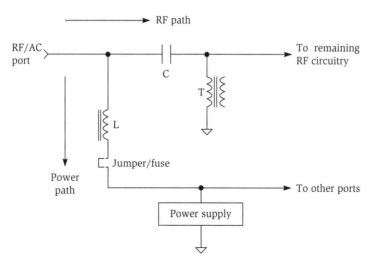

FIGURE 2.13

Power/RF separation in amplifiers.

Parametric magnetic modulation is less obvious. Consider the circuit segment in Figure 2.13. The current is tapped off the common coaxial input and sent through L to the amplifier power pack (and possibly inserted into the output coaxial cable(s) as well). Series capacitor C serves to pass the signals into the amplifier while blocking the supply voltage. Finally, T is the input winding of a typical signal-processing element, such as a directional tap, splitter, or part of a band-splitting filter.

One possible source of hum modulation is L. This component is required to exhibit very high impedance to frequencies covering the entire forward and return spectra. If the magnetic core becomes partially saturated at the peaks of the supply current, then the impedance match of the amplifier will vary accordingly, resulting in a level variation of the transmitted signal at the line frequency rate.

T is a much more sensitive component. Typically, these transformers are constructed of tiny cores that must have constant magnetic characteristics over an extremely wide frequency range. Although C nominally protects T from the supply current, there is still a displacement current to contend with. In particular, an ac current will flow through C and the primary winding of T, whose magnitude is

$$i_C = C\frac{dV}{dt} \tag{2.36}$$

When the power supply is a sine wave with a frequency of f_p and a peak voltage of E_p, the current will be

$$i_C = C\frac{d}{dt}[E_p\sin(2\pi f_p t)] = CE_p 2\pi f_p \cos(2\pi f_p t) \tag{2.37}$$

which has a peak value of $CE_p2\pi f_p$. If the voltage is a square wave with fast rise and fall times, then the displacement current can be much greater for the same peak supply voltage. To illustrate the trade-offs in design of these circuits, assume that it is desired that C have no more than 1 ohm of reactance at the low end of the upstream spectrum (generally 5 MHz) so as to affect the input match as little as possible. This requires that C be at least 0.03 μF $[X_C = 1/(2\pi f C)]$. If the supply voltage is 90-volt rms (127-volt peak) at 60 Hz, then the displacement current will be 1.4 mA. If, under square-wave powering conditions, the rise time is five times that under sine wave conditions, then the current could be as high as 7 mA. The designer's challenge is to ensure that this level of additional current in the winding of T does not change the transformer's characteristics.

In the North American NTSC analog television system, the frame repetition rate is 59.94 Hz. Since the commercial power frequency is 60 Hz, hum modulation generally appears as a horizontal bar or brightness variation whose pattern slowly moves upward with time (about 16 seconds to move the entire height of the picture). Typical coaxial components (both amplifiers and passive elements) are specified to create hum modulation at no greater than −70 dB, relative to 100% modulation, at their full rated supply voltage and pass-through current.

2.3.6 Frequency Response Variation and Impedance Match

Practical amplifiers do not amplify signals at all frequencies equally. Part of this variation is intentional and is intended to compensate for variations in cable losses and to optimize distortion performance, as we discuss in the next section. Any deviation from the intentional variation, however, is known as frequency response variation or flatness (quantified as $\pm x$ dB) or, more commonly, peak-to-valley (quantified as y dB peak-to-peak). Flatness is defined by the SCTE as the maximum gain deviation in either direction from a straight line, which represents the mean "trend line" of the frequency response of the device; the tilt of the line is defined as the "slope" of the device.[12] Figure 2.14 illustrates this definition; the peak-to-valley (P/V) is the sum of the absolute values of $+\Delta$ max and $-\Delta$ max. Arguably, for a device that is not supposed to have any slope, the reference line for determining flatness should be horizontal.

The frequency response through a network may be affected by the imperfect impedance matching between the amplifier and the attached transmission line. The effects of imperfect matches in coaxial components can best be understood in the context of their interaction. This is covered in detail in Chapter 7.

2.3.7 Practical Amplifier Design Choices

Complete amplifier stations may be simple or quite elaborate, depending on system needs. All share a common basic downstream structure consisting of several (generally two or three) cascaded gain stages, plus circuits that compensate for the loss variation of the cable before the amplifier (equalizers). Provisions are also made

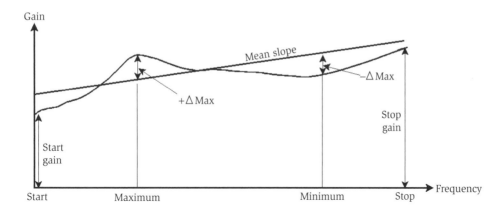

FIGURE 2.14

Definition of response variation.

for adjusting the gain of the amplifier as needed to meet system needs. Amplifiers differ in how many stages are employed, internal splitting, redundancy provisions, where operating adjustments are in the chain, automatic gain control, and the performance of each gain block. Many have provisions for automatically adjusting amplifier gain to compensate for changing input signal levels (automatic gain control).

As will be seen, optimum operation of repeatered coaxial distribution systems results when the levels of the FDM subcarriers at the output of amplifiers are not equal but increase with frequency. The variation in level across the operating range is known as *tilt*. The relationship between operating levels, amplifier response, and interconnecting transmission losses is explored more fully in Section 2.3.8.

In the upstream direction, all the amplifier designs are similar. Since cable losses are much lower in that portion of the spectrum, a single amplifier module is sufficient. Diplexers are used at each port to separate the upstream and downstream signals. All the upstream signals are passively combined and fed to the amplifier module. Unlike downstream, where all level setting takes place at the input or midstage with the aim of setting a consistent *output* level, the common upstream practice is to align the system so that the *input* level to the module is constant and to set the output gain and slope after the gain stage so that the input to the next amplifier station upstream is correct. Chapter 8 covers the alignment and operation of networks in the upstream direction.

To allow the most flexibility in application and system design, jumpers or switches allow power to enter the amplifier via any desired port and to be routed to any combination of output ports.

Early power packs used conventional transformer/linear regulator designs. Transformer taps were available to optimize the winding ratio of the transformer to limit required regulator dissipation. Modern designs almost universally use switching regulators (whose design is beyond the scope of this book) that have the property of operating at a constant high efficiency regardless of input voltage. To do so, they draw a constant *wattage* from the coaxial cable, and thus the current is inversely proportional to the supply voltage. Though this results in the greatest overall powering efficiency, it has some unexpected consequences when a number of amplifiers are powered from a common source, as will be seen in Chapter 3.

Beyond their basic functional elements, amplifier stations may be equipped with a variety of enhancements, including redundant gain modules and power supplies, status monitors and transducers, and remotely controllable upstream path disconnect. Often fiber-optic receivers and transmitters are combined with amplifier station components, creating a fiber-optic node.

Although the labels attached to different configurations are somewhat arbitrary and subject to change, the following classifications are typical:

- Trunk amplifiers are the workhorses of traditional all-coaxial cable television systems. They are optimized for long-distance, repeated signal distribution. As such, they are operated at output levels that cause only moderate distortion to allow long cascades. The gain is set as high as possible, consistent with low perstage noise addition. Typically, the output levels of the highest channels are +35 to +40 dBmV, and the gain is about 22 dB. Trunk amplifiers are not used to supply signals to taps.

- Where a local distribution circuit is also desired, a portion of the trunk signal is fed to a separate output stage known as a bridger. This amplifier generally runs at a higher output level (and distortion) to allow feeding as many customer taps as possible. Though generally configured as an optional module within the trunk station, bridgers may be contained in separate housings along with directional couplers (midspan bridgers). Figure 2.15 is a block diagram of the RF portion of a typical trunk station, including bridger.

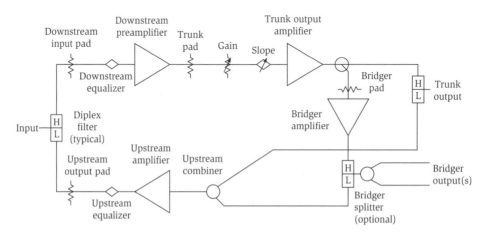

FIGURE 2.15

Typical trunk amplifier RF configuration.

■ Distribution amplifiers (sometimes called system amplifiers) are the most common active device in modern short-cascade HFC systems. They are available with two to four output amplifier modules whose output levels can be independently adjusted. Figure 2.16 shows a typical configuration with three output gain blocks.

■ Line extenders are used to allow feeding more taps than possible with just a bridger or high-level distribution amplifier port. Since they are generally operated at similar output levels, the cascade of such devices must be limited to keep distortions at an acceptable level. Line extenders are the simplest of the classifications, as shown in Figure 2.17.

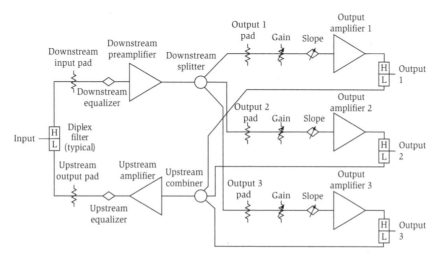

FIGURE 2.16

Typical distribution amplifier RF configuration.

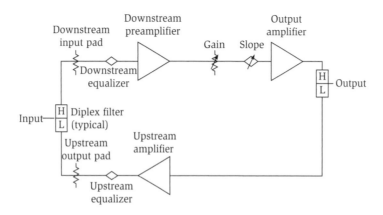

FIGURE 2.17

Typical line extender RF configuration.

2.3.8 Amplifier Operating Dynamics

The C/N degradation as a signal passes through an amplifier is related to the input signal level and the noise figure at any frequency (see Equation 2.18). On the other hand, the loss of coaxial cable increases with frequency. Thus, the amplifier need not supply the same level for channels at the bottom of the spectrum as at the top to overcome cable loss. Reducing the levels of the lower-frequency channels, in turn, reduces the amplitudes of the intermodulation products to which those channels contribute, and thus CSO, CTB, CIN, and XMOD.

The relation between cable and amplifier characteristics and operating levels can best be illustrated by considering an amplifier and its driven cable as a system (see Figure 2.18). Only the downstream path will be discussed here; Chapter 8 will deal with the equivalent upstream issues.

The preamplifier has a relatively constant noise figure and gain across the spectrum. Between the preamplifier and output stage, a slope circuit is used to adjust the frequency response so that it uniformly increases across the downstream frequency range. Typical gain slopes are 6 to 10 dB for a 750-MHz amplifier. Additionally, pads are used to adjust the overall amplifier gain. The station noise figure and slope are illustrated in Figure 2.19a.

Some combination of coaxial cable and passive RF devices is connected between this amplifier station and the input of the next station. Since both the cable and passive devices have a loss that varies across the spectrum (and, in the case of cable, increases as the square root of frequency), the variation in level reaching the next station will be reduced. Amplifier input circuits are designed to accommodate a variety of equalizers that are optimized to compensate for the residual response variation and pads that are used to set the correct drive level to the preamp input. Occasionally, external in-line equalizers may be used also, for example, as a tool to reduce the total variation of levels fed to customers.

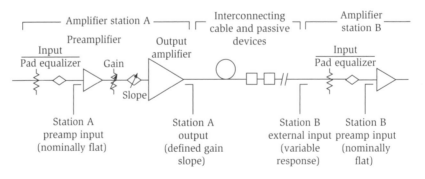

FIGURE 2.18

Downstream response and gain relationships and adjustments.

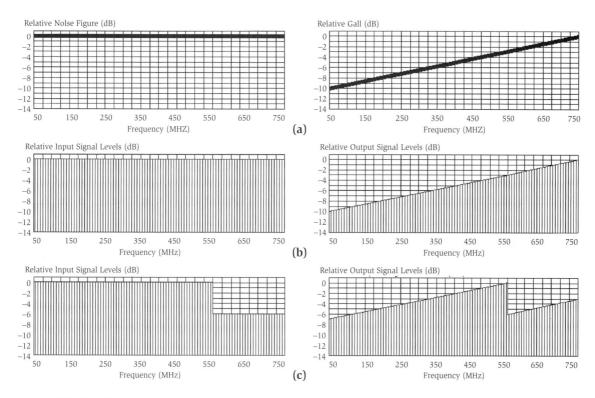

FIGURE 2.19

Amplifier gain and signal loading. (a) Amplifier characteristics. (b) Amplifier loaded with analog video signals. (c) Amplifier with hybrid analog–digital signal loading.

In station alignment, the equalizers and pads are used to align the *output* of each amplifier station as closely as possible to the optimum levels and "gain slope." Thus, the system gain and frequency response, as measured from the output of one amplifier to the output of any other similarly aligned amplifier in a series-connected string, are ideally unity. Because of the variability in interstation losses, the levels and response at station inputs will vary; however, the response at the internal preamp input will be approximately flat after equalization and padding. Amplifiers that do not feed customer taps (e.g., trunk amplifiers) are typically operated at levels several decibels lower than those that do.

By contrast to the frequency response of the system (slope), the variation in levels of the signals carried is known as *tilt*. The terms are often confused, particularly since modern amplifier performance is often specified with a tilt at amplifier outputs that matches the gain slope. Historically (with narrower-bandwidth amplifiers), it was more common to use "block tilt" with groups of channels operated at different levels. This was easier for technicians to understand since only a few levels needed to be memorized.

Modern amplifiers are generally specified under two signal-loading conditions. Figure 2.19b shows the nominal preamplifier input (after equalization) and output levels of a 750-MHz amplifier station loaded with a full spectrum of 110 video signals tilted to match the amplifier's gain slope. This is the optimum condition for carrying signals of similar format and results in approximately equal C/N degradation for each channel (because of the uniform preamp input levels) and the lowest distortion (because the outputs at the lower channels are reduced in level to approximately match interconnecting cable and component losses). Figure 2.19c shows an alternative loading condition with a superimposed −6-dB block tilt for signals above 550 MHz. The assumption is made that these signals are digitally modulated and do not require the same C/N and C/distortion as analog video channels, and so are reduced in level to reduce overall amplifier loading.

Optimum amplifier gain is a function of noise figure and output capability (for a given distortion level). By way of illustration, assume that a given amplifier has an effective noise figure of 9 dB and a CTB of −78 dB at an output level of +45/35 dBmV (the dual numbers are the individual channel levels at the top and bottom of the downstream spectrum, respectively). If the gain of the unit is set at 35 dB (at the top channel frequency) and the input level is +10 dBmV on all channels, then, from Equation 2.19, the C/N of this stage alone will be 60 dB (10 + 59 − 9). The output level will be the input level plus the gain, or +10 dBmV +35 dB = +45 dBmV, so the CTB will be the specified −78 dBmV.

If the input level is varied, the C/N will improve by 1 dB for every decibel increase in input level, whereas the CTB will degrade by 2 dB. In setting up a coaxial system, input padding is used to set the optimum operating point.

Now consider the situation if the amplifier had been designed with a gain of 40 dB. At first glance, this would seem like an improvement since such amplifiers could be spaced farther apart along the transmission line. When driven by a +10 dBmV input signal, however, the output level will be +10 dBmV + 40 dB = +50 dBmV. At that level, the CTB will be only −68 dB, having degraded by 10 dB owing to the 5-dB increase in output level. If the input level is decreased by 5 dB to restore the distortions to the specified level, the station's C/N will decrease from 60 to 55 dB. In short, the excess gain forces the user to accept either higher distortion or higher noise.

It would seem from the preceding example that reducing gain would improve performance. Although that is true, more lower-gain amplifiers would have to be cascaded to reach the same distance, and that would lower reliability and increase power consumption.

With decreasing node sizes in HFC networks, many new nodes are designed with no more than one or two (sometimes zero) amplifiers after the node launch amplifier. Since cascades are very short, amplifiers optimized for this application are designed for higher gain and output levels, allowing them to serve more taps per port with no worse distortion performance than a longer cascade of lower-output amplifiers.

The selection of optimum amplifier internal gains is very complex. The industry's choice of operational gains ranging from 20 to 38 dB (depending on technology and application) is based on the best compromise among cost, reliability, and performance.

2.3.9 Amplifier Technology Choices

As previously discussed, modern broadband solid-state cable television amplifiers are all push–pull in nature, meaning that their output stages contain two matched transistors connected in a symmetrical configuration. To the extent that any nonlinearities are also symmetrical, they will produce only odd-order distortion products. Amplifiers whose output stages each contain only a single push–pull circuit are known generally as *push–pull amplifiers*.

An improvement in distortion performance can be realized by splitting the input signal, feeding two push–pull output gain stages in parallel, and then combining the outputs into a single port. This type of amplifier, generically known as *parallel hybrid*, offers about twice the output level at the same distortion levels compared with push–pull units. Since two output stages are involved, the power consumption and dissipation are also higher than with push–pull units. Parallel hybrid amplifiers are generally used where high output powers are beneficial, such as bridgers and line extenders.

The third amplifier technology, now of mostly historical interest, is known as *feed forward*. In a feed-forward amplifier, input signals are amplified via a conventional inverting amplifier. Samples of the input and output signals, adjusted for gain, are combined and amplified in a separate inverting *error amplifier*. The output of the error amplifier is summed with the output of the original amplifier so that the errors approximately cancel.[13] Figure 2.20 shows this configuration. The delay lines are required to match the signals' phases. Feed-forward amplifiers offered about

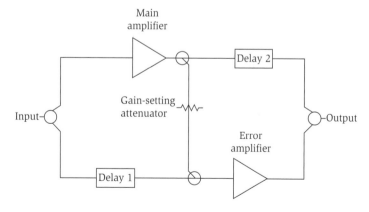

FIGURE 2.20

Feed-forward gain block.

12 dB of CTB improvement and 6 dB of CSO improvement over power doubling units at comparable operating levels, but required careful alignment. They were generally used in long trunk lines where the lower cascaded distortion was beneficial.

2.4 PASSIVE COAXIAL COMPONENTS

The nature of typical coaxial distribution systems is that the downstream path is split and resplit to create many endpoints from a common signal insertion point. In the upstream direction, the opposite is true, with signals from many potential insertion points combined at a common node. In the headend, signals from individual modulators and signal processors are combined to create the full downstream spectrum, whereas upstream signals are split to feed receivers for each service.

The signal splitting can occur either within amplifier housings or by use of stand-alone components. Those that split the signal among multiple output ports are known as *splitters*, whereas those that divert a defined portion of the input signal to a single side port (with the rest passed to an output port) are known as *directional couplers*. Finally, those that divert a portion of the input signal and then split the diverted signal to create individual customer drops are known as *taps*. All share certain characteristics and so will be treated in this section.

In general, all these are passive devices constructed using ferrite-loaded transmission lines and transmission-line transformers. They are bidirectional; that is, the same device can be used to split signals to feed multiple paths or to combine signals from multiple input ports. Important characteristics are signal loss, impedance match, and isolation between nominally isolated ports.

2.4.1 Directional Couplers

Figure 2.21 shows schematics of two directional coupler configurations. In both examples shown, the voltage transformer and current transformers have the same ratio so that, after combining, the ratio of voltage to current stays the same, meaning that the impedance of the side port is the same as the main line. The transformers sample voltage and current regardless of signal flow in the main line. The polarity of the signal as it appears at the secondary of the current transformer, however, is reversed relative to the signal at the secondary of the voltage transformer for signals traveling in one direction versus the other direction, and therefore the sampled signal, after combining, will propagate either toward the termination resistor or toward the side port, depending on the direction of signal flow. This is what gives the coupler its directivity.

By varying the turns ratio of both transformers, various values of coupling are possible. Ellis[14] has published a tabulation of coupling values as a function of turns ratios, along with a good description of coupler operation. Table 2.2 lists some commonly used values and their theoretical signal loss values (practical units will exhibit 1 to 2 dB of excess loss due to imperfect components). The coupled loss is simply due to the voltage (or current) ratio defined by the transformers, whereas

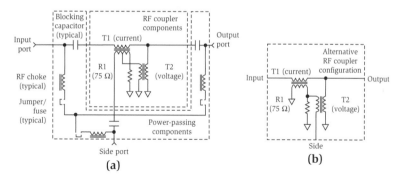

FIGURE 2.21

Directional coupler schematic. (a) Coupler plus power components. (b) Alternate RF configuration.

Table 2.2 Theoretical Directional Coupler Losses		
Turns ratio (T1 and T2)	Input to output insertion loss (dB)	Input to coupled port loss (dB)
2.5:1	0.78	7.96
3:1	0.51	9.54
4:1	0.28	12.04
5:1	0.18	13.97

the input/output loss just reflects the loss diverted to the coupled port (or isolation resistor, depending on signal flow).

As is the case with amplifiers, added components in units intended for installation in trunk and distribution cables separate power from signal voltages and send them through different paths, as shown in Figure 2.21a. Generally, means are provided to control transmission of power independently from RF signals so as to allow the greatest flexibility in system design. Note that, if ac power is transmitted through all RF ports, the displacement current through the three blocking capacitors will add in phase through the primary of the voltage transformer. Thus, couplers generate parametric-type hum modulation at levels as high as or higher than amplifiers.

The difference in sensitivity to downstream and upstream signals, as measured at the side port, is the *directivity* of the coupler. Sometimes, instead of directivity, the absolute upstream coupling factor, known as *isolation*, is specified. Numerically, directivity is simply the difference between coupling factor and isolation. As we will discuss in Chapter 7, directivity and return loss interact to cause additional system group delay and response variation.

The coupling value may not be uniform across the entire frequency range of the device. Even though the overall variation in coupling factor may not be desirable or intentional, the slope and response variation is measured separately and defined the same for passive devices as for amplifiers.

2.4.2 Splitters

Two-way splitters differ functionally from directional couplers only in that the signal splitting is equal. Other common configurations include four-way and eight-way equal splits. Three-way unequal splits are internally constructed by splitting two ways, then resplitting one of the legs from the first splitter to create a 50%:25%:25% output ratio. Equal-ratio three-way splitters are less common.

Figure 2.22 illustrates a two-way symmetrical splitter, with expansion to four-way. Figure 2.22a is the schematic diagram of a two-way unit, for which Figure 2.22b is the standard symbol, with terminology. Transformer T1 is a 2:1 impedance step-down transformer that creates a 37.5-ohm source to feed the center tap of transformer T2. T2 is a transmission-line transformer derived from a Wilkinson coupler (which is used for symmetrical splitting of high-power, narrow-band signals for

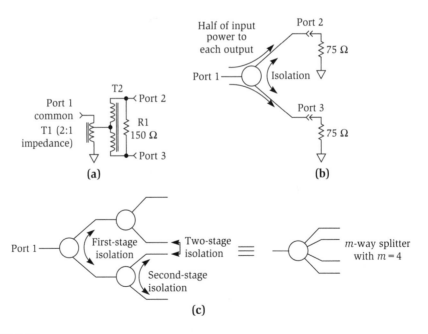

FIGURE 2.22

Splitters. (a) Schematic. (b) External power flow. (c) Multiple stages of splitting to create an *m*-way splitter with enhanced isolation among some ports.

directional antenna arrays, among other applications).[15] The two outputs at ports 2 and 3 are nominally in phase and at the same level. Resistor R1 is required to provide isolation between them.

Because power is equally divided between ports 2 and 3, the theoretical loss from port 1 to either output is 10 log (0.5) = −3.01 dB. As with directional couplers, the practical loss will be higher due to core losses in the ferrite core material in the transformers and resistive losses in the transformer wire.

The dimensions of transformers used in high-frequency applications are constrained by the necessity for the winding lengths to be a small portion of a wavelength at the highest frequency of operation. This, in turn, mandates very small cores and fine-wire gauges whose resistance is a factor in excess signal loss. The excess loss over and above that due to coupling is typically 0.5 to 1 dB to each of the output ports, making the total loss typically 3.5 to 4 dB.

Loss in a splitter is called *flat loss* because it tends not to be a strong function of frequency, as is the loss in coaxial cable. However, there is some increased loss as the frequency increases, partially due to skin effects, which increase the effective resistance of the wire as frequency increases. At higher frequencies, the ferrite core on which the transformer is wound ceases to have significant magnetic properties, but rather acts as a coil form. Some loss may be associated with it, but the ferrite material is primarily included to improve low-frequency performance. At the lowest frequencies, loss also increases because the open-circuit reactance of the transformer windings is no longer large relative to the circuit impedance.

When the splitter is used as a combiner, incoming signals on ports 2 and 3 are combined and appear at port 1. The theoretical loss from port 2 (or port 3) to port 1 is also 3 dB, the other half of the power being dissipated in resistor R1. Theoretically, no power from port 2 appears at port 3 (if all ports are properly terminated) and vice versa. The signal loss between the output ports, with all ports terminated in 75 ohms, is defined as the isolation. Typical values of isolation for commercially available splitters range from 20 to 30 dB.

Other important specifications of splitters include insertion loss, normally specified as the total loss from port 1 to port 2 with port 3 terminated (or vice versa), and the return loss at each port with the other ports terminated.

Lack of termination drastically reduces the effective isolation. For instance, power injected into port 3 is attenuated −3 dB at port 1. Should that port not be terminated, the power would be reflected into the splitter dividing equally between ports 2 and 3. Thus, the isolation from port 3 to port 2 would be only 6 dB. Similarly, the effective return loss at port 3 would be 6 dB as a result of power being reflected to that port.

Splitters having more output ports can be fabricated by combining two-way splitters in tree fashion, as shown in Figure 2.22c. Each leg of the leftmost splitter is connected to the input of another two-way splitter. At that level, four outputs exist. Each of those four can be connected to another two-way splitter, resulting in eight outputs, and so on. The practical loss at each stage will be 3.5 to 4 dB so that the four-way split loss is 7 to 8 dB. In an eight-way splitter, it is 10.5 to 12 dB and so on. In general, the loss in a multilevel splitter is given by

$$L_m = \left[\frac{L_1}{0.301}\right]\log(m) \qquad (2.38)$$

where

L_m = the loss of the m-output splitter chain in decibels
L_1 = the loss in one two-way splitter (3.5–4 dB usually)

It is also possible to construct a splitter chain with a number of outputs not equal to 2^n by simply terminating the splits early on some of the chains. Equation 2.38 must be modified in this case.

Where output port isolation is important in multiport applications (such as headend combining), one alternative is to use ports in multilevel splitters that are not derived from common stages for critical applications. As shown in Figure 2.22c, if two splitter outputs are connected to the same second-stage splitter, the isolation between them is merely the isolation of that stage. On the other hand, if two ports are not connected to the same second-stage splitter, then the isolation realized will include the effects of the first-stage splitter, as shown in the figure. Unfortunately, manufacturers may not indicate internal splitter configurations or specify nonadjacent port isolation.

Another higher-isolation alternative is to construct multiport splitters from cascaded directional couplers. Generally, side ports of adjacent, series-connected couplers will be better isolated than outputs from single-stage splitters.

2.4.3 Taps

The most common tap configuration consists of a directional coupler with the side-arm signal split two, four, or eight ways to create customer drops. Although the input and through ports are typically provided with connectors appropriate for distribution cable, the side arms are equipped with connectors appropriate for drop cable. In North American systems, this means "5/8-24" ports for input and through ports and type-F connectors for the drops.

A tap need not have a through port. At the end of the line, it is common to use a *terminating tap*, which is just a splitter whose output legs are equipped with drop connectors. Until about 1995, taps supplied RF signals, but not power, to customer drop lines and were limited in main-line current-handling capacity to 7 amperes or less since this was adequate for entertainment-based cable television systems. With the active consideration of HFC architectures for telephony service came increased demands on tap capabilities:

- Bandwidth expansion to 5 to 1000 MHz

- The ability to supply power to side-of-house active *network interface devices* (NIDs) that could provide an interface between baseband twisted-pair in-home telephone circuits and the RF carriers in the distribution system

- Provisions for changing tap values and configurations without interrupting service to customers farther along the distribution cable

■ Increased voltage and current capability, typically 90 V rms and 10 amperes, in order to allow transmission of sufficient power for both network amplifiers and NIDs over the same coaxial cables formerly used only for video service

The new generation of taps that have evolved are known as *power-passing taps* or, sometimes, *telephony taps*. In addition to normal tap capabilities, they tap into the distribution cable power and selectively provide current-limited power along with RF signals to a NID on each home. Depending on the design, this power may be multiplexed with the signals in the coaxial drop cable or carried along a separate twisted pair of copper wires in a hybrid cable configuration.

A major concern for those using the drop center conductor to carry power to NIDs is that, if arcing occurs because of a faulty center conductor contact, the arc will transfer a very significant amount of RF power to the upstream plant, likely causing interference with all users of the reverse spectrum. On the other hand, an arc often causes healing of a bad contact and thus can be self-healing.

Figure 2.23 is a circuit diagram for a typical power-passing tap that uses the drop center conductor to pass power to the NID. The RF portion of the tap consists of a directional coupler and a two-way splitter (the diagram is for a two-port tap). The directional coupler diverts a controlled portion of the downstream signal and passes it to the splitter, which divides the power to feed the subscriber ports.

Multiplexed ac power consideration in taps is similar to that on amplifiers and other network passives. Capacitors C1 and C2 isolate the multiplexed power supply voltage and current from the directional coupler RF components. Transformers T1 and T2 are built with very fine wire to permit operation at frequencies up to 1 GHz and would be unable to withstand the currents that would result if the primary of T1 were required to handle several amperes of ac current or if the primary of T2 had tens of volts of 60 Hz across it. The multiplexed ac power is shunted across the tap through the large RF choke, L1.

A choke with somewhat less current capacity, L2, provides a path for the multiplexed power that will feed the customer ports. Since this choke is shunt-connected across the main RF path, it must have a higher RF impedance than L1. The unavoidable RF loss due to this choke is one reason power-passing taps have a slightly higher through loss than normal taps.

In order to permit the tap plate (which contains most, if not all, of the circuitry) to be removed without interrupting either power or RF continuity in the hard-cable distribution plant, many modern taps incorporate a mechanical bypass switch that engages before the tap-to-baseplate connections are broken to provide continuity from input to through ports. During the removal or insertion of a tap plate, therefore, there will be a brief interval when both the bypass and main connections are made. This will cause a transient condition during which the primary of T1 will be shorted, but the primary of T2 will function normally. This momentary mismatch will cause some attenuation of the transmitted signals. Whether or not it causes a functional problem for the services offered will depend on the characteristics of the signals used.

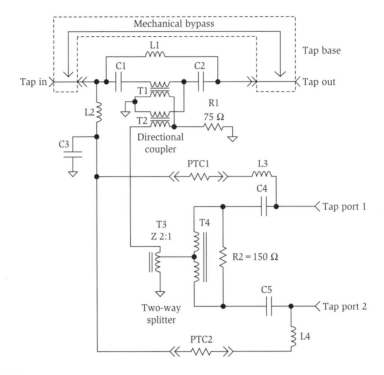

FIGURE 2.23

Power-passing tap using the drop center conductor for power delivery to a home.

Continuing with the description of the circuit, capacitor C3 is used to ensure a good RF ground on the "cold" end of L2. Positive temperature coefficient (PTC) resistors PTC1 and PTC2 limit the ac current that can be drawn through the customer ports. At normal currents, the PTC resistor (commonly called just a PTC) exhibits low resistance. As more current is drawn, its temperature increases, causing a resistance increase and effectively limiting the total current. Electronic current limiters have been proposed as an alternative to PTCs, but to date have not been widely deployed because of cost. National Electrical Code (NEC) regulations, starting in 1999, required a more sophisticated current-limiting system if the drop cable did not meet certain construction and installation criteria.

Finally, inductors L3 and L4 couple power to the two tap ports shown, again isolating the RF signals from the ac supply. As with L2, the reactance of these components must be sufficient to minimize RF losses, and their presence leads to slightly higher overall RF losses in commercially available power-passing taps.

The use of power-passing taps of the type described peaked with the use of first-generation telephone NIDs, but has decreased as operators have generally switched to DOCSIS-based voice gateways that are usually home powered, with a local battery to provide service continuity in the case of a power outage.

Another tap option is drop equalization. In this configuration, a passive device is incorporated between the directional coupler and internal splitter in each tap. Plug-in passive components can provide downstream or upstream (or both) equalization, or selectively attenuate either the downstream or upstream band while passing the other intact. As will be discussed in Chapter 8, these taps can be used to better control downstream and upstream levels to each customer.

The relationship between passive specifications and system performance will be explored in Chapter 7.

2.5 **POWER SUPPLIES**

Power supplies convert commercial power to lower voltages that are multiplexed with RF signals in the coaxial cables. Although not part of the RF circuit, certain characteristics of power supplies have an effect on the transmission of signals.

Direct current, very-low-frequency (as low as 1 Hz) ac, and 60-Hz ac have all been considered for system power, as have voltages between 30 and 90 volts. Direct current (dc) has been rejected primarily because of possible galvanic corrosion. Early cable television systems used 30 volts, but the increased power demands of wider-bandwidth, higher-output amplifiers forced the industry to convert to 60 volts for systems constructed after about 1970. Two factors have made 90 volts the default standard for new construction and upgraded systems: the desire to power larger plant sections from a single power supply to improve reliability (see Chapter 12 on HFC reliability for a detailed explanation) and the possibility of powering some terminal equipment through the distribution plant.

Along with the increase in voltage has come a requirement to increase currents as far as practical, with requirements to pass 10 to 15 amperes being common. Since current from supplies can be transmitted both ways along the cable and/or inserted into more than one cable, power supplies with a capacity of 40 or more amperes are available.

Field power supplies are roughly divided among nonstandby, standby, and UPS/standby types. The basic component of a nonstandby, line frequency power supply is the ferroresonant transformer. Though its magnetic design is beyond the scope of this book, ferroresonant transformers have a number of properties of interest to operators: (1) output voltage regulation (a typical specification is $\pm5\%$ output voltage change when the input voltage changes $\pm15\%$), (2) inherent current-limiting and short-circuit protection, (3) transient protection, and (4) 90% or better efficiency at rated output current.

Standby power supplies add a battery charger, a set of rechargeable batteries, an inverter, and a changeover switch. The charger ensures that the batteries are always held at full charge, whereas the inverter starts and supplies square wave power to replace the sine wave commercial power when it is interrupted (see Figure 2.24). Depending on the application, sufficient battery capacity may be provided for 2 to 8 hours or more of standby operation.

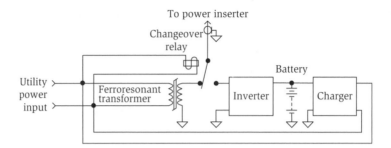

FIGURE 2.24

Basic standby power supply functional diagram.

An important parameter for operation in the standby mode is the rise and fall times of the square wave voltage. As the previously presented Equation 2.36 shows, the amount of ac power supply current that "leaks" into the low-level signal path in amplifiers and passives is directly proportional to the rise time of this waveform. The trade-off, for power supply designers, is that the efficiency of an inverter is an inverse function of the time the transistors spend in their active region (i.e., not in a saturated or cutoff condition). Also, the power lost due to slow switching is dissipated in the transistors and must be conducted away by heat sinks. Unfortunately, the industry does not have a consensus on the best compromise on rise time.

When commercial power fails, there is an unavoidable but brief interruption while the relay switches between the ferroresonant transformer output and the inverter transformer output. Typically, the time to switch is 8 to 16 ms. Most suppliers synchronize their inverters with commercial power before switching so that phase shift transients in the power supplies of the amplifiers can be avoided.

As will be discussed in Chapter 3, even with inverter phase synchronization, the short switching transient can be a problem when analyzed with respect to its effect on cascaded amplifiers. To avoid that, a third alternative is the uninterruptible power supply (UPS). Some UPS versions of field supplies avoid switching transients by utilizing the same ferroresonant transformer for both inverter and commercial power. During ac power outages, commercial power is disconnected and the inverter continues to supply power via an additional primary winding.

2.6 SUMMARY

This chapter has covered the technology behind coaxial distribution systems. The characteristics of the coaxial cable, amplifiers, passive components, and powering systems have been covered in detail, including both the theory behind operation and the performance of commercially available products.

Although other constructions are sometimes used, solid aluminum-sheathed cable of 75-ohm impedance has been seen to offer a good combination of loss, cost-effectiveness, and handling characteristics, and is in common use worldwide. Amplifier stations for cable systems are designed with unique characteristics that complement the characteristics of the interconnecting cable and passive devices. Integrated powering of active devices through the cable avoids the necessity of separately connecting each distribution system amplifier to the local utility, but requires special circuitry in every device to separate the power and signal paths.

Before the mid-1980s, cable television systems used primarily coaxial technology (sometimes supplemented by broadband microwave links) to serve their customers. Chapter 3 will cover the design of coaxial distribution systems, including both the shared portions and individual in-home "drop" wiring. As will be seen, the performance of such networks is subject to certain unavoidable limitations that become more severe as bandwidth is increased. As a result, modern systems generally use linear fiber-optic links in place of the long, repeatered coaxial trunks to interconnect small, physically separate coaxial distribution networks with shared headends. Chapter 4 and 5 will cover the technology and performance of such links. Chapter 6 will then cover the design of linear, broadband microwave links. Chapter 7 will cover the end-to-end downstream performance of the broadband network, from headend to subscriber, and Chapter 8 will deal with upstream issues.

ENDNOTES

1. *Reference Data for Radio Engineers*, 6th ed. Indianapolis, IN: Howard W. Sams, 1977, p. 6-6.

2. Frederick Terman, *Electronic and Radio Engineering*. New York: McGraw-Hill, 1955, p. 121.

3. *NCTA Recommended Practices for Measurements on Cable Television Systems*, 2nd ed. Washington, DC: National Cable & Telecommunications Association, October 1993, Part Six.

4. The size-59, -6, and -11 cables were formerly known as RG59, RG6, and RG11 because of their physical size similarity to standard military-grade 75-ohm cables carrying those designations. Since CATV cables do not attempt to adhere to military specifications, the RG notation has been dropped by the industry.

5. The SCTE is an ANSI-accredited standards-making body. It publishes a wide variety of standards covering both performance and test methods related to cable television products. In particular, SCTE-IPS-TP-011, *Test Method for Transfer Impedance*, and SCTE-IPS-TP-403, *Test Method for Shielding Effectiveness*, detail test methods for evaluating shielding integrity, whereas SCTE-IPS-SP-001, *Specification for Flexible RF Coaxial Drop Cable*, contains both mechanical and electrical minimum performance standards.

6. *Code of Federal Regulations*: C.F.R. 47 §76.5(w). Technically, the noise is defined as that occupying the band between 1.25 and 5.25 MHz above the lower band edge. Available from the Government Printing Office, Washington, DC.

7. An excellent detailed mathematical treatment of amplifier distortion based on a power-series expansion is given in *Technical Handbook for CATV Systems*, authored by

Ken Simons and published by Jerrold Electronics Corporation, Hatboro, PA (the third edition was published in 1968 and was still in print in 1978). His results were also published in the *Proceedings of the IEEE* in July 1970.

8. Schlomo Ovadia, *Broadband Cable TV Access Networks*. Upper Saddle River, NJ: Prentice-Hall, 2001, pp. 49–50.

9. Data taken from *Cable TV Reference Guide*, April 1992 edition, Philips Broadband Networks, Manlius, NY.

10. Private correspondence from Archer Taylor regarding his experiences with installed systems.

11. This treatment of CID is based on a paper by Jeff Hamilton and Dean Stoneback, "The Effect of Digital Carriers on Analog CATV Distribution Systems," 1993 *NCTA Technical Papers*, pp. 100–113. Washington, DC: National Cable & Telecommunications Association, 1993.

12. "SCTE 144 2007 Test Procedure for Measuring Transmission and Reflection." Exton, PA: Society of Cable Telecommunications Engineers, 2007.

13. A basic discussion of feed-forward gain block principles is contained in a paper by John Pavlic, "Some Considerations for Applying Several Feedforward Gain Block Models to CATV Distribution Amplifiers," *Technical Papers, Cable '83*. Washington, DC: National Cable & Telecommunications Association, June 1983.

14. Michael G. Ellis, "RF Directional Couplers," *RF Design*, February 1997, p. 33ff.

15. Robert P. Gilmore, "Applications of Power Combining in Communications Systems," *Application Note*. San Diego, CA: Qualcomm, Inc.

Coaxial Distribution System Design

3.1 INTRODUCTION

Distribution system design is, ideally, the process of specifying the most economical network that will provide the required bidirectional bandwidth to the required number of terminal points and still meet defined performance goals. The performance goals, in turn, may be derived from internal quality standards, governmental regulations, the perceived requirements for reliable signal transportation, or all of the preceding.

Typical system specifications will include noise, distortion, response variation, delivered signal levels (and their stability), hum, and a number of specifications specific to signal types carried. Reliability, another important consideration, is discussed in Chapter 12, and the effects of imperfect impedance matching among components are discussed in Chapter 7. The distribution system performance must also be considered as part of a chain that includes headend channel processing and terminal equipment effects on signals. Finally, the coaxial distribution system will usually be cascaded with a linear fiber-optic link, although occasionally microwave is used where physical plant construction is impractical. These are treated in subsequent chapters. The Excel spreadsheet entitled "Noise-Distortion Calculator.xls," available through this book's website at *www.elsevierdirect.com/companions/ 9780123744012*, includes tools for calculating cascaded C/N, C/CTB, and C/CSO as discussed in this chapter.

The final leg in the broadband distribution system is the drop wiring leading from tap ports to and throughout homes. By tradition, broadband networks are designed to meet certain goals from headend output to tap port, with an additional allowance made for the effects of in-home wiring. Modern drop systems, however, may vary widely in their complexity and quality, and in fact may constitute minidistribution networks by themselves. The final section of this chapter deals briefly with drops.

We begin by discussing basic principles and applying them to the "hard-cable" portion of the plant.

57

3.2 CARRIER-TO-NOISE RATIO

Noise is defined by the IEEE as "unwanted disturbances superposed upon a useful signal that tend to obscure its information content."[1] In many communications systems, that is a good working definition. In cable television, however, the term "noise" (without a qualifying adjective) is generally applied to thermal noise, which is treated independently from disturbances caused, for instance, by intermodulation products, ingress, or other causes. One historical reason for treating thermal noise differently from other disturbances is that the subjective effects of noise and various other types of interference to analog video signals are different. Another is that, unlike many communications systems, the sources and mechanisms by which interfering signals are generated are well understood, and a detailed independent analysis of each has proved useful. Therefore, in this book, unless otherwise stated, *noise* will be used to refer exclusively to thermal noise.

In general, thermal noise is *uncorrelated*, that is, unpredictable and nonrepetitive. Noise generated in one device or at one time is totally unrelated to noise in another device or in the same device at another time, although the *average* level of noise power may be quite predictable. Since that is the case, when the noise from two independent sources is combined, the total noise *power* will be the sum of the original noise powers.

Carrier-to-noise ratio (C/N) is defined as follows:

$$C/N \, (dB) \equiv 10 \log \left(\frac{c}{n} \right) \tag{3.1}$$

where c and n are the scalar power levels of the carrier and noise, respectively. For analog television signals, such as NTSC, the carrier power is defined as the average power during the sync tip (the highest power level in the modulated signal). Noise is defined as the average noise power measured in a defined bandwidth (4 MHz for NTSC). For QAM signals, there is no "carrier" as such, but the signal power is defined as the total in-channel, desired-signal average power level, and the noise power is measured over the entire bandwidth of the entire assigned channel (6 MHz for downstream signals and various bandwidths for upstream signals).

Equation 2.19 gives the C/N for an analog video channel transmitted through an individual amplifier, given the input signal level and noise figure. In order to design a coaxial distribution system, it is necessary to compute the C/N of cascaded amplifiers, each followed by loss equal to the gain of the preceding amplifier. For two amplifiers, the general expression for composite C/N is approximated by the equation

$$C/N_{ttl} = -10 \log \left[10^{-\left(\frac{C/N_1}{10} \right)} + 10^{-\left(\frac{C/N_2}{10} \right)} \right] \tag{3.2}$$

where C/N_1 and C/N_2 are the C/N of each of the amplifiers calculated independently using Equation 2.19 and the chain is being driven by a noise-free signal. Although this general expression is useful when cascading two dissimilar network elements, a simpler approach is useful when cascading n identical amplifiers, separated by passive network losses equal to the amplifier gain:

$$C/N_{\text{cascade}} = C/N_A - 10 \log n \qquad (3.3)$$

where

$\quad C/N_A =$ the C/N of a single amplifier
$\qquad n =$ the number of similar amplifiers cascaded and separated by losses
$\qquad\quad$ equal to their gains

These equations are quite useful, but their limitations must be emphasized.

■ Equation 3.3 is applicable only to a cascade of amplifiers and loss sections where the loss of each section equals the gain of the preceding amplifier, and each amplifier has the same noise figure.

■ Equations 3.2 and 3.3 are accurate only where the gain of each amplifier is high (a minimum gain of 20 dB is adequate to ensure reasonable accuracy).

■ Equations 3.2 and 3.3 are accurate only where the amplifier output noise power is high when compared with the thermal noise "floor" (a noise figure of 2 dB or greater combined with a 20-dB or greater gain is sufficient to ensure reasonable accuracy).

■ The input to the first amplifier contains only thermal noise.

The preceding conditions are required because the equations do not rigorously account for the effects of thermal noise, although they are adequate for analyzing typical amplifier cascades encountered in cable television systems. For other applications, a more precise set of equations is recommended.

In a simple repeatered transmission line, the designer must "juggle" three parameters to reach a required end-of-line C/N: the noise figure of individual amplifiers, the input level to each amplifier, and the number of amplifiers to be cascaded. In more complex networks, the same variables apply, but the C/N "budget" may first have been allocated among several dissimilar network sections. As will be seen, for an optimal design, noise considerations must be balanced against other requirements.

3.3 CARRIER TO DISTORTION

Unlike thermal noise, which is a function of only the transmission system characteristics and channel bandwidth, the level of distortion products depends on the signals carried. The distortion performance of amplifiers is typically specified under one or two specific channel-loading conditions. Although it would be possible to simply specify distortion with just two or three carriers, the translation to expected IM products under the unique channel loading used in cable television is not straightforward, so vendors have resorted to testing under conditions that are easily related to actual field applications.

As discussed in Chapter 2, the channel loading under which amplifiers are typically tested and specified (for CTB and CSO) consists of independently generated, unmodulated carriers at each of the visual carrier frequencies, specified in the CEA-542-B Standard frequency assignment list, that fall within the bandwidth of the device. In addition, a portion of the bandwidth may be loaded with signals that simulate the effect of QAM signals (often just band-limited white noise at a controlled level). Testing of XMOD is similar except that the carriers are simultaneously modulated.

The results of such testing do not match the distortion when systems are loaded with analog television carriers (whose sync peak carrier levels match the unmodulated carriers), but the results are much more repeatable and there are standard assumptions regarding the approximate improvement when loaded with modulated carriers: 6 dB in the case of CSO and 12 dB in the case of CTB and XMOD, though the improvement will be somewhat less with short coaxial cascades.

The buildup of distortion as amplifiers are cascaded is less straightforward than in the case of noise. If the deviations from linear response are not predictable from amplifier to amplifier, then the distortions can be considered uncorrelated, in which case they will add in the same way as noise; that is, the distortion products will increase by 10 log n, where n is the number of amplifiers. On the other hand, if every amplifier has the same general distortion shape (for instance, a flattening of the curve at voltage peaks), then the distortion will be highly correlated and the magnitude of the products will increase at a 20-log-n rate.

Since third-order distortion generally does result from symmetrical curve flattening and both CTB and XMOD arise from third-order distortion, most designs assume that these distortions increase at the 20-log-n rate, although that may be overly conservative when evaluating cascades of amplifiers with dissimilar characteristics or those that nominally cancel third-order distortion (for example, feed-forward amplifiers). Second-order distortions, on the other hand, are nominally canceled in push–pull RF gain modules. For that reason, the residual second-order distortions are not highly correlated, and many designs are based on a compromise 15-log-n buildup.

As with cascades of identical amplifiers, the buildup of distortion when cascading different network sections depends on the degree to which the distortions are correlated.[2] In general,

$$C/dist = -x\log\left[10^{-\left(\frac{C/dist_1}{x}\right)} + 10^{-\left(\frac{C/dist_2}{x}\right)}\right]$$ (3.4)

where

$C/dist$ = the resultant carrier-to-distortion ratio in dB
x = 10 to 20 depending on the degree of distortion correlation
$C/dist_1$ and $C/dist_2$ = the distortion ratios of the individual sections

Where identical amplifiers operating at the same output levels are cascaded, the expression for C/CTB can be reduced to

$$C/CTB_{cascade} = C/CTB_A - 20\log n$$ (3.5)

where

C/CTB_A = the distortion of a single amplifier
n = the number of cascaded amplifiers

The equivalent expression for CSO is

$$C/CSO_{\text{cascade}} = C/CSO_A - x \log n \qquad (3.6)$$

where

C/CSO_A = the distortion of a single amplifier
n = the number of cascaded amplifiers
x = 10 to 20 depending on the degree of second-order distortion correlation

3.4 NOISE–DISTORTION TRADE-OFF

The interplay between noise and distortion can be readily illustrated by considering a cascade of n identical amplifiers. In this network, the loss between each pair of amplifiers must be made identical to the gain of one amplifier for optimum performance. If the loss is less than that value, then each amplifier's input level (and hence output level) will be greater than the previous amplifier, and the distortions will quickly build up to a high level. If the loss is greater than the gain, then the input of each amplifier will be less than the previous amplifier and thus contribute disproportionately to the overall C/N degradation.

Given equal gains and losses, let us assume a requirement that the cascade provide an analog television C/N of 50 dB and a C/CTB of 65 dB. (We could have considered any other distortion parameter as easily, but this will serve to illustrate the trade-offs involved.) Let us also assume that each amplifier has a noise figure of 8 dB, a gain of 22 dB, and a C/CTB of 80 dB at the required channel loading and at an output level per carrier of +40 dBmV. (Again, to make it simple we will assume all carriers have the same level and the loss between the amplifiers is the same at all frequencies.)

If our cascade consists of just a single amplifier ($n = 1$), then we can calculate the minimum input level that will ensure an adequate C/N. From Equation 2.19:

$$C_i(\text{minimum}) = C/N \,(\text{dB}) - 59.2 + F_A \,(\text{dB}) = -1.2 \text{ dBmV} \qquad (3.7)$$

With a station gain of 22 dB, this corresponds to an output level of +20.8 dBmV.

Similarly, since CTB changes 2 dB for every 1-dB change in operating level, we can readily determine that we could increase the output operating level to +47.5 dBmV and stay within the distortion limit. Thus, the operating levels could vary over a 26.7-dB range while maintaining the required performance.

If additional amplifiers are cascaded, the effective noise figure increases by 3 dB for every doubling of the cascade (Equation 3.3), so the minimum C_1 (and thus output level) must increase by that amount to provide the same end-of-line C/N. Similarly,

CTB distortion increases by 6 dB for every doubling of the cascade, so the maximum allowable output level must decrease by 3 dB to maintain the same end-of-line distortion levels. Thus, the allowable range of signal levels decreases by 6 dB. Table 3.1 shows the allowable output level range as a function of cascade for this example.

If we plot the general relationships in Table 3.1 as a function of cascade, we can see that there is a maximum attainable cascade and a unique operating level that allows that cascade to be realized. Figure 3.1 illustrates the usable operating range, along with the parameters that define the noise–distortion–cascade relationship. Complete system design requires that this calculation be performed for both second- and third-order distortion, as well as noise, and that operating levels be chosen that allow all specifications to be met. Generally, composite intermodulation noise (CIN) caused by digital signals is quantified as an equivalent (but output-level-dependent) increase in noise level that must be figured into the C/N calculation.

Another way of looking at the interaction among parameters is to consider the case of a hypothetical tapped distribution line that just meets end-of-line noise and distortion specifications, as well as required signal levels at subscriber terminal equipment. The operator desires to increase the bandwidth and channel loading of this system without degrading performance.

At the new, increased upper-frequency limit, the cable loss is higher. The designer can compensate for that loss by using higher-gain amplifiers, spacing amplifiers closer together, or reducing the per-foot loss of the interconnecting cable. Additionally, the increased number of carried signals will increase the distortion products (and thus CTB and CSO) in each channel if the per-carrier level is held constant. Finally, the loss of subscriber drop wiring will increase, requiring higher tap levels or lower-loss cables.

If higher-gain amplifiers are used, then either output levels must be raised or input levels lowered; the former will further increase distortion, whereas the latter

Table 3.1 Example Cascade Effects on Allowable Amplifier Operating Levels

Amplifier cascade	Allowable output level range (dBmV)	
	Minimum (C/N limited)	Maximum (CTB limited)
1	+20.8	+47.5
2	+23.8	+44.5
4	+26.8	+41.5
8	+29.8	+38.5
16	+32.8	+35.5
21	+34.0	+34.3
>21	Not possible and still meet both noise and distortion specs	

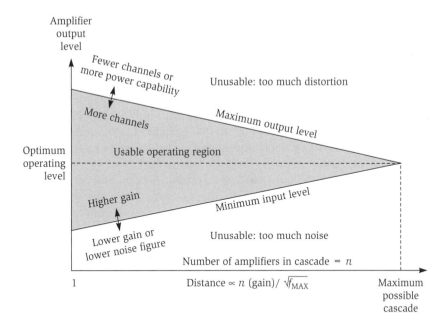

Amplifier output level

Fewer channels or more power capability

Unusable: too much distortion

More channels

Maximum output level

Optimum operating level

Usable operating region

Higher gain

Minimum input level

Lower gain or lower noise figure

Unusable: too much noise

Number of amplifiers in cascade $= n$

1

Distance $\propto n$ (gain)$/ \sqrt{f_{\text{MAX}}}$

Maximum possible cascade

FIGURE 3.1

Relationship of cascade, noise, distortion, and levels.

will cause a greater C/N degradation in each amplifier station. If amplifiers are spaced more closely together, then more will be required to reach the same physical distance, thereby increasing both noise and distortion. Even if amplifier spacing is retained, either amplifier output levels must be raised or drop cables replaced to maintain adequate subscriber equipment levels at the highest channels. Absent changes in technology, the designer is faced with an insurmountable obstacle.

Several techniques can be used to get out of this "box": (1) amplifiers with lower noise figures and/or distortions can be used; (2) both distribution and drop cables can be replaced with larger, lower-loss versions; and (3) methods can be used to transport signals to points closer to homes so that coaxial cascades can be shorter. Generally, upgrades to older all-coaxial systems employ elements of all three techniques. Usually, fiber optics is used to transport signals to short-cascade coaxial distribution networks throughout large service areas, with less noise and distortion than possible with just coaxial techniques.

3.5 **SYSTEM POWERING**

As discussed in Chapter 2, coaxial distribution systems are usually powered by multiplexing 50- or 60-Hz power with the signals and transporting both through a common cable. Through use of separate signal paths through amplifier stations and passive devices, power routing is configured independently from the signal paths.

Coaxial distribution systems may be powered from one end (centralized powering) or via power supplies located along the cable route (distributed powering). In the latter case, it is common to locate the power supply midway through the section of plant it supplies so that roughly half the current can flow in each direction from the insertion point, reducing both the current capacity requirement for components and resistive losses in the interconnecting cables. With small service areas fed from segmented nodes (as discussed further in Chapters 7 and 9), it is common to colocate power supplies with the nodes so that a single supply can power multiple small serving areas. Having a single supply per serving area increases reliability, as discussed in Chapter 12.

Figure 3.2 is a simplified schematic of a section of cable and several amplifiers extending in one direction from a power supply. From a network designer's point of view, the challenge is to minimize the number of power supplies required or, put another way, to determine the maximum number of amplifiers that can be powered from each supply.

Given a decision on system supply voltages, several parameters cannot be exceeded in making this determination: (1) the current rating of the supply, (2) the current rating of any coaxial component along the route, and (3) the minimum usable voltage at any powered component (typically around 40 volts for 60- or 90-volt systems).

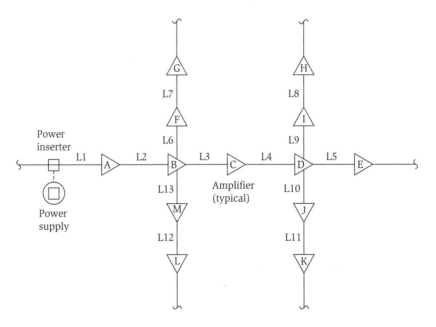

FIGURE 3.2

Example of amplifier powering.

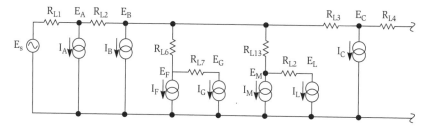

FIGURE 3.3

Equivalent circuit of a powered coaxial network.

As previously discussed, most modern amplifiers use switching power supplies. These draw current in approximately inverse proportion to the supply voltage so that the total power drawn is a constant. This allows them to maintain high efficiency and low power dissipation. It also complicates the power calculation.

Figure 3.3 is a redrafting of the first seven amplifiers in Figure 3.2 to show the power component interaction. Although it would be possible to set up simultaneous equations for each powering situation and solve for all the critical voltages and currents, a successive approximation procedure is generally used for both manual and computer calculations. The process is more or less as follows:

1. Determine the resistance of each cable leg at the maximum expected operating temperature.

2. Determine the voltage–current curve for each amplifier type to be used.

3. Determine the pass-through current ratings for each of the system components.

4. Make an initial estimate of the supply voltages at each of the amplifiers and the number of amplifiers to be served.

5. From that data, determine the current draw of each amplifier and, therefore, the total current drawn in each cable segment.

6. Using the cable currents from Step 5 and the resistances from Step 1, determine the voltage drop in each segment.

7. Starting at the power supply, subtract the first segment drop from the supply voltage to determine the voltage at amplifier 1. If different from the initial estimate, reestimate the amplifier voltages and currents and loop back to Step 6.

8. When the iterative process results in adequately consistent results (very small adjustments needed), confirm that none of the current ratings has been exceeded and that the voltage at the most distant amplifier is adequate. If not, drop one amplifier and start over.

The actual calculation is very easy on a computerized system. The "black magic" is in strategically placing power supplies and determining network power boundaries. Not only is it important to minimize the number of power supplies but, from a reliability standpoint, it is important to minimize the number of cascaded supplies that affect any given subscriber. Finally, it is important to locate power supplies where the commercial power is most reliable.[3]

A technique sometimes used to overcome both the maximum component current ratings and the voltage drop in the high-current sections near the power supplies is to add a second cable extending from power supply locations to additional strategically located power insertion points. Since these cables do not carry RF, they can be of lower characteristic impedance and thus use larger center conductors. For instance, the loop resistance of standard 0.625-inch-diameter P3 cable is 1.1 ohms/1000 feet, whereas the same-size "power feeder" cable is 0.290 ohms/1000 feet.

3.5.1 Switching Transient Effects

A consequence of the interaction among switching power supplies located along a coaxial line is that anything that causes one amplifier to draw additional current will cause all other amplifiers along the same line to also draw additional current. This is because, regardless of where it is located, the additional current supplied to one amplifier will increase the current through the first coaxial segment, which will in turn result in lower supply voltages and therefore higher currents for all other amplifiers.

Although amplifiers normally draw a constant amount of current, consider what happens when a non-UPS power supply switches between commercial and standby power. As discussed in Chapter 2, typical switching times are 8 to 16 ms. During this period, no power is supplied to the network and the input capacitors of each power pack will partially discharge.

When the power is restored, each of the amplifier power packs will attempt to draw additional current to make up for the missing 1 to 2 half-cycles. The result is that the voltage at the most distant amplifier may well drop below its operational minimum. In fact, one study has shown that power interruptions as short as 8 ms can cause service interruptions of greater than 50 ms at the fifth amplifier away from a power supply.[4] It is incumbent upon network designers to evaluate whether such interruptions are unacceptable for anticipated services and signal formats and to consider UPS switching if appropriate.

3.5.2 Hum Buildup

The mechanism for hum modulation is similar in passives and the signal-processing components of amplifier stations. Since the period of the power signal is much longer than the transit time through the network (the wavelength of 60 Hz is about

3000 miles), a conservative assumption would be that effects of the multiplexed power will be in phase throughout the system, and that consequently hum modulation due to parametric effects should build up in a 20-log fashion. As a practical matter, however, much high-voltage utility distribution is three-phase, and power supplies throughout a large service area are unlikely to all be connected to the same power phase.

To illustrate the worst-case magnitude, assume that the cascade in a distribution line includes 5 amplifier stations, 4 splitters and/or couplers, and 30 taps. If each has a hum rating of −70 dB and all components are subjected to maximum voltage and current stress, the end-of-line hum would be −70 + 20 log (5 + 4 + 30) = −38 dB, equivalent to 1.2%. Powering, however, will likely be distributed across several phases, and most components, especially end-of-line taps, are unlikely to experience anywhere close to their rated voltage and current so that total hum buildup should be well under 1% if all components are operating properly.

3.6 SIGNAL LEVEL MANAGEMENT

The requirements for level management are very different in the forward and reverse directions. In the downstream or forward direction, each amplifier receives signals from only a single source whose output is well defined. The design and operational requirements are constant amplifier output levels and adequate amplifier input levels. Additionally, to ensure that well-designed end-of-line receivers work satisfactorily, several parameters must be controlled: adequate signal strength to overcome receiver noise, avoidance of excess levels that could lead to overload, limits on adjacent channel level differences, limits on total instantaneous variation across the spectrum, and limits on changes with respect to time.

As discussed in Chapter 2, manufacturers typically specify performance with specific channel loadings and amplitudes. Since digital formats are generally more robust than analog television, it is common to specify performance under two conditions: a full spectrum of analog television signals and a defined mix of analog television and digital signals, where the digital signals are operated at a relatively lower level (as illustrated in Figure 2.19). Note that the *net gain* of the network, as measured from the output of one amplifier to the output of the next amplifier, is 0 dB in either case. The depressed levels of the digital signals relative to the analog signals are set in the headend, where they are combined.

To the extent that the positive gain slope built into amplifiers does not exactly compensate for the losses between amplifiers, *equalizers* are used to eliminate the remaining variability. To the extent that interamplifier losses (including any equalizer losses) are less than amplifier gain, attenuators (also known as *pads*) are used to set the gain block input level. Pads may be placed before the first stage (generally, the only option with line extenders) and sometimes also between stages. If the latter option is available, then in cases where excess signal level is available, operators can independently set the operating levels of input and subsequent gain blocks to optimize noise–distortion trade-offs. With amplifiers that offer multiple independent output stages, the interstage pads also allow setting of different output levels for different ports. Thus, a port that directly feeds a tapped line may be set to a higher level than one that feeds additional amplifiers and therefore needs to run at a lower distortion level.

In tapped lines, both distribution cable losses and drop cable losses must be considered. It is important that adequate and relatively uniform levels be delivered to terminal equipment. A 200-foot, size-6 drop cable has about 8-dB greater loss at 750 MHz than at 54 MHz. This differential loss tends to offset some of the intentional tilt in amplifier outputs if connected to a tap that is close to a station. On the other hand, if it is connected to the last tap in a string, it will aggravate the situation if the slope is already negative (high-end channels below the low-end channels in level). To prevent excessive level variation, in-line equalizers are sometimes inserted in tap strings or internally within taps. As a general rule, operators try to limit analog video channel level variation across the spectrum to about 10 dB. Typical design rules call for +15 to +20 dBmV analog video levels at tap ports on the highest channels, with QAM levels 6 to 10 dB lower.

Signal level management in the upstream direction is much more complex and must be treated as an overall system problem rather than as just part of the distribution network design. Signals may originate from anywhere in the system and may be of various types so that the channel loading and levels may vary continuously at any given amplifier.

The preferred approach to upstream level and gain setting is to align the system from headend out so that the *input* level to each upstream amplifier is consistent; that is, if a level of x dBmV is inserted into the input of any upstream amplifier, the level received at the headend will be the same. Pads (and, if required, equalizers) are placed in the *output* of the gain modules to set overall system gains properly.

This does not, however, mean that the required upstream transmitter output levels for terminal equipment will be consistent. Consider Figure 3.4, which depicts a typical tapped line. Following normal practice, tap values are selected to produce approximately the same downstream level at the highest channel at each home. The circuit losses depicted are based on typical manufacturers' specifications for four-port taps, the loss of 250 feet of 0.500-inch type-P3 cable between the taps, and the loss of 100 feet of size-6 drop cable connected to each tap port. As can be seen, the downstream levels at the end of the drops are all within 1 dB.

The upstream transmit levels required to reach the return amplifier, however, vary by nearly 20 dB due to the differential loss of the cable and the taps. Rather than manually setting the level of each upstream transmitter, headend RF receivers (e.g., in DOCSIS CMTSs) sense the level reaching their input ports and remotely control each device independently to equalize the received levels. Equalization internal to taps can greatly reduce the required range of upstream transmitted power levels; however, there is no uniformly accepted practice in this area.[5] Chapter 8 deals with the numerous unique issues related to upstream transmission.

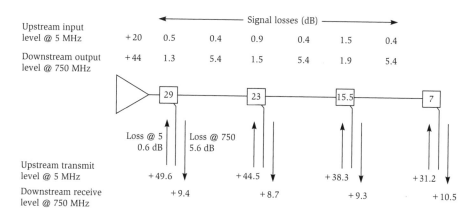

FIGURE 3.4

Signal levels in a tapped distribution line.

3.7 SIGNAL LEVEL STABILITY

As was discussed in Chapter 2, the attenuation of coaxial cable varies by about 1% per 10°F. The losses of other components, as well as amplifier gains, also vary somewhat with time and temperature. Amplifier manufacturers offer two equipment options to compensate for these variations: thermal compensators and automatic gain and/or slope control circuits (AGC/ASC).

Thermal gain compensation is *open loop*, meaning that the gain adjustment is only an approximation of the variation in interconnecting losses with temperature. AGC circuits work by sensing the level of one or more of the carried signals and controlling the gain of the station so as to maintain a constant output level for that signal. Automatic slope controls sense two signal amplitudes and control both the overall gain and the gain slope through the stage so that the levels of both signals are constant at the output port. Typical control ranges are 6 to 8 dB. Use of AGC and/or ASC circuits depends on the accuracy of headend level setting. Also, if one of the reference carriers fails, the entire distribution system can change gain sufficiently to cause serious distortion products.

The loss between amplifiers may be all cable or a combination of cable and passive devices. In the extreme case of an all-cable link whose loss is 35 dB, the loss will vary about 5.2 dB over a temperature range from +110°F to −40°F (+43°C to −40°C). Thus, every amplifier will require some sort of compensation in a trunk network.

In a tapped distribution line or one that is split several times, half or more of the loss may take place in passive devices. Thus, thermal compensation may be required only in every second or third amplifier. The trade-off is that compensation networks may have loss that reduces available gain, whereas level variations will affect C/N, CTB, and CSO. With very small nodes (cascades not exceeding two amplifiers after the node), gain management is not as critical as in legacy long-cascade nodes.

3.8 THE SERVICE DROP

So far we have dealt primarily with the portion of the distribution network that lies between the headend output and the tap ports that serve individual customers. Generally, network designers design to specifications for this portion of the network, assuming certain average performance in the headend and drop systems such that the end-to-end performance will meet regulatory requirements as well as subscriber expectations. Chapter 2 dealt with subscriber quality expectations, and Chapter 7 will cover end-to-end performance. This section will deal with the variation in drop subsystems and suggest the performance degradation that might be expected in a "standard" drop that must be taken into account in calculating end-to-end performance.

In the United States, as in many other countries, as a practical matter all or most of the drop system may not be designed, built, or maintained by the network operator. Thus, although designers must be aware of the variation in drop performance, little can be done to control quality or design within homes.

3.8.1 Simple Passive Architectures

At its simplest, the drop will consist of a flexible (either overhead or underground) cable from the distribution tap port to the building entry point, a connection to the building ground system at that point, and another flexible cable within the building that leads to a user's receiver, such as a television set or DVR. If there are multiple receiver locations, a signal splitter is used to divide the signal to feed more than one outlet.

If the loss in the interconnecting cables plus splitters is too great to ensure adequate signal level at receiver input ports, then either (1) higher tap levels must be provided, (2) lower-loss drop cable must be used, or (3) amplification must be provided in the drop system. As discussed earlier in this chapter, tap signal levels generally are difficult to increase because of the interaction among levels, noise, and distortion in the distribution network. That leaves the builder of the drop with two practical choices: reduce loss or provide gain.

In the early history of cable systems, almost all drop wiring was done with size 59 cable (originally, and incorrectly, known as RG59). When bandwidths increased beyond 300 MHz, most operators upgraded at least the portion of the drop between tap and bonding (ground) block (the point where the cable enters the dwelling) to at least size-6 and, as required, size 7 or size 11. The shift from 59 to 6 was easily justified by savings in the hard-cable plant due to lower required tap levels. The larger sizes, however, are considerably more expensive and require special connectors that add to both hardware cost and installation labor. Even in systems with size-6 outside drop cables, the inside wiring is sometimes size 59 since it is easier to handle and less obtrusive visually where exposed. Common practice is to design the hard-cable plant to have drop levels that will accommodate most situations with size-6 exterior and size 59 interior cables, and to use larger cable sizes, both inside and outside, only where required because of exceptional drop lengths and/or a high number of splits.

A Reference Drop Structure

Although there are many single-receiver households, it is increasingly common to find two (or more) television outlets in cabled homes and therefore a splitter that may be mounted at the entry point to the dwelling and that does double duty as a bonding block. Given that, we can define a *standard drop* (Figure 3.5) that will encompass the majority of current home wiring. It will include 25 to 100 feet of size-6 cable from tap to house, a four-way splitter, and size 59 connections to outlets, with lengths varying from 10 to 50 feet.

Passive Drop Transmission Characteristics

To assess the transmission characteristics of this standard drop, we need to first predict the quality of the components used, then use the tools developed in Chapter 2 to calculate their effect on the signals.

Component Quality

A prime determinant of the degree of degradation signals experience in the drop system is the quality of the components used. Unfortunately, just as there are no mandatory standards on drop wiring or design, so there are none for the components

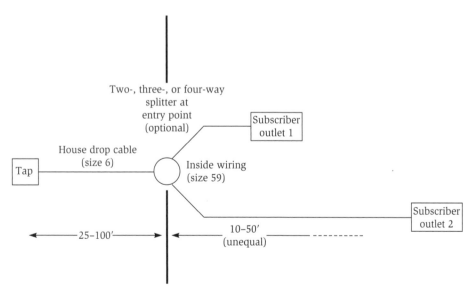

FIGURE 3.5

Typical drop configuration.

used. Historically, drop wiring was installed and maintained by cable operators (much of it still is), and they purchased reasonable-quality components because it was less expensive than the trouble calls and customer dissatisfaction resulting from inferior materials.

The Society of Cable Telecommunications Engineers (SCTE, an ANSI standards-making organization) is actively developing voluntary national standards covering virtually all drop components: cable, connectors, splitters, couplers, amplifiers, attenuators, filters, and so on.[6] When completed, these standards will cover such parameters as return losses, transmission losses, environmental requirements, shielding, surge protection, labeling, and a host of others. The specifications for amplifiers will additionally include gain, noise, and distortion. Of importance in estimating drop performance, suggested performance includes return losses of at least 18 dB, and excess loss (i.e., loss exceeding that expected from the power division ratio) in splitters and couplers not exceeding 1.0 to 1.2 dB (e.g., the loss through a two-way splitter must be no greater than 4.0 dB). Port-to-port isolation in splitters should be at least 20 dB. Cable-shielding requirements are standardized for all popular constructions. There is no assurance, of course, that existing products all meet the proposed standards or that even conforming products will continue to do so after years of exposure to weather.

Furthermore, network operators can hardly be assured that components installed by a homeowner will meet these voluntary future standards. In particular, a conservative estimate is that return losses from components may be as poor as 10 dB, port-to-port splitter isolation may be as low as 10 dB, and cable losses may, after aging if not originally, exceed nominal values (Figure 2.5) by 10%.

Drop Cable

The characteristics of various types of drop cable were discussed in Chapter 2. Within the basic size options, however, are many quality and feature options. Chief among those are shielding integrity. Cables are available with a standard dual shield (foil and braid), triple shield (foil, braid, and foil) and quad shield (foil, braid, foil, and braid), with increasing effectiveness of shielding. Of serious concern to operators are dual-shield (or worse) cables with sparse braid structures that are available in the retail market. Some of these poorly shielded cables do not adhere to SCTE tolerances for dimensions either, with the result that connectors are poorly attached, both electrically and mechanically, to the cable.

Aside from shielding options, cables are available with support messengers, with flooding compound (to prevent water from migrating through the cable structure), in a dual configuration (for dual cable distribution networks), and paired with one or more twisted copper pairs for carrying telephony or power along with RF in the same structure.

Finally, the nonmetallic portions of the cable are available with various degrees of flame resistance to meet electrical and fire codes when they are routed within some interior paths (such as plenums).

F Connectors

Whatever other components may be included in the drop, in North American cable systems, there will be at least four type-F connectors—at the tap, the input and output of the bonding block, the consumer's receiver input—and generally more. This connector, designed for low-cost mass manufacturing, is at the root of many drop problems. The female connector uses a nonprecious-metal, two-point spring clip contact for the center conductor; the male cable connector is a feed-through type that uses the center conductor of the cable itself for a pin; and the mated pair depends on a threaded joint plus a butt contact for an outer RF connection. The result is a connector family that is extremely craft sensitive in installation. Despite ANSI standardization,[7] and detailed electrochemical studies,[8] F connectors remain the leading cause of trouble calls and signal leakage in many cable systems.

In cases where power is multiplexed with RF signals on drop cables (typically to power point-of-entry telephone equipment), the limitations of F connectors are exacerbated. A less-than-perfect contact that has a reasonable capacitance may pass RF signals but will not reliably pass power. Furthermore, a loose contact, whether in the center conductor or shield, may generate electrical arcing when cables move with temperature changes or wind. These transients generally will have frequency components extending through the upstream band and into the lower downstream channels. Since they occur *within* the cable, they are tightly coupled to the transmission line in both directions and can cause severe transmission problems. The effects of electrical transients on upstream transmission are discussed in detail in Chapter 8.

In addition to inherent problems with the quality of the mating surfaces, male connectors vary in how they are attached to the flexible drop cable. Until about 1990, the most common construction used a sleeve that was pushed between the foil and braid of the cable. It was retained by use of a separate hexagonal *crimp ring*. Improved designs used a heavier, integral crimp ring. With both designs, however, field experience showed that the retention strength of the connector on the cable was reduced over time. More recent designs have featured a full annular press-fit connection that has proved to retain its strength.

The use of a feed-through design (where the cable center conductor forms the connector pin) with more than one size of cable has created problems with the mating connectors. Even with highly compliant female contact structures, once a female connector has been mated with a large cable center conductor, its ability to form a reliable contact with a small cable is reduced. The center conductor of size 11 cable is beyond the capacity of standard female ports so that special pin-type male connectors are used with it. Pin connectors are also sometimes used with size 7 cable to protect mating ports.

Traps

Historically, some combination of band-pass, band-stop, low-pass, or high-pass filters ("traps") were often inserted (and still are in some systems) into the drop circuit at the tap to control which signals reached subscribers' receivers. However they are

Table 3.2 Tap-to-Receiver Loss Ranges for Typical Passive Drop Systems

Frequency	Expected loss range	
	Minimum	Maximum
5 MHz	0.2 dB	9.5 dB
40 MHz	0.5 dB	10.5 dB
54 MHz	0.6 dB	13.0 dB
550 MHz	1.8 dB	18.5 dB
750 MHz	2.1 dB	20.0 dB

used, traps add loss. Generally, their out-of-band loss may be only a few tenths of a decibel, but their loss near cutoff frequencies can be as much as several decibels at the band edge of adjacent channels, coupled with a considerable slope through the channel. Where traps are used to control several channels individually, as many as four or five may be cascaded between tap and drop cable.

Transmission Loss

Given these variables, the total loss from tap to house will generally fall within the values given in Table 3.2, where the minimum losses result from short drop cables without a splitter and the maximum losses are based on long drops, four-way splitters, and two to three in-line traps. System designers must take into account this loss range in setting signal levels, and allowable level variation, at system taps. For example, in the "maximum" loss configuration, note that the difference in loss is 7 dB over the downstream bandwidth of a 750-MHz system. If the flatness of the signal at the tap port has a downward slope with frequency, the combination could result in widely differing signal levels being presented to receiver input ports.

Microreflections, Group Delay, and Frequency Response Variation

Cable operators are required to deliver signals directly to consumers' television receivers under some circumstances (where analog channels are unscrambled and delivered on standard channels and where customers own cable-ready digital receivers); the return loss of those receivers is essentially zero on untuned channels and may be as poor as 4 to 8 dB on the tuned channel. In any event, it is likely that an unused outlet will be left unterminated, so it should be assumed that 100% reflection occurs at each subscriber outlet. This will cause reflections whose delay and magnitude will depend on the isolation of the splitter ports and the length of the cables beyond the splitter. Using the methods that will be discussed in Chapter 7, we can estimate the worst-case reflections. Figure 3.6 shows the results at various

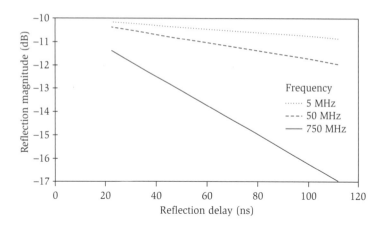

FIGURE 3.6

Worst-case microreflection magnitudes and delays in typical house wiring.

frequencies. Although operators should be prepared for occasional reflections of those magnitudes, a statistical study of actual cable systems showed 95% of all echoes, including those in the distribution plant, were more than 25 dB below carrier levels in magnitude.[9]

These reflections can lead to bit errors in digital transmissions (since delayed signals cause successive transmitted symbols to overlap at the receiver) and visible degradation of analog television pictures. As will be discussed in Chapter 7, the effects also include group delay and passband response variations. Amplitude response variations exceeding 1 dB in each channel are quite possible.

Signal Leakage and Ingress

Signal leakage is the most difficult to assess. In practice, most leakage and ingress are not associated with components or cable but rather are due to inadequate shielding in customer-owned terminal equipment and/or improperly installed or tightened drop connectors. Poor-quality connectors and poorly shielded cables may also contribute problems.

Given the statistical nature of both egress and ingress, there is no way of predicting the magnitude of ingress. The effect of ingress on upstream communications is treated, along with other upstream transmission issues, in Chapter 8.

3.8.2 Adding Amplification—The Trade-Offs

The alternative of providing gain is attractive when it is less expensive than drop cable replacement or where even the largest cables would not be adequate. However, many corollary issues are raised when amplification is added, including

- Additional noise and distortion
- Signal reliability decrease owing to the amplifier failure rate combined with the availability of its (almost always in-home) powering source
- Gain stability and flatness, hum modulation, and all other issues associated with active equipment
- Provision of a mounting location that has adequate environmental protection and available power, and yet is near where the cables to each of the outlets come together

If amplification is included in the drop system, the hard-cable plant must perform at a higher level in virtually all respects in order to ensure end-of-line quality. Drop amplifiers are frequently used in multiple-unit dwellings or commercial installations where they are, in fact, part of the distribution plant, and in single dwellings with many outlets and/or no better solution to low levels.

Occasionally drop amplifiers are used where the reverse isolation of the amplifier is needed to protect the system from ingressing signals that would otherwise travel up the drop and interfere with others' reception.

3.8.3 Integrated In-Home Wiring Systems

In response to a need to have defined performance levels and a desire to interconnect home video equipment and multiple program sources, several industry groups have designed integrated home wiring systems. These systems may use digital transmission over twisted-pair wiring, existing ac power wiring, or radiated RF, or may share use of the coaxial drop structure on nonoverlapping frequencies. This is a rapidly developing field and readers are urged to directly contact the organization developing the relevant standards and practices. Organizations and systems include the following:

- The Electronic Industries Alliance CEBus (EIA-600) standard, released in 1992, which includes options for twisted-pair, power-line, infrared, radiated-RF, and coaxial media. This standard family has been under development since the mid-1980s[10] and has its greatest success with power-line transmission. The coaxial version uses dual coaxial cables to avoid frequency conflicts with cable television signals.

- The Multimedia Over Coax Alliance (MOCA) system (*www.mocalliance.org*), which transmits digitally modulated signals at RF and shares use of the coaxial cabling in a household with cable television signals. It avoids frequency conflicts through use of frequencies above 1 GHz.

- Various digital RF standards developed by the IEEE 802.11 Committee.

- CableLabs' OpenCable Home Networking Extension.

- The HomePlug system, developed by the HomePlug Powerline Alliance, which uses in-home power wiring for transport of signals (*www.homeplug.org*).

3.9 SUMMARY

Cable television coaxial distribution systems consist of a cascade of cable, amplifiers, and passive RF components. The network typically branches in the downstream direction, using both discrete passive RF devices and devices internal to active equipment used to create the legs. The amplifiers are capable of amplifying signals flowing in both directions, with the downstream bandwidth extending from approximately the lowest broadcast television channel (54 MHz in the United States) to an upper limit determined by the bandwidth needs of the network, but typically 400 to 1000 MHz. The upstream bandwidth typically extends from 5 MHz to somewhere between 30 and 42 MHz. When over-air analog television ceases (currently scheduled for February 2009), cable operators may elect to expand their upstream bandwidth limit to around 85 MHz, simultaneously moving the start of the downstream band up to 105 MHz.

In the downstream direction, distribution networks with multiple, identical amplifiers in cascade are usually designed and operated so that the gain, measured from amplifier output to amplifier output, is unity. When systems carry only one signal type (e.g., analog video signals), their levels are often adjusted so that they increase linearly with frequency, as measured at amplifier output ports. This usually results in amplifier input levels that are approximately the same across the spectrum and creates the optimum balance between noise and distortion. QAM signals are operated 6 to 10 dB lower in level than equivalent analog video signals would be at the same frequencies.

Amplifier gains must be sufficient to offset the loss of the intervening cable and passive devices at the highest operating frequency. A combination of attenuators, positive gain slope with frequency, and special response-shaping networks is used to offset interamplifier losses. The last few amplifiers may be operated at higher levels to allow feeding more subscriber taps between gain blocks.

A distribution network will exhibit an overall downstream carrier-to-noise ratio that is inversely proportional to the logarithm of the number of amplifiers and proportional to the signal levels at the inputs to each amplifier. It will generate distortion products that are primarily determined by the amplifier output levels as well as the number of amplifiers. The bandwidth, operating levels, noise, and distortion are interdependent and, as a set, describe the essential features of the system. Other important characteristics include hum modulation, reflections, frequency response, and gain stability.

Power is carried to amplifiers over the same cables used for signals. Most commonly, 60 to 90 VAC, 60-Hz quasi sine waves are used in the United States. In the event of commercial power failure, standby power supplies replace the sine waves with trapezoidal waves. The saturation of magnetic circuits used to separate 60-Hz power from signals at each device is the largest contributor to hum modulation.

Cable television drop systems can be as simple as a single coaxial cable from tap to one television receiver or as complex as a full, integrated distribution system with multiple video sources and receivers. Today, the vast majority of cable drop configurations consist of a cable from tap to home, an optional splitter, and additional cables to one to four individual outlets.

The loss (and its variation) over this network, along with reflections from the termination points and shielding integrity, will have an effect on the overall transmission quality to consumers' receivers. In more complex networks that include amplification, the noise, distortion, gain stability, group delay, hum modulation, and so on, must be included in end-to-end performance calculations. In the case of complex in-home systems, spectral usage by internal video sources may affect compatibility with the external network.

ENDNOTES

1. *IEEE Standard Dictionary of Electrical and Electronics Terms*, 2nd ed. IEEE Std 100. New York: Institute of Electrical and Electronic Engineers, Inc., 1977.

2. Several excellent papers have been written on this subject, including Doug McEwen, et al., "Distortion Characteristics of Integrated Fibre, AML and Cable Amplifier Systems," in *CCTA Convention Papers*, 1990, Canadian Cable Television Association, Suite 400, 85 Rue Albert, Ottawa, Ontario, K1P 6A4, Canada; and Doug McEwen, et al., "Distortion Accumulation in Trunks," in *1990 NCTA Technical Papers*, Washington, DC: National Cable & Telecommunications Association, 1990.

3. An excellent treatment of this subject, along with practical recommendations, is contained in *Outage Reduction*, Louisville, CO: CableLabs, 1992, in the section entitled "Power Grid Interconnection Optimization."

4. Doug Welch, "Cable Powering into a Distributed Load," in *1995 NCTA Technical Papers*, Washington, DC: National Cable & Telecommunications Association, 1995.

5. Dean A. Stoneback and William F. Beck, "Designing the Return System for Full Digital Services," *Proceedings Manual, 1996 Conference on Emerging Technologies*, Exton, PA: SCTE, January 1996.

6. Society of Cable Telecommunications Engineers, Engineering Committee, Interface Practices Subcommittee. Released specifications and associated test procedures may be downloaded at *www.SCTE.org* (follow the link to "Standards"), or contact the SCTE at 140 Philips Road, Exton, PA 19341. Unfortunately, many specifications are still unreleased. Bonding blocks are covered by ANSI/SCTE 129 2007, while drop cables are covered by ANSI/SCTE 74 2003.

7. ANSI/SCTE 01 2006 Standard covers outdoor female F ports, and ANSI/SCTE 02 2006 covers indoor female F ports. Male feed-through cable F connectors are covered by ANSI/SCTE 123 2006, while pin-type connectors are covered by ANSI/SCTE 124 2006.

8. Brian Bauer, "F-connector Corrosion in Aggressive Environments—An Electrochemical and Practical Evaluation," in *1991 NCTA Technical Papers*, Washington, DC: National Cable and Telecommunications Association, 1991; and Brian Bauer, "Hidden Influences on Drop Reliability: Effects of Low-Level Currents on F-Interface Corrosion and Performance," in *1992 NCTA Technical Papers*, Washington, DC: National Cable & Telecommunications Association, 1992.

9. Richard Prodan, et al., "Analysis of Cable System Digital Transmission Characteristics," in *1994 NCTA Technical Papers*, Washington, DC: National Cable & Telecommunications Association, May 1994, pp. 254–262.

10. For current information on the CEBus standard, contact the Electronic Industries Association, 2500 Wilson Blvd., Arlington, VA 22201.

Linear Fiber-Optic Signal Transportation

4.1 INTRODUCTION

Although coaxial cable is used for the "last-mile" delivery of broadband services to subscribers, other technologies are frequently used to cover most of the physical distance between headend and tap. One reason for this is that the interrelationship among bandwidth, signal levels, number of cascaded devices, noise, and distortion (discussed in Chapter 3) limits the reach of purely coaxial systems. Second, large coaxial systems are best suited to delivery of a common spectrum of signals to all parts of the network, whereas many services, such as data communications, interactive video, and telephony, require a bidirectional bandwidth allocation to every customer. In order to provide this capacity in a network of attainable bandwidth, the network must be segmented (with independent signals communicated with each segment), and this requires the use of small coaxial sections, each connected by separate communications links to the headend.

In modern networks, these links almost always use linear fiber optics for at least the segment that interfaces with the coaxial network (although Chapter 6 will discuss the microwave alternative). Fiber strands have a loss that, at the optical wavelengths used by cable television systems, is approximately two orders of magnitude lower than the best coaxial cables. Furthermore, the noise and distortion added by a typical 5- to 15-mile long fiber-optic link is less than that generated in a comparable-length coaxial trunk line section.

This chapter will begin with a brief introduction to some principles of optics that are important to fiber transmission of light. Then optical fibers will be examined in detail, particularly the interaction between the fiber and the signals passing through it. Passive optical devices, comparable to their coaxial counterparts, will be treated next. Active devices will include transmitters, amplifiers, and receivers. Finally, the total performance of optical links will be examined with end-to-end performance calculations of noise and distortion. The unique characteristics of multi-wavelength systems will be covered in Chapter 5. Some of the calculations of performance parameters are fairly complex; **81** however, an Excel spreadsheet, entitled *Single-Wavelength Performance Calculator.xls*, that both calculates and plots the results is available for download from the website dedicated to this book: *www.elsevierdirect.com/companions/9780123744012*.

4.2 OPTICAL BASICS

Light "waves" are much-higher-frequency RF waves—about 300,000 times the highest frequency used in coaxial cable systems and 20,000 times the microwave frequencies sometimes used to relay cable television signals. Optical wavelengths are very short (remember that $\lambda = c/f$ in a vacuum). For instance, visible yellow light has a frequency of about 5.5×10^{14} Hz, and thus a wavelength of only 0.00000055 m, more easily expressed as 550 nm (one nanometer is one billionth of a meter)—considerably less than 1/10,000 of an inch.

At these frequencies, electromagnetic waves behave in ways that are sometimes counterintuitive. For one thing, physicists have long understood that the flow of energy is not continuous, but rather travels in "bundles" called *quanta*. In the case of light (and, for that matter, any radio waves), the carriers of the energy are massless subatomic particles called *photons* that travel, not surprisingly, at the speed of light (about 3×10^8 meters/second or, if you prefer, about 11.7 inches per nanosecond in a vacuum). The energy carried by each photon is directly proportional to the frequency of the signal, so photons at light frequencies are much more energetic than those at VHF radio frequencies. As a result, the "granularity" of VHF power transmission is extremely fine, whereas it is sufficiently coarse at optical frequencies to add measurable noise to optical transmission links.

So, is light energy carried by electromagnetic radio waves or by particles called photons? Fortunately, we do not have to answer that question. In fact, both are convenient mathematical models that explain the behavior of light under various conditions. Physicists use whichever model is most convenient to the situation at hand, and so will we.

Fortunately, we need to know but little of the broad subject called optics to understand the use of light as a carrier of signals through glass fibers. We do, however, need to understand the fundamentals of the interaction between light and materials.

4.2.1 Velocity of Propagation and Wavelength

RF signals propagate more slowly through coaxial cables than in a vacuum. Specifically (Equation 2.8), the ratio of cable propagation velocity to that in free space is $1/\sqrt{\varepsilon}$, where ε is the relative dielectric constant of the cable dielectric.

Given that light waves are simply higher-frequency radio waves, we would expect a similar phenomenon to occur in optical transmission lines, and it does. The difference is that the dielectric constant, at optical wavelengths, varies with frequency. At RF frequencies and below, the dielectric constant is dominated by molecular and atomic effects. At frequencies above the natural resonances of the molecular structures, those factors have less effect. The result is that the effective dielectric constant is both lower and wavelength dependent.

Rather than speak in terms of dielectric constant, the term *index of refraction* is used. The index of refraction of a material is numerically equal to the square root of the effective dielectric constant *at the optical frequency being considered.*

The speed of propagation through a material can be expressed as

$$v = \frac{c}{n}$$
(4.1)

where

> v = the velocity of the propagated signal in meters/second
> c = the speed of light in a vacuum (3×10^8 meters/second)
> n = the material's index of refraction (≥ 1).

The slowing of the light waves through materials is the result of a phenomenon known as *forward scattering.* When light signals travel through material, it interacts with the individual atoms. The wave model of what happens is that individual electrons get "excited" into a higher energy state and then give up that energy by generating a wave of their own. The particle model is that once in a while a photon slams into an electron, exciting it to a higher energy state. After a while, the electron returns to its former energy level, emitting a photon of equal energy in the process.

Whatever the model, the result is the same: Energy from the transmitted wave is temporarily transferred to the material and then released in the form of new waves at the same frequencies. In the uniform-density, almost-pure glass used for optical fibers, most of the new waves are transmitted in the same direction as the original wave, but delayed by the time period between excitation and re-emission (when waves are retransmitted in different directions or with varying delays, the total transmitted energy in the main wave is reduced, as will be discussed later). The new waves vectorally combine with the original wave to form a composite transmitted wave that is slightly delayed from the original. This new wave then interacts with material further along its path, adding further delay. Since this delay is proportional to the distance the wave is transmitted through the material, the result is a uniformly slower transmission speed. The index of refraction is how we express the resultant velocity relative to that in a vacuum.

The wavelength of the signal is related to the frequency, the velocity of propagation, and the index of refraction by

$$\lambda = \frac{v}{f} = \frac{\lambda_0}{n} = \frac{c}{fn}$$
(4.2)

where

> λ_0 = the wavelength in a vacuum
> f = the frequency in hertz

4.2.2 Reflection and Refraction

When light strikes a smooth, nonopaque surface, we know from common experience that some may be reflected and some may be transmitted into the material. We also observe that when light strikes a piece of glass or a still water surface at a very low angle, it is nearly all reflected, and the material resembles a mirror. At greater angles, only a small portion is reflected, and the material appears "transparent." These effects are due to the difference in index of refraction between glass and air.

Specifically, if we draw a general diagram (Figure 4.1) showing light propagating from a material on the left with diffraction index n_1 and hitting a perfectly smooth, flat interface with the material on the right (diffraction index n_2) at an angle from normal, we can express the equations governing the reflected and transmitted waves as follows.

The transmitted wave will leave the interface at an angle ϕ relative to the normal such that

$$\frac{\sin \theta}{\sin \phi} = \frac{n_2}{n_1} \qquad (4.3)$$

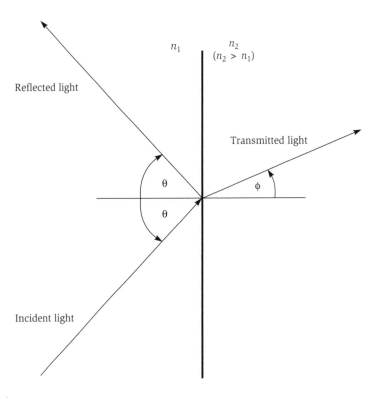

FIGURE 4.1

Light reflection and transmission at the interface between two materials.

Thus, if $n_2 > n_1$ (as in the figure), the transmitted wave will be closer to normal relative to the interface plane, whereas if $n_2 < n_1$ it will be more parallel to the interface. This relationship is known as Snell's law.

In particular, if $\sin \theta > n_2/n_1$ there is no transmitted wave, and all the energy is reflected (this is strictly true only if the n_2 material is thick). This is a crucial condition for some types of fiber transmission, as will be seen. Since the value of the sine function cannot exceed 1, total reflection is possible only when $n_1 > n_2$ (the opposite situation from that shown in Figure 4.1). The angle where total reflection occurs (the "critical angle") $= \sin^{-1}(n_2/n_1)$.

The reflected wave will leave the surface at an angle exactly opposite that of the incident wave, that is, at an angle $-\theta$ from normal. (We will see later that this effect is used to advantage in certain types of optical fiber connectors.)

The division of power between the reflected and refracted (transmitted) waves is a function of the refractive indices, the angle of incidence, and the direction of the electric fields of the incident signal. In the special case where the signal is normal to the interface, the ratio of reflected to incident power is

$$\text{relative reflected power} = \left(\frac{n_2 - n_1}{n_2 + n_1}\right)^2 \tag{4.4}$$

and the ratio of transmitted to incident power is

$$\text{relative transmitted power} = \frac{4n_2 n_1}{(n_2 + n_1)^2} \tag{4.5}$$

These results, in decibel terms that are more useful for transmission analysis, follow:

$$\text{return loss (dB)} = -20 \log \left(\frac{|n_2 - n_1|}{n_2 + n_1}\right) \tag{4.6}$$

$$\text{transmission loss (dB)} = 10 \log \left[\frac{4n_2 n_1}{(n_2 + n_1)^2}\right] \tag{4.7}$$

Thus, perfect power transmission and zero-reflected power require that $n_1 = n_2$.

As an example of less-than-perfect transmission, air has an index of approximately 1 (actually about 1.003) and common glass an index of about 1.5 at visible light frequencies, so about 96% of light striking window glass at a right angle is transmitted and 4% is reflected, a transmission loss of about 0.18 dB. These relationships are important to the design of optical connectors.

4.2.3 Light Absorption

As with coaxial cables, some of the energy in a light signal propagating through materials is converted into heat. Although an exact understanding of the mechanisms is not essential, the effect is that an optical transmission path of uniform characteristics has a loss that, as with coaxial cables, is linear (in decibels) as a function of distance.

Absorption, if it is due to atomic resonance effects, is very wavelength dependent. At the wavelengths used for signal transmission through fibers, resonances (until recently) effectively prevented the use of some of the optical spectra, whereas the effects of the resonances cause transmission characteristics at other wavelengths to be enhanced.

4.2.4 Scattering Loss and Rayleigh Scattering

Although on-axis (forward) scattering is what happens most of the time, photons may sometimes be emitted in different directions or with varying delays, leading to signal loss in the principal transmitted wave. Many mechanisms lead to this scattering, including impurities in the material, nonuniform densities, and nonlinearities due to extreme power levels. One such scattering phenomenon is known as *Rayleigh scattering*, after Lord Rayleigh, who is credited with first demonstrating that the sun's light is scattered by nitrogen and oxygen molecules in the air. Rayleigh scattering is very wavelength dependent, varying approximately as the inverse fourth power of wavelength, which is why the blue (short wavelength) end of the solar spectrum is scattered much more than the red end so that we see a sharp-edged, red-yellow sun surrounded by a diffuse blue sky.

The loss of energy in light waves transmitted through standard optical fibers is due primarily to scattering loss and secondarily to absorption and several additional minor effects.

4.2.5 Wavelength Dispersion

Except for wavelengths close to the natural atomic resonance frequencies of the material, n varies with wavelength approximately as

$$n = A + \frac{B}{\lambda^2} + \frac{C}{\lambda^4} \tag{4.8}$$

where A, B, and C are constants related to a particular material. This wavelength dependence is known as *material dispersion*. Near atomic resonances, n varies wildly, and a significant amount of absorption also takes place. Such a resonance happens to occur near the wavelengths used for optical signal transmission.

A common example of dispersion in the visible spectrum is the common glass prism (see Figure 4.2). When white light strikes a piece of glass at an angle, signals at the various colors bend *toward* the normal (right angle to the surface) at different angles, due to the difference in n across the visible light spectrum (whose wavelengths range from about 400 to 650 nm). If the glass is a flat sheet, such as a window, the reverse bending takes place on the far side, and all signal wavelengths end up restored to their original angles, and we don't notice anything. If the sides are not parallel, however, then when the light impinges upon the second interface, the angular deviation is made even greater as each wavelength bends *away* from the normal by varying amounts depending on the difference in n as a function of

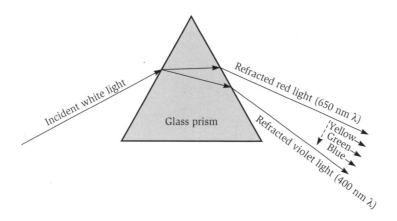

FIGURE 4.2

Chromatic dispersion of visible light in a glass prism.

wavelength, and we observe the separated spectrum. If instead of a glass prism, white light is refracted by fine droplets of water, what we see is a rainbow.

Dispersion is a major concern in optical communication cables, not primarily because of the bending effect, but because of the differing transmission speeds associated with changing n. If the components of a signal are, for some reason, generated over a range of wavelengths and transmitted through a cable whose index of refraction varies, then the components will not arrive simultaneously at the receiver. Depending on the signal format, this can lead to various kinds of distortion. The effect of dispersion is, in fact, just optical group delay (see Chapter 7) and has the same types of effects on signals.

In addition to the foregoing, the interaction of light with very small glass fibers produces some unique interactions that will be discussed in the next section.

4.3 MULTIMODE OPTICAL FIBERS

If we construct a long, smooth, narrow (but large compared with the wavelength of the light), circular-cross-section bar of glass and shine light into one end, some of the light will travel along the length of the bar and exit the far end. That will be true even if the bar isn't perfectly straight. The reason can be seen in Figure 4.3.

Since the refractive index of glass is greater than that of air, light entering the bar at a sufficiently shallow angle will be completely reflected at the glass-to-air interface and will stay in the bar, simply bouncing along from side to side and eventually exiting the far end. Light entering at a greater angle will lose some of its energy at each reflection and will quickly be dissipated. The maximum angle where all of the energy is internally reflected defines the three-dimensional *cone of acceptance* for the bar.

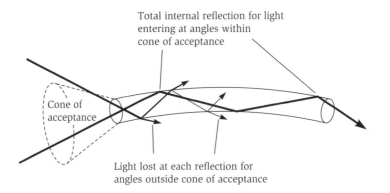

Total internal reflection for light
entering at angles within
cone of acceptance

Cone of
acceptance

Light lost at each reflection for
angles outside cone of acceptance

FIGURE 4.3

Light transmission through a bent glass bar.

If the bar is curved slowly (again, relative to the wavelength of the light), the light will still be totally reflected and will follow the curvature. If it is curved too tightly, however, some of the light will strike the outer surface at angles above the critical angle, and a percentage of the energy will be diffracted out of the bar. It is this effect that leads to minimum bending radius specifications for communications fibers.

The performance of this simple transmission line can be improved (although the cone of acceptance will be much smaller) if we coat the outside with a second layer of glass that has a slightly lower index of refraction than the core. As long as this coating is sufficiently thick, we can now handle the rod or place it next to other objects without interfering with its light transmission properties.

If the entering light is imperfectly collimated (i.e., it enters at more than one angle), it can readily be appreciated that the light traveling straight down the core will go less distance than light that is near the critical angle and bounces frequently. The difference in transmission path length will depend on the length of the bar and causes another form of dispersion (known as *modal dispersion*) that is extremely important to signal transmission.

If we modify the index of refraction so that it decreases radially from the center, light that travels at a small angle with respect to the axis will slowly be bent back toward the core as it travels farther from the center. It will, however, have traveled more quickly than light transmitted straight down the core, because it will have spent a percentage of its travel time in a medium with a lesser n and therefore greater velocity. Thus, by varying the index of refraction properly, the variation in transmission time with respect to angle can be reduced.

Now imagine that the "bar" of glass is round, with a core whose index of refraction is 1.49, whose diameter is only 50×10^{-6} or 62.5×10^{-6} m (50 or 62.5 μm, or "microns") and whose length is up to thousands of feet, and you have a typical "multimode" optical fiber. The preceding analysis, with a few exceptions, explains how signals are transmitted in such a cable. Fibers made with just a single coating are known as *step index* fibers, whereas those with a graduated index of refraction are known as *graded index* fibers.

Where the simplified analysis breaks down is that when the core of a fiber is not very large compared with the optical wavelength, only certain transmission paths are supported, whereas under the simplified analysis, light introduced at any angle within the cone of acceptance would be transmitted. The most common wavelengths transmitted through multimode fiber are 850 and 1310 nm. In glass with $n = 1.49$, these wavelengths shorten to 537 and 879 nm, respectively. Thus, the diameter of a 62.5-μm fiber core is 116 or 71 wavelengths—large but not infinite.

Little or no multimode fiber is used for cable television long-distance signal transmission because of modal dispersion. How dispersion affects signals is illustrated by Figure 4.4. If a short burst of imperfectly collimated monochromatic (all at a single frequency) light is introduced into multimode fiber at time T0, the signal will be introduced into the fiber at a range of angles (relative to the fiber axis) and, thus, travel different total distances. If the pulse is examined after it has passed through a length of fiber, we will "see" first a little light from the signal traveling parallel to the core, then from the next fastest modes, and so on, until we finally receive light from the highest angles. Similarly, at the end of the pulse, the light from the fastest modes will disappear first, and then gradually all the light will disappear.

The effect is to shorten the top of the pulse and broaden the bottom (T1). If the pulse is sufficiently short, or the fiber sufficiently long, the top will disappear entirely (T2). For still longer fibers, the leading and trailing edges of the pulse will overlap, and we will see a longer, lower-amplitude pulse (T3). If we transmit a series of pulses (representing, for instance, a digitally encoded signal), then the maximum pulse rate will be determined by when the residual effects from one pulse interfere with the onset of the next pulse. One way of expressing this maximum is the bandwidth of the fiber. If we drive the fiber with light that has been amplitude-modulated at varying rates, the bandwidth is the point where the amplitude of the demodulated signal drops by 3 dB relative to its value at low-modulation frequencies. Alternatively, the bandwidth is approximately equal to $0.35/t_r$, where t_r is the apparent rise time of the detected pulse when the input pulse has zero rise time.

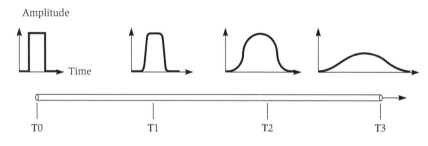

FIGURE 4.4

Pulse degradation through multimode fiber.

Multimode fibers are rated according to the amount of this length-dependent bandwidth. Typical fibers with a 62.5-micron core diameter exhibit a bandwidth-length product of 300 MHz-km at 1310 nm and 160 MHz-km at 850 nm. Fibers with a smaller, 50-micron core can reach 400 MHz-km. What this means is that a 50-micron core fiber that is 1 km long will have a bandwidth of 400 MHz, whereas one that is 10 km long will have a bandwidth of only 40 MHz.

Clearly, such fibers are not suitable for transporting 870 MHz of cable television spectrum over the long distances required in modern networks.

4.4 SINGLE-MODE OPTICAL FIBERS

If the core diameter is reduced sufficiently, fibers will support only light traveling collinearly with the axis (known as the LP_{01} mode), thereby eliminating modal dispersion. Such fibers, known as *single mode*, are almost universally used for long-distance, high-bandwidth applications.

4.4.1 Structure

The most common single-mode fiber construction consists of an 8.3-micron diameter core, surrounded by *cladding* glass with a uniform, lower index of refraction and extending out to about 125 microns. This, in turn, is surrounded by a protective layer (the *coating*) extending out to 250 microns. This outer layer is generally colored to enable easy fiber identification in bundles. This construction is known as *matched-clad, non-dispersion-shifted* fiber.

The necessary condition for suppression of higher-order modes is

$$V = \frac{2\pi a \sqrt{n_1^2 - n_2^2}}{\lambda} < 2.405 \qquad (4.9)$$

where

V = the V parameter, or normalized frequency
a = the core diameter in micrometers
n_1 = the core refractive index
n_2 = the cladding refractive index
λ = the free-space wavelength in micrometers[1]

As can be seen, this requires very small core diameters and a very small difference in the refraction coefficients for the core and the cladding.

A variant on the preceding construction is to use two layers of cladding—a lower-*n* inner cladding followed by an outer layer with an intermediate *n*. This is known as *depressed-clad, non-dispersion-shifted* fiber and is otherwise the same in construction as matched-clad fiber. With few exceptions, its performance as a transmission medium is very similar as well. Figure 4.5 shows the refraction index profile and layers of construction of both types.

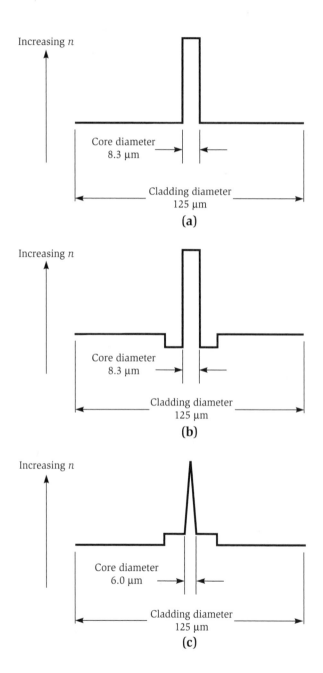

FIGURE 4.5

Cladding profiles for various fiber types. (a) Non-dispersion-shifted, matched-clad fiber-doping profile. (b) Non-dispersion-shifted, depressed-clad fiber-doping profile. (c) Dispersion-shifted fiber—one of several possible doping profiles.

With both types, the light travels mostly in the core but also partially in the cladding. The effective index of refraction is about 1.467 for each type at both of the common wavelengths used, 1310 nm and 1550 nm.

4.4.2 **Attenuation**

The total loss due to absorption and scattering is amazingly low. At 1310 nm, typical guaranteed losses for cables sold to the CATV market are only 0.35 dB/km, whereas at 1550 nm they drop to 0.25 dB/km. Otherwise stated, at 1550 nm only half the light energy is lost through a strand of glass 12 km (about 8 miles) long.

The curve of attenuation-versus-free-space wavelength is shown in Figure 4.6 (also from Ron Cotten). The local minima around 1310 and 1550 nm are known as the second and third windows of transmission, respectively. (The first is at 850 nm.) The high absorption peak around 1380 nm, known as the *water peak*, is due to absorption by hydroxyl ions. The water peak height has decreased as fiber production techniques have improved, and at least one manufacturer now offers fiber entirely free from this effect, as shown in Figure 4.7.[2]

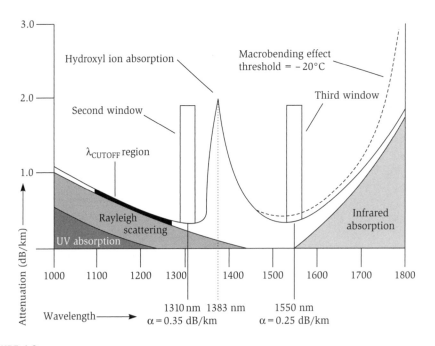

FIGURE 4.6

Fiber-optic loss as a function of wavelength.

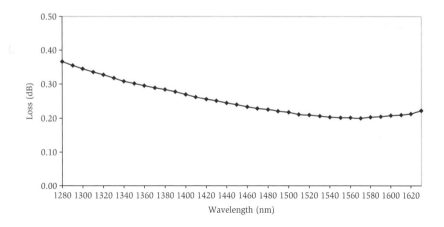

FIGURE 4.7

Typical ZWP attenuation curve.

4.4.3 **Chromatic (Wavelength) Dispersion**

With the large modal dispersion eliminated, more subtle dispersion mechanisms become the limiting factors. *Chromatic dispersion* is a measure of the degree to which the effective propagation velocity changes as a function of wavelength. It is the sum of two factors: *material dispersion*—a measure of the change in refractive index of the glass with wavelength—and *waveguide dispersion.* In optical fibers, the signal travels partially in the core and partially in the cladding, and the total *mode field diameter* changes with wavelength. Since the refractive index is different in the core than in the cladding, a change in mode field diameter also results in a change in average dispersion index and, therefore, signal velocity. The ratio of velocity change to wavelength change due to this effect is known as *waveguide dispersion*.

As with modal dispersion, chromatic dispersion is a linear function of transmission system length. The units of chromatic dispersion are picoseconds per nanometer-kilometer; that is, for a 1-nm, free-space wavelength change, this gives the number of picoseconds of delay change per kilometer of fiber length.

Standard fiber exhibits zero chromatic dispersion near 1310 nm (because the slopes of waveguide and material dispersion components are equal in magnitude and opposite in direction at that wavelength). In cases where it is important to have low dispersion at 1550 nm, the null point can be shifted upward by altering the fiber-doping profile and/or using several layers of cladding. Figure 4.5(c) gives one example of a doping profile for dispersion-shifted fiber.[3] Figure 4.8 shows a typical chromatic dispersion curve for both non-dispersion-shifted and dispersion-shifted single-mode fibers.

Typical commercial specifications for chromatic dispersion are 2.8 to 3.2 ps/nm-km from 1285- to 1330-nm wavelength and 17 to 18 ps/nm-km near 1550 nm for nonshifted fibers.[4]

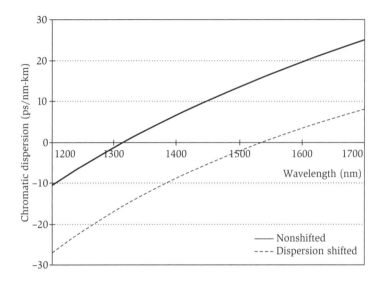

FIGURE 4.8

Chromatic dispersion for standard and dispersion-shifted fiber.

Dispersion is very important in communications circuits because the optical sources used do not transmit on a single wavelength. The interaction between various source wavelengths and network performance will be discussed later in this chapter.

4.4.4 Polarization Mode Dispersion

Light transmitted through single-mode fiber may be thought of as two separate signals (polarization modes) with their electric fields 90° apart relative to the axis of the fiber. So long as the fiber looks exactly the same to both signals, they will have the same transmission time and will arrive in phase at the detector.

Two conditions, however, can detract from equal transmission velocity: dimensional irregularities and unequal index of refraction.

■ As discussed, waveguide dispersion is a function of the mode field diameter because the signal travels partially in the core and partially in the cladding. Should the fiber core not be perfectly round, the ratio of core to cladding used for one polarity will be different from that for the other.

■ More subtly, the glass may have a dimensional preference in its atomic structure that causes n to be greater in one direction than the other. This preference is typically nonuniform along the fiber and also modified by local stresses and temperature variations.

The situation is made more complicated because energy is exchanged between the polarization modes due to imperfections in the fiber, connectors, splices, and so on.

The net effect of all these mechanisms is called *polarization mode dispersion* (PMD). PMD is typically wavelength dependent and interacts with optical transmitter wavelength changes to cause system distortion. A typical commercial specification for PMD is ≤ 0.5 ps/$\sqrt{\text{km}}$ at 1310 nm in non-dispersion-shifted cable,[5] although typical values are 0.1 to 0.2 ps/$\sqrt{\text{km}}$. At these values, PMD does not add materially to total system distortion in most cable networks.

4.4.5 Attenuation in Bent Fibers

As with the waveguides used for microwave signal transmission lines, single-mode fibers may not be sharply bent without causing signal loss. Two classifications of bends are normally considered. *Microbends* are microscopic imperfections, often introduced in the manufacturing process, such as irregularities in the core material or in the interface between core and cladding. Losses due to microbending are included in manufacturers' specifications for cable performance.

Macrobends are the bending of the completed fibers. If the radius of a macrobend is sufficiently small, significant amounts of the light will be transmitted out through the cladding and be lost. For that reason, manufacturers specify cable and individual fiber-bending radii that must be respected.

The fact that light is not constrained to remain within the fiber when bent has been exploited by manufacturers of light insertion and detection (LID) fusion splicers. They bend the incoming fiber sufficiently to insert light on one side of the splice location (light can "leak" into, as well out of, fiber when it is bent), and then bend it on the other side and detect the leaked light. By manipulating the position of the fibers at the joint for maximum transmission before fusing, splice loss can be minimized. One ambitious manufacturer even reached the field trial stage with a fiber-to-the-curb (FTTC) telephone and cable television distribution system that used bent-fiber couplers to extract and insert light at every node.[6] Their first version used multimode fiber, but later versions used single-mode fiber.

A typical commercial fiber-bending specification is 0.05-dB maximum loss at 1310 nm and 0.10 dB at 1550 nm for 100 turns of fiber wound around a 75-mm (2.95-inch) diameter mandrel. The specified loss for a single turn around a 32-mm (1.26-inch) diameter mandrel is 0.5 dB at 1550 nm.[7] In general, bending losses are higher at 1550 nm than at 1310 nm.

4.4.6 Stimulated Brillouin Scattering

When the power level of monochromatic light transmitted into a long fiber strand is increased, the output power increases proportionately until a threshold is hit. Beyond that level, the received power stays relatively constant, and energy reflected toward the source increases dramatically. The signal-to-noise and signal-to-distortion ratios of the received signals both degrade. This phenomenon is known as *stimulated Brillouin scattering* (SBS).

SBS occurs because glass is electrostrictive—that is, an electrical field causes a mechanical stress on the material. When the field associated with the light signal reaches a certain amplitude, only some of the energy from excited electrons is returned as forward-transmitted waves. The remainder is translated into an acoustic wave that propagates through the material. This acoustic wave, in turn, modulates the index of refraction due to the sensitivity of the index of refraction in glass to pressure. The varying index of refraction then causes the main light wave to alternately slow down and speed up, causing the detected signal to have increased distortion. A portion of the reflected light is re-reflected at acoustic wavefronts due to the change in index of refraction, and the random phase relationship between the original and double-reflected signal, as received at the detector, causes increased noise.

SBS is a function of fiber geometry, loss, and length, as well as transmitted power. It is also a wavelength-specific process, in that energy at light frequencies separated by as little as 20 to 100 MHz behaves independently, so when light is transmitted at several wavelengths each experiences about the same Brillouin threshold.

The basic equation for the single-wavelength SBS threshold is

$$P_{SBS} = \frac{21A\alpha}{\gamma(1 - e^{-\alpha L})} \tag{4.10}$$

where

P_{SBS} = the threshold power of SBS scattering in mW
A = the cross-sectional area of the fiber core (approximately 80×10^{-12} m^2 for non–dispersion-shifted fibers and 50×10^{-12} m^2 for dispersion-shifted fibers)
γ = the Brillouin gain coefficient (2–2.3×10^{-14} meters/mW, depending on the degree of polarization randomness in the signal)
α = the fiber's attenuation in dB/km $\times 2.3 \times 10^{-4}$ (numerically equal to twice the attenuation in nepers/m)
L = the fiber's length in meters[8]

Figure 4.9 shows typical SBS threshold values for standard (Std) fibers at both 1310 and 1550 nm and for dispersion-shifted (DS) fibers at 1550 nm.

Power higher than the monochromatic SBS threshold can be transmitted if divided among optical carriers whose frequencies differ by more than the SBS line-width. Some vendors use spectrum-spreading techniques to allow transmitted powers as high as +17 dBm (50 mW) at 1550 nm in standard fiber without significant distortion. Clearly SBS extension becomes a balance between widening the spectrum sufficiently to avoid the Brillouin limit while keeping it sufficiently narrow to avoid significant chromatic dispersion. One method commonly used is to phase-modulate the source with a sufficiently high amplitude and frequency to adequately spread the spectral power while creating added modulation sidebands that fall above the highest RF signal carried by the system.[9]

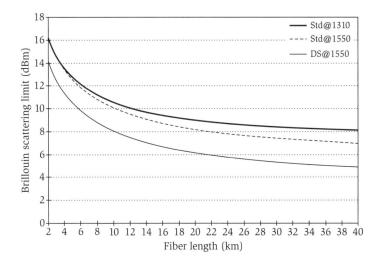

FIGURE 4.9

Brillouin scattering limit for monochromatic light as a function of fiber length, type, and operating wavelength.

4.4.7 Self-Phase Modulation Interacting with Dispersion

Another power-related effect that occurs in optical fibers is known as *self-phase modulation* (SPM). This is caused by the fact that the index of refraction, n, is slightly modulated by variations in the instantaneous intensity of the transmitted light. This causes a different propagation velocity (as the instantaneous power varies), and thus an effective envelope distortion, resulting in phase modulation as seen at the detector. The nature of the distortion will be affected by whether the wavelength is centered on the fiber's dispersion null or on one side of the null.

In general, the effect of SPM will be an increase in the level of composite second-order (CSO) distortion through the link. Although the analysis is not straightforward, the C/CSO will be degraded under the following circumstances:

- Chromatic dispersion is higher.
- Fiber is longer.
- RF carrier frequency is higher.
- Wavelength of the light is longer.
- Average light level is higher.
- Optical modulation index (OMI—the intensity variation due to the modulating waveform) per carrier is higher.
- Core diameter of the fiber is smaller.
- Fiber attenuation is lower.

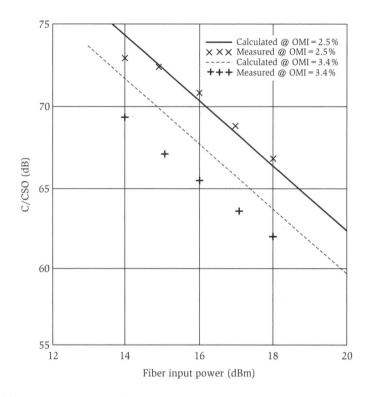

FIGURE 4.10

CSO degradation due to self-phase modulation.

Figure 4.10 shows the measured and calculated C/CSO degradation due to SPM as a function of average optical power level under the following conditions[10]:

- Length = 50 km of non-dispersion-shifted fiber with a power coefficient of diffraction, index equal to $2 \times 10^{-20} m^2/W$, attenuation of 0.0576 nepers/km, and chromatic dispersion at 1553 nm of 17 ps/nm-km.
- Channel loading = 77 RF carriers, with OMI/carrier approximately 2.5% (top curve) and 3.4% (lower curve).
- C/CSO measured on top channel (547.25 MHz).
- The transmitter is an externally modulated DFB laser at 1553 nm (optical transmitter characteristics are discussed later in this chapter).

In Figure 4.10, the solid lines are the calculated results, and the discrete points are measured data. The referenced paper offers no explanation for the deviation between calculated and measured data at higher OMI values.

Figure 4.11 shows the variation as a function of length for a fixed +18-dBm optical power level. For lengths greater than 50 km, the signal was amplified after the first 50 km and transmitted through the additional fiber length. The solid line is the calculated performance, while the *x* marks are measured data. As can be seen

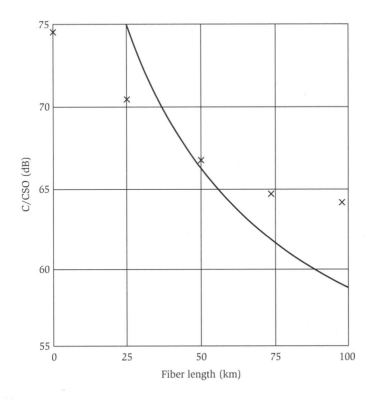

FIGURE 4.11

CSO degradation due to SPM as a function of fiber length.

in these graphs, at higher optical levels, the degradation in C/CSO is significant. In some cases, this may be a compelling argument for the use of dispersion-shifted fiber for long 1550-nm analog links.

In systems containing components other than fiber, SPM also interacts with any response variation to produce additional distortion components. This is covered in more detail in Chapter 5, since wavelength division multiplexers are often the primary contributors to this additional CSO source. Because self-phase modulation affects the transmission properties of a link, it is one of the mechanisms that limits performance when more than one optical signal (on different wavelengths) shares a fiber—a phenomenon known as *cross-phase modulation*, also discussed in Chapter 5.

4.5 NETWORK PASSIVES

In coaxial distribution systems, passive devices are used for various signal-splitting and combining functions. Optical equivalents exist for many of the same functions, with the obvious exception of multiplexing of 60-Hz power with signals. Discussed next are the essential passive components used in linear optical links.

4.5.1 Connectors

Methods for joining fibers fall into three general classes: fusion splices, mechanical splices, and connectors. *Fusion splicing* consists of carefully preparing the end of each of the fibers to be joined and then bringing the ends together carefully and literally melting them. Automated and semiautomated fusion splicers have evolved that consistently produce splices with less than 0.1 dB of loss.

Mechanical splices generally involve similar fiber-end preparation. The difference is that the fibers are brought into proximity and embedded in a gel-like material whose index of refraction closely matches that of glass. A mechanical sleeve holds the fibers in position. Although the loss at such splices is higher than at fusion splices (typically 0.1 to 0.2 dB), they are quick to manufacture and are favored for rapid field repair tasks in cases where a fusion splice crew can later replace the temporary fix.

A wide variety of connector families have been developed by various vendors. These are used for interfacing between active equipment and fiber lines and for patch panels that allow test points and reconfiguring of systems. Typical connector losses are higher than mechanical splices (about 0.25 to 0.5 dB) and are variable with remating.

The difficulty in improving connectors lies in their imperfect fiber-to-fiber interface. As discussed at the beginning of this chapter, signals lose approximately 0.18 dB at each fiber–air interface. Unless the fiber ends are in intimate contact, a mated connector pair will have two such interfaces and a loss of 0.36 dB due to the two fiber–air interfaces alone. Worse, the return loss from each interface could be as bad as 14 dB.

A number of different connector families have been used over the years, and more will likely be developed in the future. The SC series is currently popular in North America. This is a small push-on–pull-off connector that is capable of low insertion loss and good return loss if the fiber ends are properly polished and kept clean. A zirconia ceramic ferrule is used to align the two fibers. It has a central capillary hole into which the fiber is cemented, following which the end is polished. Connectors may be attached in the field or supplied preattached to fiber pigtails that can be fusion-spliced in the field.

Ultra-Polished and Angle-Polished Connectors

SC connectors, as well as some other series, come with either flat, highly polished tips or angle-polished tips. The flat (SC/UPC) version allows for somewhat better insertion loss when cleaned properly but has typically 5-dB worse return loss than the angled (SC/APC) version.

The reason for the lower reflections from the APC version is shown in Figure 4.12. Whatever light is reflected at the fiber end (due to alignment errors between the fibers, air gaps, imperfect polishing, or differences in the index of refraction) is returned at an angle equal to twice the end angle of the fiber, which is 8° to 12°. The reflected light is outside the cone of acceptance of the fiber and so is not transmitted toward the source.

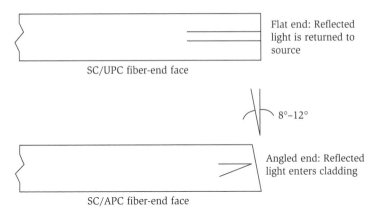

Flat end: Reflected light is returned to source

SC/UPC fiber-end face

8°–12°

Angled end: Reflected light enters cladding

SC/APC fiber-end face

FIGURE 4.12

UPC versus APC connector.

By contrast, the UPC connector requires a higher degree of polishing, which results in lower insertion loss, but with the disadvantage that whatever light is reflected will propagate back toward the source. Because of this difference, the return loss of an imperfectly cleaned UPC connector degrades more quickly than that of an APC connector.

The preoccupation with return loss levels in optical circuits, which are much lower than the 16 dB typical for coaxial components (as discussed in Chapter 2), is because directly modulated laser diode transmitters are very sensitive to reflections, as discussed in Section 4.6. Generally, optical return loss values must be significantly better than 40 dB to avoid problems.

Connector-Cleaning Issues

Proper cleaning of optical connectors is mandatory for good performance. Many problems in optical links are caused by dirty connectors. Proper installation and maintenance practices call for careful cleaning and inspection of all connectors before mating or remating, preferably using inspection microscopes made for that purpose. Recent experiments have shown that, even when connectors on new equipment were carefully cleaned and capped for protection, they were unacceptably dirty when uncovered for use after undergoing a simulated shipping environment.[11]

If dirty connectors are mated, it is possible that the foreign material, if abrasive, can damage the polish of the fiber-end faces, permanently degrading the performance. In that case, the only remedy is to install a new connector.

Two methods of cleaning are currently accepted. In the first, a slightly abrasive tape is wiped across the connector end face. The tape is contained within a cartridge and is advanced after a set number of cleanings. This method has been found effective with SC/UPC connectors; however, its use on SC/APC connectors is questionable since excessive use can damage the angle polish.

The second method uses at least 91% pure isopropyl alcohol applied with a lint-free swab, followed by a dry swab and then blowing it dry using canned air. This method seems to be adequate for any type of connector. Standard "rubbing alcohol" is not acceptable because of impurity levels that may leave a residue.

4.5.2 Signal Splitters

Signal splitters can be made with virtually any splitting ratio. Excess losses (i.e., the difference between input light power and the sum of the powers appearing at all output ports) are generally less than 1 dB. Often, multiple splitters are packaged together to create 10 or more legs.

4.5.3 Wavelength Division Multiplexers

WDM couplers are the optical equivalent of RF diplex filters. They are used to route light to the correct port on the basis of the optical wavelength. The simplest versions divide 1310-nm light from that at 1550 nm. More complex WDM couplers can separate multiple wavelengths that differ by as little as 0.8 nm. Such systems are known as *dense WDM*. Wavelength division multiplexers are discussed in greater depth in Chapter 5.

4.5.4 Attenuators

Optical attenuators are used both as test equipment and for absorbing excess light in some transmission links. Both fixed and variable units are available. A variety of techniques, including controlled bending of an internal fiber, are used to create the desired signal loss.

4.6 LINEAR OPTICAL TRANSMITTERS

Transmitters generate optical carriers and intensity-modulate those carriers with wideband RF spectra. In addition to linearity and noise requirements that are analogous to those placed on RF amplifiers, optical transmitters must exhibit optical characteristics that are compatible with the interconnecting fiber strands.

4.6.1 General Characteristics

In general, optical transmitters use an electrical signal to modulate the power of a light source. The most common application is simple on–off modulation used to convert high-speed binary signals to light pulses. At the receiving end, detectors need only detect the presence or absence of light to accurately reproduce the original digital stream. Digital modulation is a conceptually simple and robust format, and relatively high noise levels can be tolerated. At the present state of the art, speeds in

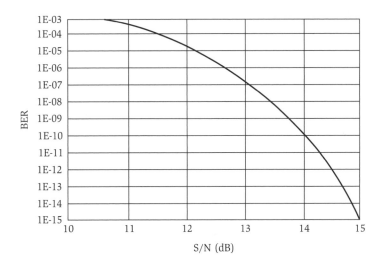

FIGURE 4.13

Bit error as a function of signal-to-noise ratio for a binary digital transmission system.

excess of 10 gigabits per second (Gb/s) are commercially deployed and 100 Gb/s is under development, whereas optical losses of 30 dB can be tolerated between transmitters and receivers.

Figure 4.13 shows theoretical bit error rate as a function of signal-to-noise (S/N) ratio for a baseband, binary transmission system.[12] Quite moderate S/N ratios (compared with those required for modulated analog NTSC or QAM signals) yield very good bit error rates. Baseband digital modulation is frequently employed in fiber-deep architecture (fiber-to-the-curb or fiber-to-the-home) due to the lower cost of the transmitters relative to those commonly used in HFC systems. Chapter 11 discusses fiber-deep architecture in detail.

By contrast, transmission of an FDM analog signal spectrum is much more complex. In the usual cable television application, the composite headend output waveform (with spectral components extending from 50 to 750 MHz or more) is used to control the light intensity in a proportional manner. The modulation must be highly linear or, more correctly, must complement exactly the demodulation characteristic so that the total link is highly linear. In addition, the end-to-end C/N of each multiplexed RF signal must be compatible with signal-quality requirements. Typically, the fiber-optic link is required to provide a C/N of 50 dB or greater for each analog video carrier with composite distortion products 60 to 65 dB down, and C/(N+I) in the low 40s for QAM signals. Since stimulated Brillouin scattering and other nonlinear fiber effects limit the maximum transmitted power to +10 to +17 dBm, and receiver power levels of about 0 dBm are required to sufficiently overcome "shot noise" (see Section 4.8) at the receiver, this limits practical optical budgets for typical wideband links.

In fact, optical transmitters and receivers are not linear devices but "square-law" devices; that is, the instantaneous light output *power* of a transmitter is proportional to the input *current* and thus to the square root of the input signal power. At the other end of the circuit, the RF output power from the detector is proportional to the square of the optical power received, so the total link is nominally linear (predistortion is often used to overcome residual nonlinearities). As will be seen, however, the square-law transfer function has an effect on noise and distortion addition. In particular, because of the square-law detector transfer function, a change of 1 dB in optical loss will result in a 2-dB change in detected RF power, leading to the common, but incorrect, statement that "optical decibels are twice as big as RF decibels."

From a system standpoint, and regardless of the technology used to generate the signals, transmitters can be characterized by their wavelength, spectral purity, and stability, and by their bandwidth, linearity, and noise levels. These interact with the fiber and detector characteristics to determine the total link quality.

4.6.2 Directly Modulated Fabry–Perot Laser Diodes

Although a number of technologies can produce the roughly monochromatic light required for optical transmitters, few meet the dual requirements of sufficient power output along with a linear relationship between input voltage or current and light output power.

One that does is the Fabry–Perot semiconductor laser, named for the French scientists Charles Fabry and Alfred Perot. In a Fabry–Perot (F-P) laser, light is reflected and re-reflected between two "mirrors" at either end of a semiconductor material that has been biased electrically. The material and two mirrors form a resonant cavity that roughly determines the wavelength of the light produced. One of the mirrors is only partly reflective, allowing some portion of the light to "leak" out into an external fiber, whereas most is internally reflected. This is directly analogous to a "high-Q" resonant L-C tuned circuit in the RF domain, where the circulating energy is much higher than that coupled into a load.

Physical processing limitations dictate that the spacings between the mirrors form a resonant chamber long enough that oscillation can take place at any of several frequencies (longitudinal modes) for which the cavity length is an integer number of half wavelengths. Although the total output power of F-P diodes is relatively constant (for a given bias current), that power fluctuates randomly among several modes, each with a slightly different wavelength. For typical 1310-nm F-P diodes, the spectral lines are spaced at about 1 nm, and the energy is spread among several such lines. When this signal is transmitted through a fiber, light at each of these frequencies transmits at a slightly different speed due to chromatic dispersion. At the detector, the randomly varying transmission times translate into noise.

In addition to this *mode partition noise*, F-P diodes exhibit a certain amount of instability in their total optical power, known as *relative intensity noise* (RIN), and typically deviate slightly from an ideal square-law transfer curve. For all these reasons, F-P diodes are not generally used for wideband downstream transmission, although their moderate cost makes them attractive for upstream links that are relatively short and not heavily loaded with signals.

4.6.3 Directly Modulated Distributed Feedback Laser Diodes

A modification of the basic F-P laser uses a diffraction grating (which serves as an optical tuned circuit) along the length of the cavity to restrict oscillation to a single mode. Known as a *distributed feedback* (DFB) laser, this is the most common light source used in downstream optical transmitters. High-grade DFB lasers may have linewidths (the width of the optical spectrum in the absence of modulation) as narrow as 1 MHz. As will be seen, source linewidth is an important factor for certain noise-generating mechanisms.

The key characteristics of F-P and DFB lasers are covered next. Although this discussion applies generally to either type, the typical values given will be applicable to DFB units optimized for direct modulation unless otherwise specified.

Linearity as a Directly Modulated Source

The typical transfer curve showing the relationship between driving current and light output power for a DFB is shown in Figure 4.14. In modern diodes that are designed for analog modulation, an end-to-end C/CSO of 60 dB or better and a C/CTB of 65 dB or better are common for a signal loading of 80 unmodulated carriers and for signals that stay within the linear portion of the curve. The sharp discontinuity at low currents, however, causes abrupt clipping of applied waveforms that are too large. This is discussed later in this chapter.

Relative Intensity Noise

The light from laser diodes has some random amplitude fluctuation. This is generally expressed in terms of the noise power in a 1-Hz bandwidth compared with the average optical power level. Typical values for quality DFBs are approximately -160 dB/Hz, provided that there is no reflected light. Any light reflected from the load, however, will degrade this quickly. For that reason, high-performance DFB sources are connected to fibers through optical isolators that serve to reduce the level of reflected light reaching the laser diode.

In order to assess the effect of source RIN on link C/N, we need to compare it to the modulation of the light source by each carrier. The optical modulation index (OMI) is defined as the peak optical power variation from the unmodulated level divided by the difference between the unmodulated level and the threshold level (A/B in Figure 4.14). Since the device is highly linear, OMI can also be defined as the peak deviation from the bias current level relative to the difference between bias and threshold current levels.

We can speak of the total modulation of the transmitter by the sum of all the RF carriers or of the modulation by some individual carrier. Although it is important that the total modulation not exceed 100%, to keep the signal from being clipped, we are also frequently interested in the performance of individual channels. The peak

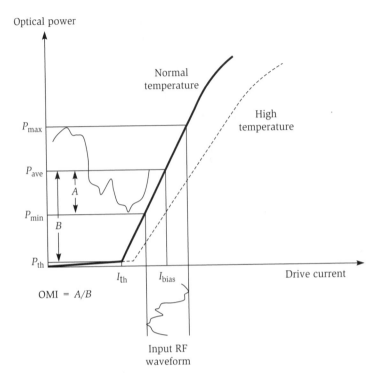

FIGURE 4.14

Laser diode transfer function.

modulation of the optical carrier by an individual carrier is abbreviated m_i, which will be an important factor in calculating the per-channel noise performance of an optical link.

The RIN contribution to total link C/N as a function of source RIN, m_i, and channel bandwidth is expressed by the formula

$$C/N_{RIN} = -\text{RIN} - 10 \log(\text{BW}) + 20 \log\left(\frac{m_i}{\sqrt{2}}\right) \qquad (4.11)$$

where

$\quad C/N_{RIN}$ = the contribution of the source noise to the C/N of a signal, expressed in dB

$\quad\quad\quad$ RIN = the source noise level (relative to the unmodulated light power), expressed in dB/Hz

$\quad\quad\quad$ BW = the receiver noise bandwidth, in Hz, for the communications channel being evaluated

$\quad\quad\quad m_i$ = the peak modulation of the light source by each RF signal

As an example, if a source has an RIN of -160 dB/Hz and is modulated 3% (typical for a 77-channel system) by an NTSC video channel whose noise is measured in a 4-MHz bandwidth, the C/N will be approximately 60.5 dB. This puts a length-independent ceiling on the performance of a fiber-optic link (which will be further degraded by detector and postamplifier noise, as discussed later).

Incidental Wavelength Modulation (Chirp)

When the current through a directly modulated laser diode changes as a result of modulation, there is also a small effect on the instantaneous wavelength of the produced light. This incidental FM is known as *chirp*. In typical laser diodes, the rate of frequency shift can vary over a range from approximately 50 to 500 MHz/mA with a total shift of ±1.5 to ±15 GHz, with DFBs exhibiting lower shifts than F-Ps and 1550-nm lasers exhibiting higher shifts than 1310-nm lasers.[13]

Chirp has several important effects on link performance. First, it spreads the energy over a range of wavelengths, which increases the effective Brillouin scattering threshold and thus allows higher optical power levels to be transmitted. On the other hand, it interacts with chromatic dispersion to cause a decrease in C/CSO. Finally, it interacts with reflected light to degrade the effective source RIN.

Because the energy of a directly modulated DFB source is spread over a wider spectrum, it is possible to transmit at higher power levels without reaching the Brillouin scattering threshold. Experience has shown that launch powers in excess of 25 mW into standard 1310-nm fiber are possible without a discernible increase in noise or distortion.

CSO Caused by Chirp Interacting with Dispersion

Over the relatively small wavelength shifts associated with chirp, the fiber's index of refraction will shift in an approximately linear manner. Thus, as the instantaneous modulating signal swings in one direction, the light will shift to a wavelength that travels slightly faster, whereas at the other polarity the generated light will travel slightly slower. Because the variance is approximately linear with modulation, the resultant distortion in the detected signal will affect one peak of the RF waveform exactly opposite of its effect on the other peak.

As was discussed in Chapter 2, distortion with this characteristic causes only even-order products, of which the dominant is C/CSO. The relationship between chirp, RF frequency, fiber dispersion, and link length is given by the following formula:

$$C/CSO_{\text{CHIRP-D}} = -20 \log\left(DL\,\Delta\lambda\,f_{RF}\,2\pi\,10^{-6}\right) - 10 \log(N_2) + 3 \qquad (4.12)$$

where

$C/CSO_{\text{CHIRP-D}} =$ the ratio of the level of the visual carrier in question to the level of the CSO products falling in that channel

$D =$ the fiber chromatic dispersion, in ps/nm-km, at the optical frequency used

$L =$ the length of the fiber in km

$\Delta\lambda$ = the laser chirp per channel, in nm, as a result of modulation
f_{RF} = the frequency of the CSO product being analyzed, in MHz
N_2 = the number of second-order products in the composite beat
that falls in the channel being analyzed (see Equation 4.25)[14]

The CSO affects channels differently because (1) a given amount of time shift represents more degrees of phase shift at higher frequencies, and (2) the number of second-order products falling into channels varies.

If the laser chirp per channel is known in terms of optical frequency rather than wavelength, it can be converted to wavelength chirp using

$$\Delta\lambda \text{ (nm)} = \left(2.42 \times 10^{-4} + 4.17 \times 10^{-6}\lambda\right)\Delta f\text{(GH}_Z\text{)} \tag{4.13}$$

where λ = the operating wavelength in nm.

For example, typical 1310-nm DFBs exhibit about 100-MHz/mA incidental frequency modulation. If such a laser were modulated at 2 mA/channel and the signal transmitted through 20 km of standard fiber with a chromatic dispersion of 3 ps/nm-km, the chirp-related C/CSO at a channel with 31 upper-side, second-order products would be 60.6 dB.

Directly modulated 1550-nm DFBs tend to have higher chirp values—typically 250 MHz/mA. If such a source were modulated at the same 2 mA/channel and the light transmitted through the nonshifted 20-km fiber described earlier, the C/-CSO would decrease to 35.8 dB due primarily to the 18-ps/nm-km chromatic dispersion at that frequency. Thus, directly modulated DFB transmitters are only suitable for multichannel FDM video transmission when operated near the zero-dispersion wavelengths of fibers, when driving very short fiber cables, or when modulated by an RF spectrum of less than an octave so that the second-order products fall out of band.

Effects of Reflected Light

When light is reflected back into a DFB (or F-P) laser from a connector, passive component, receiver, or the fiber itself due to Raleigh backscattering, it can have a significant effect on RIN. Because the wavelength of the laser changes with modulation, it is almost certain that its wavelength will be different from that of the reflected signal due to the round-trip transmission time from transmitter to point of reflection.

If the laser wavelength is close to that of the reflected signal, it will try to lock its present oscillation to the frequency of the returned light. However, this is not the frequency the laser "should" be on, based on the modulating signal. The result is similar to that of an electronic oscillator that is receiving energy at a frequency close to, but not exactly on, its own frequency. The oscillator "pulls" toward the incoming frequency, resulting in a noisy output. The same thing happens with a laser and results in spurious emissions and an overall degradation in effective RIN. Some protection is afforded where optical isolators (components that exhibit low forward loss but typically greater than 30 dB of isolation in the reverse direction) are installed in laser diode output fibers, but attention to reflections from the driven optical circuits is also required. The jumps in frequency also add a degree of uncertainty to the calculation of interferometric intensity noise (see Section 4.9.1).

Temperature Effects

The current-versus-light transfer function for diodes shown in Figure 4.13 is stable at any single temperature. As the temperature changes, the curve shifts horizontally and may also change slope. Since this could result in a shift of the operating point from the optimum value, lasers used for wideband, downstream transmission are almost always connected to thermoelectric coolers (TECs) that act to maintain a constant chip temperature.

While the use of TECs is desirable in all linear modulation applications, the cost and power consumption have resulted in the use of noncooled transmitters in many lower-performance upstream transmitters.

4.6.4 Externally Modulated Continuous Wave Sources

Externally modulated transmitters consist of a continuous wave light source whose intensity is varied through the use of an external device that is driven by the FDM waveform. This configuration offers several advantages, including:

- Freedom from the incidental wavelength modulation (chirp) associated with direct modulation of laser diodes (although modulators have some residual shift of their own)
- Improved isolation of the source from reflections in the transmission system, thereby decreasing effective source RIN
- The ability to use a variety of optical sources without regard to their ability to vary light output in proportion to an electrical modulating signal

The most common external modulator is a Mach–Zehnder (M-Z) device constructed on a lithium niobate ($LiNbO^3$) substrate. In an M-Z modulator, the incoming light is divided proportionately between two outputs in response to an electrical stimulus. The transfer function to each output is very nearly sinusoidal, as illustrated in Figure 4.15. When used as a linear transmitter for cable television distribution, the predictable symmetric curvature of the transfer function (which causes large odd-order distortion products) is compensated for by predistortion in the driver circuit.

The transfer function of M-Z modulators provides one important additional advantage over directly modulated sources: The distortion is symmetrical about the inflection point of the transfer function, offering significantly improved second-order distortion products (see Section 2.3.3 for discussion of distortion in coaxial systems).

Externally modulated transmitters can be constructed at either 1310 or 1550 nm. At 1310 nm, the usual source is a relatively high-powered (80-mW typical) YAG oscillator. This device, whose wavelength is actually 1319 nm, exhibits a low RIN and optical linewidth. YAG-sourced devices are of primarily historical interest.

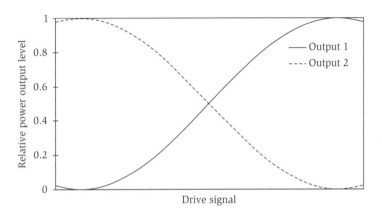

FIGURE 4.15

Transfer function, external optical modulator.

At 1550 nm, it is more common to use a DFB diode for the light source and then to amplify to the desired power level using optical amplifiers. Because an unmodulated DFB has a spectral width of less than 100 MHz, this makes Brillouin scattering a concern.

Regardless of the light source, when an FDM spectrum extending up to between 500 MHz and 1.0 GHz is used to amplitude-modulate the light, the optical spectrum will have sidebands extending to the maximum modulating frequency on each side of the unmodulated optical center frequency. It might be expected that this would effectively raise the Brillouin limit. An analysis, however, has shown that 99% of the energy is still concentrated at the unmodulated wavelength, and actual measurements have demonstrated a negligible increase in scattering limit.[15]

High launch powers are possible, however, if the total optical power is spread more evenly over a range of wavelengths. Two methods are commonly used: phase modulation in the same external modulator used for amplitude modulation and, in the case of DFB sources, intentional chirp generated by modulating the DFB's operating point with a constant frequency. In either case, the wavelength spreading must be sufficient that the beats between the optical frequencies fall above the highest modulating frequency. Manufacturers who employ SBS extension techniques commonly claim the ability to launch +16 to +17 dBm into long single-mode non-dispersion-shifted fibers with acceptably low levels of CSO degradation at either 1310 or 1550 nm.

4.7 OPTICAL AMPLIFIERS

Optical amplifiers boost the level of amplitude-modulated light without requiring the optical-to-electrical conversion, RF amplification, and remodulating otherwise required in a repeating location in a network. Understanding the process requires

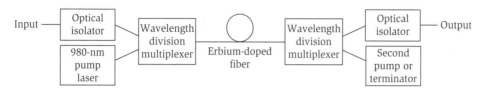

FIGURE 4.16

Schematic of an EDFA.

knowledge of atomic physics that is beyond the scope of this book, but a broad explanation of the principles follows.

The most common form of amplifier is the 1550-nm *erbium-doped fiber amplifier* (EDFA). In an EDFA, the incoming signals are combined, in a WDM coupler, with a high-power unmodulated signal at 980 nm* from one or more "pump" sources. The two signals are then sent through a special length of fiber that is "doped" with erbium (i.e., a carefully controlled amount of erbium is added). The pump signal causes electrons in the erbium atoms to jump to a higher energy band. When they return to their normal state, the difference in energy boosts the signals at 1550 nm. Figure 4.16 shows one of several possible basic schematics of a dual-pump EDFA.

The magic of EDFAs is that they have completely different characteristics than coaxial amplifiers with respect to noise and distortion. Even though they operate in a saturated mode (where a normal coaxial amplifier would produce high harmonic and IM content), EDFAs add no measurable distortion to the modulated signal. Not only that, but they can be overdriven, if desired, so that their input noise level is small compared with the signal to be amplified. The C/N contribution from an EDFA is given by

$$C/N_{EDFA} = 86.2 + P_i + 20 \log(m_i) - NF_{EDFA} \qquad (4.14)$$

where

C/N_{EDFA} = the carrier-to-noise ratio per channel (measured in a 4-MHz bandwidth) in dB
P_i = the optical input power to the EDFA in dBm
m_i = the optical modulation index (OMI) per carrier
NF_{EDFA} = the noise figure of the amplifier

The noise figure of a standard EDFA depends somewhat on input power. Figure 4.17 shows typical variations in NF based on several manufacturers' specifications.

Commercial amplifiers are available with saturated power output levels up to several hundred milliwatts. The highest-powered units use two or more pump sources, injecting light into both ends of the doped fiber (actually, four pumps are possible,

---

*980 nm is the most commonly used pump wavelength. Older devices used 1480-nm pumps, and other wavelengths, such as 850 nm, are possible.

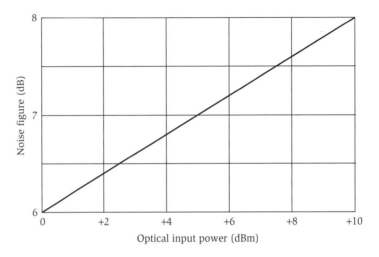

FIGURE 4.17

Noise figure variation in an EDFA as a function of drive level.

two at each end, if they are cross-polarized), while multiple-stage devices are also common. Increasing pump power increases the available output power since more energy is stored in excited electrons that can be tapped to produce optical emissions. A modified technology uses erbium and ytterbium doping and an 800-nm pump wavelength, and achieves even higher powers.[16]

Unfortunately, the efficiency and performance of an optical amplifier are accidents of the properties of specific atomic elements. Although 1550-nm amplifiers are a mature technology, it has proved much more difficult to produce commercially practical units at 1310 nm. Experimental results, though, include a +20-dBm unit with a 22-dB small signal gain and 6-dB noise figure. This unit uses praseodymium doping.[17]

4.8 OPTICAL RECEIVERS

Unlike transmitters, optical detectors are relatively standardized. The incoming light impinges on the active area of a photodiode that has a very precise square law transfer curve (i.e., the output current is proportional to input optical power). Typical responsivity (the slope of the received optical power versus output current transfer function) is 0.8 to 1.0 mA/mW.

The noise performance of an optical receiver is limited by the noise current of the diode (shot noise due to the statistical variation in arriving photon distribution) and by the noise of the following coaxial amplifier. Since the inherent impedance of the detector diode is not 75 ohms, either an impedance-matching transformer or an active circuit is required to match it to the gain stages. Sometimes a *transimpedance amplifier* is used. Although these amplifiers have an excellent noise figure, they have limited dynamic range, with the result that the light level reaching a receiver must typically be controlled within a few decibels of 0 dBm for the best balance between noise and distortion for amplitude-modulated links. It is common for manufacturers of analog broadband fiber-optic terminal equipment to specify link performance at or near 0-dBm received power.

The formula for the C/N contribution due to shot noise is

$$C/N_{SHOT} = P_r + 20 \, \log\left(\frac{m_i}{\sqrt{2}}\right) + 10 \, \log(R) - 10 \, \log(BW) + 154.94 \qquad (4.15)$$

where

C/N_{SHOT} = the C/N of an individual carrier due to shot noise in the detector, expressed in dB

P_r = the received optical power level in dBm

m_i = the peak modulation of the light source by the carrier

R = the responsivity of the receiving diode in amperes per watt (or mA/mW)

BW = the noise susceptibility bandwidth of the channel in Hz

For example, if the OMI per carrier is 3%, the diode response is 0.9 A/W, the received optical power is 0 dBm, and the video bandwidth is 4 MHz, then the C/N contribution due to shot noise will be approximately 55 dB.

Added to that must be the contribution from the postdetector amplification system. If a transimpedance amplifier is used, its C/N contribution can be calculated using

$$C/N_{POSTAMPLIFIR} = 2P_r + 20 \, \log\left(\frac{m_i}{\sqrt{2}}\right) + 20 \, \log(R) - 10 \, \log(BW)$$
$$+ 10 \, \log(R_z) - F + 137.91 \qquad (4.16)$$

where

$C/N_{POSTAMPLIFIER}$ = the C/N of a signal due to thermal noise generated within the postamplifier, expressed in dB

R_z = the postamplifier transimpedance in ohms

F = the postamplifier noise figure in dB

Note that the C/N varies 2:1 with received optical power (the factor $2P_r$) because of the square-law nature of the detector, as opposed to C/N_{SHOT}, which varies 1:1 with optical power because it occurs in the optical domain (before detection).

If, in the previous example, the detector diode is attached to a postamplifier having a 3-dB noise figure and 1200-ohm transimpedance, the C/N contribution due to postamplifier noise will be 65.3 dB. Transimpedance amplifiers, however, have very limited dynamic range. In commercial optical receivers optimized for cable television applications, a variety of means are used to couple photodiodes to postamplifiers, including both direct and impedance-matching transformers. A more general way to calculate postamplifier noise uses the total postamplifier equivalent thermal noise (which includes both the irreducible noise due to the impedance and the excess noise generated within the amplifier).

If Equation 4.16 is reconfigured to use equivalent amplifier thermal noise input current, the postamplifier C/N contribution can be calculated using[18]

$$
\text{C/N}_{\text{POSTAMPLIFIER}} = 2P_r + 20 \log\left(\frac{m_i}{\sqrt{2}}\right) + 20 \log(R) - 10 \log(\text{BW})
$$
$$
- 20 \log(I_r) + 180
$$

(4.17)

where

$\quad$ C/N$_{\text{POSTAMPLIFIER}}$ = the C/N of a signal due to thermal noise generated within the postamplifier, expressed in dB

$\quad\quad P_r$ = the received optical power level in dBm

$\quad\quad m_i$ = the peak modulation of the light source by the signal being evaluated

$\quad\quad R$ = the responsivity of the photodiode in amperes/watt (or mA/mW)

$\quad\quad I_r$ = the postamplifier equivalent input noise current density in pA/$\sqrt{\text{Hz}}$

$\quad\quad 180$ = a factor that results from converting the input power to milliwatts from watts and the amplifier noise to picoamperes from amperes

For example, if we use the same parameters as in the last example but assume instead that the amplifier input noise current density is 7 pA/$\sqrt{\text{Hz}}$ (typical values will be 6 to 8), we can calculate that the postamplifier C/N for an analog video channel will be 62.7 dB.

4.9 INTERACTIONS AMONG TRANSMITTERS, FIBERS, AND RECEIVERS

In addition to the noise and distortion that take place within transmitters and receivers, signal degradation takes place because of the interaction of fiber characteristics with the characteristics of the optical transmitter and receiver. These additional effects can have a significant effect on link performance, which is why it is important that fiber-optic equipment be specified and tested through actual fiber links, not just attenuators.

4.9.1 Double Rayleigh Backscattering: Interferometric Intensity Noise

Some portion of light that is scattered backward through the fiber due to Rayleigh scattering will be rescattered in the forward direction and will combine with the normally transmitted light. Since the double-scattered light from various points along the fiber will not be coherent with the principal optical signal, the effect when both reach the optical detector is that they mix to produce products at the differences in optical frequencies (and multiples thereof) and will show up as an effective increase in link noise. This *interferometric intensity noise* (IIN) is spread across a spectrum that is about twice the total effective linewidth of the transmitter (including the effect of chirp if present). The effective link IIN is given by

$$\text{IIN} = 10 \log \left[\frac{3.6 \times 10^{-14} \left[L - \frac{1}{2\alpha} \left(1 - e^{-2\alpha L} \right) \right]}{\Delta f_{RMS}} \right] \qquad (4.18)$$

where

    IIN = the level of double-scattering-caused noise relative to the unmodulated light level, in dB/Hz

    L = the length of the fiber in km

    $\alpha = 1 - 10^{-\alpha_0/10}$

    α_0 = the loss of the fiber in dB/km

    Δf_{RMS} = the total rms effective linewidth (In the case of directly modulated transmitters, this is the total wavelength spread (chirp) of the source as a result of modulation; in the case of externally modulated transmitters, this is the linewidth of the unmodulated source if not dithered or phase-modulated.)[19]

For affected frequencies, IIN can be related to in-channel C/N in the same way as transmitter RIN:

$$C/N_{IIN} = \text{IIN} - 10 \log(\text{BW}) + 20 \log \left(\frac{m_i}{\sqrt{2}} \right) \qquad (4.19)$$

where

    C/N_{IIN} = the contribution of the IIN effects to the C/N of a signal, expressed in dB

    IIN = the interferometric noise level (relative to the unmodulated light power), as calculated in Equation 4.18 and expressed in dB/Hz

    BW = the receiver noise bandwidth, in Hz, for the communications channel being evaluated

    m_i = the peak modulation of the light source by the signal

Figure 4.18 shows an example of the effect of IIN on video C/N as a function of fiber length for several optical linewidths at 1310 nm. The assumed OMI per carrier was 3%.

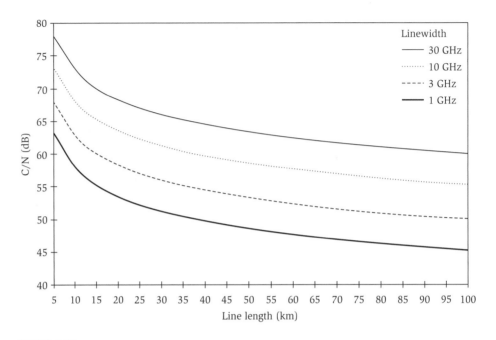

FIGURE 4.18

C/N degradation due to IIN.

For externally modulated sources, absent SBS suppression techniques that cause considerable line spreading, the linewidth is so narrow that IIN noise density is very high and is concentrated at very low frequencies. In order to avoid severe IIN degradation to television channel 2, which starts at 54 MHz, the linewidth must be either less than a few megahertz or artificially spread to levels at least comparable with those found with directly modulated lasers. Since a wider spectral line may be required as part of SBS suppression techniques, the latter approach is generally taken.

Finally, IIN may affect long upstream DFB links in a different way. The unmodulated linewidth of a typical DFB is approximately 10 MHz. Since an upstream link may not be used continuously, when it is idle there may be a significant level of IIN extending up to about 20 MHz much of the time. A possible answer is to apply a "dithering" modulation to the laser continuously to ensure a wider chirped linewidth.[20]

4.9.2 Phase Noise Contribution to Link Performance

Even though DFB diodes oscillate in only a single longitudinal mode, they still exhibit some residual frequency instability. As in F-P diodes, this variance interacts with dispersion to create link noise.

The relationship between source phase noise and link C/N is given by the formula[21]

$$C/N_{PM-AM} = 398.55 - 10 \log\left(\Delta v \, \text{BW}_{RF} \, D^2\lambda^4 f_{RF}^2 L^2\right) + 20 \log\left(\frac{m_i}{\sqrt{2}}\right) \qquad (4.20)$$

where

C/N_{PM-AM} = the contribution to channel C/N (in dB) due to the phase noise in the optical source being converted to amplitude noise in the detector

Δv = the source linewidth in MHz

BW_{RF} = the noise susceptibility bandwidth of the channel in Hz

D = the fiber dispersion constant in ps/nm-km

λ = the operating free-space optical wavelength in nm

f_{RF} = the modulating frequency in MHz

L = the fiber length in km

m_i = the OMI per RF carrier at f_{RF}

The 398.55 factor is the result of converting the various parameters to common engineering units.

As can be seen, the noise affects the RF channels unequally, increasing as the square of the RF channel frequency. It also increases as the square of the fiber length.

Phase-related amplitude noise is generally not of concern in 1310-nm links using nonshifted fiber but may be significant in cases of long fiber links using non–dispersion-shifted fiber at 1550 nm. As an example, assume a 750-MHz analog video channel used to externally modulate (OMI/ch = 3%) an amplified 1550-nm DFB whose optical linewidth is 1 MHz. The signal is then transmitted through a 60-km fiber whose chromatic dispersion is 17 ps/nm-km. The detected signal will exhibit a C/N due to PM–AM conversion of 53.8 dB.

4.10 END-TO-END FIBER-OPTIC LINK PERFORMANCE

The characteristics of the transmitter, interconnecting fiber, receiver, and, optionally, any amplifiers work together to determine the link performance. In particular, the interaction between the signals and the transmission media is much more complex in optical than in coaxial links.

4.10.1 Noise Performance

The total link C/N will have contributions due to transmitter RIN, detector shot noise, and postamplifier noise, as well as due to the IIN interaction among laser linewidth, double scattering, and detector mixing. These noise effects are uncorrelated and so will add on a power basis:

$$C/N_{\text{LINK}} = -10\log\left[10^{-\left(\frac{C/N_{RIN}}{10}\right)} + 10^{-\left(\frac{C/N_{IIN}}{10}\right)}\right.$$
$$\left. +10^{-\left(\frac{C/N_{SHOT}}{10}\right)} + 10^{-\left(\frac{C/N_{POSTAMPLIFIER}}{10}\right)}\right] \tag{4.21}$$

where

$$C/N_{\text{LINK}} = \text{the net per-channel C/N}$$
$$C/N_{\text{RIN}} = \text{the per-channel transmitter relative intensity noise (Eq. 4.11)}$$
$$C/N_{\text{IIN}} = \text{the per-channel interferometric intensity noise (Eq. 4.19)}$$
$$C/N_{\text{SHOT}} = \text{the per-channel shot noise at the detector input (Eq. 4.15)}$$
$$C/N_{\text{POSTAMPLIFIER}} = \text{the per-channel postamplifier noise contribution (Eq. 4.16 or}$$
$$4.17)$$

If the end-to-end C/N of a simple DFB link is plotted as a function of optical loss, the curve will typically have three asymptotes, as shown in Figure 4.19 (the effects of IIN are not readily plotted on the same chart because they vary not with received optical power but with line length).

For high received power levels, the transmitter RIN will dominate, and the C/N will be independent of path loss; at lower received levels, the shot noise will begin

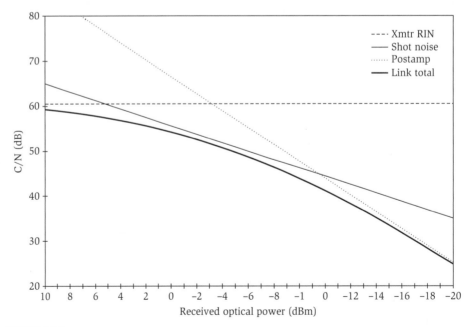

FIGURE 4.19

Typical fiber-optic link C/N contributions.

to dominate and the link C/N will change 1 dB for every decibel of reduction in received power level. At some point, the postamplifier noise will begin to dominate, and the link will begin to degrade 2 dB for every decibel of loss, due to the square-law receiver response. The range of receiver power over which each of these effects dominates depends, of course, on the quality of the individual components. For typical links, the slope of C/N versus level near 0-dBm received power is about 1:1.

In addition to the factors shown in Equation 4.21, other elements and interactions may affect the end-to-end C/N. For instance, if an EDFA is used, its C/N must be included within the parentheses as an additional factor. In long 1550-nm links, residual phase noise may be a factor.

The companion software applications available on the website dedicated to this book (*www.elsevierdirect.com/companions/9780123744012*) include an Excel spreadsheet, entitled *Single-Wavelength Performance Calculator.xls*, that allows simple calculation of the C/N and CSO of most linear optical links in which only a single optical signal is transmitted through each fiber. A separate calculator, discussed in the next chapter, predicts cross-modulation among multiple optical signals sharing a fiber.

4.10.2 Small-Signal Distortions

Directly modulated DFB transmitters behave similarly to single-ended RF amplifiers, generating both second- and third-order distortion whose amplitudes, as a function of RF drive level, increase roughly 1 dB/dB (in the case of second-order products) and 2 dB/dB (in the case of third-order products). As with their coaxial counterparts, CSO products tend to be the limiting distortion. As discussed earlier, typical specifications for such transmitters are 60 to 62 dB for C/CSO and 65 dB for C/CTB under normal operating conditions with a loading of 77 unmodulated carriers. These distortions arise from the combination of small transfer function nonlinearities and large signal clipping.

Externally modulated transmitters exhibit symmetrical distortion and are thus similar to conventional push–pull coaxial amplifiers in that regard. That, combined with the predictability of the nonlinearities, allows C/CSO and C/CTB values of 65 or better with channel loadings of 77 unmodulated carriers.

Distortion occurring in the optical receiver must be added to that generated in the transmitter. Like the transmitter, the detector–postamplifier combination behaves like a single-ended amplifier, with dominant second-order distortion. Often manufacturers specify link performance with a given received power, rather than individually specifying transmitter and receiver.

When the link loss includes fiber, the CSO degradations due to both chirp-induced dispersion and SPM must be included in the calculation of end-to-end performance. Since the CSO distortion mechanisms are synchronized primarily with the modulating waveform (with the exception of the small-signal DFB nonlinearities), the various CSO contributions could be expected to add on a voltage (20 log) basis rather than a power basis. Although this is true, the chirp and SPM effects may, in fact, be of opposite polarity and tend to cancel each other rather than add. Nevertheless, an assumption of voltage addition is the most conservative approach to link design.

One technique for reducing the effects of chirp, SPM, and receiver-generated CSO is to transmit both outputs of a Mach–Zehnder type modulator through parallel networks to the receiver. If the two signals are separately detected and then combined out of phase at RF, these second-order effects will tend to cancel, just as they do in push–pull RF amplifiers. C/CSO values of greater than 70 dB have been reported using this technique, known commercially as a Harmonic Link Extender. As an added benefit, when the signals are combined, the noise will be largely uncorrected (except for the contribution from transmitter RIN) and so will add on a power basis, whereas the signals will add on a voltage basis, resulting in a net 3-dB increase in C/N in the link. Link performance of 55-dB C/N over 50-km links at 1550 nm has been reported.[22]

4.10.3 Clipping Distortion

The ratio of peak-to-average absolute voltage in a simple unmodulated carrier is about 1.6:1. When two equal-amplitude unrelated carriers are summed, however, the relationship is not as simple. Figure 4.20 shows three possible waveforms resulting from the simple addition of two sine waves when one is exactly twice the frequency of the other. Depending on their relative phases, the peak voltages can vary by nearly a factor of 2.

The case when many signals are summed is much more complex. When many summed signals are randomly distributed in both frequency and phase, the peak-to-average level seldom exceeds 14 dB, as discussed in Chapter 7 (although with occasional higher peaks). The downstream spectrum of cable systems is not random, however. The most extreme case occurs when a large number of carriers are harmonics of a common root frequency (as in the CEA-542-B HRC channelization

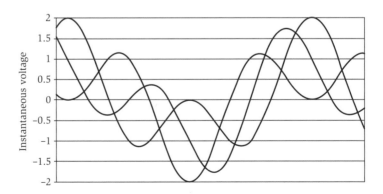

FIGURE 4.20

Addition of two sine waves with various phase differences.

plan) and all the carrier phases are aligned. In that case, the time domain waveform can resemble a string of impulses spaced by a time interval equal to the period of the common root frequency. This is not a surprising result since the Fourier transform of an infinite string of zero-width pulses is an infinite string of carriers.[23]

In the more commonly used CEA-542-B Standard frequency plan, most of the visual carriers are offset by approximately 1.25 MHz from harmonics of 6 MHz and are neither frequency nor phase related. Despite this, the composite waveform has characteristics that are close to harmonically related carriers if the carrier phases do happen to align at some time. Figure 4.21 shows the resultant instantaneous voltage of the standard channels between 54 and 550 MHz, with each assigned a frequency at random within its tolerance range but with the signal phases aligned at $t = 30$ ns on the horizontal scale. The peak-to-average voltage is approximately 34:1. If we look at the same waveform later in time, however, the phases slowly move out of coincidence and the peak voltage decreases. Figure 4.22 shows the condition at $t = 15$ μs. By 20 to 30 μs, the pulses are no longer distinguishable. Figure 4.23 shows a typical situation with truly random phase relationships.

Observations of actual headends carrying NTSC-modulated carriers have confirmed that peak-to-average ratios generally vary from about 3.5:1 to greater than 7:1. When some subset of carriers happen to phase-align, the result is voltage peaks spaced approximately 167 ns apart (the inverse of the 6-MHz channel spacing), which build up to a peak over a few tens of microseconds and then decrease again as the carriers move out of phase coincidence.

The importance of this occasionally occurring peak voltage condition is that, depending on the OMI, the optical transmitter may be driven into hard limiting (clipping) when a sufficient number of carriers are in phase alignment. This is

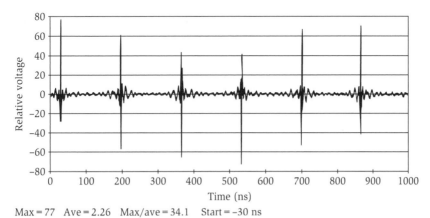

Max = 77   Ave = 2.26   Max/ave = 34.1   Start = –30 ns

FIGURE 4.21

Instantaneous voltage from the addition of 77 FDM carriers with standard frequency assignments and tolerances with phases aligned at $t = 30$ ns.

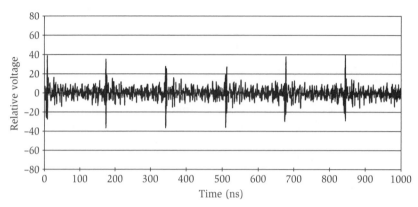

Max = 39.1   Ave = 4.46   Max/ave = 8.8   Start = 1.5ns

FIGURE 4.22

Spike degeneration after 15 μs.

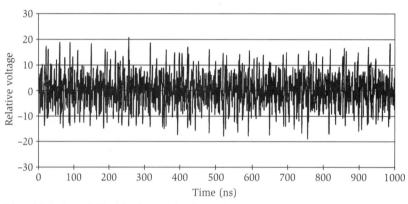

Max = 20.4   Ave = 5.00   Max/ave = 4.1   Start = 3ns

FIGURE 4.23

Typical headend output waveform.

particularly true in the case of directly modulated laser diodes, where a sharp knee occurs in the transfer function below which the light output is extinguished. When that occurs, intermodulation products are generated. As Figure 4.24 shows, both even- and odd-order distortion products are generated when one polarity of a sine wave is clipped off (although second-order products are always the largest). Thus, both CTB and CSO will show an increase when clipping happens with sufficient frequency to be statistically significant. Since clipping produces a string of pulses with the characteristic 167-ns spacing, the largest components produced will fall at harmonics of 6 MHz (which is at the position of the lower CSO beat when the

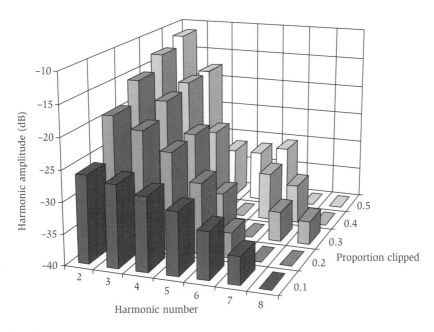

FIGURE 4.24

Harmonic content of a clipped sine wave.

CEA Standard or IRC channel allocation scheme is used, and at the video carrier frequency when the CEA HRC channel scheme is used). With highly linear diodes, clipping may, in fact, be the principal contributor to IM products.

In the case of Mach–Zehnder external modulators, the nonlinearities are symmetrical, and the limiting is "softer," resulting in less clipping and primarily odd-order resultant distortion.[24] Regardless of the modulation method used, the visible effect on analog video channels is that, as OMI is increased, "dashes" resembling electrical interference begin to appear on the displayed picture. These visible effects are due to the integrated effect of a group of pulses (the spacing of which is closer than the television can resolve).

In the case of high-order digitally modulated carriers sharing a linear link with a comb of analog television carriers, the result of clipping is an increase in bit error rate (BER). Data taken by one of the authors found that the BER through a fiber link loaded with 80 normally modulated video channels and one 64-QAM data channel (whose signal level was 10 dB below the video channels) was approximately 1.3×10^{-10}. As the OMI was increased, the BER did not change until a critical threshold was reached, whereupon the BER increased to 7.6×10^{-8}, a 600:1 degradation, with an OMI increase of less than 1 dB. This confirms findings of other researchers in this field. The observations of researchers using normal NTSC video signals were that the BER increased to unacceptably high values before any degradation was visible in displayed analog pictures.[25]

The crucial question is how often clipping occurs. This has been explored by a number of authors. David Grubb and Yudhi Trisno suggested that if OMI per channel is held to $0.348/\sqrt{N}$ (where N is the number of channels), the voltage will exceed the clipping threshold about 2.5×10^{-5} of the time.[26] That analysis, however, was based on unmodulated, randomly phased carriers. They noted, however, that optimal phasing of harmonically related carriers can reduce the theoretical peak voltage. The ratio of theoretical maximum voltage to the maximum achievable with phases aligned optimally is $(\sqrt{N})/1.5$. If the signals feeding an optical transmitter were so related, the modulation index could be increased to $0.67/\sqrt{N}$, or about 5.7 dB higher. This would translate directly to an achievable C/N increase in the link (whose exact amount is related to the relative contribution of transmitter, shot, and postamplifier noise, as discussed earlier in this chapter).

Another factor is video modulation. Since NTSC signals are at maximum carrier level only a small percentage of the time (during synchronizing peaks), the sum of the instantaneous voltages of a number of randomly timed video channels is almost always lower than that of unmodulated carriers. As with carrier phasing, however, the key word is *almost* since the synchronizing pulses for multiple channels will occasionally drift into alignment. Stuart Wagner and colleagues have measured clipping noise and its effect on the BER of a digital signal carried along with 40 randomly timed analog video channels in a fiber link. They found that the peak OMI per analog carrier could be increased by approximately half the average difference in power level (in decibels) between the unmodulated and modulated carriers with no increase in noise or BER.[27] As discussed in Chapter 2, the usual assumption is that average power levels are about 6 dB below peak levels. In particular, the black level of a video signal is about 2.5 dB below sync, so with random video timing it should be possible, on average, to raise peak OMI per channel by about 3 dB compared with the unmodulated carrier case.

On the other hand, with optimum video timing it should be possible to keep the total carrier power close to the average power by minimizing instances where carriers are simultaneously at peak levels. In that case, it should be possible to increase OMI by the difference between peak and average power, 6 dB, without increasing clipping distortion.[28] That increase will lead to a similar increase in link C/N.

4.11 SUMMARY

Linear fiber-optic links are capable of transporting the full spectrum of cable television services over distances exceeding 20 miles without amplification. Amplification, readily available at 1550-nm wavelength, can extend the attainable distance several-fold, with only a minor impact on end-to-end performance.

The basic C/N performance of optical links is limited by transmitter intensity noise, optical shot noise, the interaction between transmitter linewidth and doubly scattered light in the fiber, and receiver postamplifier noise. The interaction between transmitter residual phase noise and the fiber can further reduce the noise under some conditions.

Distortion is fundamentally limited by both small-signal nonlinearities in the transmitter and clipping caused by large-signal peaks. Additionally, interaction between incidental transmitter FM and fiber dispersion can cause second-order distortion, as can interaction between peak power levels and the glass material itself.

Increasing the optical modulation index per carrier in an optical link will improve C/N at the expense of distortion; increasing operating levels in a coaxial network will have the same effect. Similarly, decreasing the number of carriers will allow higher C/N and lower distortion per channel, as in a coaxial network.

Chapter 5 will discuss multi-wavelength transmission through shared fibers. Chapter 7 will discuss the total end-to-end performance of cascaded fiber-optic and coaxial broadband distribution networks; Chapter 10, various HFC architectures; Chapter 11, fiber-deep architecture; and Chapter 12, the reliability of various HFC architectures.

ENDNOTES

1. Ronald C. Cotten, *Lightwave Transmission Applications.* Louisville, CO: CableLabs, September 1993, pp. 80–84.
2. Data provided by CommScope, Inc., Hickory, NC.
3. *AT&T Generic Specification: Fiber-Optic Outside Plant Cable,* Issue 11. Norcross, GA: AT&T Network Cable Systems, December 1995.
4. *CommScope Fiber Optic Cable Catalog.* Hickory, NC: CommScope, Inc., September 1995.
5. *AT&T Generic Specification.*
6. Claude Romans and David Large, "Optical Bus Architecture for Co-Deployment of Telephone and CATV Services in the FRG," in *Conference Record, Globecom '89.* IEEE Communications Society, November 1989, pp. 37.5.1–37.5.9.
7. *AT&T Generic Specification.*
8. David Grubb III and Yudhi Trisno, "AM Fiber Optic Trunks—A Noise and Distortion Analysis," in *1989 NCTA Technical Papers.* Washington, DC: National Cable & Telecommunications Association, May 1989.
9. F.W. Willems, W. Muys, and J.S. Leong, "Simultaneous Suppression of Stimulated Brillouin Scattering and Interferometric Noise in Externally Modulated Lightwave AM-SCM Systems," *IEEE Photonics Technology Letters,* vol. 6, no. 12 (December 1994). See also S.W. Merritt, G.J. McBrien, and E.R. Yates, "Integrated Optic Modulators for 1-GHz HFC Systems," *CED,* February 1996.
10. Dogan A. Atlas, "Fiber-Induced Distortion and Phase Noise to Intensity Noise Conversion in Externally Modulated CATV Systems," in *1996 NCTA Technical Papers,* Washington, DC: National Cable & Telecommunications Association, 1996.
11. AT&T Corporation, *LGX Broadband Fiber Management System Application Guide.* Norcross, GA: AT&T Network Systems, 1995.
12. Dan Harris, "Primer on Baseband Digital Transmission on Single-Mode." *Communications Technology,* August 1996, pp. 92–98.

13. Cotten, *Lightwave Transmission Applications*, p. 148. More recent laser diodes have significantly lower chirp coefficients.

14. Henry A. Blauvelt, et al., "Optimum Laser Chirp Range for AM Video Transmission," in *1992 NCTA Technical Papers*. Washington, DC: National Cable & Telecommunications Association, pp. 79–85.

15. X.P. Mao, et al., "Brillouin Scattering in Lightwave AM-VSB CATV Transmission Systems." Paper presented at OFC '92 Conference, San Jose, CA, February 1992. Digest paper in *Technical Digest—Optical Fiber Communication Conference* (Washington, DC: Optical Society of America, 1992).

16. Roger Brown, "Wave of New Products Set to Break," *CED*, September 1996, pp. 26–30.

17. Vincent Morin and Edouard Taufflieb, "Improved Optical Fiber Amplifier for 1.3-μm AM-VSB CATV Systems." Presented at NCTA National Conference and published in *1998 NCTA Technical Papers*. Washington, DC: National Cable & Telecommunications Association, 1998.

18. This equation is identical to that used by Cotten in *Lightwave Transmission Applications*, Equation 16, p. 171, but with the input variables converted to more common engineering units and with the bandwidth kept as a separate factor to allow the formula to be applied to various bandwidth services.

19. Blauvelt, "Optimum Laser Chirp Range."

20. Donald Raskin and Dean Stoneback, *Return Systems for Hybrid Fiber/Coax Cable TV Networks*. Upper Saddle River, NJ: Prentice-Hall, 1998, pp. 152–154.

21. Atlas, "Fiber-Induced Distortion." Modified after consultation with Dr. Dan Harris of Corning Fiber to give the result per channel and to convert the units to engineering units more familiar to cable engineers.

22. Patrick Harshman, "Applying Push-Pull Technology to Optical Networks," *CED*, September 1996, pp. 56–61.

23. Athanasios Papoulis, *Circuits and Systems: A Modern Approach*. New York: Holt, Rinehart & Winston, 1980, pp. 331–389. Fourier transforms are used to convert between time domain waveforms and their equivalent frequency content.

24. D. Raskin, et al., "Don't Get Clipped on the Information Highway," in *1996 NCTA Technical Papers*. Washington, DC: National Cable & Telecommunications Association, 1996.

25. David Large and Rex Bullinger, "Downstream Laser Clipping: Field Measurements and Operational Recommendations," in *Proceedings Manual, 1997 Conference on Emerging Technologies*. Washington, DC: Society of Cable Telecommunications Engineers, January 1997.

26. Grubb and Trisno. "AM Fiber-Optic Trunks—A Noise and Distortion Analysis."

27. Stuart S. Wagner, Thomas E. Chapuran, and Ronald C. Menendez, "The Effect of Analog Video Modulation on Laser Clipping Noise in Optical Video-Distribution Networks," *IEEE Photonics Technology Letters*, vol. 8, no. 2 (February 1996), pp. 275–277.

28. David Large, "Reducing Distortions Using Video Timing Techniques," *CED*, June 1989, pp. 114–119.

Wavelength Division Multiplexing

5.1 INTRODUCTION

Chapter 4 covered the basics of linear fiber-optic signal transport. These are applicable to situations in which just a single optical signal is sent through each fiber. Fibers, however, are capable of carrying multiple independent optical signals on different wavelengths simultaneously with a minimum of mutual interaction. The general term for such shared use of fiber is *wavelength division multiplexing* (WDM). A network design may choose to use WDM as an economical alternative to installing more fibers or as a means for combining signals that will be detected simultaneously by a common receiver. Both techniques have applications in cable systems.

This chapter will deal with the technology and performance issues encountered in various linear WDM applications, including component performance, mutual interaction in fibers, and link design trade-offs. Readers should first be familiar with the material covered in Chapter 4 because only the incremental information related to multi-wavelength use of fibers will be covered here. The calculations required to predict the degree of crosstalk between signals modulated on different wavelengths in shared signals are fairly complex. To aid the user, two spreadsheets are available for download from the website for this book, *www.elsevierdirect.com/companions/ 9780123744012*. *Optical Crosstalk-Individual Mechanisms.xls* calculates the effect of each mechanism separately and plots the results as a function of one or more parameters, while *Optical Crosstalk Summary.xls* calculates the net effect on one signal of all of the crosstalk mechanisms among 16 DWDM carriers sharing a single fiber.

5.2 WAVELENGTH MULTIPLEXING: WWDM, CWDM, AND DWDM

The optical spectrum is divided into "bands": 1260 through 1360 nm, including the zero-dispersion wavelength in standard fiber, is referred to as "O-Band"; 1360 to 1460 nm, which includes the water peak (see Figure 4.6), is "E-Band"; 1460 through **127**

1530 is "S-Band"; 1530 through 1565, including the lowest attenuation wavelengths and most currently used close-spaced wavelengths, is "C-Band"; and 1565 through 1625 is "L-Band."

Wavelength multiplexing refers to any application in which multiple optical signals on different wavelengths share the use of common fibers. Within that general definition, however, there is a considerable range of applications and wavelength usage plans. Various abbreviations are applied, somewhat inconsistently, to these plans to distinguish them. For our purposes, we will distinguish among three wavelength plans.

1310/1550 dual-wavelength plans—WWDM: The earliest WDM plan involved just two wavelengths: one in the 1310-nm window and one in the 1550-nm window. A typical cable application might involve transporting two signals over a shared link where they would be separated at the far end, or sending two signals modulated with nonoverlapping RF spectra to a common detector where they would be detected and combined in a single operation. Although WDM generally refers to any level of multiplexing, the term is sometimes applied to 1310/1550 multiplexing, as distinguished from the more dense plans discussed later. ITU draft standard ITU-T G.671 considers any channel spacing greater than 50 nm to be *wide wavelength division multiplexing* (WWDM); we will use that designation here.

20-nm-spaced plans—CWDM: An optical industry interim standard uses up to eight wavelengths, spaced 20 nm apart and centered approximately at 1550 nm. The wavelengths are 1470, 1490, . . . 1610 nm and include all of the S-, C-, and L-Bands. Generally, this scheme is referred to as *coarse wavelength division multiplexing* (CWDM), in accordance with ITU-T G.671 (any channel spacing between 8 and 50 nm). ITU-T Recommendation G694-2, approved in June 2002, extends this down to 1270 nm (18 wavelengths), anticipating the ready commercial availability of fiber with no "water peak" of loss between the 1310-nm and 1550-nm transmission windows,[1] as discussed in Chapter 4. Such an extended-wavelength plan is, of course, applicable only to nonamplified systems until such time as optical amplifiers with similarly extended bandwidths are developed.

Subnanometer-spaced plans—DWDM: The International Telecommunications Union (ITU) has defined a usage plan that can scale to as many as 45 wavelengths in the third window and whose spacings have been further split in some systems to yield twice that number. The defined channel designations are for channels spaced 100 GHz apart (about 0.8 nm). Regardless of whether 200-GHz, 100-GHz, or 50-GHz spacings are used, the usage plan is referred to as *dense wavelength division multiplexing* (DWDM).

A few properties are common to all the plans, each with obvious parallels in RF technology.

- The closer the wavelengths are spaced, the harder (and more expensive) it is to separate them in the demultiplexers and simultaneously achieve adequate adjacent channel isolation, minimal in-channel flatness variation, and low insertion loss.

- The closer the wavelengths are spaced, the more frequency stability is required of the transmitters.

- The closer the wavelengths are spaced, the better the signal transmission velocities will match. Four-wave mixing and cross-phase modulation are both maximum when the signals travel at nearly the same velocity. The degree of matching is, of course, also dependent on fiber dispersion, with standard fiber having high dispersion at 1550 nm but low dispersion at 1310 nm. By contrast, close wavelength spacing leads to reduced crosstalk from stimulated Raman scattering. These mechanisms are discussed later.

- The more wavelengths that share a fiber, the lower must be the power per wavelength for a given amount of mutual interaction due to nonlinear glass properties.

Figure 5.1 shows the relationship of bands, CWDM channels, and DWDM channels. Cable systems using linear DWDM technology generally use 200-GHz-spaced channels from among the set of 20 listed in Table 5.1, though a few vendors offer 100-GHz spacing. For network designs that use fewer than 20 of the listed wavelengths, various vendors have chosen to offer different subsets. Most offer C21 through C35

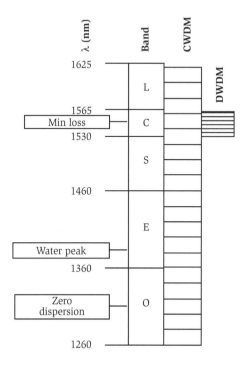

FIGURE 5.1

Relationship of wavelength bands.

Table 5.1 Commonly Used DWDM Channels

Wavelength	ITU channel designation
1560.61	C21
1558.98	C23
1557.36	C25
1555.75	C27
1554.13	C29
1552.52	C31
1550.92	C33
1549.32	C35
1547.72	C37
1546.12	C39
1544.72	C41
1542.94	C43
1541.35	C45
1539.77	C47
1538.19	C49
1536.61	C51
1535.04	C53
1533.47	C55
1531.90	C57
1530.33	C59

as the first eight, but one vendor offers C39 through C53 as the second eight, another offers C45 through C59, and a third has chosen to offer C37 through C51. This is obviously inconvenient for operators who wish to have multiple sources for optical transmitters and DWDM multiplexers.

5.3 COMPONENTS FOR WDM SYSTEMS

Constructing WDM systems requires the use of some components not required for single-wavelength links and tighter control over the specifications of other components.

5.3.1 **Wavelength Multiplexers**

Essential to shared use of fibers is a means by which to combine incoming signals at the transmit end and to separate them at the receiving end. It is possible to use simple wideband splitter/combiners or directional couplers to combine optical signals at the transmit end, and some applications do just that. The trade-off is that a broadband optical combiner (e.g., an RF combiner), has a minimal theoretical insertion loss of about 3 dB per two-way splitting level, with practical devices having losses 0.5 to 1.5 dB higher, whereas a 2-wavelength multiplexer may have a loss of under 2 dB, and a 20-wavelength multiplexer a loss of under 4 dB.

At the current state of technology, the retail cost of a broadband combiner is about 10 to 15% of the cost of a 200-GHz-spaced WDWM multiplexer with an equivalent number of ports. Thus, the decision as to whether to use wavelength-specific or broadband combining at the transmit end of a WDM link must be driven by consideration of the overall link design, including the passive loss and the relative cost of obtaining higher-power transmitters as compared to the cost of wavelength-specific multiplexers.

At the receiving end, however, there is no alternative to using wavelength-specific demultiplexers if the signals are to be detected separately, because detectors are generally insensitive to minor changes in wavelength, with the result that all of the RF spectra modulated onto all of the received optical signals, along with beats among the optical spectra, will otherwise appear at the detector output port.

The technology used to build WDM filters is developing rapidly, with corresponding improvements in both performance and price.[2] Table 5.2 shows typical performance specs for 16- or 20-wavelength, 200-GHz channel-spacing filters. Not generally specified is the maximum in-channel transmission slope, which is crucial to calculating how various phase modulation mechanisms convert to noise and second-order distortion.

Table 5.2 Performance Specifications	
Adjacent channel isolation	27–30 dB
Nonadjacent channel isolation	30–40 dB
Total insertion loss, including connectors	3.8–4.0 dB
Differential insertion loss	1.0 dB
In-channel loss variation	0.5 dB
Polarization-dependent loss variation	0.5 dB

5.3.2 Gain-Flattened Optical Amplifiers

Not only fibers but optical amplifiers are capable of handling multiple optical signals on separate wavelengths. In single-wavelength applications, they are almost always operated in saturated mode and thus have a constant output power regardless of drive level (over a defined range, of course). Thus, any variation of gain with wavelength is not an important consideration. When operated in saturated mode while amplifying multiple wavelengths, however, the total output power will be divided among all the signals, so if one input level changes or a signal is removed or added, the level of all the other signals will also change, which is obviously unacceptable in analog optical links where the RF output power of a detector is a function of both modulation level and optical power level.

Manufacturers avoid this problem by offering products that can optionally be operated in constant-gain-per-wavelength mode. As with coaxial amplifiers, however, the uniformity of gain with (optical) frequency is an essential factor. In general, amplifiers designed to handle a single wavelength do not exhibit a sufficiently flat response. Not only that but their optical frequency response varies as a function of input level. Thus, a class of amplifiers known as *gain-flattened* has been developed for DWDM applications. These devices are designed to operate in a fixed-gain mode of operation and offer a much flatter frequency response. Typical specifications for such a device include gain flatness within 1 dB peak to peak from 1530 to 1565 nm and over a composite power input range of −6 dBm to +6 dBm. Typical devices offer a maximum total power output of up to 20 dBm, gain of 17 to 26 dB, and a noise figure of 5 to 5.5 dB.[3]

The imperfect frequency response of the optical channel (the total of multiplexer, demultiplexer, and amplifier variation) interacts with each source's incidental wavelength modulation (chirp) to produce distortion products. To the extent that the response variation is approximately linear across the transmitter's modulated linewidth (the usual case), the result will be CSO degradation in the demodulated RF signals. If the response variation is noticeably nonlinear, third-order products will be produced as well.

Second, the imperfect in-channel frequency response will interact with any cross-phase modulation occurring before the device to produce cross-amplitude modulation, as discussed later.

Finally, the broader response variation (the total of wideband variation in amplifier response and multiplexer/demultiplexer channel-to-channel insertion loss variations) will also make the various optical signals arrive at their detectors at different levels, resulting in a less-than-optimum balance between noise and distortion for some of the wavelengths.

5.4 WDM-SPECIFIC DESIGN FACTORS

Figure 5.2 illustrates the two generic applications of WDM. In the first application, optical signals on multiple wavelengths are generated by independent transmitters, multiplexed together, transmitted through a shared fiber, optionally amplified,

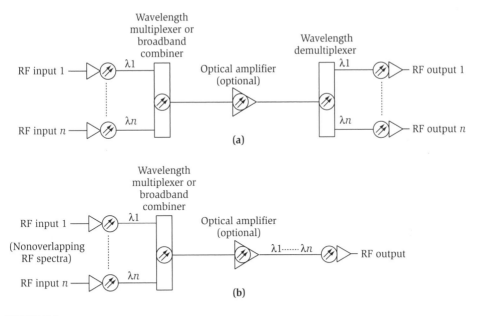

FIGURE 5.2

Separate transmitters and receivers (a) versus separate transmitters and a shared receiver (b) in WDM applications.

demultiplexed at the receiving end, and detected by independent receivers. In the second application, the signals are not demultiplexed but rather fed to a common receiver.

A typical example of the first application would be the transmission of multiple node-specific digital programming from a headend to a hub, where the signals destined for each node would be separated before detection. The second application is frequently used for combining common RF spectra modulated on one wavelength (e.g., 50 to 550 MHz modulating a 1310-nm transmitter) with node-specific programming (using some portion of the spectrum above 550 MHz modulating a 1550-nm transmitter) and then detecting both at the node using a common detector. Sometimes these applications are cascaded, as will be discussed in Chapter 10.

In the first application, the following performance parameters must be considered, in addition to those discussed in Chapter 4:

- Detectors are largely wavelength independent. Thus, to the extent that light from other wavelengths is not perfectly excluded from the desired wavelength output of the demultiplexer, the recovered RF spectrum will also contain some level of the signals modulated on other wavelengths.

- As discussed in Chapter 4, optical signals parametrically modulate the properties of the glass through which they pass. More specifically, the refractive index varies slightly in proportion to the instantaneous optical power level (known as the *optical Kerr effect*, or OKE). In multiple-wavelength systems, these variations lead to various inter-wavelength effects: *cross-phase modulation* (XPM), *four-wave mixing* (FWM), and *cross-polarization modulation*. These, in turn, interact with the properties of both the fiber and the discrete devices along the transmission path to produce noise and cross-modulation in the detected RF signals. Additionally, the presence of each signal can cause the fiber to exhibit incremental gain or loss to other signals through a process known as *stimulated Raman scattering* (SRS).

- To the extent that the optical frequency response of each channel (including the multiplexer, any amplifiers, and the demultiplexer) is not flat, that will combine with any transmitter chirp to generate in-band second-order distortion products in the recovered RF spectrum.

When a common detector is fed more than a single wavelength, some additional parameters must be considered:

- Since there is no way to filter the RF output spectra before combining, each portion of the final spectrum will be degraded by broadband noise from both optical links.

- Similarly, each portion of the spectrum will be degraded by distortion components arising from among signals at other wavelengths and RF frequencies that fall in the RF spectrum of the first link.

- The final balancing of RF levels among those transmitted on each link will be a combination of the *optical modulation index* (OMI) and the relative optical received levels, and thus cannot be adjusted at the receiving site. When WWDM is used in a split-band downstream transmission, the difference in attenuation at 1310 versus 1550 nm will make level balancing dependent on the length of the fiber, and thus prevent two links of different lengths fed by a common transmitter from both being properly balanced.

Each of these will be considered in detail later.

5.5 CROSSTALK MECHANISMS

The first set of factors to be considered are those that lead to crosstalk—defined as the level of postdetection products and wideband noise relative to desired signals that are caused by the presence of modulated optical signals, other than the one whose performance is being considered, and that share use of a common optical network segment that may include multiplexers, fiber, amplifiers, and/or demultiplexers.[4]

Some of the calculations discussed later are rather complex or, at the least, contain so many terms that they require careful manipulation. To make it easier, the Excel workbook entitled *Optical Crosstalk-Individual Mechanisms.xls*, available for download at *www.elsevierdirect.com/companions/9780123744012*, provides easy-to-use, parameterized calculations of major crosstalk mechanisms affecting the performance of a multi-wavelength link. These degradations can be added to the single-wavelength calculations discussed in the previous chapter (most of which are in the spreadsheet entitled *Single-Wavelength Performance Calculator.xls*) to determine total link performance.

5.5.1 Imperfect Demultiplexer Wavelength Isolation

Imperfect multiplexer isolation affects the amount of light from each source that shows up at the wrong output port(s), but otherwise it has no effect on link operation. Imperfect demultiplexer isolation, however, allows some light from undesired wavelengths to impinge on the detector along with light at the desired wavelength. This is not a cross-modulation effect, but does contribute to total crosstalk performance.

In the detector, each of the incoming optical signals will be detected, resulting in a composite RF spectrum that contains elements of the modulating spectra of all the signals. Since the detector is a square law device, the contributions from undesired signals will be lower than the desired RF output by twice the difference in optical levels at the detector input, assuming similar received optical power levels and modulation indices (the assumption throughout this chapter, unless stated otherwise).

Thus, if the adjacent channel isolation in a DWDM demux is 30 dB and OMIs are similar, then the modulated RF signals carried on each of the adjacent wavelengths will appear about 60 dB below the desired signal after detection. If the modulation is analog video and the same nominal channel frequencies are used for each link, then the undesired video carriers will appear close to the desired carriers and have the same effect as ingressing signals. If the modulation on both desired and adjacent signals is digital, then the undesired RF output will appear noise-like and the two adjacent signals together will generate a contribution to the total link C/N of 57 dB.

More generally, if the link were carrying a total of n wavelengths, each modulated with a similar spectrum of signals, the adjacent channel isolation were A dB, and the nonadjacent isolation were B dB, then the total link C/I contribution (for all but the shortest and longest wavelengths) due to imperfect demultiplexer isolation would be

$$C/I_{\text{ISOLATION}} = -10 \log\left[2 \times 10^{-A/5} + (n-3) \times 10^{-B/5}\right] \qquad (5.1)$$

For the highest and lowest wavelengths, there is only one adjacent wavelength, so the equation becomes

$$C/I_{\text{ISOLATION}} = -10 \log\left[10^{-A/5} + (n-2) \times 10^{-B/5}\right] \qquad (5.2)$$

where

$C/I_{\text{ISOLATION}}$ = the ratio of the desired to the total undesired RF signal power in the demodulated spectrum of the victim optical carrier in dB

A = the adjacent optical channel isolation of the WDM demultiplexer in dB

B = the nonadjacent optical channel isolation of the WDM demultiplexer in dB

n = the number of optical carriers

Assuming an environment where all optical signals are at the same nominal level and optical modulation index (the usual case), the level of postdetection cross-talk interference will be independent of the average optical levels and modulation frequency; thus, this is considered a linear degradation factor.

5.5.2 Cross-Phase Modulation Combined with Fiber Dispersion

Recall from Chapter 4 that self-phase modulation (SPM) results from the fact that the refractive index of optical fiber changes slightly in the presence of high electrical fields. Thus, a sufficiently high-amplitude signal will cause the index of refraction to vary as the square of its own instantaneous electrical field strength, resulting in incidental phase modulation, because the velocity of propagation varies inversely with the index of refraction.

When two or more optical signals share a fiber, whatever modulation of the index of refraction takes place affects all of the signals. Thus, the amplitude variations of each of the individual signals result in some degree of phase modulation of the other signals. In a perfect transmission path and with a perfect broadband detector, this phase modulation would have no effect on performance. The cross-phase-modulated signal, however, travels through fiber that exhibits chromatic dispersion to create cross-intensity modulation in the optical signal and, thus, cross-amplitude modulation in the detected RF signals.

Assuming equal optical modulation indices, crosstalk from each interfering modulated optical carrier due to the interaction of cross-phase modulation with fiber dispersion is given by

$$C/I_{XPM-D}(\text{dB}) = -20 \log \left(\frac{4\pi n_2 \beta \Omega^2 P_{20} \rho_{XPM}}{\lambda_2 A \left[\alpha^2 + (d_{12}\Omega)^2 \right]} \right) - 10 \log \left(1 + e^{-2\alpha z} - 2e^{-\alpha z}(1 - \alpha z) \right.$$

$$\left. \cos(d_{12}\Omega z) - 2z[\alpha + d_{12}\Omega e^{-\alpha z} \sin(d_{12}\Omega z)] + \left[\alpha^2 + (d_{12}\Omega)^2 \right] z^2 \right)$$

(5.3)

where all variables are in a consistent set of units. In meter-kilogram-second (MKS) units:

C/I_{XPM} = the ratio, in dB, of desired to undesired RF signal powers in the demodulated spectrum of the victim optical carrier (assuming equal optical modulation indices of both optical signals)

n_2 = the nonlinear refractive index of the fiber, typically 2.6×10^{-20} m^2/W

$\beta = -(\lambda_2{}^2 D)/(2\pi c)$

λ_1 = the wavelength of the victim optical carrier, generally between 1.53×10^{-6} and 1.56×10^{-6} m

λ_2 = the wavelength of the interfering modulated optical carrier, in meters

D = the dispersion coefficient of the fiber in sec/m^2 (For standard fiber near 1550 nm, this is typically 17 ps/nm-km = 17×10^{-6} sec/m^2.)

e = the speed of light in a vacuum = 3×10^8 m/sec

Ω = the frequency of the modulating RF signal in radians = $2\pi f_I$, where f_I is the modulating frequency in Hz

P_{20} = the power level of the modulated interfering optical signal, in watts

ρ_{XPM} = the effective polarization overlap between the interfering and the victim optical carriers (This varies from 1 for copolarized signals to $1/3$ for cross-polarized signals. At $45°$ it is $2/3$.)

A = the effective mode cross-sectional area of the fiber core, about 80×10^{-12} m^2 for non-dispersion-shifted fibers and 50×10^{-12} m^2 for dispersion-shifted fibers

α = the fractional power attenuation of the fiber per meter of length = $1 - 10^{-(\alpha 0/10,000)}$, where $\alpha 0$ is the attenuation in dB/km (A typical value of $\alpha 0$ for standard fiber at 1550 nm is 0.21 dB/km, for which $\alpha = 4.835 \times 10^{-5}$ per meter.)

z = the length of the shared fiber, in meters

d_{12} = the group velocity mismatch between the interfering and victim optical carriers $\approx D(\lambda_1 - \lambda_2)$

Converting this to more common engineering units and assuming operation near 1550 nm, we get

$$C/I_{XPM-D}(\text{dB}) = 459.5 - 2P_I - 20 \log\left(\frac{f_{RF}^2 DL^2 \rho_{XPM}}{A[X^2 + Y^2]}\right) - 10 \log\left(1 + e^{-2X} - 2e^{-X}\right)$$

$$(1 - X)\cos(Y) - 2X - 2Ye^{-X}\sin(Y) + X^2 + Y^2) \qquad (5.4)$$

where

P_I = the launch power of the interfering optical carrier in dBm

f_{RF} = the modulation frequency in MHz

D = the fiber dispersion in ps/nm-km (For non-dispersion-shifted fiber near 1550 nm this is typically 17.)

L = the length of the fiber in km

ρ_{XPM} = the effective polarization overlap between the interfering and victim optical carriers (This varies from 1 for copolarized signals to $1/3$ for cross-polarized signals and is $2/3$ for $45°$ relative polarization.)

A = the effective cross-sectional area of the fiber core. For non-dispersion-shifted fiber this is typically 80×10^{-12} m^2

α = the fractional power attenuation of the fiber per km = $1 - 10^{-(\alpha 0/10)}$, where $\alpha 0$ is the attenuation in dB/km (A typical value of $\alpha 0$ for standard fiber at 1550 nm is 0.21 dB/km, for which $\alpha = 0.047$.)

$\Delta\lambda$ = the difference in wavelength between the interfering and victim optical carriers in nm

X = the "loss parameter" αL (For fiber with a loss of 0.21 dB/km, this is $0.047L$, where L is the length of the fiber in km.)

Y = the "walk-off parameter" $D \Delta\lambda(2\pi f_{RF})L$ (For fiber with a dispersion of 17 ps/nm-km, this is $1.068 \times 10^{-4} \Delta\lambda f_{RF} L$.)

The amount of optical cross-phase modulation, and thus intensity modulation after interaction with the dispersion, varies linearly with the level of the interfering optical signal. Thus, after detection this degradation factor will vary 2 dB for every 1-dB change in the level of the interfering optical signal.

The amount of optical cross-phase modulation also varies according to the polarization match between the interfering and victim optical signals in the fiber. For cross-polarized signals, the cross-modulation is one-third that for copolarized signals.

Due to dispersion in the fiber, the interfering and victim optical signals will travel at slightly different velocities. This property, also known as *walk-off*, reduces the peak cross-phase modulation because the peak amplitude of the interfering signal "slides" along the victim signal rather than synchronously acting on the same spot in time. The greater the wavelength difference, the faster the walk-off occurs, resulting in less peak cross-phase modulation.

The effects of cross-phase modulation are greatest at higher RF frequencies. One reason is that a constant level of phase deviation versus frequency results in an optical frequency deviation that linearly increases with modulating frequency, and it is the frequency change that interacts with dispersion to create the crosstalk.

Figure 5.3 shows the maximum and minimum expected crosstalk from this mechanism for a single copolarized interfering carrier whose launch power is +7 dBm and whose optical carrier is 1.5 nm away from the victim carrier, with both transmitted through 30 km of standard fiber.

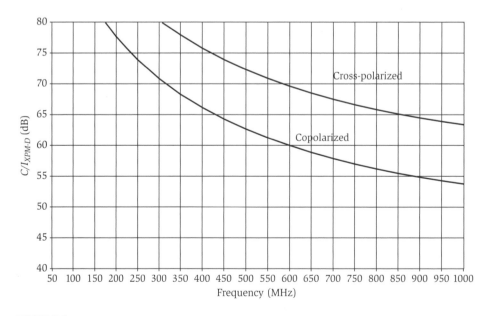

FIGURE 5.3

C/I due to cross-phase modulation interacting with fiber dispersion.

5.5.3 Stimulated Raman Scattering (SRS or "Raman Crosstalk")

At a sufficiently high optical signal level, one optical signal can act as a "pump" so as to provide gain (either positive or negative) to other signals sharing the fiber. If the pump signal has a wavelength that is shorter than the victim signal, then the gain will be positive, whereas if the pump signal is longer, the gain will be negative (in other words, loss). The gain is maximum for WDM channels with optical frequencies separated by about 13 THz and is proportionately lower for narrower separations. Another way of looking at this phenomenon is that power is transferred from the shorter-wavelength optical carrier to the longer-wavelength carrier as they travel through the shared fiber; but since they are both modulated, the SRS gain follows the instantaneous carrier levels and results in mutual cross-amplitude modulation.

Assuming equal optical modulation indices, crosstalk from each interfering modulated optical carrier due to stimulated Raman scattering is given by

$$C/I_{SRS}(dB) = -10 \log\left[\left(\frac{\rho_{SRS}g_{12}P_{20}}{A}\right)^2 \left(\frac{1 + e^{-2\alpha z} - 2e^{-\alpha z}\cos(\Omega d_{12}z)}{\alpha^2 + (\Omega d_{12})^2}\right)\right] \quad (5.5)$$

where the units are the same as for Equation 13.3, with the following additions:

C/I_{SRS} = the ratio of desired to undesired RF signal powers in the demodulated spectrum of the victim optical carrier in dB (assuming equal optical modulation indices of both optical signals)

ρ_{SRS} = the effective polarization overlap between the interfering and victim signals (This equals 1 for copolarized signals and less than 0.1 for cross-polarized signals.)

g_{12} = the Raman gain coefficient (positive if the interfering signal is of shorter wavelength than the victim signal and negative if the interfering signal is of longer wavelength = $g_{SRS}c(\lambda_2 - \lambda_1)/(\lambda_2\lambda_1)$, where g_{SRS} = the Raman gain slope for the fiber—typically 5×10^{-27} m/W-Hz)

Converting this to more convenient engineering units, we get

$$C/I_{SRS}(dB) = 304.1 - 2P_I - 20 \log\left(\frac{\rho_{SRS}\Delta\lambda L}{A}\right)$$
$$-10 \log\left(\frac{1 + e^{-2X} - 2e^{-X}\cos(Y)}{X^2 + Y^2}\right) \quad (5.6)$$

where the units are the same as for Equation 5.4, with the following additions:

C/I_{SRS} = the ratio of desired to undesired RF signal powers in the demodulated spectrum of the victim optical carrier in dB (assuming equal optical modulation indices of both optical signals)

ρ_{SRS} = the effective polarization overlap between the interfering and the victim optical carriers (This varies from 1 for copolarized signals to less than 1/10 for cross-polarized signals. At 45° relative polarization, it has a value of 0.5.)

As with XPM crosstalk, SRS varies 2 dB for every 1-dB increase in optical carrier level; however, the degree of SRS "coupling" between the signals is more highly dependent on the polarization match between them and drops to less than a tenth for cross-polarized signals, meaning that the RF crosstalk can vary more than 20 dB.

Crosstalk due to SRS is maximum at low modulation frequencies, but decreases in a nonlinear way, with a periodic variation superimposed on the general decrease as a function of frequency due to the walk-off between the interfering and victim channels. The variation exhibits more cycles across the modulation frequency spectrum when the optical channels are more widely separated, since the velocity mismatch is then greater.

Figure 5.4 shows the maximum and minimum expected crosstalk from SRS for a single interfering carrier whose launch power is +7 dBm and whose optical carrier is 24 nm away from the victim carrier, with both transmitted through 30 km of standard fiber.

SRS crosstalk is typically the most serious of the crosstalk mechanisms at wide wavelength spacings and low modulation frequencies, with the crosstalk at 50 MHz being worse than for any other mechanism at any other frequency. One researcher has suggested reducing the effect of SRS by transmitting pairs of closely spaced optical carriers, modulated 180° out of phase, so that the SRS crosstalk on a third carrier from one would approximately cancel the crosstalk from the other. Experimental data confirms a reduction of about 30 dB at 50 MHz and 15 dB at 800 MHz for 1-nm-spaced interfering carriers, with 4- to 5-nm spacing to the victim carrier. Whether this is a cost-effective solution to the problem is questionable.[5]

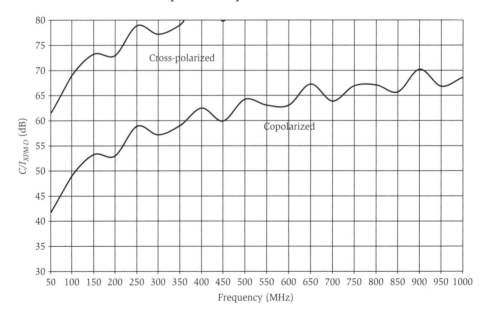

FIGURE 5.4

C/I due to stimulated Raman scattering.

5.5.4 Cross-Phase Modulation Combined with Transmission Slope

Aside from the conversion from XPM to intensity modulation that takes place in the fiber itself, the phase-modulated victim signal also reacts with any device whose transmission slope is not flat with frequency (*transmission slope*, or TS). Generally, the least flat component is the wavelength demultiplexer. This gives rise to a slope-detection conversion from phase to amplitude modulation. Assuming equal modulation of the two carriers, the crosstalk is given by this equation:

$$C/I_{XPM-TS}(\text{dB}) = -20 \log \left(\left[\frac{1}{T_0} \frac{\partial T}{\partial f} \right] \frac{2n_2 \Omega P_{20} \rho_{XPM}}{\lambda A} \right)$$
$$- 10 \log \left(\frac{1 + e^{-2\alpha z} - 2e^{-\alpha z} \cos(d_{12}\Omega z)}{[\alpha^2 + (d_{12}\Omega)^2]} \right) \tag{5.7}$$

where all variables have the same units and meanings as in Equation 5.3, with the following additions:

T_0 = the linear transmission coefficient of the component in question (i.e., the ratio of output power to input power)

$\partial T / \partial f$ = the differential of the linear transmission coefficient at the wavelength being used with respect to frequency (i.e., change in ratio of output power to input power divided by change in optical frequency)

The product of these, in MKS units, can be calculated using

$$\frac{1}{T_0} \frac{\partial T}{\partial f} = 1 - 10^{-S/10^{-9}} \tag{5.8}$$

where S is the transmission slope of the demultiplexer or other component in dB/GHz.
In more common engineering units, this reduces to

$$C/I_{XPM-TS}(\text{dB}) = 313.5 - 2P_I - 20 \log \left(\frac{S_T f_{RF} \rho_{XPM} L}{A} \right)$$
$$- 10 \log \left(\frac{1 + e^{-2X} - 2e^{-X} \cos(Y)}{X^2 + Y^2} \right) \tag{5.9}$$

where the units are the same as for Equation 5.4, with the following additions:

$S_T = 1 - 10^{-S/10}$
L = the length of the fiber in km

Unfortunately, the in-band transmission slope of wavelength demultiplexers is seldom specified. One researcher has found typical devices to have a slope that averaged 0.02 dB/GHz but some were as high as 0.11 dB/GHz.[6]

As with crosstalk, due to the interaction between cross-phase modulation and fiber dispersion, XPM-TS is greater at higher modulating frequencies and higher

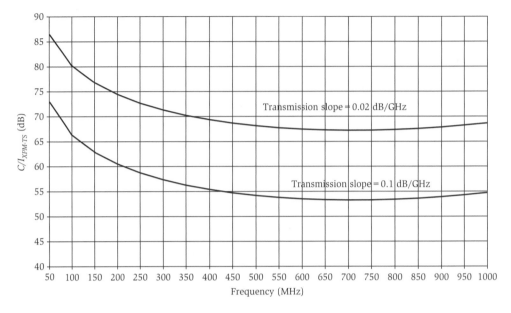

FIGURE 5.5

C/I due to cross-phase modulation interacting with imperfect demux channel flatness.

optical powers, but is reduced at wider optical channel spacing and higher fiber dispersion. Figure 5.5 shows the variation with frequency for two copolarized signals spaced by 1.5 nm and launched at 7 dBm. Curves are plotted for 0.02 dB/GHz and 0.1 dB/GHz, which represent the typical range of measured values for commercially available DWDM demultiplexers.

XPM-TS can add either in phase or out of phase with XPM-D, depending on the slope of the filter loss.

5.5.5 Optical Kerr Effect Combined with Polarization-Dependent Loss

As seen already, both XPM and SRS are maximum when the polarizations of the interfering signals are aligned with the target signal and minimum when they are cross-polarized. When they are at some other relative polarization, however, the polarization as well as the gain and phase of the target signal are modulated.

This can be understood if the target signal is viewed as the vector addition of two signals, one copolarized with the interfering signal and one cross-polarized with it. The one that is copolarized undergoes much greater cross-amplitude and cross-phase modulation than the one that is cross-polarized, with the result that the vector sum of the two has a net polarization that varies with the amplitude of the undesired signal.

As with XPM, in a perfect network followed by a perfect detector, the OKE would have no effect on the detected signals. When either the fiber or a discrete device has a *polarization-dependent loss* (PDL), however, it is converted to amplitude modulation. One researcher found a typical WDM demultiplexer to have a

PDL of 0.03 to 0.17 dB[7]; however, as noted earlier, typical specifications for production devices are of the order of 0.5 dB.

Assuming equal optical modulation indices, crosstalk from each interfering modulated optical carrier, due to the interaction of the optical Kerr effect with polarization-dependent loss in a terminating component, is given by the following general equation:

$$C/I_{OKE-PDL}(\text{dB}) = -10 \log \left[\left(\frac{\Delta T \rho_3 t_3}{3 \left(1 - \frac{\Delta T}{2} (1 - t_2)\right)} \right)^2 \left(\frac{4\pi n_2 P_{20}}{\lambda A} \right)^2 \right.$$
$$\left. \left(\frac{1 + e^{-2\alpha z} - 2e^{-\alpha z} \cos(d_{12} 2\pi f_{RF} L)}{\alpha^2 + (d_{12} 2\pi f_{RF})^2} \right) \right] \tag{5.10}$$

where the units are the same as for Equation 5.3, with the following additions:

$C/I_{OKE-PDL}$ = the ratio of desired to undesired RF signal powers in the demodulated spectrum of the victim optical carrier in dB, for a single interfering carrier

ΔT = the transmission difference, as a function of polarity, through the terminating device, as a percentage of the maximum transmission = $1 - 10^{-\text{PDL}/10}$, where PDL is the polarity-dependent loss through the device in dB

ρ_3 = the effective polarization overlap factor for this mechanism (This varies from 0.75 at 45° relative polarization to 0 for signals that are either co-polarized or orthogonally polarized.)

t_2, t_3 = transmission parameters that can vary over the range from +1 to −1 (Crosstalk is maximum for $t_3 = 1$ and $t_2 = -1$.)

Converting this to more common engineering units and calculating the maximum possible crosstalk, we get

$$C/I_{OKE-PDL}(\text{dB}) = 263 - 2P_I - 20 \log \left[\frac{\Delta T L \rho_3}{A} \right]$$
$$- 10 \log \left[\frac{1 + e^{-2X} - 2e^{-X} \cos(Y)}{X^2 + Y^2} \right] \tag{5.11}$$

where the units are the same as for Equation 5.4, except that ΔT and ρ_3 are the same as in Equation 5.9.

Although the maximum possible OKE-PDL effect can be calculated, the level in practical applications can vary widely due to two factors. First, the degree of cross-polarization modulation varies with the relative polarizations between the interfering and victim signals. Second, the conversion from polarization modulation to amplitude modulation depends on the polarization of the victim signal relative to the maximum slope of loss versus polarization in the demultiplexer. One researcher found that the experimental C/I from this effect was 6 dB better than the minimum predicted and that the median C/I was 9 dB better.[8]

interfering signal is at a shorter wavelength, they add to produce crosstalk greater than either mechanism alone. On the other hand, SRS crosstalk increases, while XPM decreases, as the difference in wavelengths increases, resulting generally in a broad minimum as the wavelength spacing approaches zero, whereas OKE-PDL has a broad maximum with small wavelength spacing and prevents XPM and SRS effects from canceling completely at any spacing.

XPM-TS, like OKE-PDL, can add constructively or destructively with the net of XPM and SRS, depending on the slope of the response of the device, which is generally not predictable. Finally, crosstalk due to imperfect demultiplexer isolation will add constructively with XPM-D crosstalk.

Thus, the most conservative calculation of optical cross-modulation in a two-wavelength system, assuming four-wavelength mixing can be ignored, would require adding the worst-case demultiplexer isolation and XPM-D magnitudes, then adding or subtracting (depending on relative wavelengths) the SRS magnitude, and then adding the XPM-TS and OKE-PDL magnitudes to the absolute value of the previous calculation. More formally,

$$C/I_{\text{CROSSTALK}}(\text{dB}) = -20 \log\left[\left| 10^{-I/20} + 10^{-C/I_{XPM-D}/20} \pm 10^{-C/I_{SRS}/20} \right| \right.$$
$$\left. + 10^{-C/I_{OKE-PDL}/20} + 10^{-C/I_{XPM-TS}/20}\right] \tag{5.12}$$

where the plus sign is used where the interfering carrier is at a shorter wavelength than the victim carrier and the minus sign otherwise, and where

$C/I_{\text{CROSSTALK}} =$ the net crosstalk occurring between two optical carriers similarly modulated

$I =$ the isolation of the WDM demultiplexer at the wavelength of the interfering carrier in dB

$C/I_{XPM-D} =$ the crosstalk due to cross-phase modulation interacting with fiber dispersion in dB

$C/I_{SRS} =$ the crosstalk due to stimulated Raman scattering in dB

$C/I_{OKE-PDL} =$ the crosstalk due to the optical-Kerr-effect-caused cross-polarization modulation interacting with polarization-dependent loss in the WDM demultiplexer in dB

$C/I_{XPM-TS} =$ the crosstalk due to cross-phase modulation interacting with imperfect channel flatness in the WDM demultiplexer in dB

Such a calculation will overstate the total cross modulation if worst-case levels are assumed for all mechanisms, because the OKE-PDL magnitude cannot be maximum at the same input-signal relative polarization that maximizes SRS and XPM. To be safe, the calculation can be run with relative polarizations of $0°$ (where OKE-PDL is zero) and also at $45°$ (where OKE-PDL is maximum) to see which one results in the worst-case crosstalk.

In practical headend and field installations, relative polarizations will not be known or controlled and can be assumed to vary randomly. Since XPM crosstalk varies by about 10 dB with polarization and SRS varies by 20 dB or more, at best this calculation will yield an approximation of the total likely cross-modulation.

In systems of more than two wavelengths, the calculated cross-modulations between various pairs of optical carriers will vary due to different channel spacings, different numbers of lower and higher interfering channels relative to each victim channel, different qualities of optical demultiplexer channels (combined with transmitter wavelength tolerance relative to nominal channel center wavelength), and random polarization combinations. In addition, it is not uncommon in CATV systems for at least part of the spectrum to be common to multiple transmitters driving a common fiber. This means that, potentially, multiple interfering carriers could be modulated synchronously over at least part of the RF spectrum, and therefore that the cross-modulation effects could add vectorially rather than randomly. One researcher has found that ignoring possible synchronous effects (i.e., by adding the calculated distortion from each interfering carrier on a power, rather than voltage, basis) agrees with experimental results within 7 dB at all frequencies and within 3 dB above 500-MHz modulation in an eight-wavelength system.[11]

Using this approach, Figure 5.7 shows the maximum likely contributions of each crosstalk mechanism and the net crosstalk affecting the longest and shortest

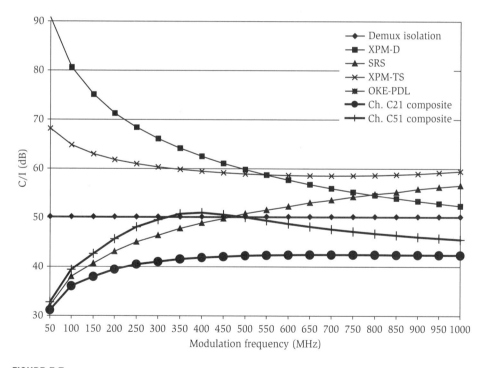

FIGURE 5.7

Maximum composite C/I: 16 wavelengths copolarized, shortest and longest wavelengths.

imposed by the demux isolation, with typical C/I probably falling somewhere in the 42- to 45-dB range for the conditions specified. Whatever the case, it is clear that the various cross-modulation effects combine to make long, multi-wavelength links inadequate to carry analog video channels.

5.5.8 Linear versus Nonlinear Crosstalk

Among the preceding crosstalk mechanisms, only demultiplexer isolation is linear—that is, results in the simple addition of desired and undesired modulated RF spectra after detection. Each of the other mechanisms results in one modulated lightwave signal being modulated, in turn, by the amplitude variations in one or more other lightwave signals. This process results in the generation of products (and therefore RF signals after detection) that were not part of either modulating spectra.

To quantify this effect, keep in mind that the equation for a conventional amplitude-modulated signal is

$$[1 + A \sin(\omega_1 t)]\sin(\omega_c t) \tag{5.13}$$

where

A = the modulation depth (1 = 100% modulation)
ω_1 = the modulating frequency in radians/second
ω_c = the carrier (in this case, optical carrier) frequency in radians/second

When a carrier-amplitude is modulated, sidebands are generated that are $-20 \log (A/2)$ dB relative to the carrier and spaced on either side of it by the modulating frequency.

If this modulated signal is now multiplied (as happens in nonlinear crosstalk) by the amplitude of a second modulated optical signal $[1 + B \sin(\omega_2 t)]C$ (where B is the modulation level of the undesired signal and C is the cross-modulation level), we get not only sidebands spaced at $\omega_c \pm \omega_1$ at level $-20 \log(A/2)$ dB (from the original modulation), and $\omega_c \pm \omega_2$ at level $-20 \log(BC/2)$ dB (as you would expect from linear crosstalk), but also terms at $\omega_c \pm \omega_1 \pm \omega_2$ at level $20 \log(ABC/4)$ dB—in other words, at the sum and difference between the original and crosstalk modulating frequencies. After detection, the linear crosstalk RF products will be at a level of $-20 \log(BC/A)$ relative to the desired signals, while the new cross-modulation RF products will be $-20 \log(BC)$ relative to the level of the original modulating signals.

What this means is that, if two nonoverlapping spectra are transported over two different wavelengths sharing a common fiber, there can still be mutual in-band interference generated. For example, if the 5- to 40-MHz return band is transmitted using a single wavelength, and a 50- to 870-MHz downstream band is transmitted using another wavelength, the finite isolation of the demultiplexer would not lead to mutual interference (assuming the detected spectra is appropriately filtered to eliminate the unwanted out-of-band signals). On the other hand, the nonlinear effects quantified before would lead to generation of new in-band RF products extending from 10 to 40 MHz in the return band and from 50 to 865 MHz in the forward band that cannot be removed by simple RF filtering.

If both forward and reverse signals were modulated by multiple RF signals with the same 3% modulation index per RF signal, and the crosstalk level were 1% (40 dB), the products at the difference frequencies would be $-20 \log(0.01 * 0.03) = 70.5$ dB below the desired signals after detection and not a problem for either analog or QAM signals. If, on the other hand, the return band were 100% modulated by a single sine-wave signal, the products at the difference frequencies would be only $-20 \log (0.01) = 40$ dB below the desired signals. Thus, some caution is advised when fibers are shared among modulated lightwave signals with significantly different modulation levels and, in particular, with baseband digital signals where the lowest bit rate is not at least twice the highest desired signal frequency.

5.5.9 An Illustration: Dense WDM near 1310 nm

Recently, several manufacturers have begun to develop equipment designed to transport several wavelengths in O-Band. This application is worth discussing because it illustrates some of the trade-offs in designing multi-wavelength applications. The motive for such systems is cost. If more than two wavelengths need to be transported, each to be modulated by the full spectrum of downstream signals, there is only one other option—externally modulated transmitters at 1550 nm, which cost several times as much as directly modulated transmitters. Directly modulated transmitters at 1550 nm are not a solution since their chirp will interact with fiber dispersion to cause unacceptable CSO, while use of multiple wavelengths at 1310 nm with standard wavelength plans will cause a high level of four-wave mixing, cross-phase and Raman crosstalk, and other problems.

One proposed scheme uses a careful balancing of crosstalk effects, chirp compensation, and superior demultiplexer performance to achieve acceptable performance over a 25-km link, transporting four wavelengths.[12] Part of the solution is wavelength choice—1323.003, 1324.172, 1325.783, and 1327.249 nm were used, with the result that all FWM products (second as well as third order) fell between the original wavelengths. Compensation for the 200-MHz/mA transmitter chirp, combined with a demultiplexer slope below 0.1 dB/nm, and wavelengths below 1328 nm resulted in chirp-TS–induced C/CSO of 70 dB or better (see Section 5.6 for a derivation of this effect). Keeping the total wavelength span to just over 4 nm, combined with some "grooming" of the RF signals driving the transmitters, limited Raman crosstalk to acceptable levels. Similarly, control over demultiplexer in-channel flatness, combined with the widest wavelength spacing possible, given Raman crosstalk, yielded acceptable values of cross-phase modulation effects. The total link exhibited a C/N of 50.5 dB, a CSO of 63 dB, a CTB of 70 dB, a BER (256 QAM) of 10^{-7}, and a MER of 37.5 dB.

5.6 CSO DUE TO TRANSMITTER CHIRP COMBINED WITH IMPERFECT CHANNEL FLATNESS

Directly modulated DFB transmitters exhibit an incidental wavelength modulation, known as *chirp*. Additionally, due to the Kerr effect, each optical carrier generates self-phase modulation (SPM), which adds an additional component of wavelength variation. When transmitted through fiber with appreciable dispersion, these cause second-order distortion in the demodulated signals because the transmission rate through the fiber then varies as a function of the modulation level. Both of these phenomena are covered in Sections 4.6.3 and 4.4.7.

In DWDM systems, however, another factor arises due to the variations in channel amplitude response as a function of optical frequency. Various components may contribute to this, including the optical multiplexer, the optical amplifiers, and the demultiplexer. Transmitter chirp interacts with this imperfect channel response to add another stage of optical modulation. Since each modulation is proportional to the modulating current and the modulation stages are effectively in series, the current at the output of the detector will have a component that is proportional to the square of the input current, and this creates the second-order distortion mechanism *chirp + transmission slope* (CHIRP-TS). For systems carrying analog video channels exclusively, the calculation is relatively simple.

First, given a change in modulating current Δi_M, the optical power will vary by $\Delta P_{\text{OPT}} = k_1 \, \Delta i_M$, where k_1 is the modulation slope of the laser diode. The frequency of the optical carrier will also vary by $\Delta f_{\text{OPT}} = k_2 \, \Delta i_M$, where k_2 is the chirp slope of the laser diode in GHz/mA. The changing optical frequency interacts with the transmission slope of the channel T_S, in dB/GHz, to produce a change in optical power of $\Delta f_{\text{OPT}} T_S = k_2 \Delta i_M T_S$ dB.

In order to calculate the total effective modulation on the signal as received at the detector, it is necessary to convert this second stage of modulation back into a scalar quantity and to multiply it by the normal laser modulation. When we do that we get

$$\Delta P_R = k_i \Delta i_M 10^{\left(\frac{k_2 \Delta i_M T_S}{10}\right)} \tag{5.14}$$

where

ΔP_R = the change in optical received power resulting from a change in modulating current
k_1 = the modulation slope of the transmitter diode in mW/mA
Δi_M = the change in modulating current in mA
k_2 = the chirp slope of the transmitter diode in GHz/mA
T_S = the transmission slope of the channel in dB/GHz

Multiplying the change in power by the responsivity of the detector gives us the change in output current as a function of the change in input current and, thus, the equation for the transfer function of the system:

$$\Delta i_o = R k_i \Delta i_M 10^{\left(\frac{k_2 \Delta i_M T_S}{10}\right)} \tag{5.15}$$

where

R = the detector diode responsivity in mA/mW

This can be simplified by converting the power of 10 to a power of e and then taking the first two terms of the Taylor expansion of $e^x = 1 + x + x^2/2! + x^3/3! \ldots$. This is equivalent to assuming that, over small changes in wavelength, the multiplication of the chirp slope and the transmission slope results in linear modulation as a function of input current. With that simplification, the transfer function becomes

$$\Delta i_o = Rk_i \Delta i_m + Rk_i 0.23026 k_2 T_S \, \Delta i_m^2 \qquad (5.16)$$

Referring to the derivation of CSO in Chapter 2, this is in the form of Equation 2.20, but expressed in terms of current rather than voltage, where $i_o = Ai_M + Bi_M^2$, with $A = Rk_1$ and $B = 0.23026 \, Rk_1 k_2 T_S$. From the analysis in Section 2.3.3, we know that the amplitude of the fundamental is Ai_M and that the amplitude of the individual second-order products is Bi_M^2, and therefore that the ratio of amplitudes of the fundamental and second-order products is A/B, or $1/(0.23026 \, k_2 T_S I_M)$, where I_M = the peak input-modulating current. Since power is proportional to the square of current and the composite second-order product will be determined by the power sum of products, we can write an equation for composite second-order distortion from this mechanism:

$$C/CSO_{\text{CHIRP}-TS} = -20 \log(0.23026 k_2 T_S I_M) - 10 \log N \qquad (5.17)$$

where

$C/CSO_{\text{CHIRP}-TS}$ = the ratio of the desired carrier on the channel being evaluated to the composite power in the second-order products resulting from the interaction of transmitter chirp and the flatness of the transmission channel

k_2 = the chirp slope of the transmitter diode in GHz/mA

T_S = the transmission slope of the demultiplexer channel in dB/GHz

I_M = the peak per-channel modulating current in mA

N = the number of second-order beats falling in a cluster affecting the channel being evaluated (from Equation 2.25).

As was shown in Chapter 4, the CSO level resulting from the use of directly modulated 1550-nm DFB transmitters combined with transmission through long strands of standard fiber was sufficiently high to render this combination unusable for analog video transmission when the spectrum was greater than an octave. The same is true for transmitter chirp when combined with a typical WDM filter transmission slope. For example, a transmission slope of 0.05 dB/GHz (a very moderate assumption because it is typical of just the DWDM demux) combined with the typical DFB chirp of 0.25 GHz/mA and 2-mA/channel modulating current results in second-order products that are 44.8 dB below the desired signal. The power addition of the 31 upperside products affecting the highest channel in a 550-MHz system would result in a C/CSO of only 29.8 dB.

When the RF modulation consists wholly or partially of QAM signals, however, the second-order products are no longer narrow. The low-side product of a QAM channel mixing with an analog video channel exhibits a flat, noise-like spectrum 6 MHz wide, centered 1.75 MHz above the lower channel boundary, since the analog carrier is 1.25 MHz above the lower channel boundary and the QAM channel is 3 MHz above the lower channel boundary. The second-order products resulting from the mixture of two QAM channels will be noise-like, centered on the boundary between two channels, but 12 MHz wide (assuming the mixing channels were each 6 MHz wide) with a triangular spectral shape. When a continuous spectrum of adjacent QAM channels is carried, these products will overlap, leading to a relatively flat composite intermodulation noise (CIN) floor whose level can be approximated using the earlier formula, even though the level arises from products each of whose average noise-like density is spread over two channels. For the case of 45 QAM channels extending from 600 to 870 MHz, each modulated at 2 mA/channel, the magnitude of the second-order intermodulation noise per 6 MHz of bandwidth falling near channel 2 would be 29.2 dB below the level of the digital signals. This is 20 dB worse at channel 2 than the CSO, due to chirp interacting with just fiber dispersion (Equation 4.12); it shows that the degradation due to discrete components often is the limiting factor in system performance. The import of this severe level of CSO will be discussed later when composite transmission systems are considered.

While this mechanism has been described in the context of the composite optical channel response, it has been investigated by others considering only the response of an optical amplifier, with results that are consistent with the preceding analysis. One experimenter found C/CSO levels as poor as 40 dB for wavelengths between 1535 and 1565 nm but rising to worse than 30 dB at 1525 nm.[13]

5.7 DEGRADATION IN SHARED-DETECTOR, MULTI-WAVELENGTH SYSTEMS

When a shared detector is used to demodulate multiple optical signals on different wavelengths, it not possible to process the modulating signals on each wavelength before RF combining. In particular, wideband noise and discrete distortion products that have been generated by passing each signal through its optical path, and which lie in the spectral space occupied by the signals modulating the other link, will act to degrade the performance.

5.7.1 Postdetection White Noise and CIN Addition

When two optical signals modulated with nonoverlapping RF spectra are combined and then fed to a common detector, each portion of the detected spectrum will be affected by broadband noise from both transmitters. In the general case, the optical modulation levels of the two transmitters will be different and the relative optical levels and modulation indices will be adjusted at the transmit end so that the levels of the detected signals are in the proper proportion.

As an example, suppose that the signals consist of a spectrum of analog video channels covering the spectrum from 50 to 550 MHz modulating one transmitter and a spectrum of 45 QAM digital signals covering the spectrum from 600 to 870 MHz modulating a second transmitter. It is desired that, after detection, the power level of the QAM signals be 6 dB below the sync peak levels of the analog video signals.

It is common to set the optical modulation index (OMI) of an externally modulated analog transmitter carrying 78 signals to approximately 3% per channel. This represents a typical compromise among C/N, C/CTB, C/CSO, and clipping probability in the link. It is similarly desired to set the OMI of the QAM transmitter as high as possible, consistent with low clipping probability, to maximize C/N in that portion of the spectrum. When a spectrum consists of many noncoherent signals, the overall peak-to-rms current ratio tends to be independent of the number of signals.[14] Therefore, the probability of clipping remains relatively constant if the total RF drive power remains constant. Since the optical modulation index varies as the drive current, an approximation of the maximum usable per-channel OMI of a transmitter is related to the number of carried channels by

$$m_i = \frac{26.5}{\sqrt{N}} \tag{5.18}$$

where

m_i = the maximum per-channel optical modulation index percentage
N = the number of equal-power RF channels in the modulating spectrum

The constant represents the commonly achievable performance as of the writing of this book. With improved linearization techniques and advanced techniques such as phase control of the modulating carriers and timing control of modulation, it is possible to increase the optical modulation per channel. Given this relationship, the maximum acceptable OMI for the 45 QAM channels in the example is approximately 3.95%.

After detection, each of the recovered RF carriers will be at a level proportional to the square of the OMI, so if the optical carrier levels were the same at the input to the detector, the QAM channels would exceed the analog video channels by 20 log (5.3/3.0) = 2.37 dB. Since we want those carriers to be lower than the analog carriers by 6 dB, we need to reduce the relative level of the optical signal carrying the QAM channels by about 4.2 dB [(2.37 + 6)/2]. Designing analog optical links with a received power of 0 dBm is typical, so the QAM carrier level for proper post-detection level matching would be −4.2 dBm. With the optical system levels now determined, we can calculate the effective C/N for each portion of the spectrum.

In Section 4.10.1, we calculated the C/N of a single optical carrier link. Of the four factors considered, however, only transmitter RIN and IIN are related to each optical signal as received at the detector. The other two, shot noise and postamplifier noise,

- Clipping distortion products (discussed in Section 4.10.3)
- If relevant, CSO due to directly modulated DFB transmitter chirp interacting with WDM demux in-channel response slope (discussed in Section 5.6)

In estimating the probable link performance, it is necessary to consider how the effects add. There is no obvious correlation between residual transmitter/receiver nonlinearities and other effects.

The three CSO effects, on the other hand, will either be in phase or directly opposite in phase (depending on the direction of the response slope of the WDM demux). While the probability that clipping will occur is fairly predictable, the magnitude and polarity of individual clipping distortion products are very difficult to predict. The most conservative approach is to assume in-phase addition of all calculable products and thus a "20 log" combination.

Having estimated the worst-channel CTB and CSO products among the analog carriers, Section 2.3.3 discussed the number of products falling in each channel. In the case of CSO products, Equation 2.25a–c can be used to calculate the number of products in each channel, including above the analog spectrum, and it can be assumed that the number of third-order products will be greatest near the middle of the analog spectrum and that the greatest magnitude of CTB distortion will fall higher in the spectrum.

Knowing the worst-case distortion and the number of distortion products as a function of frequency, the magnitude of C/CTB and C/CSO distortion in any channel can be calculated by assuming that the distortion magnitude will vary as "10 log (n)," where n is the number of products in that channel. Finally, the ratio of digital carrier to analog C/CSO or C/CTB products will be lower (worse) than the foregoing, by the ratio of analog signal levels to QAM signal levels in the combined RF spectrum (typically 6 dB).

Only the upper-side CSO products (2.5 MHz above the lower channel boundary) need be considered because only those products extend above the analog spectrum and because the lower-side products fall between standard channel boundaries. CTB products will fall 1.25 MHz above the lower channel boundary.

If we look at the previous example of a 30-km optical link and assume that the analog signals, occupying 50 to 550 MHz, modulate an externally modulated transmitter operating in the 1550-nm range with a launch power of +17 dBm, we get the following contributions to distortion:

- The transmitter/receiver pair will typically generate upper-side C/CSO and C/-CTB of 65 dB on the most affected channels.
- Self-phase modulation will interact with the fiber to produce C/CSO at a level of about 70 dB.

At worst, the CSO effects will add on a voltage basis to produce a total C/CSO of 61 dB at the highest analog channel. Assuming the digital spectrum occupies 600 to 870 MHz, the level at the lowest digital channel will be 0.4 dB higher relative to the analog carriers (from Equation 2.25 and assuming that CSO varies as 10 log(n), where n is the number of high-side products), but will be higher relative to the QAM signals that are run at 6-dB lower levels than analog, giving a net C/CSO in the lowest QAM channel of 54.6 dB.

The analog CTB will be highest somewhere above the center of the analog spectrum, and fall off by approximately 2 dB at the upper edge of the analog spectrum and by about 3 dB at the lowest QAM channel. As with CSO, however, we need to account for the 6-dB difference in levels between analog and QAM signals, giving us a net C/CTB for the lowest QAM channel of about 62 dB.

Given a typical end-of-line $C/(N + I)$ spec of 40 dB, the levels of CTB and CSO products resulting from use of a common detector are seldom a problem, provided externally modulated analog transmitters are used.

5.8 SUMMARY

Wavelength division multiplexing has become standard in the engineering of cable television and similar networks because it facilitates the delivery of switched services to small groups of customers. It does this by allowing the transport of many independent signals over shared fibers and through shared optical amplifiers.

Unfortunately, optical signals on separate wavelengths interact as they travel through the fiber, and those interactions, sometimes in conjunction with discrete optical components in the circuit, generate various levels of crosstalk. Depending on the parameters of a given link, these mechanisms can have a serious effect on recovered RF signal quality. As our analysis shows, the quality of discrete components in general, and of the wavelength demultiplexer in particular, is typically the limiting factor in achieving acceptable low levels of crosstalk interference.

The analysis also shows that the achievable quality for 16-wavelength DWDM circuits with lengths approaching 30 km will not be acceptable for analog video (assuming those signals differ among the optical signals) but will be adequate for at least 256 QAM signals with adequate component quality.

ENDNOTES

1. Bernard Eichenbaum, "Coarse WDM Applications, Architectures, and Scalability for HFC and FTTH Digital Broadband Access," *Proceedings Manual and Collected Technical Papers*, Cable-Tec 2002 Expo, SCTE, Exton, PA, June 2002, pp. 19–38; "New Global Standard Set for Metro Networks," *IEEE Spectrum*, August 2002, pp. 21, 24.

2. For a brief, nonmathematical summary comparing wavelength multiplexer technologies, see Schlomo Ovadia, *Broadband Cable TV Access Technologies*. Upper Saddle River, NJ: Prentice-Hall, 2001, Sec. 6.1.1.

3. Based on data sheets for current products from Cisco and Arris (both located in Atlanta).

4. Much of the material in this section related to XPM, OKE-PDL, and SRS is based on the excellent and clearly explained work of M. R. Phillips (sometimes copublished with D.M. Ott), various of whose papers covering optical cross-modulation are referenced in subsequent endnotes.

5. K.Y. Wong, et al., "Nonlinear Crosstalk Suppression in a WDM Analog Fiber System by Complementary Modulation of Twin Carriers," *OFC2001* Conference, Optical Society of America, 2000, pp. WV5-1–WV5-3.

6. Mary R. Phillips and Daniel M. Ott, "Crosstalk Caused by Nonideal Output Filters in WDM Lightwave Systems," *IEEE Photonics Technology Letters*, vol. 12, no. 8 (August 2000).

7. Mary R. Phillips and Daniel M. Ott, "Crosstalk Due to Optical Fiber Nonlinearities in WDM CATV Lightwave Systems," *Journal of Lightwave Technology*, vol. 17, no. 10 (October 1999).

8. Ibid., p. 1788.

9. Ibid., p. 1790.

10. Kyo Inoue, "Four-Wave Mixing in an Optical Fiber in the Zero-Dispersion Wavelength Region," *Journal of Lightwave Technology*, vol. 10, no. 11 (November 1992): 1553–1561; James J. Refi, "Optical Fibers for Optical Networking," *Bell Labs Technical Journal*, January–March 1999, pp. 246–261.

11. M.R. Phillips, "Crosstalk in an Eight-Wavelength WDM Analog Lightwave System: Measurement and Analysis." Optical Fiber Communication Conference and Exhibit, 2001, *OFC 2001*, vol. 3, pp. WCC1, 1–3.

12. Tim Brophy, Fernando Villarruel, and Kuang-Yi Wu, "A Delicate Balance: Alternatives for Multi-Wavelength Systems, *Communications Technology*, vol. 25, no. 1 (January 2008): 33–37.

13. C.Y. Kuo and E.E. Bergmann, "Erbium-Doped Fiber Amplifier Second-Order Distortion in Analog Links and Electronic Compensation," *IEEE Photonics Technology Letters*, vol. 3, no. 9 (September 1991): 829–831.

14. Section 17.3 of *Recommended Practices for Measurements on Cable Television Systems* (Washington, DC: National Cable & Telecommunications Association, 2002) contains an excellent tutorial on this subject. It shows that the probability of exceeding a given peak-to-rms voltage ratio is essentially unchanged as the number of summed signals increases beyond 10.

Linear Microwave Signal Transportation

6

6.1 INTRODUCTION

Although linear amplitude-modulated fiber-optic links are the favored trunking methodology for most applications, there are situations where they are simply not cost-effective. For example, physical barriers, such as waterways, may make cable construction very expensive. Alternatively, the network may need to serve several small outlying communities that are so widely separated that the cost of the interconnecting links affects the economic viability of the project. Finally, network operators sometimes need to transport signals through areas where rights-of-way are either unavailable or very expensive to acquire. In any of these cases, point-to-point or point-to-multipoint broadband amplitude-modulated microwave links (AMLs) may offer a superior solution.

This chapter will cover the basic operation of this equipment and the essential calculations and methodology required to engineer AMLs. No attempt is made to present a comprehensive manual on either internal designs of microwave equipment or the many subtleties of path engineering. However, an Excel spreadsheet entitled "Micro.xls" is available for download from the website for this book, *www.elsevierdirect.com/companions/9780123744012*; it includes all essential calculations from path design through nominal performance to predicted link availability. Several standard reference books on the subject are available for those desiring to pursue the subject in greater depth.[1]

Microwave may be used for relay of individual channels or for transport of the entire FDM spectrum. Channelized microwave (which often employs digital or frequency modulation) is sometimes used for transportation of individual signals at the headend/hub level, but the discussion here will be limited to links that transport the entire spectrum and are part of the broadband distribution network.

6.2 U.S. REGULATION OF MICROWAVE TRANSMISSION

Regulation of radio transmission will vary by country, although broad spectrum planning is harmonized worldwide through international conferences. In the United States, the essential regulations pertaining to AML systems are contained in the FCC's rules.[2] In particular, Part 17 covers towers, whereas Part 78 covers microwave licensing, channelization, and performance. Operators of microwave systems are required to have current copies of the rules on hand and to comply with detailed requirements regarding licensing, log books, posting of stations, periodic performance tests, and the like. Maintenance of tower lighting, where required, is a matter of concern because of aircraft safety issues.

The FCC has set aside the frequencies extending from 12.7 to 13.2 GHz for cable television relay service. Additional spectrum is assigned at 18 GHz and 31 GHz as well. Within the 12-GHz band, several acceptable channelization schemes are given for both frequency and amplitude modulation: A, B, and K channels for FM, and C, D, E, and F designations for AML. Each channel in each scheme is given a unique identifier.

In the case of the AML bands, each channel group represents a direct translation of the FDM cable spectrum to a different portion of the assigned microwave band as follows:

- Group C maps 54 through 300 MHz to 12,700.5 through 12,946.5 MHz.
- Group D maps 54 through 300 MHz to 12,759.7 through 13,005.7 MHz.
- Group E maps 54 through 300 MHz to 12,952.5 through 13,198.5 MHz.
- Group F maps 54 through 240 MHz to 13,012.5 through 13,198.5 MHz.

Transmission of an 80-channel spectrum is possible through the use of a combination of Groups C, D, and E channels (with some minor shifts from nominal microwave frequencies) occupying the full 500-MHz-wide 12-GHz CARS band. Without some form of frequency reuse, no combination of available 12-GHz channels is adequate for systems whose bandwidth exceeds 500 MHz.

In general, the FCC limits the microwave power level delivered to the antenna system to 5 watts per channel and the radiated power to +55 dBW EIRP.* Microwave frequencies must be accurate within ±0.005%, and the original cable channel frequencies must not shift by more than ±0.0005% through the link.

6.3 GENERAL OPERATIONAL PRINCIPLES

The basic principle of operation of an AML link is simplicity itself. At the transmitter, the incoming cable spectrum is simply mixed with an unmodulated signal (the

---

*Equivalent isotropically radiated power—the product of transmitter power and isotropic antenna gain.

microwave local oscillator, or LO) whose frequency is equal to the difference between the original channel frequencies and the translated microwave frequencies. At the receiver, the microwave spectrum is mixed with another unmodulated carrier at the same LO frequency, resulting in recovery of the original cable spectrum.

In order to preserve the frequency accuracy of the VHF spectrum, as well as provide the required microwave frequency accuracy, a crystal reference oscillator operating at 1/171 of the offset frequency is used to directly phase-lock the transmitter local oscillator. A sample of the reference frequency (which falls in the VHF spectrum between cable channels 4 and 5) is also up-converted and sent along with the remainder of the cable spectrum through the microwave link. At the receiver, the reference signal is recovered and used to phase-lock the microwave LO there. Since both LOs are locked to a common reference, the recovered VHF spectrum is frequency coherent with the transmitted spectrum, while the accuracy of the microwave spectrum depends on the accuracy of the reference oscillator. Figure 6.1 is a basic functional diagram of an AML. Table 6.1 summarizes the frequencies for various bands, and Table 6.2 shows the combination of AML channels used to transport a 54- to 552-MHz cable spectrum.

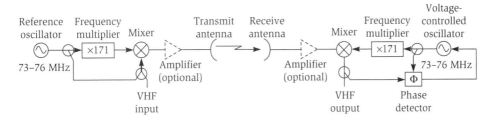

FIGURE 6.1

Basic AML principles of operation.

Table 6.1 Frequency Relationships in AML Links (in MHz)

FCC channel group	Cable spectrum		Microwave spectrum		Offset frequency	Reference oscillator
	Start	Stop	Start	Stop		
C	54	552	12,700.5	13,198.5	12,646.5	73.956140
D	54	300	12,759.7	13,005.7	12,705.7	74.302339
E	54	300	12,952.5	13,198.5	12,898.5	75.429824
F	54	240	13,012.5	13,198.5	12,958.5	75.780701

6.4 PATH DESIGN

Microwaves travel approximately along "line-of-sight" paths, meaning that, unlike low-frequency AM broadcast stations, they do not bend significantly to follow the earth's curvature (although a slight bending in the direction of the earth is typical). Like light waves, however, they can be reflected from multiple intermediate surfaces between the transmitter and receiver. Under some atmospheric conditions, micro-wave signals can temporarily shift from their normal path, either toward or away from the earth's surface. Such bending, discussed in Section 6.6, can cause the trans-mitted signal to completely miss the receiving antenna and is one of the factors limiting link reliability.

Designing a microwave path between two fixed points consists of determining the distance and direction between the points and then examining the path to make sure there is adequate clearance from any objects near the direct line between trans-mitting and receiving antennas.

6.4.1 Path End Coordinates

The locations of the path ends are described by four parameters: the longitude and latitude define the location on the earth's surface, while the altitude of the base of the antenna tower and the mounting height of the antenna on that tower define the vertical location of the antenna relative to sea level.

The longitude is usually expressed as the sum of the number of degrees, minutes, and seconds that the location is east or west of the prime meridian, which passes through Greenwich, England. The latitude is the sum of the number of degrees, min-utes, and seconds that the location is north (positive) or south (negative) of the equator.

Since there are 60 minutes in a degree of arc and 60 seconds in a minute of arc, we can convert the longitude and latitude of the transmitter and receiver antenna locations to decimal degrees as follows:

$$\text{longitude or latitude (decimal degrees)} = \text{degrees} + \frac{\text{minutes}}{60} + \frac{\text{seconds}}{3600} \quad (6.1)$$

For the remainder of this chapter, we will assume that this conversion has been done and that the transmitting location is at a west longitude of W_T and a north lati-tude of N_T, while the receiving antenna is at a west longitude of W_R and a north latitude of N_R, where all numbers are in decimal degrees. Minor modifications of the formulas will be required for links located in the southern hemisphere and/or eastern longitudes.

6.4.2 Path Length

Path calculations are based on an average earth circumference of 24,857 statute miles. Thus, each degree of arc along that surface represents $24,857/360 = 69.047$ statute miles.

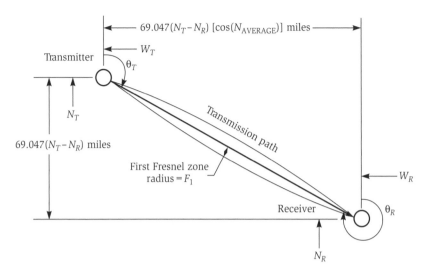

FIGURE 6.2

Microwave path horizontal parameters.

We can approximate the path length by calculating the length of the diagonal of a hypothetical rectangle whose corners are located at the transmit and receiver locations, as shown in Figure 6.2. In the north–south direction, the distance in miles is just the difference in the latitude values times 69.047, because latitude lines are all the same length. In the east–west direction, however, one degree represents that distance only at the equator. At any distance away from the equator, the distance is shortened by the cosine of the latitude. The formula for path length is

$$D\,(\text{statute miles}) = 69.047\ \text{arccos}[\sin(N_T)\ \sin(N_R) \\ + \cos(N_T)\ \cos(N_R)\ \cos(W_T - W_R)] \tag{6.2}$$

If the path length is desired in nautical miles for some reason, then use 60 rather than 69.047 to convert degrees of arc to distance (nautical miles are based on an earth circumference of exactly 21,600 miles).

6.4.3 Path Azimuth

The next required value is the compass heading (azimuth) for the antennas, in order to align the path. Compass headings are measured in degrees clockwise from true north. The first step is to calculate the angle θ using

$$\theta\,(\text{degrees}) = \text{arccos}\left[\frac{\sin(N_R) - \sin(N_T)\ \cos(D/69.047)}{\sin(D/69.047)\ \cos(N_T)}\right] \tag{6.3}$$

If W_R is less than W_T, then the transmit antenna azimuth $\theta_T = \theta$. If W_R is greater than W_T, then $\theta_T = 360° - \theta$.

The azimuth for the antenna at the receive site is the opposite of that at the transmit site; that is, for θ_T between 0° and 180°, $\theta_R = \theta_T + 180$ degrees, whereas for θ_T between 180° and 360°, $\theta_R = \theta_T - 180°$. Note that azimuth headings are based on a true north reference, not the heading on a magnetic compass; the magnetic north pole and the axis of the earth's rotation differ slightly.

6.4.4 Path Clearances

Having determined the horizontal distance and azimuth, the next step is to check for adequate clearances along the path. In the horizontal direction, this requires a calculation of a factor known as the *Fresnel zone*; in the vertical direction, it additionally requires consideration of the topology of the land, the height of features, such as trees and buildings, and the effective curvature of the earth.

Fresnel Zone Calculations

The primary path from transmitting to receiving antenna is a nominally straight line. It is possible, however, for the signal to be reflected from objects that, although not in the direct path, are close enough that they are within the beamwidth of the antennas. If that happens, whatever portion of the transmitted signal is reflected toward the receiving antenna will arrive there after the direct signal because of the longer path length involved. The impact of this reflected wave will depend on the nature of the surface from which the signal is reflected, on the difference in path length, and on the pattern of the transmitting and receiving antennas.

The first Fresnel zone is defined as a series of imaginary rings surrounding the centerline of the direct path such that the distance from the transmitting antenna to each ring plus the distance from the ring to the receiving antenna is equal to one-half wavelength more than the direct path between the antennas. Subsequent Fresnel zones are defined as larger imaginary rings, where the difference in path lengths is $n\lambda/2$, where n is an integer larger than 1 and λ is the free-space wavelength of the signal.

The radius of the first Fresnel zone at a point D_1 miles along the direct path from the transmitting to the receiving antennas is

$$F_1 = 72.1\sqrt{\frac{D_1 D_2}{fD}} \qquad (6.4)$$

where

$F_1 =$ the radius of the first Fresnel zone in feet
$D =$ the total direct path length in miles
$D_1 =$ the distance from the transmitting antenna in miles
$D_2 =$ the distance from the receiving antenna in miles $= D - D_1$
$f =$ the operating frequency in GHz

Figure 6.2 shows how the width of the first Fresnel zone varies along the transmission path.

Although higher-order Fresnel reflections can cause problems with highly reflective surfaces that are oriented optimally (such as smooth, flat terrain or calm water), the general rule of microwave design is that it is sufficient to clear objects by $0.6F_1$.

Additional Vertical Clearances

In the vertical plane, it is necessary to add the Fresnel zone clearance to the effective height of objects that lie under the direct path. Factors to be considered include the curvature of the earth, peaks in the terrain, and/or any objects, such as buildings and trees. Traditionally, such analyses were done graphically, although they are more likely to be done with a computer today. Figure 6.3 illustrates how the terms add up.

The flat line at the bottom of the figure represents a straight line drawn through the earth from mean sea level at the transmit location to mean sea level at the receive location. At the transmit end, a vertical line represents the elevation of the ground at the base of the antenna tower, as surveyed or shown on a topographical map. The units are feet *above mean sea level* (AMSL); we have designated this elevation as $AMSL_T$ to identify which site is referenced. The elevation of the center of the transmit antenna relative to the ground is *above ground level*, or AGL_T. The sum of the ground height and antenna mounting height we have designated as H_T. At the other end of the path, the equivalent values are $AMSL_R$, AGL_R, and H_R.

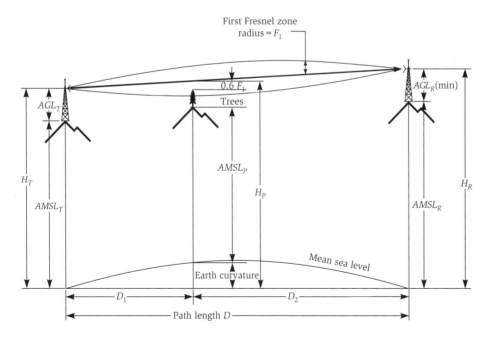

FIGURE 6.3

Microwave path vertical clearances.

The curved line that intersects the ends of the flat line represents the effective curvature of the earth between the endpoints. The effective curvature may not equal the actual curvature, however, because the microwave beam may be slightly bent due to atmospheric conditions. While the beam most commonly bends in the same direction as the earth's curvature (thereby allowing greater clearance over obstacles in the path), occasionally the reverse is true. These effects are taken into account using a factor called the K factor. K is the ratio between the effective and actual earth radius. The effect of earth curvature along a path of length D miles can be calculated using

$$h = \frac{D_1 D_2}{1.5\,K} \qquad (6.5)$$

where

h = the virtual height, in feet, due to effective earth curvature
D_1 = the distance to the transmitting antenna in statute miles
D_2 = the distance to the receiving antenna in statute miles
K = the K factor

Under normal atmospheric conditions, K is approximately $4/3$. Conservative path design, however, frequently calls for calculating clearances using $K = 2/3$. K for any specific location is determined from a factor known as the *August mean radio refractivity* and the path elevation above mean sea level.

In the special case of equal-height antennas transmitting over a smooth surface (so that the maximum interference point is midway along the path), Equation 6.5 reduces to

$$h_{\text{max}} = \frac{D^2}{6\,K} \qquad (6.6)$$

where

h_{max} = the effective height increase, in feet, at the midpoint of the path
D = the total path length in miles

The next step is to examine the vertical path profile. Generally this is done using topographical maps, such as those available from the U.S. Geological Survey (USGS). Rather than plot the entire profile, it is sufficient to plot selected points that represent elevation maxima. For simplicity, we have shown a single peak, located at distance D_1 from the transmit antenna, whose effective height is $AMSL_P$ plus the effective curvature of the earth at that distance along the path.

Added to this effective peak height must be anything that projects above the ground level at the peak. In wooded areas, for instance, it is common to add a number of feet that represent the maximum height of trees in that area; in a more urban setting, it might be a specific building. Finally, we must add $0.6\,F_1$, the required clearance to the first Fresnel zone, to get H_P, the total effective height of the peak.

Using the height of the transmit antenna, the effective height of the peak, and its distance from the transmit antenna, we can calculate the minimum mounting height for the receive antenna using

$$AGL_R(\text{ft}) \geq (H_P - H_T)\left(\frac{D}{D_1}\right) + H_T - AMSL_R \qquad (6.7)$$

So long as the receive antenna mounting height above ground is greater than this value, the path should be acceptable from the standpoint of vertical clearances.

Note that in the special case of a flat landscape covering much of the distance between antennas, it may not be obvious where along the path the greatest potential interference occurs. A reasonable approximation requires first calculating the effective difference, ΔH, in elevation between the transmit antenna and the flat ground along the path:

$$\Delta H(\text{ft}) \simeq AMSL_T + AGL_T - AMSL_P - \text{Trees} - 21.63\sqrt{\frac{D}{f}} \qquad (6.8)$$

where

$AMSL_T$ = the elevation at the base of the transmit tower
AGL_T = the mounting height on the tower
$AMSL_P$ = the elevation of the flat land between the antennas
Trees = the allowance for foliage and objects on the flat land
D = the total distance between the antennas in miles
f = the operating frequency in GHz

The only approximation in Equation 6.8 is the last term, which calculates the Fresnel clearance on the assumption that the highest point will be roughly in the center of the path. Obviously, to the degree that the total heights of the transmitting antenna and of the receiving antenna are different, this will be in error.

Given the effective difference in elevation between the transmit antenna and the flat area, the maximum distance that a signal can travel from the transmitter and still clear the ground and obstructions by the required Fresnel clearance amount is

$$D_1 \simeq 69.047 \, \arccos\left(\frac{R_E K}{R_E K + \Delta H}\right) \qquad (6.9)$$

where

D_1 = the distance from the transmitter, in miles, to the point where the signal just clears the ground by the required amount
R_E = the radius of the earth in feet = 20,888,284
K = the K factor
ΔH = the effective elevation difference calculated earlier

D_1 can now be plugged into Equation 6.7, along with the other factors, to determine the required mounting height of the receive antenna.

6.5 PERFORMANCE CALCULATION

In order to predict the performance of an AML, we first need to define the details of the complete signal path from the transmitter to each receiver. Then we start with the transmitter output RF power per channel and add up all the signal losses and gains (in dB) from the path elements to determine the nominal power level at each significant point. Knowing the performance of each circuit element, we then calculate the cascaded noise and distortion of the link under normal weather conditions. Finally, using charts of expected weather disturbances, we estimate the reliability of the circuit.

6.5.1 Signal Path Definition

The first step in performance calculation is to carefully list every circuit element in the path between transmitter and receiver. Since a single transmitter may feed more than one receiver, the first element may well be a signal splitter. Following that will usually be sections of waveguide. Since elliptical waveguide is more lossy than circular, it is not uncommon to use circular waveguide to feed up tall towers and then to transition to elliptical guide for the last few feet at both ends of the transmission line to allow flexibility for dish adjustments and equipment placement.

The dish will have a defined gain, followed by the path loss through the air and then by the gain of the receiving antenna. There may be a low-noise amplifier at the output of the receive antenna, followed by some combination of waveguides down the tower, finally terminating at the receiver input. All the applicable circuit elements should be listed separately for each section of the path and a separate list made up for each path fed from a transmitter. The left two columns of Table 6.3 show a sample list of circuit elements for a typical AML path at 13 GHz.

6.5.2 Power Budget Calculation

In the first row of the fourth column of the table is the transmitter power output per channel in dBm. Unlike coaxial cable distribution networks, where the reference for power measurements is 1 millivolt in a 75-ohm impedance (dBmV), the reference for microwave power is the milliwatt (10^{-3} watts). Thus, the power in dBm is $10 \log(P)$, where P is the power in milliwatts. AML transmitters are available with rated power output levels per channel varying from about -12 dBm to $+33$ dBm.

Next come any splitters used to feed multiple receive sites. Manufacturer's data sheets will give the loss of these. As a first approximation, the loss will typically be a few tenths of a decibel higher than the theoretical splitter ratio loss (e.g., a four-way splitter has a theoretical loss of 6 dB and an actual loss of about 6.5 dB to each port). Enter the appropriate loss in the third column of the worksheet as a negative number (representing "negative gain" in that path element).

Table 6.3 Sample AML Performance Calculation

Network element	Quantity/property	Gain (dB)	Cumulative power (dBm/channel)	C/N (dB)	CTB (dBc)	CSO (dBc)
Transmitter			+10.0	61.0	−65.0	−70.0
Splitter	2-way	−3.5	+6.5			
Circular waveguide	200 ft	−2.8	+3.7			
Elliptical waveguide	50 ft	−1.9	+1.8			
Transmit antenna	10 ft dia.	+48.8	+50.6			
Free-space loss	24 mi	−146.5	−95.9			
Excess loss allowance		−2.0	−97.9			
Receiving antenna	10 ft dia.	+48.8	−49.1			
LNA	3 dB NF	+17.0	−32.1	55.9		
Circular waveguide	300 ft	−4.1	−36.2			
Elliptical waveguide	´50 ft	−1.9	−38.1			
Receiver	13 dB NF			56.9	−70.0	−61.0
Total link performance				52.6	−61.1	−58.4

After the splitter are the waveguides connecting the splitter output port to the antenna. As a general rule, circular waveguide has a loss of about 0.014 dB/ft at 13 GHz, while elliptical waveguide has a loss of about 0.038 dB/ft at the same frequency. The losses of transmission lines used at other frequencies will be given in the manufacturer's literature or in commonly available design tables. For each type of transmission line, multiply the line length by the loss per unit length and enter the net loss into the third column, again as a negative gain number.

Next enter the transmitting antenna gain, which will be positive relative to an isotropic radiator. The antennas used for CARS band are almost always constructed with prime-focus feeds. Diameters commonly range from 4 to 10 feet. While actual antennas will vary slightly, a typical gain for a circular antenna with a parabolic cross-section and a prime-focus "button-hook" feed is

$$\text{parabolic antenna gain (dBi)} = 20 \log(d) + 20 \log(f) + 6.5 \qquad (6.10)$$

where

d = the diameter of the antenna in feet
f = the operating frequency in GHz

The loss suffered as a result of sending the signal through the air, the *free-space loss*, is dependent on both path length and operating frequency. Under normal atmospheric conditions, free-space loss is

$$\text{path loss (dB)} = 96.6 + 20 \log(f) + 20 \log(D) \qquad (6.11)$$

where

f = the operating frequency in GHz
D = the path distance in statute miles

Next, it is common to add an additional loss allowance of about 2 dB to account for aging, imperfect alignment of equipment, and so on (sometimes known as the *field factor*).

The receive antenna will have a gain that will also be calculated in accordance with Equation 6.10. If an LNA is mounted at the back of the receive antenna feedhorn, as is common, enter its gain at this point. Now, as at the transmitter end, enter all the feedline losses between the antenna or LNA and receiver input.

In the fourth column, calculate the power at each point in the circuit, adding power gain values and subtracting losses in dB. The final number is the receiver input level, in dBm, under normal atmospheric conditions.

6.5.3 Carrier-to-Thermal-Noise Calculation

As discussed in Chapter 2, the room-temperature thermal noise power in the 4-MHz bandwidth used to calculate NTSC analog video performance is about −59 dBmV. However, 0 dBmV is approximately equal to −49 dBm, so the noise level referenced to 1 mW is −108 dBm. For QAM signals, the noise susceptibility bandwidth may be as high as 6 MHz, in which case the thermal noise will be 1.8 dB higher, or approximately −106 dBm.

Thus, the equivalent NTSC video input noise floor of any device is equal to −108 dBm + F_A, where F_A is its noise figure. Its C/N contribution (the difference between the driving signal level and the equivalent input noise level due to the device itself) can be calculated using

$$C/N_{\text{Device}}(\text{dB}) = 108 - F_A(\text{dB}) + P_{\text{IN}}(\text{dBm}) \qquad (6.12)$$

where

$$C/N_{\text{Device}} = \text{the carrier-to-noise ratio contribution of the device}$$
$$F_A = \text{the noise figure of the device in dB}$$
$$P_{\text{IN}} = \text{the driving power level in dBm}$$

There are three principal contributors to link C/N: the transmitter, the LNA (if used), and the receiver. The transmitter C/N is generally given by the manufacturer for various channel-loading conditions. Since the input levels and noise figures of both LNA and receiver are known, their C/N contributions are readily calculable. All three C/N values are entered into column five of the worksheet.

The link C/N is calculated using the methodology of Equation 3.2:

$$C/N_{ttl} = -10 \log\left(10^{-\left(\frac{C/N_T}{10}\right)} + 10^{-\left(\frac{C/N_L}{10}\right)} + 10^{-\left(\frac{C/N_R}{10}\right)}\right) \qquad (6.13)$$

where C/N_{ttl} is the carrier-to-noise ratio of the entire link and C/N_T, C/N_L, and C/N_R are the carrier-to-noise contributions of the transmitter, LNA, and receiver, respectively.

For links carrying QAM signals or a mixture of QAM and analog video signals, an additional calculation must be done for composite intermodulation noise (CIN), which is due to low-level mixing of various combinations of analog and digital signals and which manifests itself as frequency-shaped noise products. Manufacturers of transmitters, amplifiers, and receivers should be consulted for CIN performance of their equipment. The CIN level should be added as a term in Equation 6.13 to get the total equivalent link C/N.

6.5.4 Distortion Calculation

For analog video, the CTB and CSO distortion levels are given by the manufacturers for various channel loadings and power levels. In most cases, the LNA will contribute only slightly to the overall distortion levels.

Addition of second- and third-order distortion levels is discussed in Chapter 3. The link performance numbers in the worksheet were calculated using the most conservative assumption, which is

$$C/CTB_{\text{Link}} = -20 \log\left(10^{-\left(\frac{C/CTB_T}{20}\right)} + 10^{-\left(\frac{C/CTB_R}{20}\right)}\right) \qquad (6.14)$$

where

$$C/CTB_T = \text{the transmitter third-order distortion in dB}$$
$$C/CTB_R = \text{the receiver third-order distortion in dB}$$

A similar formula is used to calculate link CSO performance. Manufacturers should be consulted for the specific microwave equipment chosen to determine whether Equation 6.14 is appropriate for calculating cascaded distortion.

Second, it is necessary to determine the rainfall rate that will result in attenuation per kilometer greater than M'. The relationship between signal attenuation and rainfall rate can be approximated[4] using

$$Y_R = kR^\alpha \tag{6.18}$$

where

Y_R = the attenuation along the signal path in dB/km
R = the rainfall rate in mm/hr
k and α = "constants" that are a function of frequency, polarization, and vertical path angle

In turn, k and α are determined using the following formulas:

$$k = \frac{k_b + k_v + (k_b - k_v)\cos^2\theta\,\cos 2T}{2} \tag{6.19}$$

$$\alpha = \frac{k_b\alpha_b + k_v\alpha_v + (k_b\alpha_b - k_v\alpha_v)\cos^2\theta\,\cos 2T}{2k} \tag{6.20}$$

where k_b, k_v, α_b, and α_v are determined from Table 6.4 and

θ = the path elevation angle in degrees (zero for a horizontal path)
T = the path polarization tilt angle in degrees: $0°$ for horizontal polarization, $90°$ for vertical polarization, $45°$ for circular

For relatively flat paths and horizontal polarization, $k = k_b$ and $\alpha = \alpha_b$; for relatively flat paths with vertical polarization, $k = k_v$ and $\alpha = \alpha_v$.

The maximum allowable rainfall rate can be calculated by solving Equation 6.18 for R and substituting M' for Y_R:

$$R_{\max} = \left[\frac{M'}{k}\right]^{\frac{1}{\alpha}} \tag{6.21}$$

The probability that the rain rate exceeds this value in any given climate region is given by[5]

$$U_R = 10^{-4}\left[\frac{R_{0.01}}{R_{\max}}\right]^b e^{u(R_{0.01}-R_{\max})} = 10^{-4}\left[\frac{e^{(u)R_{0.01}+(b)\ln(R_{0.01})}}{e^{(u)R_{\max}+(b)\ln(R_{\max})}}\right] \tag{6.22}$$

where u depends on the climate region and is given in Table 6.5 and

U_R = the time-averaged probability that the rainfall rate exceeds $R_{\max}$
$R_{0.01}$ = the rainfall rate, in mm/hr, that is exceeded in any given climate region for 0.01% of the time (0.86 hr/yr), with an integration time of 1 min

Table 6.4 Rainfall Attenuation Constants as a Function of Frequency

Frequency (GHz)	k_h	k_v	α_h	α_v
1	0.0000387	0.0000352	0.912	0.888
2	0.00154	0.000138	0.963	0.923
4	0.00065	0.000591	1.121	1.075
6	0.00175	0.00155	1.308	1.265
7	0.00301	0.00265	1.332	1.312
8	0.00454	0.00395	1.327	1.310
10	0.0101	0.00887	1.276	1.264
12	0.0188	0.0168	1.217	1.200
15	0.0367	0.0335	1.154	1.128
20	0.0751	0.0691	1.099	1.065
25	0.124	0.113	1.061	1.030
30	0.187	0.167	1.021	1.000
35	0.263	0.233	0.979	0.963
40	0.350	0.310	0.939	0.929
45	0.442	0.393	0.903	0.897
50	0.536	0.479	0.873	0.868
60	0.707	0.642	0.826	0.824
70	0.851	0.784	0.793	0.793
80	0.975	0.906	0.769	0.769
90	1.06	0.999	0.753	0.754
100	1.12	1.06	0.743	0.744

(As with u, it is given in Table 6.5. In both cases, the applicable climate region is determined from one of the maps constituting Figures 6.4 through 6.6.[6])

b is determined from

$$b = 8.22(R_{0.01})^{-0.584} \tag{6.23}$$

Table 6.5 Rainfall Variable by Climatic Region

Region	u	$R_{0.01}$
A	−0.2391	8
B	−0.0050	12
C	0.05669	15
D	0.10252	19
E	0.03726	22
F	0.04652	28
G	0.07652	30
H	0.04081	32
J	0.1082	35
K	0.0444	42
L	0.03368	60
M	0.04087	63
N	0.02924	95
P	0.02477	145

Once the probability of rainfall exceeding the value needed to attenuate the signal below the specified performance threshold is determined, the annual number of hours of rainfall-caused outage can be determined simply by multiplying U_R by 8760.

Finally, once the rainfall and multipath unavailability probabilities are determined, the total unavailability can be expressed as yearly hours of outage using

$$\text{unavailable hours} = 8760(U_M + U_R) \qquad (6.24)$$

Alternatively, the overall path availability can be calculated using

$$\text{path availability} = 1 - U_M - U_R \qquad (6.25)$$

Typical link specifications vary from 0.999 availability for noncritical video applications to 0.99999 or even higher for some telephony applications. 0.9999 availability (equivalent to 53 minutes per year average outage time) is a typical goal for a cable television trunking application.

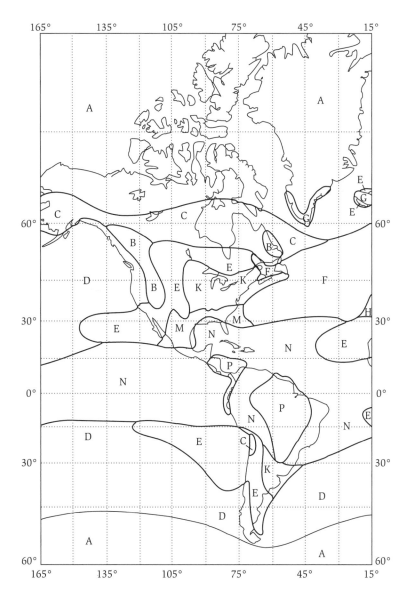

FIGURE 6.4

Rain zones: the Americas and Greenland.

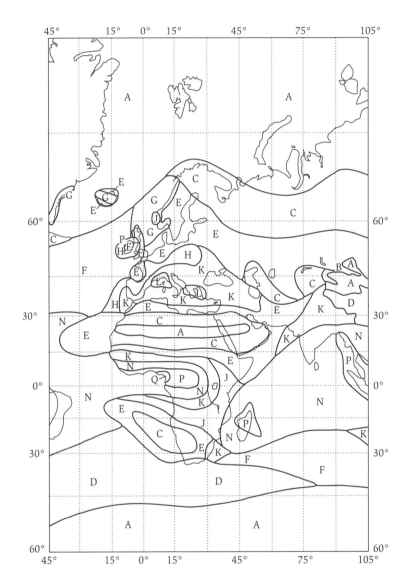

FIGURE 6.5

Rain zones: Europe and Africa.

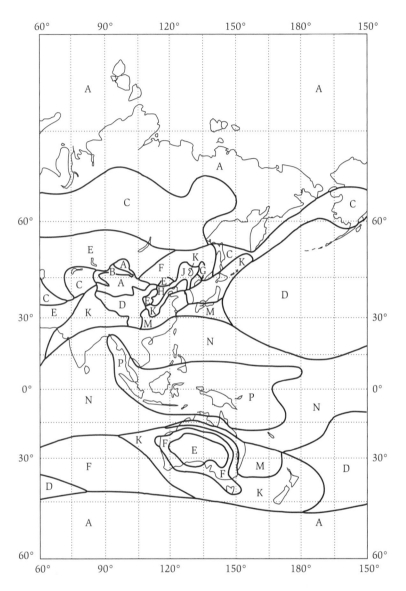

FIGURE 6.6

Rain zones: Asia and Australia.

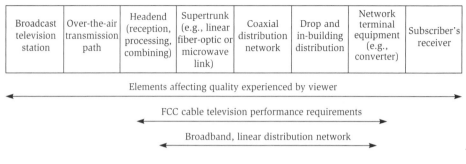

Broadcast television station	Over-the-air transmission path	Headend (reception, processing, combining)	Supertrunk (e.g., linear fiber-optic or microwave link)	Coaxial distribution network	Drop and in-building distribution	Network terminal equipment (e.g., converter)	Subscriber's receiver

Elements affecting quality experienced by viewer

FCC cable television performance requirements

Broadband, linear distribution network

FIGURE 7.1

Various performance measures for a typical broadcast television channel.

(used to combine visual and aural signals) and antenna will affect the frequency response, whereas visual transmitter incidental carrier phase modulation (ICPM) limits attainable stereo audio performance.

In the case of a digital broadcast signal, a host of other factors come into play, such as digital compression artifacts that are, in turn, determined by how aggressive the compression is. Other factors include relative delays in the sound versus the picture paths through the studio and various linear picture distortions that occur when source video is stretched to fit a different ratio of picture width to height.

The source-to-headend path, if the headend is receiving the signal via antenna, might include multipath distortion (echoes resulting from signals bouncing off objects to create more than one transmission path), frequency response variations due to receiving antenna characteristics, electrical noise interference, and a host of other factors.

Within the headend complex, the signal may be demodulated, digitized, switched, amplified, combined with other signals, modulated, redigitized, and/or shifted in frequency. In some cases, signals may be received at a different location from where they are finally combined into the RF spectrum that is transmitted to customers, adding more layers of processing and transmission. In that case, the term *headend* is intended to include everything from first reception by the network operator to generation of the modulated FDM signal complex for transmission to customers. Each of the processing steps within the headend complex adds a measure of degradation.

Finally, the complete frequency spectrum enters the broadband, linear distribution network, where, among others, noise, intermodulation distortion, cross-modulation, hum distortion, and group delay are added.

Analog (and sometimes digital) video signals may be directly connected to subscribers' receivers, or they may pass through a network termination device, such as an analog or digital set-top terminal. If a signal passes through a set-top terminal, it may be demodulated, descrambled or decrypted, and remodulated—each an imperfect process.

Finally, the subscriber's own television receiver will add a measure of degradation. In addition to noise and distortion, it may be inadequately shielded so that off-air signals are mixed with the cable-delivered signals, creating a special form of crosstalk known as *direct pickup* (DPU) interference. DPU results in a variety of visible picture defects in analog signals and may reduce the bit error rate for digital signals.

As shown in Figure 7.1, the viewer sees and hears the composite effect of everything that happens to the signal from the source to his or her screen and speakers (or other end application).

Obviously, both the chain of network elements and the required quality of signal will be different for analog video, downstream digital services (generally 64 or 256 QAM), and upstream digital services (generally QPSK, 16 QAM or 64 QAM, but some simpler modulations are still in use).

Although no end-to-end formal standards are in effect for U.S. television distribution, the Deutsche Bundespost (DBP, or German post office—the responsibilities for cable television have since been transferred to Deutsche Telecom) long ago published standards covering all segments of its entire network from camera to viewer.[1] The standards were very complete, with 19 quality measures covered. By contrast, the FCC regulates few aspects of television broadcast stations (primarily those that ensure a lack of interference among stations) but many parameters of cable television systems (including drops if installed and maintained by network operators) and set-top terminals (again, only if owned by the network operator). Performance standards for subscriber receivers vary according to how they are marketed, with only minimal requirements for analog receivers not specifically labeled "cable-ready" or digital receivers not specifically labeled "unidirectional receiving devices." FCC performance standards cover downstream analog and digital video, but require regular testing of only analog video and shared network performance parameters. There are no FCC standards covering the quality of drop materials available for purchase by end users, although voluntary SCTE standards are being developed for both component performance and standardized testing procedures.

FCC standards applied to cable television systems generally specify the total allowable signal degradation from acquisition at the headend to delivery of the final signal to subscribers' receivers (although there are exceptions). This range of coverage is shown by the second horizontal line in Figure 7.1. The quality parameters are applicable (with a couple of minor exceptions) to every analog and digital video signal at every subscriber equipment terminal under all normal operational conditions.

It is important to recognize that the FCC's requirements apply to performance when the network is carrying normally modulated signals. Although these parameters relate directly to subscriber picture-quality perception, the nature of NTSC video is such that some parameters (e.g., IM distortion products) are difficult to measure precisely under normal signal conditions because they vary depending on instantaneous levels, carrier phase relationships, and timing of video modulation. Since the total RF power in most cable systems is dominated by analog NTSC video signals, networks are designed and initially tested using unmodulated carriers in place of each expected visual carrier. This yields higher, but more consistent, levels of distortion. Various conversion factors are used to estimate performance under normal signal-loading conditions. In-service systems are tested using normal modulated signal loading, with precision sacrificed to avoid the subscriber service interruption that would be required to perform unmodulated signal testing.

The FCC's operational standards for television broadcasters are contained in the Code of Federal Regulations, Section 47, Part 73; the cable television regulations are contained in Part 76 and are summarized in Tables 7.1 and 7.2. Regulations pertaining to both set-top terminals and subscriber receivers are contained in Part 15.[2]

Table 7.1 FCC Rules for Analog Signals in U.S. Cable Television Systems

Parameter/FCC rule paragraph	Performance limit
Visual carrier frequency §76.612	No specific requirement except that carriers within the specified aeronautical bands (108–137 and 225–400 MHz) be offset from communications channels with a frequency tolerance of ±5 kHz (see rule for details). However, CEA-23-A requires operators to maintain channels within ±25 kHz of nominal assignments as listed in CEA-542
Aural/visual carrier frequency difference §76.605(a)(2)	4.500 MHz ± 5 kHz
Minimum visual signal level §76.605(a)(3)	≥+3 dBmV at the end of a reference 100-foot drop cable connected to any subscriber tap port, and ≥0 dBmV at the input to each subscriber's receiver
Visual signal level stability §76.605(a)(4)	≤8 dB pk–pk variation in visual carrier level over the sum of two 24-hour tests, one taken in July or August and one taken in January or February
Adjacent visual signal level difference §76.605(a)(4)(i)	≤3 dB
Total variation in levels among all visual signals §76.605(a)(4)(ii)	≤10 dB pk–pk for systems with an upper frequency limit of 300 MHz or less, plus 1 dB for each additional 100-MHz increment, or fraction thereof (e.g., for a 550-MHz system, the allowed variation is 13 dB)
Maximum visual signal level §76.605(a)(4)(iii)	Below the TV overload point (level not specified); however, CEA-23-A specifies +20 dBmV maximum, while ANSI/SCTE 105 specifies +15 dBmV maximum
Level of aural signal relative to visual signal §76.605(a)(5)	−10 to −17 dB (−6.5 dB maximum at the set-top terminal output)
In-channel visual frequency response variation §76.605(a)(6)	≤4 dB pk–pk from 0.5 MHz below the visual carrier to 3.75 MHz above the visual carrier; includes set-top terminal response

Visual signal carrier-to-noise ratio §76.605(a)(7)	$\geq$43 dB, measured in a 4-MHz bandwidth
Composite triple beat (CTB) and composite second-order (CSO) IM product levels, relative to visual signal level §76.605(a)(8)	$\leq$−51 dB, time averaged, except $\leq$−47 dB for products that are frequency coherent with the visual carrier in HRC and IRC systems
Hum modulation §76.605(a)(10)	$\leq$ 3% pk–pk modulation of the visual carrier ($\leq$ 1.5% modulation by the conventional definition)
Relative chrominance/luminance transmission delay (chroma delay) §76.605(a)(11)(i)	$\leq\pm$170 ns, not including the contribution of any set-top terminal
Differential gain §76.605(a)(11)(ii)	$\leq\pm$20%, not including the contribution of any set-top terminal
Differential phase §76.605(a)(11)(iii)	$\leq \pm$10 degrees, not including the contribution of any set-top terminal
Undesired signal amplitudes	No FCC requirement; however, ANSI/SCTE 105 requires a receiver to tolerate undesired out-of-channel signals up to the following amplitudes: 5–30 MHz +42 dBmV 30–41 MHz +24 dBmV 41–48 MHz 0 dBmV 48–54 MHz −10 dBmV $\geq$54 MHz +20 dBmV

In addition to the FCC's regulations, negotiations between the cable television and consumer electronics industries have resulted in supplemental voluntary standards applying to both cable systems and consumer receivers. In particular:

- Standard CEA-23-A includes test procedures for determining receiver compliance with various Part 15.118 performance standards. It also includes some minor additions to the FCC's rules for cable operators.

- Standard ANSI/SCTE 105 2005 specifies additional requirements on cable-compatible receivers (both analog and digital) and, by doing so, applies additional requirements on cable operators.

Regardless of their official status, these performance guidelines represent good engineering practice in ensuring that cable television signals are compatible with most consumer electronics receivers. Both sets of requirements are reflected in the preceding table and Table 7.2, which follows.

Table 7.2 FCC Rules for Digital Signals in U.S. Cable Television Systems

Parameter/SCTE 40 paragraph	Performance limit
Carrier-to-noise ratio [$C/(N + I)$], Table B, line 4 (includes both noise and all discrete products and interfering signals)	$\geq$ 27 dB for 64 QAM $\geq$ 33 dB for 256 QAM
Burst noise, Table B, line 14	$\leq$ 25 µs at 10-Hz repetition rate
Phase noise, Table B, line 11	$\leq$ −88 dBc/Hz at 10 kHz offset (relative to the center of the QAM signal spectrum); however, ANSI/SCTE 105 requires receivers to tolerate −86 dBc/Hz
Group delay variation, Table B, line 9	$\leq$ 0.25 µs/MHz across a 6-MHz channel
In-channel visual frequency response variation, Table B, line 12	$\leq$5 dB pk–pk
Microreflections (dominant echo), Table B, line 12	−10 dB at $\leq$0.5 µs −15 dB at $\leq$1.0 µs −20 dB at $\leq$1.5 µs −30 dB at $\leq$4.5 µs (Longer reflections are included in the C/(N + I) limit)
Delivered signal level, Table B, line 15	64 QAM: −15 to +15 dBmV 256 QAM: −12 to +15 dBmV
Level relative to analog signals, Table D	64 QAM: −10 ± 2 dB 256 QAM: −5 ± 2 dB

Adjacent signal level difference, Table E	Desired	Adjacent	D/U max
	Analog	64 QAM	−1 dB
	Analog	256 QAM	−6 dB
	64 QAM	Analog	−21 dB
	64 QAM	64 QAM	−6 dB*
	64 QAM	256 QAM	−21 dB
	256 QAM	Analog	−16 dB
	256 QAM	64 QAM	−11 dB
	256 QAM	256 QAM	−6 dB*

Hum modulation, Table B, line 8	$\leq$ 3% pk–pk modulation of the visual carrier ($\leq$ 1.5% modulation by conventional definition)

From ANSI/SCTE 105—not an FCC requirement.

Not included in either U.S. government regulations or interindustry agreements are specifications covering several aspects of the sound accompanying NTSC signals (such as loudness level and stereo separation), although these are included in the DBP model. An issue with both over-the-air broadcast and cable-generated video programming has been the perceived loudness variations among channels and within channels (e.g., between the main program and commercials). Despite several attempts by both government and industry groups, it has never been successfully resolved.

In addition to the requirements for the delivery of analog and digital video signals, the CableLabs *Data over Cable Service Interface Specification* (DOCSIS) describe assumed downstream RF channel transmission conditions. Those that are more strict than, or that supplement, equivalent parameters in Tables 7.1 and 7.2 include:

- In-band amplitude ripple $\leq$ 3.0 dB
- In-band group delay ripple $\leq$ 75 ns total

7.3 PERFORMANCE ALLOCATIONS AMONG SECTIONS OF CABLE SYSTEMS

Among the listed parameters, clearly some are determined exclusively (or primarily) in one element of the transmission chain, whereas others (such as carrier to noise ratio) are cumulative as the signal travels through the sections. Specifically:

- The visual carrier frequency is initially determined at the point of RF modulation, but may be modified by subsequent frequency conversions. In most set-top terminals, the video signal is demodulated and remodulated (if delivered as an RF signal) so that the frequency of the signal delivered to the subscriber's equipment is not related to that on the network. In that case, the FCC's frequency standards apply to both the headend output and the output of each terminal.

- The difference between visual and aural carrier frequencies is also determined at the point of modulation and is unaffected by subsequent frequency conversions that modify the entire channel's spectrum (or the entire RF spectrum, such as in an AML transmitter). Similarly, the deviation of the aural carrier of an analog video signal (and therefore the "loudness" of the detected sound) is determined at the last point of modulation, be that the over-the-air transmitter, headend, or set-top terminal. Here again, the FCC's rules apply at the last point of modulation.

- The levels of signals delivered to subscribers' homes are primarily a function of the broadband distribution system but are also affected by changes in the head-end. Where set-top terminals are used, however, the RF signal levels reaching subscribers' receivers may have no relationship to system operating levels. The FCC rules on levels delivered to subscriber equipment apply both before and after any operator-supplied terminal equipment. In addition to the Part 76 rules covering cable television, specifications in Part 15 further limit the allowable output RF power range of terminals.

- In-channel frequency response variation, relative visual/aural carrier-level difference, chroma delay, differential gain, and differential phase in a properly operating cable system are primarily determined in the headend and only slightly modified as a result of variations in the response of the broadband network. As with visual levels, however, set-top terminals significantly modify all these parameters.

- Intermodulation distortions (CTB, CSO, XMOD, and CIN) primarily occur in the broadband distribution network, but can be further degraded by set-top terminals.

- Hum modulation can occur at any place in the network, although in a properly maintained system it will primarily occur because of the side effects of ac power being carried over the same coaxial system as RF signals—a combination of power pack ripple and parametric modulation of magnetic components.

- Noise is added at all stages in the process, although not in equal amounts.

In summary, the primary impediments that occur in multiple sections of cable systems are distortion (occurring in both broadband distribution network and terminal equipment) and noise (with a contribution from headend, broadband distribution network, and terminal equipment). With this understanding, we can discuss allocations of the allowable degree of cable system signal degradation among the various major network sections and within the subparts of the broadband distribution section.

7.4 NOISE AND DISTORTION ALLOCATIONS IN CABLE SYSTEMS

Although there are many parameters of interest, the two of fundamental importance in designing a linear, broadband distribution system are added noise and the generation of distortion products. They are treated in this section and are interdependent since they are inversely affected by variations in operating levels.

7.4.1 Carrier-to-Noise Ratio

Applying Equation 3.2 to the elements of a cable system, it can be seen that the total C/N measured from signal acquisition to the input of subscribers' receivers is

$$C/N_{ttl} = -10 \log \left[10^{-\left(\frac{C/N_b}{10}\right)} + 10^{-\left(\frac{C/N_s}{10}\right)} + 10^{-\left(\frac{C/N_d}{10}\right)} + 10^{-\left(\frac{C/N_t}{10}\right)} \right] \qquad (7.1)$$

where

C/N_{ttl} = the system C/N, considering only noise contributions from the headend input to the input of subscribers' receivers

C/N_b = the C/N of the headend, considered alone

C/N_s = the C/N of the supertrunk (generally fiber-optic or microwave link), considered alone

C/N_d = the C/N of the coaxial distribution, considered alone

C/N_t = the C/N of the terminal equipment (e.g., set-top terminal), considered alone

Although this formula appears somewhat complex, it reflects the conversion of each section's relative noise level to a scalar value, adding the normalized noise levels, and reconverting to familiar logarithmic (dB) terms. The initial factor of 10 and the 10 used to divide each of the original C/N values reflect the fact that the thermal noise generated in each section is noncorrelated and so adds on a power rather than a voltage basis. A shorthand way of stating this relationship is to state that the "cascade factor" is "10 log."

One eminent cable engineer has suggested the use of a shorthand notation to express such equations, which we have slightly modified to make it more universal.[3] Using this notation, Equation 7.1 can be written more simply as

$$C/N_{ttl} = C/N_b \oplus C/N_s \oplus C/N_d \oplus C/N_t : 10 \log \qquad (7.2)$$

where the $\oplus$ symbol indicates the conversion to scalar values, addition, and reconversion to dB form, and the term after the colon indicates the cascade factor, which may vary from 10 log (totally uncorrelated power addition) to 20 log (voltage addition). We will use this notation throughout this section. An Excel spreadsheet entitled *Noise-distortion calculator. xml* is included on this book's companion website, which includes the required calculations for composite noise and distortion among cascades of similar and dissimilar elements in the chain between headend and subscriber.

Analog

Typical set-top terminals that handle analog input signals have noise figure specifications ranging from 10 to 13 dB. Since cable operators are only required to deliver analog television signals at levels of 0 dBmV (and typically deliver many channels at close to that level), we can use Equation 2.19 to determine that, with the noisiest terminals and minimum signal levels:

$$C/N_t = 0 \text{ dBmV} + 59.2 \text{ dB} - 13 \text{ dB} \simeq 46 \text{ dB} \qquad (7.3)$$

At the other end of the chain, individual modulators and signal processors will generally exhibit 60-dB C/N or better. That is degraded, however, by the out-of-band noise from other modulators when many channels are passively combined. The various summing and isolation amplifiers add additional noise as well, so that the typical C/N of individual channels as measured at the input to the broadband distribution network is on the order of 57 dB.

Assuming that the goal is simply to meet the FCC's required analog television C/N_{ttl} of 43 dB, we can find the minimum composite C/N of the supertrunk (generally fiber) and coaxial distribution together using

$$\begin{aligned} C/N_s \oplus C/N_d &= C/N_{ttl} \ominus C/N_b \ominus C/N_t : 10 \log \\ &= 43 \ominus 57 \ominus 46 = 46.4 \text{ dB} \end{aligned} \qquad (7.4)$$

where the $\ominus$ symbol indicates that the scalar quantities are subtracted rather than added.

What Equation 7.4 shows is that our worst-case terminal has effectively used up half the total noise budget of the system. Although most modern terminals have lower noise figures, set-top terminals still contribute significantly to total noise.

Typical design specifications for the supertrunk plus coaxial distribution portion of the plant call for 48 to 49 dB analog video C/N. The margin of about 2 dB provides an allowance for such operating variations as errors in setting operating levels at the headend, aging of components, and imperfect frequency response through chains of amplifiers. The variation in frequency response is known as peak-to-valley (P/V) and is a measure of the peak-to-peak (pk–pk) variation, in decibels, from the ideal. Although fiber-optic links are typically flat within a few tenths of a decibel, the usual allowance for coaxial distribution networks is $N/10 + 2$, where N is the number of cascaded amplifiers.

Digital

Digital reception differs in several regards. For one thing, QAM signals are never passed through a digital set-top box with only RF processing. At the least, the signal is demodulated, decrypted as required, and re-modulated. Most commonly, however, the signal is delivered to customers' receivers in one of several baseband formats. In any case, however, there is never the cascaded noise addition that happens with RF analog converters.

The goal of cable operators is therefore to meet the 33-dB $C/(N + I)$ requirement from SCTE 40 at tap ports with an adequate margin for operational variations. For *QAM signals, 40-dB end-of-line $C/(N + CIN)$** is a typical design spec and is consistent with 48-dB analog signal to noise, with digital signals depressed 6 dB from analog and a correction of 1.8 dB for the noise susceptibility bandwidth, *provided* that the noise floor is similar across the analog and digital spectrum. As will be discussed in Chapter 10, this is not always the case with modern, bandwidth-scalable architectures. In addition to operational variables, 40 dB provides a margin for the composite power level of intermodulation products.

In the future, few analog or combination analog/digital set-top terminals will likely be deployed, as systems will probably carry all programming in digital form (and may or may not elect to simulcast an analog video service for basic-only outlets). Digital-only terminals are significantly less expensive, the programming is more secure, and the incremental cost to add a digital video recorder (DVR) to a box is lower.

The allocation of noise budget between supertrunk and coaxial distribution depends on both architecture and technology. Typical downstream fiber-optic links driven by directly modulated DFB transmitters will exhibit C/N values of 51 to 54 dB, as will broadband AML microwave links. In a simple architecture, a 49-dB supertrunk/coaxial C/N requirement might be met by cascading fiber-optic and coaxial sections, each independently providing 52-dB C/N. More complex architectures might need cascaded supertrunk links, requiring better performance in each section.

7.4.2 CTB and CSO

Since headend levels can be carefully optimized and premium amplifiers used, intermodulation distortion within the headend is minimized, and most distortion occurs in

---

*This includes thermal and intermod noise, but not discrete distortion products, and is sometimes expressed as noise power ratio (NPR). It differs from $C/(N + I)$, which includes discrete products such as CTB and CSO products from analog video signals.

the supertrunk, coaxial distribution, and set-top terminal. As discussed in Chapter 3, however, the calculation is not straightforward. Continuing the example of a simple HFC network, the distortion mechanisms in the directly modulated DFB laser, the balanced RF amplifiers, and the input stages of the set-top terminal have some characteristics in common (all exhibit some form of limiting and small-signal distortions) and others that are different (the predominance of second-order distortion in optical links, but third-order distortion in coaxial amplifiers, and the differing effects of signal limiting when it occurs).

Using the same notation as in Figure 7.1, we can write a general equation for the composite distortion:

$$C/dist_{ttl} = C/dist_s \oplus C/dist_d \oplus C/dist_t : n \log \qquad (7.5)$$

where *dist* could indicate CTB or CSO and n is the cascade factor, which can vary from 10 to 20. When the dominant distortion mechanism is similar in the cascaded elements, for instance symmetrical compression in cascaded push–pull amplifiers running at the same output levels, the cascade factor will be close to 20, which was the number traditionally used for CTB in large all-coaxial networks. Research in the performance of dissimilar cascaded sections, however, has shown that distortions often combine at less than a voltage addition rate (see Endnote 2, Chapter 3). In occasional cases, in fact, the distortion may build up at a less than 10 log rate when distortions partially cancel.

As discussed in Chapter 3, the broadband distribution network is specified, designed, and (often) tested using unmodulated carriers in place of analog video signals and, increasingly, broadband noise in the spectrum that will be occupied by QAM signals. The use of unmodulated carriers results in CTB and XMOD product design levels that are worse than average operational values by about 12 dB, whereas CSO products will be worse than operational values by about 6 dB, although the difference may not be that great for very short cascades or where the modulation on multiple channels is synchronized.

Although there are no standards in this area, common industry practice has been to design for about 53 dB C/CTB and C/CSO for analog video signals in the broadband network (supertrunk plus coaxial distribution) under test (unmodulated-carrier-plus-white-noise loading) conditions. Even when combined with typical analog set-top terminal distortion levels (57- to 65-dB C/CTB and 60-dB C/CSO), the total distortion under operational conditions is well within FCC requirements, even with the most conservative cascade factor assumptions, as shown in the following equations:

$$C/CTB_{ttl} = (53 \oplus 57 : n \log) - 12 \text{ dB} = 60.8 \text{ dB for } n = 20 \qquad (7.6)$$

$$C/CSO_{ttl} = (53 \oplus 60 : n \log) - 6 \text{ dB} = 55.8 \text{ dB for } n = 20 \qquad (7.7)$$

With NTSC analog signal loading, and with digital signals depressed by 6 dB relative to analog signals, the level of CTB products falling in the most-affected QAM channel would be $-53 - 12 + 6 = -59$ dBc, while the level of CSO products would be $-53 - 6 + 6 = -53$ dBc, for a combined level of -52 dBc. That, combined with

S = the suppression of digital signal levels relative to analog video (in dB)

B = the noise susceptibility bandwidth of the digital receiver (in MHz)

margin = the expected variation from design performance due to aging, P/V, and operational tolerances (in dB)

As an example, if $C/N_s \oplus C/N_d$ is 48 dB, the signals are run 6 dB below video, the bandwidth is 6 MHz, and we allow a 2-dB margin, the worst-case $C/N_{digital}$ would be 38.2 dB.

7.5.2 Intermodulation Products from Discrete Carriers

As discussed earlier, typical broadband networks (supertrunk plus distribution) are designed to provide C/CTB and C/CSO levels of at least 53 dB under unmodulated-signal-plus-noise test conditions. Combined with hypothetical set-top terminal distortion levels and adjusted for the difference between unmodulated carriers and normal television signals, worst-case C/CTB will be about 61 dB, whereas C/CSO will be about 56 dB.

As with C/N, a further allowance must be made for imperfect frequency response (P/V) and for operational variances and aging of components. Errors in setting signal levels will cause larger differences for CTB since the distortion product amplitudes change by 3 dB for every 1-dB change in desired levels, whereas CSO products change by only 2 dB. Furthermore, the levels of each video signal and the total peak RF power carried will change over time as average picture brightness changes and as the various video-modulating waveforms drift into and out of time synchronization. The result is that the observed product clusters affecting any one channel will vary by several decibels over time (the FCC allows time-averaged tests in evaluating operational systems). If we allow 5 dB for the total of these effects on CTB and 3 dB for the CSO effects, we can predict that the worst-case C/CTB on any channel at any time will be about 55 dB, whereas the worst-case C/CSO will be about 53 dB.

The improvement in performance experienced by subscribers who are near optical nodes is not as great as for C/N since the largest contributor to CSO is the optical transmitter, whereas the largest contributor to CTB is generally the last amplifier (or two) that drives each subscriber tap string.

In the case of digitally modulated signals sharing the cable network with analog television signals, some intermodulation products will fall into the digital spectrum. If the same channelization is used, then the products will appear in the same relative positions within each channel. That is, for CEA-542 Standard channels, they will occur at harmonics of 6 MHz and 1.25 and 2.5 MHz above those harmonics, with the first and third of those being CSO products and the middle being the CTB product. Scaling from the analysis just done for video signals, adjusting for the 6 dB of level difference, and eliminating the contribution from the set-top terminal (since digital signals do not pass in the RF domain through set-top boxes to other equipment), we would expect that the worst-case operational C/CTB might be as low as 54 dB, and the worst-case C/CSO as low as 50 dB. When combined with the

38.3-dB worst-case C/N calculated earlier, this leads to a predicted worst-case $C/(N + I)$ of 37.9 dB, still comfortably above the 33-dB minimum required by SCTE 40.

Given the distribution of CSO products with frequency (see Figure 2.8), the only significant CSO products are those occupying the highest frequency in each set (2.5 MHz above the harmonics of 6 MHz) when digital signals are placed at the top end of the spectrum. CEA-542 Standard channels (except for channels 5 and 6, which are offset) are protected against lower-side CSO products because they occur only at the boundary between channels.

Although other CEA-542 channelization alternatives are declining in popularity, it should be mentioned that with the HRC system, all the second- and third-order products will fall exactly on harmonics of the reference oscillator (generally 6.0003 MHz), as will the visual carrier if present. Since the products are frequency coherent, they do not cause visible beats in analog channels and so are less visible. With the IRC system, the products have approximately the same frequencies as with Standard channelization, except that each product group is frequency coherent. Because the second-order products are not coherent with the visual carrier, second-order beats may become visible in analog channels carried in IRC systems before third-order beats in some cases.

7.5.3 Composite Intermodulation Noise

As discussed in Chapter 2, intermodulation products among digital signals and between digital signals and analog visual carriers add "bands" of noise-like products, which add to thermal noise to raise the effective noise floor of the system. The frequency distribution of these products is a function of the distribution and relative power levels of both the analog and digital signals. Fortunately, when the average power density of digital signals is suppressed by 5 dB or more relative to visual carriers, the effective C/N degradation for the visual signals is typically less than 1 dB.

7.5.4 Laser Transmitter Clipping Distortion

As discussed in Chapter 4, downstream laser-clipping distortion is a statistically rare event in a properly adjusted, directly modulated DFB transmitter. When external modulation methods are used, clipping is even rarer since other nonlinearities limit average modulation levels before clipping probability becomes significant. Thus, it can reasonably be expected that laser clipping will have no measurable, visible, or audible effect on analog NTSC channels under normal operating conditions. Should the optical modulation levels be adjusted too high, however, horizontal black streaks will appear in pictures.

Studies of clipping-induced errors in 64-QAM data signals that share DFB optical transmitters with a full spectrum (54 to 550 MHz) of analog video signals have shown that, with proper transmitter adjustment, bit error rates due to clipping are less than 10^{-9} even without forward error correction. If, however, the modulation is set too high, the BER can increase to the order of 10^{-7} or even higher before affecting subjective picture quality. Once the threshold of clipping is approached, the decline in performance with increasing modulation is very steep.

7.5.5 Hum Modulation

Hum modulation occurs both in powered equipment (due to imperfect power supply filtering) and as a result of parametric modulation of magnetic components in both amplifiers and passive devices. As discussed in Chapter 2, even though the FCC allows 3% pk–pk modulation levels, systems seldom exceed half that in practice. Modulation due to power supply ripple should logically be more or less independent of RF frequency. To the extent that parametric modulation of magnetic components is a factor, however, its effects may vary with frequency. The primary mechanism is that magnetic cores may partially saturate at peaks of the ac current. This will affect their impedance at RF and so create a change in return and transmission loss that will vary at a 60-Hz rate. Since the impedance change may vary with frequency, as may the effect of the impedance change, there is no way of predicting how the modulation percentage will vary across the spectrum. At a given frequency, however, the percentage modulation of a video signal should be the same as that of a digitally modulated signal, although the latter may be able to tolerate a higher modulation percentage.

7.5.6 Microreflections

Microreflections can occur anywhere within the broadband coaxial network (or, for that matter, in the optical link), but are most severe where components are mounted within a few hundred feet of each other—namely, in the tapped coaxial feeder lines and drop structure. Even though component quality (and thus impedance match, isolation, and directivity) is higher in the "hard-cable" plant (that is, the coaxial portion on the network side of subscriber taps), that is partially offset by the lower per-foot cable losses and greater reflection delays.

The mechanisms by which microreflections occur were analyzed in Chapter 2. Drops were analyzed in Chapter 3. In summary, occasional microreflections should be expected whose magnitude can vary from as large as −10 dBc at zero delay to a maximum amplitude that will decline in accordance with round-trip cable losses at the frequency in question.

Such large reflections, however, can only occur in the trunk and distribution network in the case of a major cable or component fault, poor-quality passive components, or a terminating tap, all of whose subscriber ports are unterminated. If any tap port is terminated, even by connection to a drop cable, the reflections will be significantly smaller. In the drop structure, reflections from receivers and unterminated outlets are partially compensated for by the larger attenuation of the interconnecting cables. As a practical rule, most delayed signals should be at least 20 dB below direct signals, with delays ranging from 0 to about 500 ns. In addition to reflections in tapped lines and within the drop structure, mismatches occurring in long, untapped cable spans (trunk or express feeder lines) can result in smaller reflections ($\leq$ −40 dBc) with delays as long as 5 μs.

Microreflections can cause various picture degradations in analog transmitted signals, ranging from subjective softening or overemphasis of vertical lines (depending on the relative polarity of the reflected signal) when delay times are short, to visible ghosts when the delay time is sufficient that the reflected picture is distinguishable from the direct picture. Because the subjective degradation of analog video signals as a result of reflections is greater for long delays, standard practice is to connect equipment through either very short cables (thereby keeping any reflections below visibility due to short time delay) or quite long cables (thereby taking advantage of cable losses to reduce the magnitude of reflections to below visibility).

With QAM signals, the reflected signal may be interpreted in a number of ways. In the time domain, the effect is to create an amplitude uncertainty in detected amplitude and phase as the delayed and direct signals add at the detector. In the frequency domain, these same effects can be interpreted as group delay and in-band response variations. Reflections up to a certain threshold are compensated for by the receiver's internal equalization networks. The FCC's digital transmission quality requirements and the SCTE's digital receiver standards offer guidance on the maximum tolerance of QAM receiving devices.

7.5.7 Group Delay and In-Band Response Variations

To review, the return loss of a component is the ratio between the signal impinging on a port (with all other ports properly terminated) and the signal reflected from that port:

$$R \text{ (dB)} = L_i \text{ (dBmV)} - L_r \text{ (dBmV)} = 10 \log \left[\frac{P_i}{P_r}\right] \qquad (7.9)$$

where

$R =$ the return loss in dB
L_i and $L_r =$ incident and reflected power levels in dBmV (or any other consistent logarithmic units)
P_i and $P_r =$ incident and reflected power levels in mW (or any other scalar quantities)

Another way of quantifying the mismatch recognizes that the voltage due to the reflected wave will, at some points along the transmission line, add to the incident wave, whereas at others it will subtract from it. The ratio of maximum to minimum combined voltage is known as *voltage standing wave ratio* (VSWR). Note that although at any point the voltage will vary in a sinusoidal fashion at the frequency of the signal, the *ratio* of voltages along the line will not change—hence, a "standing" wave ratio. The relationship between VSWR and return loss is

$$\text{VSWR} = \frac{(1 + 10^{-R/20})}{(1 - 10^{-R/20})} \qquad (7.10)$$

Figure 7.2 illustrates the standing waves resulting when a transmission line is terminated in a pure resistance equal to half its characteristic impedance. When a line

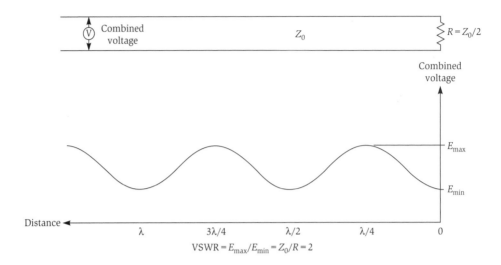

FIGURE 7.2

Standing wave pattern.

is terminated in a pure resistance of any value, the VSWR is Z_0/R or R/Z_0—whichever is greater.

As can be seen, for purely resistive terminations, the standing wave pattern has a maximum value at distances that are odd multiples of one-quarter wavelength from the termination and a minimum value at distances that are even multiples. The reverse would be true if R were greater than Z_0. If the termination is complex (not a pure resistance), the distance to the first minimum or maximum will be other than one-quarter wavelength. Regardless of the termination, however, the maxima and minima will be exactly one-quarter wavelength apart at the frequency of the signal.

The phase shift, ϕ, through a length of cable, in radians, is $2\pi L/\lambda$, where L is the length and λ is the wavelength in the cable. Substituting for λ from Equation 2.9:

$$\phi = \frac{2\pi Lf}{984V_P} \qquad (7.11)$$

where

ϕ = the phase shift in radians
L = the distance, in feet, over which the phase shift is measured
f = the frequency in MHz
V_P = the relative velocity of propagation in the cable

We would like to know what frequency shift, Δf, would be required to cause a relative phase difference of 2π radians through a fixed length, L, of cable. If we solve Equation 7.11 for f and let $\phi = 2\pi$, we get

$$\Delta f = \frac{984 V_P}{L} \qquad (7.12)$$

If a direct signal and one delayed by being transmitted through a cable of length L are mixed, as through a reflection, then Δf is known as the ripple frequency.

Reflections Due to Mismatches in Trunk and Distribution Plant

To see how this affects amplitude response and group delay, let us examine a portion of a typical tapped distribution line (Figure 7.3). Signals exit the source, which might be an upstream tap or amplifier. They travel through cable 1 and enter the tap. Signals exiting the tap through-port travel through cable 2 to the next downstream component, labeled *load*, which might be another tap or the input to a following amplifier.

The following parameters will be used in the calculations:

- Length of cable 1 in feet $= L_1$
- Length of cable 2 in feet $= L_2$
- Source return loss in dB $= R_s$
- Load return loss in dB $= R_L$
- Tap return loss in dB $= R_T$
- Attenuation of cable 1 in dB $= A_{C1}$
- Attenuation of cable 2 in dB $= A_{C2}$
- Tap directivity in dB $= D$
- Frequency in MHz $= f$

Reflected power will be coupled into the drop by two primary mechanisms (although secondary reflections will also contribute):

- A portion of the signals that are reflected from the tap input will be re-reflected from the source and combined with the direct signals delayed by the transit time through $2L_1$ feet of cable. The difference in level between the desired and reflected signals, R_1 (in dB), will be $2A_{CI} + R_s + R_T$.

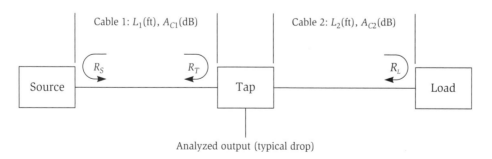

Analyzed output (typical drop)

FIGURE 7.3

Sample tapped line segment.

- A portion of the signals that are reflected from the load will be coupled into the drop due to the finite directivity of the tap. These signals will be delayed relative to the desired signals by the transit time through $2L_2$ feet of cable. The difference, R_2, in level between the desired and delayed signals in this case will be $2L_{C2} + R_L + D$.

The ratio of the scalar magnitudes of the desired, E_F, and delayed, E_D, signal voltages appearing at the drop port will be $10^{R_1/20}$ and $10^{R_2/20}$, respectively.

The presence of the reflected/delayed signal affects the desired signal in three ways. First, the delay, if longer than the symbol period of a digital transmission, will reduce the error threshold by interfering with the following symbol. In the case of an analog television signal, the visible effect is a horizontally offset image whose visual appearance depends on the amplitude and delay time, as covered previously.

Second, the frequency-sensitive nature of the VSWR pattern between the direct and reflected signals will affect the apparent amplitude-versus-frequency response of the system. Using Equation 7.10, the pk–pk change in amplitude response can be calculated to be

$$\text{ripple (dB pk–pk)} = 20 \log \left[\frac{(1 + 10^{-R/20})}{(1 - 10^{-R/20})} \right] \tag{7.13}$$

This ripple will occur at the incremental frequency rate calculated in Equation 7.12, where L is either $2L_1$ or $2L_2$ depending on the dominant coupling mechanism.

Finally, the vector combination of the desired and delayed signals incrementally affects the phase shift through the system and thus the group delay. Figure 7.4 shows the relationship between the magnitudes of the desired and reflected signals, the angle between them, and the angle and magnitude of the resultant signal. In general,

$$\theta = \arctan \left[\frac{E_D \sin \phi}{E_F + E_D \cos \phi} \right]$$

$$= \arctan \left[\frac{10^{-R/20} \sin \left(\dfrac{2\pi L f}{984 V_P} \right)}{1 + 10^{-R/20} \cos \left(\dfrac{2\pi L f}{984 V_P} \right)} \right] \tag{7.14}$$

We can restate the definition of group delay (see Equation 2.32) in similar units:

$$\text{group delay (ns)} \equiv \frac{1{,}000}{2\pi} \frac{d\theta}{df} \tag{7.15}$$

where

θ = the incremental phase shift in radians

$d\theta/df$ = the rate of change of phase shift through the device as a function of frequency in units of radians per MHz

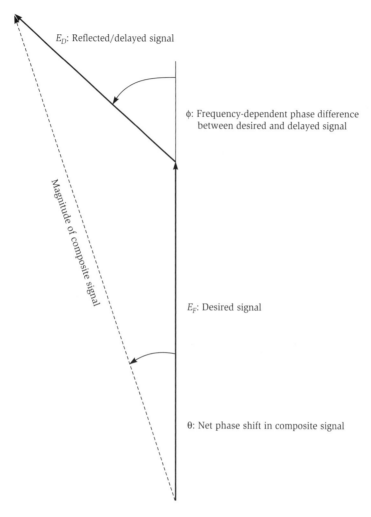

E_D: Reflected/delayed signal

ϕ: Frequency-dependent phase difference between desired and delayed signal

Magnitude of composite signal

E_F: Desired signal

θ: Net phase shift in composite signal

FIGURE 7.4

Vector addition of desired and reflected/delayed signals.

This allows us to solve for the pk–pk delay variation due to the presence of the reflected signal:

$$\text{group delay variation (ns pk}-\text{pk)} = \left[\frac{2.032L}{V_P}\right]\left[\frac{10^{R/20}}{10^{R/10}-1}\right] \quad (7.16)$$

where

$L =$ the incremental cable length through which the reflected signal is transmitted in feet

V_p = the relative propagation velocity (dimensionless)
R = the ratio of the desired to the reflected signal strength as measured at the drop port and expressed in dB

A practical example may be useful in quantizing the effects of reflected signals in typical coaxial distribution lines. Typical amplifiers and passives have return loss specifications of about 16 dB when properly terminated, with the worst performance near the ends of the passband, as can be expected. The specified directivity of taps varies as a function of both frequency and tap value. In general, the worst values are also at the extremes of the passband (especially at the low end of the upstream frequency range) and at high tap values, where the absolute coupling between ports limits the isolation. For most values, the directivity in the downstream spectrum is 10 to 15 dB, whereas the return band directivity is 6 to 9 dB. Finally, most distribution lines use cable whose loss is about 1.6 dB/100 feet at 750 MHz and varies, as we have seen, as the square root of frequency. The relative velocity of propagation for these cables is about 0.90.

Given these parameters, assume that an amplifier and two taps are spaced at 100-foot increments along a cable. At 750 MHz, the following will be the situation under proper operating conditions:

- The signal reflected from the first tap and re-reflected from the amplifier will be attenuated by $16 + 16 + 2(1.6) = 35.6$ dB and delayed by $200/[(0.984)(0.9)] = 226$ ns. The signal transmitted through the first tap, reflected from the second tap and coupled into the drop due to a directivity (which we will assume to be 12 dB), will be attenuated by 31.6 dB and also delayed by 226 ns. We will use this larger delayed signal for calculating the effects.

- If a digital data stream is being transmitted, one effect of this "microreflection" is that, if a pulse is transmitted, an echo of that pulse will create a voltage amplitude uncertainty of about 2.6% in the signal 226 ns later.

- The amplitude response will have a "ripple" versus frequency. The frequency of the ripple will be 4.42 MHz (meaning a full cycle plus in every 6-MHz channel), and the amplitude will be 0.45 dB pk–pk.

- The group delay will also have a variation versus frequency at the "ripple" rate. The delay variation will be 11.7 ns pk–pk.

Many cable operators, on the other hand, do *not* terminate unused tap ports, but only cover them to prevent undue weathering of the connectors. Their reasoning has been that a loose type-F terminator acts as both a radiator and a signal pickup point, reducing the shielding integrity of the system. The consequences for reflected signals, however, can be serious. In the case of a terminating 4-dB tap (actually just a two-way splitter), for instance, the return loss when unterminated is typically <5 dB. If the preceding calculations are made assuming a 5-dB return loss, the delayed signal will be only 20.2 dB below the desired signal, causing the delayed voltage uncertainty to increase to 9.8%, the amplitude response variation to increase to

1.7 dB, and the group delay variation to increase to 45 ns. Although none of the results from a properly terminated system would significantly degrade most signal formats, the second set of values is large enough to be of concern.

If we do a similar calculation at 10 MHz in the upstream band, the principal differences are that the cable loss is much less and that tap directivity, and sometimes return loss, is degraded. Figures 7.5 and 7.6 show the amplitude and group delay variations for some typical situations based on an average of several manufacturers' component specifications.

Although the preceding calculations are simplified to a single reflection, in actual systems many reflections occur. Since a tapped distribution line can easily contain a

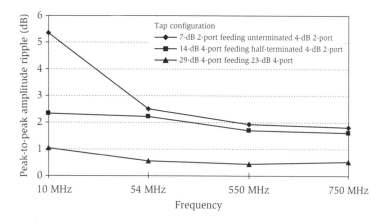

FIGURE 7.5

Passband frequency response as a function of the tapped-line configuration.

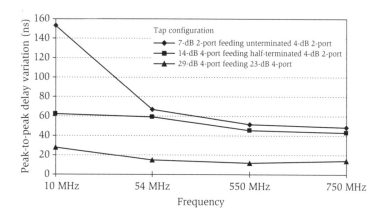

FIGURE 7.6

Group delay as a function of the tapped-line configuration.

to the lowered cable loss and, frequently, worse component matches at the lowest frequencies. Upstream transmission is discussed in detail in Chapter 8.

Other In-Band Frequency Response Variations

In addition to response variations at the ripple frequency associated with multiple reflections, channels will experience in-band variations from three causes: the intentional gain/frequency slope of amplifiers (typically 8 to 12 dB across the full downstream spectrum depending on bandwidth), the variation in cable loss with frequency (in both distribution and drop cables), and the precision with which the various loss variations can be compensated for within each amplifier (P/V).

In addition to the other effects discussed, individual drops may be subject to additional amplitude and group delay degradation when filters and traps are inserted to tailor the spectrum delivered to customers. With a gradual industry shift to all-digital transmission, the need for such devices will slowly diminish.

It is rare for the total in-band response variation within any single 6-MHz channel to exceed 1.0 dB pk–pk in a well-maintained cable system, not including the effects of drop filters.

7.5.8 Local Oscillator and Other Interfering Signals from Receivers

Based on measurements made on a sampling of analog production television receivers in 1993 and on current FCC regulations for one-way, cable-ready digital receivers, local oscillator signals transmitted out the antenna terminals of receivers may have amplitudes as high as -10 dBmV, but are more likely to be -20 dBmV or lower.[4] These signals may be coupled into the downstream signal paths feeding other receivers via the imperfect isolation between tap or splitter output ports. Assuming 20 dB of isolation in such devices and short interconnecting cables, the likely maximum undesired carrier levels at the input to an adjacent receiver are about -40 dBmV, or 40 dB below the minimum acceptable analog desired signal, and thus 34 dB below the level of a 256-QAM signal that is suppressed 6 dB relative to analog signals. This is above the threshold for interference for analog signals and would also likely cause the total FCC-specified $C/(N + I)$ limit of 33 dB for 256-QAM signals to be exceeded.

The probability of such interference to any given channel, however, is slight. With normal single-conversion television design (41- to 47-MHz intermediate frequency), it occurs only when the receiver generating the interference is tuned exactly seven channels lower than the affected receiver and is connected directly to the cable drop (as opposed to through a converter). When it does occur, the interfering carrier will appear 5 MHz above the lower band edge or 3.75 MHz above the desired luminance signal and very close to the chrominance signal, where the threshold of visibility is great.

7.5.9 Antenna-Conducted Ingress from Receivers

Another potential source of interference is over-the-air signals that are picked up by the internal wiring of consumer receivers, by poorly shielded or faulty drop components (including cable and connectors), or coupled across antenna selector switches owing to finite isolation between ports. Such signals can affect the reception at the inadequately shielded receiver, but they can also be conducted out of the antenna terminals and back up the drop cable (thus "antenna-conducted"). Assuming that drops are properly installed using quality components, the largest effect is due to the finite shielding of consumer receivers.

If the source of the off-air signal is a VHF television analog broadcast station (until these cease transmitting in February 2009), then the interfering signal will be close in frequency to the corresponding CEA-542 Standard-scheme channel. Often, in fact, analog cable channels are phase-locked to the corresponding strong off-air VHF stations to reduce the visibility of co-channel interference by eliminating the difference in frequency "beat" lines that otherwise occur. A major disadvantage of IRC and HRC channelization plans is that this mechanism for improving subjective picture quality in the presence of ingress interference is unavailable since the visual carriers in each case are phase-locked to a master headend frequency source. The potential for interference is especially severe in HRC systems, where the difference between off-air and cable visual carriers is 1.25 MHz and results in a highly visible diagonal line pattern on viewers' television screens when the interfering carrier levels are suppressed by less than about 55 dB below the desired signal.

If the interfering signal is a UHF television analog broadcast station, then its visual carrier will fall 3.25 MHz above the lower channel boundary of the overlapping Standard cable channel (cable channels 73 to 128 overlap the spectrum used for UHF broadcasting). To the extent that other external radiators cause interference, the frequencies will differ. For instance, cable channel 19 is often affected by such services as paging transmitters.

Although the probability of destructive interference from external ingress is still relatively low, the interference, when it occurs, is likely to persist since it is not related to the tuning of the inadequately shielded receiver. Tests conducted on typical receivers that were immersed in an external field of 100 mV/m showed that most antenna-conducted egress levels from this cause were −20 dBmV or less.[5] Thus, like local oscillator interference, the probable maximum levels at adjacent receivers exposed to this field strength are about −40 dBmV. It must be pointed out, however, that significant areas in the country are exposed to much higher field strengths.[6] In some cases, well-shielded converters are connected between drop outlets to serve the dual purpose of converting all channels off the off-air frequency in the downstream direction while isolating the cable system from antenna-conducted receiver egress in the reverse direction.

7.5.10 Signal Levels and Stability

Cable systems typically have little problem meeting the various signal level, spectral flatness, and stability requirements imposed by the FCC's rules. In part this is because it would be difficult to meet the noise and distortion requirements if signal levels varied far from optimum levels. It is unlikely, for instance, that total variation across the delivered downstream spectrum will exceed 10 dB, while individual carrier levels will probably not vary by more than 5 dB with time and temperature.

The implications of the expected levels and their variation of required video receiver performance are as follows:

- The receiver front end may be exposed to as high as +35 dBmV total RF power across the downstream spectrum (100 channels at +15 dBmV), but more probably 5 to 10 dB less than that. Additionally, the receiver may be exposed to individual signals as high as +40 dBmV in the return band.

- The receiver must tolerate signals appearing at the image frequency (assuming a standard 41- to 47-MHz IF band) that exceed the desired signal level by 10 dB.

- The receiver must tolerate adjacent video channels whose levels exceed those of the desired channel by 3 dB.

- The level of desired analog signals could be as low as 0 dBmV or as high as +20 dBmV, but will likely not vary by more than 5 dB over time (the FCC allows 8 dB), while the level of desired 256-QAM digital signals can vary from −12 dBmV to +15 dBmV (64-QAM signals may be as low as −15 dBmV).

7.6 SUMMARY

Typical HFC broadband distribution networks provide a broadband thermal noise floor at a level of approximately −45 dBc relative to normal video levels, as measured at the entry point to buildings and referenced to a 4-MHz bandwidth. The noise level in other bandwidths, after set-top terminals, or relative to other signal levels is easily calculated.

Various signals may occur adjacent to or within standard 6-MHz channels as a result of network nonlinearities, normal signal loading, and/or attached subscriber receivers. These are summarized in Figure 7.8. For reference, the levels are expressed relative to an analog video desired signal. The approximate level of suppression required to maintain a subjectively good analog NTSC picture is shown as a dotted line.

The threshold of destructive interference to digital signals is dependent on the total amount of noise and discrete signal interference in the channel, but the voluntary ANSI/SCTE 105 standard, *2005 Unidirectional Receiving Device Standard for Digital Cable,* requires compliant receivers to work correctly with a combination of impairments, including 36-dB C/N. Assuming that the signal is delivered from the cable operator with a C/N of 40 dB, the total power of all interfering products cannot exceed −38.2 dB relative to a digital signal. If digital signals are suppressed 6 dB relative to analog signals, that means that the threshold of interference is about −44 dB in Figure 7.8, shown as a horizontal dotted line.

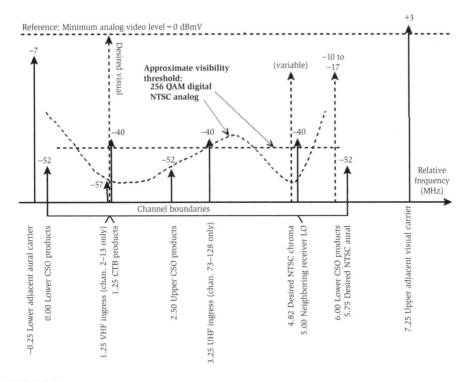

FIGURE 7.8

Maximum expected levels of extraneous signals in or near CEA-542 Standard television channels as received at the input ports of terminal equipment.

Finally, downstream signals transmitted through the network will be subjected to the following:

- Hum modulation that may be as high as 3% pk–pk, but is unlikely to exceed 1.5%.

- Microreflections that can be as high as −13 dBc, but are unlikely to exceed −20 dBc, with delays ranging from 0 to 500 ns, with smaller echoes having delays as long as 5 µs.

- Sinusoidally varying group delay (as a function of frequency) with an amplitude as high as 100 ns pk–pk but unlikely to exceed 30 to 50 ns. The periodicity of the delay variation will typically be in the 2- to 5-MHz range. Additionally, channel 2 (in a standard low-split system) may be subjected to chroma delay as high as 170 ns but more likely 100 to 150 ns owing to the diplex filters. Finally, individual subscriber drops may experience additional group delay due to the effects of any installed filters.

- In-band frequency response variations arising from microreflections, differential cable losses, intentional amplifier response slope, and imperfect frequency response.

The total variation from all these causes is unlikely to exceed 1 dB pk–pk in any 6-MHz channel. As with group delay, however, the use of drop filters may add considerable response variations to some channels.

- Received analog video signal levels ranging from 0 to +20 dBmV at subscriber outlets, with variations within that total range as large as 8 dB (but more likely less than 5 dB) over time and temperature. Digital signals will be suppressed 6 to 10 dB relative to analog signals.

As seen in Chapter 8, signals transmitted in the reverse direction (from the subscriber toward the headend) are subject to channel conditions that are less well defined.

ENDNOTES

1. Hans Stekle (Hrsg.), *Breitbandverteilnetze der Deutschen Bundespost*. Heidelberg: Decker, 1988.
2. *Code of Federal Regulations, Section 47*, available from the U.S. Government Printing Office, Washington, DC, in several volumes covering the entire FCC set of regulations, Parts 0 through 80.
3. Private correspondence from Archer Taylor of the Strategis Group. Taylor does not claim to have invented it. We have modified Archer's suggested notation to add a variable cascade factor to broaden its applicability.
4. *Customer Premises Equipment Performance and Compatibility Testing*, CableLabs, Louisville, CO (undated but published in late 1993). Part 4: Receiver Performance. The FCC regulations that apply to unidirectional digital cable-ready receivers are contained in C.F.R.47 §15.118(c)(5). While the FCC standards allow −15-dBmV levels above 450 MHz, they also mandate average performance across all channels of −20 dBmV or lower.
5. Ibid.
6. Ibid., Part 2, Potential Impact of Direct Pickup Interference. The report concludes that about 20% of U.S. households will be exposed to external field strengths of at least 100 mV/m from at least one VHF television broadcast station, while 41% will be exposed to that magnitude of signal from at least one UHF station operating at or below 550 MHz. Television receivers, however, are usually placed within buildings that provide some attenuation of the external signal.

Upstream Issues

8

8.1 INTRODUCTION

This chapter covers a number of topics of interest to those using return plant or needing to understand the issues involved in the operation of return plant. Return, or upstream, signal levels must be managed differently from downstream signal levels, and this topic is covered in some depth. Return laser characteristics are covered, along with methods used to determine the proper level at which to operate return lasers. Finally, noise on the return path is dealt with. Several methods of analyzing the problem are presented, as are some alternative countermeasures.

Limited two-way cable plant has been built since the mid to late 1970s. As early as 1972, the FCC required that plant be built to be "two-way ready." It was not until the mid-1990s, however, that adequate applications appeared to justify widespread deployment. Previously, the only applications were provision of a return path for impulse-pay-per-view (IPPV) set-top terminals, some of which used an RF return path, and a few status-monitoring applications. Return analog video was and is practiced, but most links involve trunk runs only and are limited to local backhaul applications. Beginning in the mid-1990s, these applications were joined by HFC-based high-speed data transmission and telephony. More sophisticated status monitoring was deployed in the plant, though its required data rate remains modest. Interactive video in the form of video conferencing is becoming more widely employed.

The enabling technology that made the widespread use of the return path possible was the introduction of the smaller, fiber-based, nodal architecture in place of the older tree-and-branch architecture. This made feasible the control of noise buildup and also made it possible to realize adequate bandwidth to support marketable services. Thus, by the mid-1990s, the technology and applications had both arrived to make return plant practical and economically justifiable.

Because of demands on the upstream spectrum, there is new talk in North America about transitioning to a higher split ratio, abandoning the low cable channels in favor of more upstream bandwidth. For example, one possible split is 88/120. This sacrifices channels 2 to 6 as well as the channels in the FM band and just above (channels 95 to 99) in favor of expanding the upstream band from a maximum frequency of 42 MHz to a maximum of 88 MHz. However, this move has some potential problems. The TV IF band in North America covers 42 to 47 MHz, so signals transmitted in this band have the potential to interfere with TV operation. In addition, according to the FCC's current (as of this writing) list of digital off-air frequency assignments, there will be 37 TV stations transmitting on channels 2 to 6 after analog transmissions are turned off. They pose potential ingress interference in the expanded upstream band.

Useful upstream bandwidth may be somewhat less than the entire return bandwidth. On the low end, ingress often is the limiting factor below 15 or 20 MHz. The subject is covered in more detail later. As you approach the upper end of the return band, group delay increases owing to the characteristics of the diplex filters. Whether the group delay is a problem or not depends on the number of diplex filters in cascade, the rate of cutoff of the diplex filter, and the type of modulation used. Thus, the usable bandwidth of the return plant may be lower than the reverse passband.

8.4 GROUP DELAY OF DIPLEX FILTERS

Of concern with two-way plant is the group delay of the diplex filters used to separate the upstream and downstream frequency bands. The narrower the crossover region, the worse the problem becomes. In the upstream direction, the effect is to introduce group delay to the data signals that are typically carried in that direction. Group delay can produce intersymbol interference, the error in a signaling symbol produced by adjacent data symbols. If bad enough, the bit error rate of the signal is adversely affected. Cable modems from DOCSIS 1.1 on include preequalizers that compensate for the group delay from each modem to the headend. The CMTS calculates the needed preequalization and sends the information to the modem. In addition, the CMTS can perform individual modem equalization. Group delay is discussed in more detail in Chapters 2, 3, and 7.

8.4.1 Upstream Group Delay

Figure 8.2 illustrates the upstream group delay of an amplifier having a 42/52 split.[1] The left vertical scale shows the absolute group delay (defined in Equation 2.35), and the right scale is the differential group delay in a 1-MHz frequency span. (If we were concerned about carrying NTSC video, we would measure the differential group delay over a frequency span of 3.58 MHz, and we would call it chroma/luma delay.) Note that at the high end of the return path, the differential group delay increases

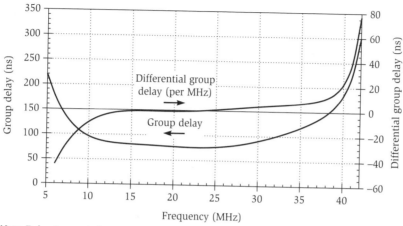

FIGURE 8.2

Upstream group delay due to a diplex filter.

significantly, as the frequency is approaching the low-pass cutoff of the diplexer. If the differential group delay is too great, then some spectrum at the high end of the band may not be usable. "Too much" group delay is a function of the modulation type and the particular system being used. Higher-density modulation systems (i.e., those having a higher bandwidth efficiency) are generally more susceptible to group delay and other impairments than are lower-density modulation systems.

The group delay increase at the low end of the band is a result of a high-pass filter included in the amplifier measured. The high-pass filter is advantageous in that noise below the 5-MHz low cutoff is not as much of a factor in loading the return system. Additionally, the AC bypass coils used to extract power are a major source of group delay at the low end of the upstream band.

Note that the chart in Figure 8.2 reflects the group delay per station. Multiply the group delay shown by the number of stations in cascade. Optical nodes will exhibit somewhat less group delay because they have only one diplex filter (see Figure 8.1). Figures 2.15 through 2.17 show that two diplex filters are cascaded in an amplifier. Furthermore, amplifiers need more crossover attenuation than do nodes to avoid the stability issue described in Chapter 2.

8.5 SPLITTING THE NODE IN THE UPSTREAM DIRECTION

Demand for upstream bandwidth is increasing rapidly, driven primarily by the needs of DOCSIS modems. Each voice call requires about 128 kb/s in the upstream direction. While this is not a high data rate itself, if you have 50 simultaneous conversations, you are tying up 6.4 Mb/s of the roughly 8 Mb/s of upstream payload with

16-QAM (at 2.56 Msymb/s) upstream modulation. Peer-to-peer applications consume a lot of upstream bandwidth. Furthermore, the large picture, audio, and video files being uploaded today demand higher speeds. Competition with fiber-to-the-home systems, which typically have an upstream bandwidth of 1 Gb/s or more spread over only 32 homes, is also putting more pressure on the upstream. This pressure on upstream bandwidth has generated several technologies for splitting the node in the upstream direction, without using more fibers to get data back to the hub or headend. Splitting the node also helps with noise-funneling issues.

8.5.1 Block Conversion

Capacity may be increased, and noise buildup reduced, by splitting the return into several sectors (frequently based on multiple cables branching from the node) and using a separate return transmitter for each. Rather than using multiple return transmitters, block conversion has been used as an alternative. A block conversion system takes several return paths and converts all except one to a unique block of frequencies. The blocks are combined and transmitted to the headend using one return optical transmitter.

Figure 8.3 illustrates block conversion in a common configuration that uses a 200-MHz return optical transmitter. Typically, this circuitry would be housed in

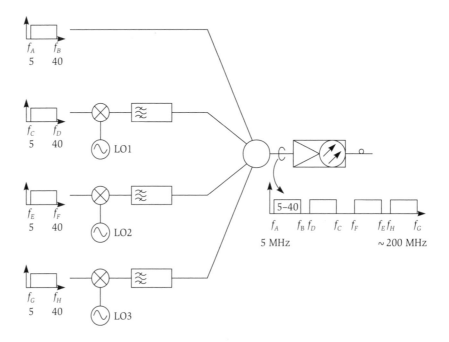

FIGURE 8.3

Block conversion at a node.

a node, though it might be housed in an ancillary housing. Up to four return paths may be accommodated. The first is coupled directly to the optical transmitter. The other three are up-converted to other frequencies up to about 200 MHz and combined with the unconverted spectrum to supply signals to a return transmitter. At the headend, the process is reversed, developing four individual 5- to 40-MHz spectra to be supplied individually to receivers. Alternatively, it is possible to build return receivers that tune to 200 MHz, eliminating the need for down-conversion in the headend.

Single conversion is used for economy. For other applications, double conversion might be used if it is necessary to put many blocks close together, but the cost is higher. The single conversion results in inversion of the spectra of the three converted bands, so that what was the low end of the band becomes the high end of the converted band. The conversion back in the headend will re-invert the spectrum. Inversion is brought about by the practical need to use high-side local oscillators.

In some cases, it is necessary to provide very accurate frequency conversion in the node and headend, such that the frequency to which a signal is restored in the headend is very close to the frequency at which it existed before conversion at the node. If this is required, then most commonly the oscillators in the node will be phase locked to those in the headend, or vice versa. A pilot tone is transmitted between the node and headend to allow phase locking.

Node splitting increases the bandwidth available per customer and reduces noise funneling without requiring more optical transmitters and receivers. However, since the one optical transmitter is loaded with more signals in block conversion systems, the performance of that transmitter must be higher or the OMI must be reduced. This reduces the carrier-to-noise ratio (C/N) available in the optical portion of the return path. The use of block conversion will force use of a DFB return laser designed for this type of service rather than a lower-cost F-P laser, and may prove critical to set up.

8.5.2 Wavelength Division Multiplexing

An alternative to block conversion is wave division multiplexing (WDM). Each branch coming back to the node is supplied to a different optical transmitter operating on a different wavelength. At this time, there are no standard wavelengths, though one manufacturer does suggest 1470, 1490, 1510, 1530, 1550, 1570, 1590, and 1610 nm. A WDM is used to combine the wavelengths on a single fiber for transmission to the headend or hub. A second WDM is used at the headend or hub to separate the individual wavelengths before they are supplied to individual optical receivers.

The preceding wavelength assignments are known as coarse wavelength division multiplexing (CWDM) because of the relatively large spacing between transmitters. Closer wavelengths can be used, and this technique is known as dense wavelength division multiplexing (DWDM). As wavelengths used get closer together, laser wavelength drift becomes more of a problem—you cannot let the laser drift out of its wavelength assignment or the signal will not go through the WDMs, and in extreme cases you might even find one upstream transmitter interfering with another.

8.5.3 **Digital Return**

Yet a third technology for combining signals is available: digitize the return band at the node and transport the digitized signals to the headend. At the headend, the digitized signals are converted again to RF in order to allow interface with legacy headend systems.

Figure 8.4 illustrates a digital return system. Compare it with Figure 8.1, which shows the same node with RF return on two separate fibers. In the digital return system, the outputs of the two diplexer low-pass sections are individually digitized in the two *analog-to-digital* (A/D) converters, and then applied to a multiplexer (mux), which alternately passes data from one A/D converter and then from the other. The data are serialized and supplied to a digital transmitter for transport to the headend. At the headend, the data is demultiplexed into two signal streams, which are converted to RF in *digital-to-analog* (D/A) converters. The RF signals can then be supplied to the normal headend upstream receiving equipment, such as DOCSIS CMTSs for data.

To avoid the potential of destroying data, it is necessary to sample data at more than twice the highest frequency present. If the high end of the return band is

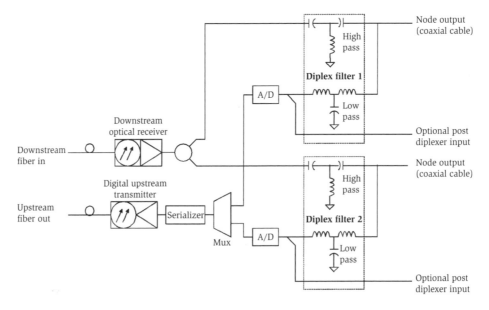

FIGURE 8.4

Digital return system.

42 MHz, then the sampling rate must be above 84 megasamples per second (Ms/s). A convenient sampling frequency is 100 Ms/s. Commonly, a 10-bit digital system is used. This means that the data rate from each of the two A/D converters is 1 Gb/s (100 million samples each second times 10 bits per sample) before any protocol overhead is added. Two A/D converters multiplexed together yield a data rate of 2 Gb/s before adding overhead. This fits nicely into an OC-48 transmitter, which runs at a wire rate (the actual data rate) of 2.488 Gb/s. Transmitters and receivers for this data rate are commonly available.

There are several advantages to using digital return transmission. The first is cost. A digital transmitter is lower in cost than an analog transmitter because power levels can generally be lower and because the specifications on a digital transmitter are much looser. Furthermore, by comparing Figures 8.1 and 8.4, you see that only one return transmitter is required rather than two. Of course, somewhat offsetting the cost reductions is the need for two high-speed A/D converters and the other digital processing circuitry. But you do realize net savings in many cases, at least where you need more than one return path.

Digital returns can be particularly advantageous in longer-distance paths because the NPR curve does not degrade with distance, at least not until you hit the well-known wall, beyond which digital signals do not work at all. Yet another advantage is gain stability, since the signal received at the headend is not dependent on the optical signal level received. This is important for system balance and alignment.

As many advantages as digital return has, there are limits to its application. As the demand for upstream bandwidth increases, there is pressure to raise the upstream RF bandwidth beyond 42 MHz. This will push the sampling speed of the A/D converters higher, increasing the cost of the A/D converters and increasing the bandwidth required on the fiber. This in turn increases the cost of the digital transmitter at the node and the digital receiver and D/A converter at the headend or hub. These issues plus progress in WDM systems are limiting the application of digital return systems.

8.6 RETURN SIGNAL LEVEL ISSUES

Of paramount importance to the operation of the return path is the proper handling of signal levels. The issue is far more complex in the upstream direction than it is in the downstream direction. In the upstream direction, you deal with many transmitters located on or in subscribers' homes, with each signal path having a different gain between the home and the headend. Several conditions must be addressed in setting the level of the transmitters. Designing and balancing the reverse and forward paths are equally important. If you balance the forward plant and let the reverse fall where it may, reliable return performance will not be obtained.

occupied bandwidth, and some analyzers are not equipped with IF filters wider than 1 MHz. Also, if adjacent channels are occupied, it may be necessary to reduce the bandwidth of the analyzer in order to avoid interference from those adjacent signal(s).

Some spectrum analyzers use IF filters with relatively high shape factors (the ratio of bandwidth at high attenuation to bandwidth at low attenuation). Such filters tend to ring less and can allow accurate measurements to be made faster. However, it does mean that the resolution bandwidth may need to be less than the occupied bandwidth in order to reject adjacent channel power. Other analyzers use filter shapes that are more squared (somewhat as illustrated in Figure 8.5). These filters, if available in the correct bandwidth, do a better job of rejecting adjacent channel signals, but they tend to ring more, introducing yet another source of error.

Making the measurement with a significantly narrower spectrum analyzer bandwidth can yield a fairly accurate average channel power measurement *if* return signals are present for a long time (with respect to the settling time of the IF filter in the spectrum analyzer). This can be useful in checking that a long-loop ALC system is set to operate at the desired level.

In summary, it is difficult to make accurate measurements of the amplitude of TDMA signals in a real network. Gross errors can often be spotted fairly easily, but very accurate measurements are hard to make. The *NCTA Recommended Practices* document, referenced earlier, defines the "level" as being what would be measured if the signal were on continuously. It further requires the manufacturer of a signal-measuring device to publish a valid procedure to allow a user to translate the level indicated to the defined level. However, this is not always easy to do.

Measurement of the level of return signals using more advanced techniques, such as code division multiplexing and multiple carriers, is not covered here. The vendor of such systems should provide guidance for making the required measurements.

8.6.2 Long-Loop Automatic Level Control

Figure 8.6 illustrates the critical points in the return-signal–level control issue. Return services include a long-loop automatic level control (ALC), wherein the signal level is measured in the headend (Lvl 1 in Figure 8.5) and a signal is sent to the home transmitter, TX4, to adjust its output such that the "correct" level is received at the headend. This corresponds to some level at the tap, Lvl 5, and to other levels at each RF amplifier (Lvl 4) and at the node, Lvl 3. The point is that, once the system controls the signal level at Lvl 1, all other signal levels are set according to the design of the system.

The most critical level is that at the return optical transmitter, Lvl 3. The dynamic range (the amplitude range from maximum signal level down to noise level) tends to be relatively low for return path optical transmitters, both due to technology and cost. Dynamic range is explored in more detail later. See Chapter 4 for a detailed discussion of optical technology.

The system must be set up to optimize the level at Lvl 3. However, Lvl 3 cannot be directly observed by the adjusting system. Instead, the gain between the point

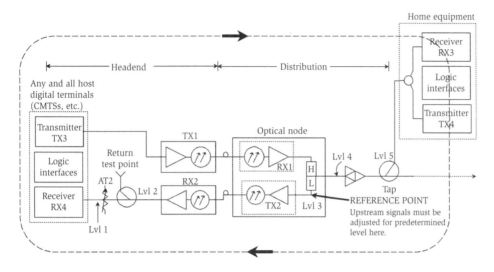

FIGURE 8.6

Pertinent points in return signal level control. An ALC loop is set up between the headend and each individual home system. The headend senses the return signal level and adjusts the upstream transmitter such that the correct level is received at the headend receiver. The most critical level is at the reverse optical transmitter, Lvl 3.

marked Lvl 3 and that marked Lvl 1, where the level observation is made, must be known and must be stable. The target value of Lvl 1, to which the system is adjusted, is set based on the desired value of Lvl 3. At the same time, it is necessary to set the gain in the system such that the input and output signal levels at all amplifiers, represented by Lvl 4, are correct. Attenuators and equalizers are often provided in the return amplifiers for this purpose and must be properly selected during system alignment. "Correct" is based on the manufacturer's specified operating levels for the conditions under which the amplifier is being used. When these levels are set (by design and alignment of the system), then the level at the tap, Lvl 5, will be set by the tap value and the gain from there to the node.

A few systems have attempted to use automatic gain control (AGC) in return path amplifiers or the node. This is not recommended for a number of reasons. First, it fights the long-loop setting of levels as described earlier. Second, at times it may be normal for the number of carriers in the reverse direction to change. For example, some services employing time division multiple access (TDMA) may permit signal dropout as a normal condition at times. Further, as return services are added and deleted, it is not desirable that gain in the return path change. Next, real return paths often branch and have a different number of amplifiers in each branch. AGC can significantly complicate the operation of such systems.

In some cases where reverse AGC has been employed, it has been done with a pilot tone generated somewhere near the end of the system and detected by all amplifiers and the node. This may work, but raises many questions when downstream signals branch after leaving the node. With branches having a different number of amplifiers in cascade, where do you put the pilot tone generator? You would logically place it at the end of one of the branches, but that leaves the other branches with no coverage.

8.6.3 Working with Long-Loop ALC

Upstream transmitters in subscribers' homes all use a long-loop automatic level control. The receiver in the headend has a target level it expects to see for return signals. When it sees a level other than this target level, a signal is sent to the upstream transmitter, telling it to correct its level until the target level is measured in the headend. This long-loop ALC is necessary in order to keep signal levels within reasonable bounds, but it is confusing to work with. Long-loop ALC results in some very nonintuitive behaviors in the network. This section lays some theoretical groundwork for understanding long-loop ALC; later we will explain how to deal with it.

Thermal Gain Control

It is often desirable to provide thermal control of return path equipment. Even at return frequencies, cable exhibits some variation in loss with temperature, and it may be desirable also to compensate for variations in the operating point of lasers. This is often done by using thermistors (temperature-sensitive resistors) to sense temperature level inside the return optical transmitter and adjust gain based on temperature variation. It is also practiced at times to cool the laser, as mentioned in Section 8.7.

Return Signal Levels at the Tap

Of interest to those designing or using systems needing the services of the return path is the issue of the signal level at the tap, Lvl 5, needed in order to produce the desired level at Lvl 3. Intuitively, we might assume that the difference between the lowest and highest levels would be about the same as the difference between the lowest and highest tap value in the system. Tap values are chosen such that the downstream level at the tap is more or less constant, fixed by system design. This calculation is done at the highest frequency of interest, where cable loss is maximum. At the return band, cable loss is much lower, so the level required at the tap, Lvl 5, is lower at lower tap values. Generally, those lower-value taps are located farther from an amplifier (in the downstream direction).

Analysis of the return gain characteristics of real nodes, however, shows that this line of reasoning is oversimplified. Sometimes low-value taps are located at the end of a long cable run, so there is little upstream loss at the low frequencies composing the return band. Other times, though, low-value taps are located after a directional coupler and near an amplifier. At those locations, the loss is primarily flat (not a function of frequency), and the required output at Lvl 5 will be higher.

Figure 8.7, from the analysis of one real node, shows the levels found to be required at the tap (Lvl 5 of Figure 8.6) in order to produce a level of 0 dBmV at the node (Lvl 3). Each dot represents a tap of the value shown on the *x*-axis, which requires the *y*-axis level at any tap port. Note that low tap values exhibit a wide variation in level required, with the level range tending to compress slightly as you move to higher tap values. This slight compression is a result of having few places to use high-value taps other than shortly after an amplifier. This data is from one node, but examination of other nodes owned by the same and other cable operators shows the same tendency.

It is not necessarily desirable to have a node that requires low signal levels at the return input. It is desirable to require the highest level that can be supported by the reverse amplifiers that supply signals to the node. This will help minimize the effect of noise entering the plant (primarily from homes). Of course, you must ensure that the requisite signal levels are available at the home transmitter. The use of 0 dBmV as the input to the node is intended not as a real case but rather as a convenient normalized reference point.

Figure 8.8 illustrates the signal level issue another way. The population of taps having certain level requirements is plotted for the node of Figure 8.7. The distribution of levels appears to be a very crude approximation to a normal distribution. It illustrates that, though there is a clumping of levels, a significant number of taps will require a higher or lower level. The product designer must plan for the required

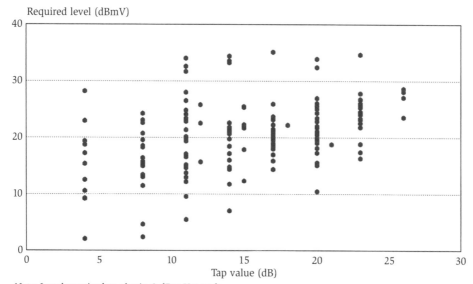

Note: Level required to obtain 0-dBm Vat node.

FIGURE 8.7

Required signal level as a function of tap value.

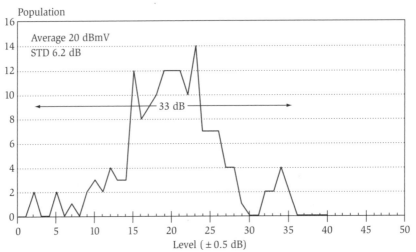

FIGURE 8.8

Distribution of tap signal levels.

level range, also allowing for variations from system to system, errors, and variations with temperature. Note that the level of the signals at the home will vary because of temperature-dependent changes in gain in the system. When the signal level received at the headend changes, this will cause the signal level commanded from the home to change due to operation of the long-loop ALC.

Reducing the required tap return level range would be desirable, in that a reduced level range specification would provide some reduction in cost and would enhance performance in at least some cases. Homes with the lowest signal level requirement are also the homes that have the greatest potential to introduce noise into the return path. A wide level range implies high output level capability from the device, which implies possible high noise emission when the level is set low. It also implies rather larger current drain since the output amplifier must have the capability to handle large signals with minimum distortion.

8.7 OPTIONAL WAYS TO SPECIFY RETURN LASERS

At least four types of return transmitters are in common use at this time: digital, cooled distributed feedback (DFB) lasers, uncooled DFB lasers, and Fabry–Perot (F-P) lasers. The list is in the order of decreasing performance (and decreasing cost). It is required to select the correct laser for each application, bearing in mind the eventual loading, not just the initial loading. Refer to Chapter 4, which discusses laser technology.

8.7.1 Data- or Video-Grade Classification

An early method of classifying return transmitters (and receivers) was to classify them according to data grade or video grade, with the implication that video-grade lasers are better. This method has proved unsatisfactory because it does not take into account the real requirements placed on the system. A return path with many data signals requires at least as good a laser as does a return path with one analog video signal. Further, there are no standard criteria for classifying lasers. In at least one case, a manufacturer interpreted "data grade" to mean capable of handling one FSK return signal only. When it was used with multiple QPSK return signals, it was incapable of handling the job.

8.7.2 Discrete Carrier Testing and Classification

An older method of measuring the performance of return components is taken directly from downstream measuring practice. Either two or four CW carriers are used to excite the laser, and the results are measured on a spectrum analyzer. The second- and third-order beat products are recorded.

Figure 8.9 illustrates the method. Two or four oscillators are combined, with identical output levels, to produce a spectrum, usually on the highest upstream carrier frequencies used by the system. The performance of the system is reported as the composite second- (CSO) and third- (CTB) order beats and the cross-modulation, as if this were a miniature downstream system. Typically, lasers tend to be more second-order than third-order limited, so CSO becomes the dominant specification.

The attenuators and bandpass filter are shown for practical reasons. The attenuators help isolate the signal sources to prevent intermodulation distortion in the

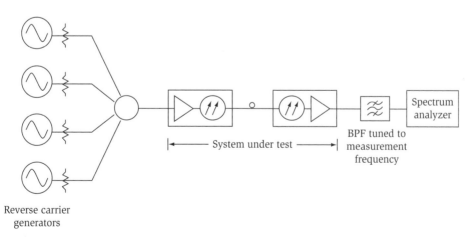

Reverse carrier
generators

FIGURE 8.9

Four-tone measurement of a return optical system.

output circuits of the generators. The bandpass filter (BPF) tuned to the frequency of measurement prevents overload of the spectrum analyzer.

In evaluating the performance of the system for carrying a limited number of signals, some practitioners have tried to predict the frequencies at which the maximum distortion is present. These frequencies are then avoided in order to maximize the performance of the link. The cost of doing this is that many potentially useful frequencies are excluded, and you are left with lower capacity and less ability to move carriers to avoid noise. Another problem with this approach is that, as we will show, when the laser goes into clipping, the normal model used for predicting the frequencies of distortion components is invalid. Also, this technique fails to stress the laser the same as it would be stressed with a number of real digital signals. Again, this is explained later.

Yet another problem encountered in comparing specifications among manufacturers by using discrete test tones is that some manufacturers, following downstream practice, quote specifications with equal-level carriers. Others assume that some number of the carriers represent analog signals and others represent digital signals that are carried at a lower level. They reduce the level of some of the signals when making measurements.

Still another problem in comparing specifications is that manufacturers may choose different channels on which to place the carriers. Depending on the placement, differing numbers of composite beat products will exist on the measurement frequencies. Only the most careful reading of the data sheet can reveal the exact conditions under which the measurements were made.

With a small number of tones, each has a large relative contribution to any beat products. This means that the measured amplitude of the beat products will be inconsistent, as the individual components of the composite beat go in and out of phase. This tends to be not as much of a problem in the downstream direction since you are dealing with a large number of beat products on each frequency.

8.7.3 Noise Power Ratio Testing and Classification

A newer method of characterizing systems has become common practice. It comes much closer to testing the laser as it will be operated in service. The technique is not really new, as it has been used in the telephone industry for years to characterize linear systems, such as FDM (frequency division multiplex) coax and radio systems. HFC systems are FDM systems because they employ multiple frequencies to carry different information.

Figure 8.10 illustrates the so-called noise power ratio (NPR) testing technique. A broadband white noise generator is used to simulate a spectrum filled with data signals. Data signals generally have a flat spectrum over the occupied bandwidth of the signal, so simulating them with a white noise signal is reasonable. ("White noise" simply means that the spectrum is flat over the frequency range of interest.) A bandpass filter limits the spectrum to that for which the system under test is rated.

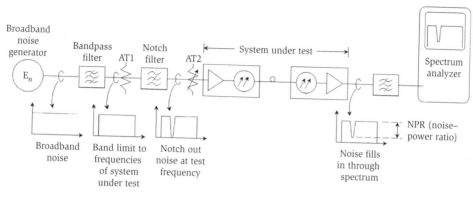

FIGURE 8.10

Noise power ratio of a return path transmitter.

An attenuator is used to isolate the bandpass filter from a notch filter that follows. The notch filter removes the white noise in the measurement bandwidth. The total power in the signal is important, and would be measured using, ideally, a thermocouple-type power meter. The variable attenuator is used to adjust the signal level supplied to the system under test.

A spectrum analyzer, protected if necessary by a bandpass filter tuned to the notch frequency, is used to observe the output. The notched frequency will be somewhat filled in by the system under test. At low signal levels, the filled-in noise is due to noise introduced by the system under test. At higher signal levels, it is filled in by distortion introduced by the system under test. It is not possible to look at the filled-in level and tell whether the fill is due to noise or distortion or both. The ratio of noise on the flat portion of the spectrum and that in the notch is called the noise–power ratio (NPR). Some practitioners have called it carrier to noise plus intermodulation noise, or C/(N + IMD).

Use of NPR to Set the Operating Level

If we were to plot the NPR against the power supplied to the laser, we would obtain a plot similar to that of Figure 8.11. The total power supplied to the transmitter is plotted on the x-axis. Often the quantity plotted will be the power spectral density, which is the total power divided by the bandwidth over which the power exists.

At low signal levels, the NPR is noise limited. One would expect the NPR to increase 1 dB for every decibel increase in total power into the laser. In practice, there will often be a region on the left of the diagram in which the NPR increases faster than decibel for decibel.[3] This is especially true for unisolated distributed feedback (DFB) lasers feeding long fiber-optic cables. The reason is that at low signal levels, lasers are susceptible to reflections from the optical cable due to Rayleigh

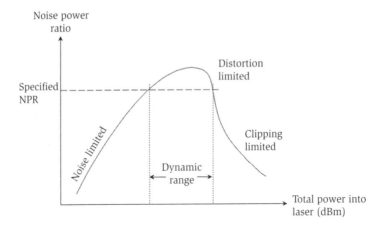

FIGURE 8.11

NPR as a function of total power into the transmitter.

backscatter. The reflected light "pulls" the laser wavelength, creating noise. As the drive to the laser increases, the laser tends to "chirp" (change in wavelength with instantaneous drive) more, reducing the pulling by reflected light. The reflected light is a function of the length of optical cable used: the longer the cable, the more reflection. DFB lasers tend to be more susceptible than are F-P lasers because their wavelength is chirped less by modulation, making them more susceptible to wavelength pulling by reflected light. Many modern lasers are isolated and tend to change NPR at about a 1:1 rate with signal level.

Wavelength pulling by reflected light is a phenomenon similar to the tendency of an oscillator to oscillate off of its normal frequency if a signal at a close frequency is supplied to the circuit. The more the separation between the two frequencies, the less the tendency to pull. Chirp refers to the changing of frequency (wavelength) of an oscillator (or light source) with applied modulation.

At some drive level, the NPR is maximized. Above this level, the NPR drops quickly. The initial drop may be due to distortion, primarily second order, but you quickly enter a region in which the primary effect is from laser clipping. Clipping noise tends to be the dominant mechanism by which the NPR is reduced on the right side of the graph; it is covered in greater detail later in this chapter.

NPR should not be confused with carrier-to-noise ratio. C/N represents the ratio of a signal to the noise lying under that signal. It is a function of signal level and the total noise provided from thermal sources plus the excess noise generated in real electronics. On the other hand, the noise in the notch of an NPR measurement either is a function of the thermal and excess noise or, at higher levels, is caused by distortion, which transfers noise from other frequencies into the notch. The mechanism may be the familiar second- and third-order distortion, or much of the noise fill in the notch may be clipping noise from the laser (or electronic amplifiers). Do not look for a simple and universal relationship between NPR and C/N. Later in this chapter, we show how to compute C/N from NPR.

One convenient way to establish the level at which to operate the laser is to determine the range of input signal levels across which some specified minimum NPR is obtained, as indicated in Figure 8.11. The laser should be operated with total power within this "dynamic range." The engineer might be tempted to operate the laser at the total power that represents the highest NPR. This will work, but because the dropoff in performance is so steep on the right side, he or she may want to operate with slightly less power (to the left of the maximum NPR). (In some lasers, the slope on the right side has a region of gentler slope, where it is limited by second-order distortion. In other lasers, the slope tends to be quite steep just to the right of the peak. This indicates that the laser performance is limited more by clipping than by second-order distortion.)

A noise power ratio test has several advantages over a four-tone test. Noise has an amplitude probability distribution that is different from that of four carriers, but is similar to that of a number of digital carriers added together. The central limit theorem from statistics states that, when a number of independent variables having any arbitrary distribution are added together, the resultant distribution is normal. A normal distribution also describes the amplitude distribution of noise.

Further, the measurement is independent of the measurement bandwidth (the resolution bandwidth of the spectrum analyzer) so long as the measurement bandwidth is significantly less than the notch width. It is also independent of the characteristics of the spectrum analyzer detector, so repeatability is good. The only other instrument (besides a spectrum analyzer) needed is a thermocouple power meter, which is low in cost and very accurate.

Use of BER to Set the Operating Level

An alternative way to look at the optimum laser operating point recognizes that the vast majority of signals likely to be carried in the reverse direction use low-density digital modulation (though this could change with pressure on upstream data bandwidth). The return spectrum is loaded much as is shown in Figure 8.10 except that a modulated (usually QPSK) signal is added into the notched frequency band. The bit error rate is plotted against the signal level.[4]

Figure 8.12 illustrates the principle. At low signal levels, the bit error rate (BER) is poor owing to noise corruption. As the signal level increases, the BER gets better (lower on the y-axis denotes better BER). In the central part of the diagram, the BER is so good it is below the chart. Toward the right side of the graph, the BER again begins to deteriorate due to clipping. The operating total signal level into the laser is set to be somewhere in the middle of the range where the BER is extremely good.

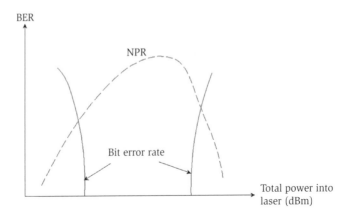

FIGURE 8.12

BER versus signal level.

8.8 CHARACTERISTICS OF RETURN LASERS

Two basic types of laser diodes are used in return path service today: Fabry–Perot (F-P) and distributed feedback (DFB) lasers. Chapter 4 provides additional information on lasers used in cable TV work. DFB lasers may be either cooled, with an integral thermoelectric cooler, or uncooled. F-P lasers tend to have lower performance but are lower in cost. Since lasers perform somewhat more poorly at high temperatures, a cooled laser can offer better performance at higher optical output levels. The cooler can also reduce the shift in transfer function of the laser with temperature. However, the cooler increases power consumption and usually increases cost. Electronic circuits have been developed that compensate for the changes in laser characteristics with temperature. Coolers tend to be used only in dense wavelength division multiplexing applications. Besides use of analog returns and block conversion, digital return systems have been developed whereby the entire return path is digitized and returned to the headend. At the headend, the signal is turned back into RF form so that signals may be supplied to legacy systems.

8.8.1 Fabry–Perot Lasers

Fabry-Perot lasers have their frequency controlled by the spacing of mirrors at each end of the laser. The frequency control mechanism is such that the laser can oscillate simultaneously, or jump in rapid succession, to several wavelengths that are close to each other. This is sometimes called *mode hopping*. Each wavelength propagates through the fiber at slightly different velocity due to chromatic dispersion in the fiber.[5] As shown in Chapter 4, this results in restricted performance in terms of C/N or NPR on the low side.

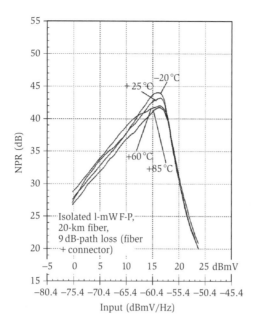

FIGURE 8.13

NPR performance of an F-P return laser diode.

Figure 8.13 illustrates NPR performance of a real F-P laser diode using the NPR test described earlier. On the left side of the graph, performance is limited by inherent noise in the device. It increases almost precisely 1 dB for every decibel increase in signal level. Above the level of peak NPR performance, the drop in performance is precipitous as the laser rapidly enters the region in which the signal is clipped.

Note that Figure 8.13 is the same plot as in Figure 8.11 except that this figure is for a real laser. A strategy for setting the level into the laser is to operate just to the left of the point of maximum NPR. You would apportion total power at the operating point, perhaps +15 dBmV for the transmitter shown, over the actual occupied bandwidth of all signals. This subject is covered more fully later in this chapter.

8.8.2 Distributed Feedback Lasers

DFB lasers operate in a similar manner to F-P lasers except that a diffraction grating restricts the operating wavelength of the laser primarily to a single mode (wavelength) of oscillation. This means that, relative to an F-P laser, the DFB laser exhibits a lot less noise and distortion as a result of multiple propagation speeds in the fiber.

Figure 8.14 illustrates the NPR of an uncooled DFB return laser diode on the same NPR scale as the F-P laser of Figure 8.12. (The absolute values on the *x*-axis are irrelevant and may vary from one transmitter to another.) Both diodes (Figures 8.13 and 8.14) were measured using the same 9-dB path loss. The increase

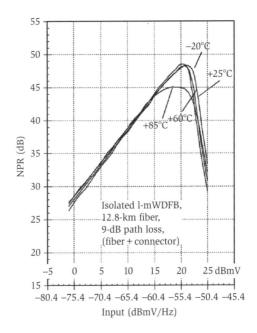

FIGURE 8.14

NPR performance of a DFB return laser diode.

in NPR with increasing signal level on the left side is only slightly greater than decibel for decibel in Figure 8.14 because the laser is isolated. In brief, optical power reflected to the optical transmitter due to Rayleigh backscatter is diverted in an isolator and not allowed to enter the laser. Chapter 4 explains Rayleigh backscatter and the deleterious effect that it can have on transmitter operation.

As shown in Figure 8.14, the laser's NPR performance is somewhat better in terms of C/N and dynamic range at room temperature and below than at high temperatures. For this reason, cooled DFB lasers are sometimes used in return path operation and may be necessary where high power levels are required. However, the added cost and power drain (which adds heat to the node) often argue against adding a cooler. The performance of uncooled DFB lasers is considered adequate for many purposes, although long, heavily loaded paths may benefit from a cooled laser. The laser of Figure 8.14 was embedded in a temperature-compensated transmitter module. Had it not been, the performance range with temperature would have been worse.

Effect of Distance on DFB Link Performance

Figure 8.15 compares the NPR curves for one isolated DFB transmitter with different lengths of fiber, expressed as the loss of the fiber and connectors. Shown are 3-dB through 15-dB links. As expected, with longer fiber lengths, the peak NPR curve drops as a result of lower received signal level. Had the test been done with

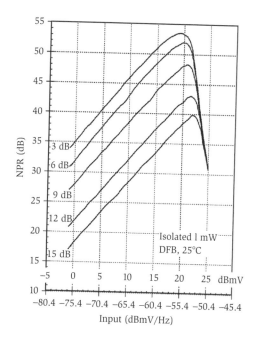

FIGURE 8.15

NPR performance of a DFB laser for various return path lengths.

nonisolated lasers, the performance on the left would have dropped off much faster as a result of Rayleigh backscatter noise reflecting into the laser.[6]

Figure 8.16 shows the NPR curve for a 10-bit digital return system on the same scale as is used for the analog return systems shown earlier. The temperature variation is a reflection of the inevitable shift in operating point of the A/D converter and perhaps a function of RF components preceding the A/D converter. It is not a function of shifts in the laser operating point, as is the case in analog transmission. The familiar precipitous drop on the right side is due to saturation of the A/D converter rather than to clipping in the laser.

8.9 RETURN PATH COMBINING AT THE HEADEND

To avoid the cost of multiple RF receivers in the headend, it is a frequent practice to combine several reverse path signals into one. This can work if adequate total data capacity (called "bandwidth" by data communications engineers) is available to service multiple nodes as one. This combining is usually done electrically so that there is one optical receiver for each node. RF combining (in the headend, after the optical receiver) can be done satisfactorily as long as adequate C/N is maintained, considering both thermal noise and ingress. *Very important: The gain from the electrical reverse input to the node, to the combined output in the headend,*

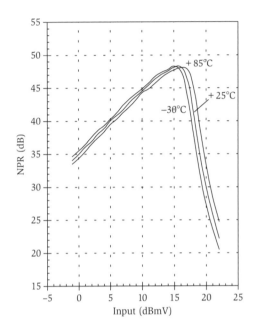

FIGURE 8.16

NPR curve for a 10-bit digital return path.

must be the same for all return paths that are combined. Otherwise, the return operating level of at least one of the nodes will be incorrect.

However, some operators like to do optical combining to further save the cost of optical receivers. Optical combining must be done carefully, if at all, because if the lasers operate at close to the same wavelength, interference (beats) between the lasers will develop in the receiver. These can increase the noise level much more than would be expected from the addition of incoming noise from each transmitter. The term *optical beat interference* (OBI) is sometimes applied to this phenomenon. Also, the received power from each return laser must be the same. Optical combining is not a recommended practice.

Yet another problem with combining lasers is that with time and temperature, the laser wavelength may drift. Thus, when you set up a combining situation, things may look fine because the lasers are sufficiently separated in wavelength. But hours, days, or months later, they may drift close to each other, creating OBI.

Since DFB lasers have relatively narrow ranges of operational wavelengths, it may be possible to combine them. You must ensure that the wavelengths will stay sufficiently separate over life, temperature, and modulation. Because F-P lasers have a less well-defined wavelength operating range, optical combining when F-P lasers are being used is particularly dangerous. Optical combining may work when it is first implemented, but if at a later date the two lasers drift to the same wavelength, the link could fail.

Of course, any node combining will exacerbate the effects of noise funneling because more noise sources are being summed. Also, the more nodes you combine, the lower the bandwidth per subscriber. Because of these factors, it is becoming less common to combine nodes and more common to split nodes into several distinct return paths.

8.10 SPURIOUS SIGNALS IN THE RETURN PATH

Of paramount concern to operators of two-way plant is noise induced into the return path. Anecdotal and numerical evidence points to the house as being the prime contributor of noise, with the drop contributing the next largest amount. Most practitioners contend that the hard-line plant is not responsible for many noise problems with the exception of common path distortion.

Considerable investigation has gone into this problem of noise on the return plant. Figure 8.17[7] illustrates a fairly typical result. This is a three-dimensional plot

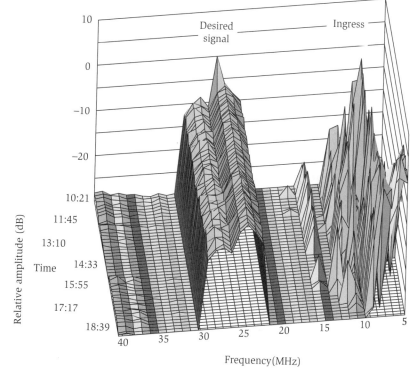

FIGURE 8.17

Interference versus frequency and time.

of the frequency and time of interference in the return band. Frequency is plotted along the bottom of the chart, progressing from right to left. Along the left edge is plotted time over a period of about nine hours. The vertical axis represents the relative level of signal observed. These data were taken with a special-purpose receiver, which can sample signals sequentially at a number of frequencies. The data was stored on a computer for later analysis. Other investigators have used a spectrum analyzer interfaced to a computer. A third method for obtaining the data is to capture the return spectrum on a high-speed digital oscilloscope and do a fast Fourier transform (FFT) on the resultant waveform. (An FFT is a mathematical way of computing the frequency spectrum of a complex waveform.)

Figure 8.17 shows considerable interference at lower frequencies. The frequency spectrum below about 7 MHz is relatively invisible in the upper right-hand corner of the box, but shows less occupancy (by interfering signals) in the morning than in the afternoon. This is consistent with typical off-air usage patterns on these frequencies, which exhibit better propagation characteristics during the later parts of the day and at night. The large energy content between about 22 and 30 MHz is an intentional return signal. The other energy content represents ingress. Above about 15 MHz, this node is essentially ingress free. Below this frequency, interference is substantial and has the distinct probability of causing serious interference with communications.

That the spectrum below about 15 or 20 MHz is relatively "dirty" and the higher spectrum tends to be much cleaner is a fairly typical result. Traditional services, such as status monitoring and return signals from set-top terminals, use relatively robust signaling methods, such as FSK and QPSK, at low data rates. These are transmitted in this lower portion of the band, where interference is worse. The nature of the transmissions is that if one transmission doesn't get through, the system will try again and nothing is lost.

8.10.1 Plant Unavailability Analysis Based on Undesired Signals

Measurement of the quality of the upstream signal path is complicated by the absence of a spectrum of steady-state known signals and by the varying nature and presence of the undesired signals.

Generally, the dominant interfering signals are common path distortion (CPD), discrete ingress signals, and electrical transients (impulsive noise). The first two result in signals that may be present for relatively long periods but occupy narrow frequency bands, whereas transients are present for a very short duty cycle, but may have broad spectral content. Even though they have a broad spectral content, they may *appear* on a spectrum analyzer to have a narrow spectral content. For example, consider a circuit that arcs at the peak of an ac waveform. It puts out a broad spectrum when it is arcing, but is quiet the rest of the time. When you look at the interference on an oscilloscope, you may see a relatively narrow spike of power at whatever frequency the spectrum analyzer is sweeping when the arc occurs. On different sweeps, the signal may appear at different frequencies unless the analyzer is synchronized to the ac line (in the example). You can determine that this is what is happening by slowing the analyzer's sweep speed down very low, in which case you will start to see the broad spectrum that really exists.

It is important to be able to measure these two classes of signals (discrete and impulsive) separately since their effects and the required countermeasures are different:

- Because discrete signal interference varies with time and frequency, the most effective countermeasure is often the ability of a service to shift the upstream frequencies as required to avoid these signals. In order to do that, the headend equipment must continually monitor the spectrum from each node and keep a list of available frequency bands.

- Because electrical transients are typically very brief in duration, the most effective countermeasure is often some combination of interleaving (to prevent one transient burst from affecting more bits than can be corrected by the error-correction capability of the FEC) and adequate FEC techniques to correct isolated errors. FEC is a technique whereby additional bits are added to a transmitted packet in order to allow errors in the transmitted packet to be detected and corrected. Interleaving is a technique whereby the order of bits in a transmission is changed to improve the effectiveness of FEC in the case of a noise burst. Neither FEC nor interleaving is something that you can affect in the field—it must be, and usually is, designed into the transmission system.

The following two measurement techniques are offered as examples of industry practice in this area. The first measures the entire spectrum and range of possible operating levels but includes only discrete signals, whereas the second measures multiple types of interference but on only a single channel at a single defined operating level.

8.10.2 Discrete Interfering Signal Probability

An NCTA-recommended practice for quantification of discrete interfering signals is discrete interfering signal probability (DISP).[8] This procedure was developed by Large and Bullinger as a result of extensive field testing.[9]

Continuous spectrum analyzer measurements are taken over the entire upstream spectrum. The operating parameters are set to reject transients so that the measurements reflect only discrete signals. The level reading at each frequency on each sweep is downloaded to an attached computer for analysis. Each reading is compared with several predefined thresholds to create a three-dimensional matrix whose axes are frequency, time, and level, and whose values are the probability that a signal is present, at a given frequency and time, whose amplitude exceeds a given threshold.

From this matrix, postprocessing is used to derive overall discrete signal/CPD performance of the system as a function of threshold, system availability as a function of frequency and operating level, channel availability as a function of time and operating level, and other data as required.

8.10.3 **Plant Unavailability Analysis Based on Threshold Boundaries**

Studies have been made of the availability of return plant using a CW tester developed at Cable Television Laboratories (CableLabs).[10] The technique uses a CW carrier in the return band and analyzes the characteristics of the signal received at the headend to predict the error rate of a signal at that frequency and with that bandwidth. From the data, we can predict the percent availability of a channel. Whereas the DISP measurement was based on interference amplitude measurement, the CableLabs technique analyzes the errors in location of a point in the data constellation (the data constellation is a graphical display of the discrete steps of a digital transmission).

Figure 8.18 illustrates the CW tester block diagram and the resulting constellation. A CW carrier is added somewhere in the node to be studied. At the headend, the carrier is up-converted to the normal TV IF of 44 MHz and passed through a SAW filter. After AGC (not shown), the signal is supplied to a phase-locked loop, which generates quadrature demodulating carriers.

The outputs of the demodulator are supplied to a digital sampling oscilloscope and to a window comparator that determines when the signal is outside the accurate decoding window. The accurate decoding window, as shown in Figure 8.18, is the decoding window for 16 QAM. While the constellation point is in the window, the correct state

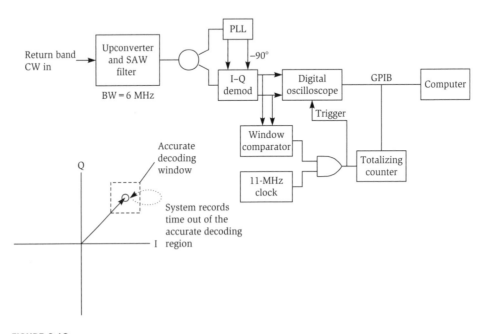

FIGURE 8.18

CW tester and constellation.

is decoded. While it is outside the window, a totalizing counter counts pulses from an 11-MHz clock. The output of the totalizing counter is accumulated by a computer, along with output data from the oscilloscope.

The constellation diagram at the bottom of the figure illustrates the data point crossing the threshold to the region occupied by another state. Assume for a moment that the study concerns use of 16-QAM modulation on the return carrier. The box defining the threshold region, in which the signal will be correctly demodulated, is shown. If a disturbance of any kind causes the carrier to go outside the box, the totalizing counter is started and measures the total time the signal is out of the box. From this information, we obtain the symbol error rate (SER), equal to the proportion of time out of the accurate decoding region. If we assume that the channel is available when the SER is below some level (10^{-5} in the example shown), then we can chart the percent of unavailability of the channel.

Note that the parameter measured is called the *symbol* error rate rather than the *bit* error rate. This is because it is the symbol that is subject to error and typically each symbol comprises two or more bits.

Figure 8.19 illustrates the symbol error rate and consequent percentage of unavailability of nodes in several cable systems based on one set of tests. Each was observed for about 1 week. To the left is a logarithmic scale showing the symbol

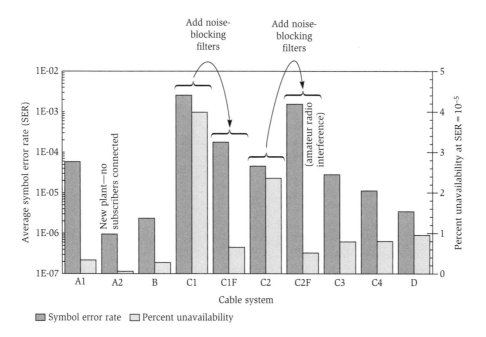

FIGURE 8.19

SER and percent unavailability of selected nodes.

error rate, and to the right is a scale showing the percent of unavailability. Note node A2, which was a new node with no subscribers. Its good performance is evidence of the observation made by others that drops and house wiring tend to be responsible for many return path problems.

Nodes C1 and C2 were studied with and without noise-blocking filters. Noise-blocking filters are high-pass filters placed on taps to prevent in-home–generated noise from reaching the return path. In node C2, interference developed from an amateur radio operator during the testing; nonetheless, the percent of unavailability dropped significantly when the filters were added. The symbol error rate and unavailability improved dramatically in node C1 when the filters were added. This observation again lends credence to the hypothesis that the home is responsible for most of the problems in return path operation. It also attests to the efficacy of noise-blocking filters (covered in more detail later in this chapter).

8.11 CHARACTERISTICS OF A COMPOSITE REVERSE SIGNAL

A sinusoid (CW signal) has a well-known peak-to-average ratio given by $20 \log \sqrt{2} = 3$ dB. A composite signal composed of n carriers of equal level and randomly phased has a total average power n times the power of one carrier, or $10 \log n$ dB greater than one carrier.[11] The peaks add on a voltage basis (because at some time they will all add in phase), so the peak power is $10 \log(2n^2)$ dB greater than the average power of a single carrier. As more carriers are added, the peak power compared with the average power increases, though the peak is reached for progressively shorter times.

This peak-to-average ratio argues again for the characterization of return lasers using NPR techniques rather than discrete carriers. When a number of carriers are combined, as for transmission on a return optical transmitter, the composite signal is noise-like in its amplitude and frequency characteristics. A noise-like signal has a well-defined and measurable average power, but it does not have a distinct peak value. Very occasionally, a high peak comes along, which will cause the laser (and electronic amplifiers) to clip.

As we add more carriers to the signals applied to a laser, the more noise-like the signal becomes in terms of peak-to-average ratio. Figure 8.20 illustrates the addition of carriers. Plotted on the x-axis is the probability (percentage of time) that the waveform will exceed the average value by the number of decibels shown on the y-axis. For example, look at the x-axis value of 10%. Following it up to the three-carrier line shows that a signal consisting of three (sinusoidal) carriers exceeds its average value by just over 4 dB for 10% of the time. If the total signal comprises more than three signals, it will exceed its RMS value by at least 4.5 dB for 10% of the time.

As the graphs level off (toward the left side of the figure), it is proper to speak of the y-axis as representing the peak-to-average ratio. For three carriers, the

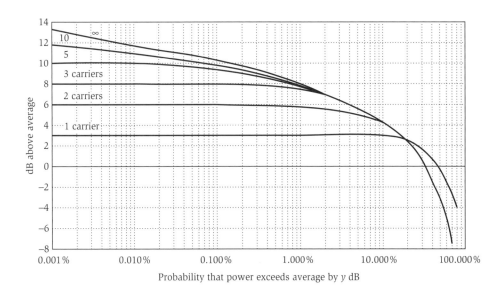

FIGURE 8.20

Peak-to-average ratio of multiple CW carriers.

peak-to-average ratio is about 8 dB; for five carriers, it is about 10 dB. We cannot see the peak-to-average ratio for a larger number of carriers because it occurs for a smaller fraction of the time than 0.001%, the leftmost value on the graph.

As the number of carriers is increased, the curve approaches that of random noise, which has a distribution equal to the infinite curve. This is a confirmation of the central limit theorem from statistics. Stated in engineering terms, the central limit theorem may be expressed as follows:

> *The sum of independent variables, X_j, will be normal for $n \to \infty$, even if the X_j each have a different distribution, provided that ... the variance of any one term is negligible compared to the variance of the sum. If this is not so, the term whose variance is not negligible will predominate in the sum and its distribution will still be apparent in that of the sum.[12]*

This demonstrates one of the shortcomings of evaluating the return laser with four CW carriers, as described earlier. The peak-to-average ratio of four carriers is around 9 dB, much less than the peak-to-average ratio of random noise or, equivalently, a large number of independent signals sharing the return spectrum. A composite signal consisting of 10 carriers will have a peak-to-average ratio of about 13 dB, within 2 dB of the peak- (probability 10^{-8}) to-average ratio of random noise, so this signal may be acceptable for testing purposes.[13] However, in terms of peak-to-average ratio, random noise remains the most appropriate test signal (and is readily available from test equipment).

8.12 REACTION OF ACTIVE COMPONENTS TO SIGNAL CHARACTERISTICS

The "peaky" nature of the signals has caused a great deal of concern within the engineering community regarding the reaction of laser transmitters to the peaks in the signal. The issue is receiving renewed attention with DOCSIS 3.0 systems, which add to the load of the upstream path, using very noise-like signals.

8.12.1 Effect of Laser Clipping—Frequency Domain View

The effect of laser clipping in the frequency domain can be analyzed as done by West.[14] Figure 8.21a illustrates no laser clipping. The laser transfer characteristic curve shows that, with laser bias current (the x-axis), there is no light output until a threshold current is reached, above which the light output power is proportional to the current through the laser. The input signal is shown below the transfer curve,

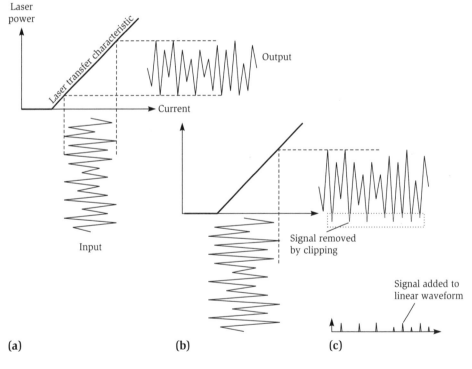

(a) (b) (c)

FIGURE 8.21

Laser in the linear region and in mild clipping. (a) No clipping. (b) Clipping. (c) Quasi-impulse of the clipping signal.

and the output is shown to the right. So long as the input signal remains such that the light output never drops to zero, changes in the output light are proportional to changes in the input current.

As shown in Figure 8.21b, if the input signal current is such that the light output ceases for a portion of the input signal, then the light output "clips" the signal. The portion of the signal represented by the dotted line is not really transmitted, so the signal is distorted. One way to model this is to assume that the signal was converted to light with no clipping, but then a signal was added exactly equal in amplitude and opposite in phase, to the portion of the signal clipped. This "added" signal is shown in Figure 8.21(c). It represents a series of near-impulses, which have a frequency spectrum that extends from some very low frequency equal to the lowest beat note between any elements of the input signal to very high frequencies. Thus, the spectrum of the clipping energy extends from very low frequencies to frequencies generally exceeding the bandwidth of the return path. The result is noise degradation, as represented by the degradation in NPR on the right side of Figure 8.16 and earlier figures.

8.12.2 Amplifier Characteristics

RF amplifiers tend to react similarly to the peaky nature of the return signals. Typically, the dynamic range in which satisfactory performance is achieved is somewhat better than with return lasers, but many of the same concerns apply.

8.13 COMMON PATH DISTORTION

Common path distortion (CPD) manifests itself as a series of beats in the return spectrum, located at multiples of 6 MHz (for North American systems using 6-MHz channel spacing). The distortion is a result of intermodulation of the downstream signals. The cause has usually been found to be mechanical connections at passive components in the common path of the upstream and downstream signals. Examples of such points are connectors, taps, drops, and terminators. These components handle the combined upstream and downstream signals, as opposed to amplifiers and nodes, which separate signals bound in the two directions.

Any mechanical junction is potentially a source of CPD if it handles signals in both directions. If the junction exhibits any nonlinearity, then intermodulation develops. Corrosion on the mating surfaces will typically create such a nonlinearity. Mitigation consists of careful selection of materials on mating surfaces to minimize corrosion and to ensure that the connections are airtight, meaning that they are held in place with so much force that there is a region never in contact with air so that corrosion cannot take place. (Corrosion requires water, which can, and usually does, come from humidity, or water in the air. You cannot keep water out of the air, so you must keep air out of the connector, at least at a particular spot.)

This latter criterion is not easy to achieve. Often, because of temperature fluctuations or mechanical vibrations, a point on a contact that is airtight at one time will at another time be exposed to air. Corrosion can develop whenever water (in the air) is present. This mechanism has been called *fretting corrosion*.

There have been reports of components that were assembled with small contacts between—for example, ground components such as a terminating resistor. Small contacts with relatively little force holding them together are particularly susceptible to fretting corrosion, especially if inappropriate materials are used. However, the majority of devices using mechanical connections work quite well today; manufacturers have had extensive experience with the problem and are able to control it well.

8.14 RETURN PATH INTERFERENCE MITIGATION TECHNIQUES

A number of proposals have been made for noise mitigation on the return path. Some operators who have reasonably new and properly installed plant feel that noise mitigation of any sort is unnecessary. However, it is not possible for the cable operator to maintain control over in-house wiring over time since the subscriber has the legal right to provide his or her own wiring. Traditionally, the availability of poor-quality coaxial cable and connectors in the consumer market, coupled with lack of proper training and installation tools, has resulted in degradation of in-home wiring over time. Some success has been achieved by operators who make available installation kits having high-quality components and, perhaps, instructions for proper installation. Some operators have also worked with local retail establishments to ensure that they carry quality components.

Figure 8.22 summarizes a number of mitigation techniques. They involve putting something in the hard line between amplifiers or at the drop (or in some cases at a splitter in the house). Several approaches have been proposed, and they are summarized here. While in-home mitigation interference is still important, arguably the situation is getting better as the industry moves to ever-smaller nodes in order to increase data capacity. This has the added benefit of less opportunity for noise funneling. On the other hand, there are more noise-generating devices in the home than ever.

8.14.1 Option 1: Drop Filters

Drop filters can be used to remove return band energy that might be coming out of the house. Two alternatives, 1a and 1b, are shown in Figure 8.22. Option 1a is a high-pass filter that cuts off below about 54 MHz, the low end of the forward band. It is intended for use at homes not taking any services requiring two-way communications. With typically 25 to 40 dB of attenuation in the return band, the filter does not allow return band signal power in the home to reach the hard-line plant.

Filter option 1b is similar to 1a except that a bypass is added to allow signals in a narrow band to pass. These are used when the home has a video-on-demand (VOD)

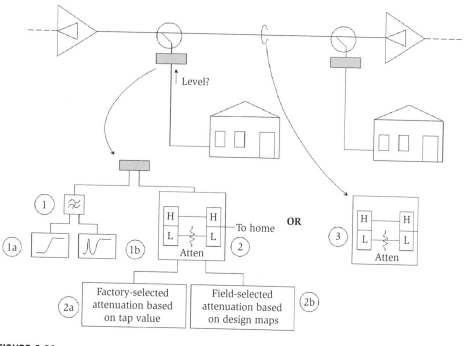

FIGURE 8.22

Options for in-home interference mitigation.

set top or a cable modem, both of which must communicate back to the headend on these frequencies. Interference from the home that occurs in the passband obviously appears in the hard-line plant, but interference coming out of the house at other frequencies is blocked.

Filters are usually placed at the tap, though they may be placed at the side of the home in some cases. They are sometimes seen as a stopgap measure because they do not remove the root cause of the problem, and they interfere with provision of modern two-way services in the home. Since customers can purchase two-way hardware (such as a cable modem) at retail and install it themselves (a desirable way to sell data services), the filter can cause particular difficulties. In addition, the filter is seen by some as an undesirable expenditure at homes not paying for enhanced two-way services. Countering this last argument is the thought that use of the filters postpones the day that homes *not* taking two-way services will have to have their internal distribution wiring improved.

Even when two-way services are added to the home, it may be possible to split signals at some point, with a new cable supplying only the device requiring return facilities. The filter can then be placed in the path to all services not requiring two-way facilities.

8.14.2 Option 2: Return Attenuation

A second interference mitigation option is to provide, in the tap or externally, two diplex filters, which separate the upstream frequency band (5 to 42 MHz) from the downstream band (54+ MHz). An attenuator is inserted into the low side of the diplex filter chain so that the loss is increased in the return direction while not changing the loss in the forward direction. The rationale is that tap values are selected to yield the correct signal level at the highest downstream frequency. Since cable loss is roughly proportional to the square root of the frequency, the loss in the upstream direction is considerably lower than in the downstream direction. Thus, whereas the *downstream received* level is the same at all houses (within a certain range), the *upstream transmit* level is significantly different between homes.

Figures 8.7 and 8.8 illustrate the range of levels that can be expected in a particular node that was analyzed for return level. Generally, as you move downstream from an amplifier, the tap value is reduced to compensate for signal loss at the high end of the downstream band. Since return signals suffer much less loss, the required upstream transmit level is reduced as you move downstream from an amplifier. Since the taps farther from an amplifier require a lower transmit level, they also admit more potential interference from the house.

The thought behind adding the attenuator in the return direction is that this will bring taps requiring a low signal level up to requiring a higher signal level. In the process, it will attenuate interference coming out of those homes. It would not deter return services from being installed, as might filters. However, the diplexers would add some group delay. You can in many cases add attenuation at reverse amplifiers and accomplish the same good without using additional diplexers. This option demands major caution: if an attenuator is to work to reduce noise, it must be added such that noise is reduced but the demanded signal levels from all upstream transmitters stay within their design values. Putting an attenuator just before an upstream transmitter in a node and then increasing the gain of the node, for example, will not do you any good—you cannot improve the C/N once it has been degraded.

Option 2a: Factory Selection of Attenuation Based on Tap Value

Within the spectrum of options for the return band attenuators is the possibility that the value of return attenuation is selected at the factory, based on the tap value. This would not place any additional burden on field installation personnel, who treat the tap as they would any other tap. The problem with this approach, however, is that the range of transmit levels required at any particular tap value (Figure 8.7) is so great that factory selection of an attenuator value would be very difficult.

Figure 8.23 illustrates an attempt in one real node to add reverse attenuation. In this example, all tap values 23 dB and less had reverse attenuation added such that the total attenuation in the reverse spectrum equaled 23 dB. (Figure 8.23 is plotted the same way as Figure 8.7.) Dots show the required levels before addition of the reverse attenuation, and the + signs show the required levels after. Note that after adding attenuation, some of the low-value taps now require the highest return

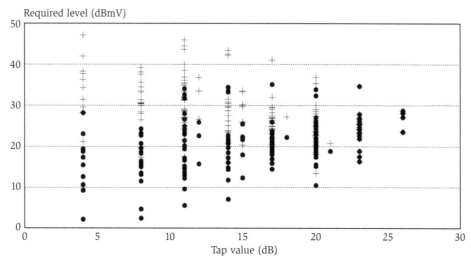

Required level (dBmV)

● Without attenuators   + With fixed attenuators

Note: Level required to obtain 0 dBmV at node.

FIGURE 8.23

Required tap level with and without reverse attenuation.

levels. The reason is that some low-value taps are placed after a lot of cable attenuation, so they benefit from a lot of added attenuation. Other low-value taps follow a directional coupler so that the loss is primarily flat (frequency-insensitive) loss, and the return signal level required after addition of the attenuation is high. This is not a good condition since it could require excessive output level from a transmitter.

Preliminary analysis has raised questions about the efficacy of factory selection of attenuator values. If the amount of attenuation added is low enough to prevent possible excessive level requirement, the benefit derived is minimal.

Option 2b: Field Selection of Attenuation Based on Design Maps

The other option for attenuators in taps is to provide a plug-in attenuator that is selected in the field, based on computed gain back to the previous amplifier. This technique shows considerable promise to improve the ingress problem while permitting return transmitters to be designed with a very narrow return signal range. The problem is that additional burden is placed on field installation personnel, who first have to select the tap based on system design and then have to select the correct attenuator value to plug in. After the tap is installed, it is not possible to inspect the attenuator for the correct value. If the tap value is changed later, the new tap may not be equipped with the optimum attenuator value.

8.14.3 Option 3: Move Diplexers and Attenuator to Midspan

Others have suggested that the diplexer be moved from the tap to approximately midspan between amplifiers, and that the attenuation used be selected to make the transmit levels required downstream of the diplexer roughly equal to those before the diplexer. This would reduce the number of diplexers required by somewhere around a factor of three or four, compared with putting them in taps. It does necessitate inserting another device into the hard-line cable. Co-locating the diplexers with an equalizer has been suggested, but this does not seem to be optimum.

Preliminary analysis indicates that such placement, combined with optimum attenuation selection in the field, would significantly reduce the signal level range required of transmitters. However, the estimated improvement in ingress is not particularly good, raising questions about the efficacy of the technique.

Note that the industry has not firmed up its philosophy for applying these ingress countermeasures. Future work may reveal advantages that are not obvious at this time and may result in newer techniques that yield more benefit. Also, it is possible that the industry will learn how to improve performance of problem homes without having to use any of the techniques shown in this section.

8.14.4 Option 4: Use Frequency Hopping

Many services that use return plant service have provisions for frequency hopping. They can move from one frequency to another if their original frequency develops interference problems that make communications unreliable. The problem with this, of course, is that as the return band is filled, fewer options for frequency hopping exist.

8.14.5 Option 5: Use Error Correction

Error correction is often added to digital data streams to allow correction of any bits that are corrupted in transmission. The effect is to sharpen the curve of error rate versus carrier-to-noise (or interference) ratio. As noise increases, the recovered signal retains its quality longer, but at some point the quality will collapse rapidly with worsening carrier-to-noise ratio.

8.15 UPSTREAM SIGNAL POWER APPORTIONMENT

We showed earlier that an optimum operating level (the power sum of all upstream signals) for a return path laser exists—at the peak of the NPR curve. It is desirable to set the actual operating level as close to this as possible without going over the limit where clipping gets to be a significant issue. The operator must take into account temperature effects, errors in level setting, and laser loading due to ingress. He or she must also account for future services that may be added; it is not good to go back and readjust operating levels to accommodate a new service.

8.15.1 **Power Apportionment Philosophy**

After the operating point has been determined by selecting an appropriate operating point on the NPR curve, it remains to apportion power among multiple services intelligently. This section gives two examples of how an upstream optical transmitter should be operated under different conditions. The philosophy we are following for setting return path levels is a little different from that followed by some, but we feel this optimizes each return path signal, giving it the same probability of getting through (absent interference) while preventing excessive clipping in the laser. The philosophy is to first determine the operating power level of the upstream transmitter by referring to the NPR curves of Figures 8.13 through 8.16 (in the real world, you would refer to the transmitter manufacturer's published curves). NPR curves are published by transmitter manufacturers. The optimum operating point is assumed to be slightly to the left of the peak in the NPR curve. Ideally, you would want to operate at the peak of the curve, but considering the number of variables in the real world, and considering the consequences of accidentally getting into clipping, we choose to operate a few dB to the left of the optimum point in order to give headroom.

Once the optimum operating power point is determined from the NPR curves, we must apportion the power to each service using the return path. We apportion the power as follows:

- For a given modulation type, allocate signal power proportional to the bandwidth of the signal, since a wider bandwidth signal requires more power than a narrow one—the amount of noise admitted to the detector is proportional to the bandwidth of the receive filter, and the receive filter bandwidth is proportional to the bandwidth of the signal (taking into account filter shape factors, of course). This is sometimes called the *constant power density* method of power allocation.

- For different modulation types, we adjust the amplitude according to the need of the modulation. For instance, 16-QAM modulation requires about 4 dB better C/N than does a QPSK signal of the same bandwidth.[15] Thus, a 16-QAM signal will be carried at 4-dB greater amplitude than will a similar-bandwidth QPSK signal.

At the book's website, *www.elsevierdirect.com/companions/9780123744012*, there is a spreadsheet that will do the work for you. In addition, it will compute the level your spectrum analyzer should show for each signal. You put in the NPR operating point and the types of signals you are putting on the upstream path; the spreadsheet lists and provides a graph of the signals, their occupied spectrum, the total level of the signal, and the level reading shown by a spectrum analyzer (assuming you can trigger it on the desired signal). In addition, it computes the C/N *of the optical portion of the return path only.* You will need to combine the C/N of the optical portion with the rest of the network using Equation 3.2. Instructions for using the spreadsheet are on the website. The following examples are calculated using this program, but we have added annotation to the graphs, that cannot be displayed in the spreadsheet.

8.15.2 Example 1: Few Return Services, F-P Laser

The first example illustrates the apportionment of signal power for a fairly simple node having only a few return path services and using a Fabry–Perot (F-P) laser. The chosen operating point is a total signal power into the transmitter of +15 dBmV (−60.4 dBmV/Hz), where the laser exhibits about 42 dB NPR at room temperature. In practice, you may want to operate slightly lower on the curve to allow more room for error, but we assume this point for illustration.

The services assumed include the following:

1. A status-monitoring carrier using FSK modulation at a center frequency of 10 MHz, with an occupied bandwidth of 250 kHz (total, not plus and minus), conforming to ANSI/SCTE 25-1 2002. We will assume that the C/N required is the same as for a BPSK carrier. The actual performance of an FSK carrier depends on the deviation, but our assumption will be close.

2. A set-top return carrier conforming to SCTE 55-2 at 18 MHz, with an occupied bandwidth of 1.5 MHz, QPSK modulation. QPSK needs about 3 dB better C/N than does a BPSK signal at the same bandwidth.

3. A DOCSIS 2.0 RF return using QPSK, centered at 22 MHz.

4. A DOCSIS 2.0 RF return using 16-QAM, centered at 30 MHz, with an occupied bandwidth of 3.2 MHz. 16-QAM requires about 4 dB better C/N than QPSK, or 7 dB better C/N than BPSK for the same bandwidth.

A significant omission from this list (intentional to keep the example simple) is an allocation for future expansion. It is essential that all future services be allocated the amount of power they will need when added. Failure to do so can result in extreme laser clipping later, and possibly a situation where a node that previously worked no longer does. Also, we have not allowed for ingress. It is advisable to allow some power for ingress.

The signal levels are set such that the total signal power is equal to the total at the operating point of the NPR curve, for example, +15 dBmV. The signals must be added on a power basis. If the levels of the four signals are L1, L2, L3, and L4, in dBmV, then the power must add to the target power, in this case +15 dBmV (equivalent to −60.4 dBmV/Hz if the noise bandwidth at which the NPR is measured is 35 MHz):

$$\text{total power} = 10 \log\left(10^{L1/10} + 10^{L2/10} + 10^{L3/10} + 10^{L4/10}\right) = +15 \text{ dBmV}$$

Note that although signal level is expressed in dBmV, as is customary in the cable television industry, we are actually manipulating signal power, expressed in dBmV in a 75-ohm system. We can get away with this sleight of hand because we are working in a constant-impedance environment. Dividing each level by 10 rather than by 20 lets us effectively add powers. One cannot add power when that power is expressed in decibels. In the inner expression—taking the signal level, dividing by 10, and raising

10 to the power of the result—we are taking the antilog of the level expressed in dBmV. We have legitimate power units, though they are not commonly used units such as milliwatts. Signal level in dB is always a POWER ratio (with respect to some stated reference). For example, 0 dBmV refers to the *power* produced by a 1-mV rms signal across the working characteristic impedance (75 ohms in our case).

Figure 8.24 shows the levels of the signals in the example. In each case, the top—thicker—line is the actual level of the return signal, and the lower level is what shows on the spectrum analyzer, assuming the spectrum analyzer settings shown. The figure is not to be taken as a spectrum analyzer display: it is very hard to display the return spectrum on a spectrum analyzer because every signal is not always present. Either you would have to run the spectrum analyzer in peak detect mode for a long time, with slow sweep speed, or you would have to synchronize it with the return signal in order to get a display that looks like the lower lines on this display.

We have two QPSK signals, but one gets more total power than the other does because its occupied spectrum is wider (because the data rate is higher). We also have two signals 3.2 MHz wide, but one gets more power than the other does because it is of more complex modulation (16 QAM versus QPSK), and the more complex modulation needs better C/N to deliver error-free performance.

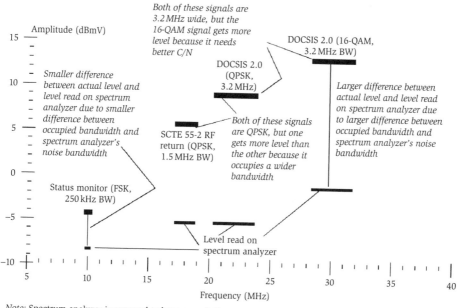

Note: Spectrum analyzer is assumed to have a resolution bandwidth of 100 kHz and a noise bandwidth of 120 kHz.

FIGURE 8.24

Signal-level apportionment, F-P laser, limited services.

Note that the example did not include an allowance for ingress, nor did it include an allowance for errors in level of the various return signals. As shown in Section 8.6, the signal levels at the return laser transmitter are controlled from the headend. Inevitably there will be some error in the control of the levels. Finally, allowance was not made for future services; you would be wise to allow for such future expansion of offerings.

8.15.3 Example 2: More Return Services, DFB Laser

The next example involves a DFB return laser carrying a greater number of signals. Power is apportioned first to the analog signal, giving it the level required to allow it to operate at the desired C/N. Next, the remaining signal capability of the laser is apportioned to the digital signals using a philosophy of constant power per Hertz within a type of modulation. As in the first example, the power per Hertz allocated to a signal is offset based on the modulation type, with denser modulation formats receiving a proportionately larger share of the power per Hertz to allow for their greater sensitivity to noise.

For the DFB transmitter, we will select an input level of 18 dBmV and a corresponding NPR of 47 dB as our operating point.

The following signals are included in this example:

1. A set-top return carrier (according to SCTE 55-1) at 7.5 MHz, with an occupied bandwidth of 192 kHz, QPSK modulation.

2. A DOCSIS 2.0 RF return using 16 QAM, centered at 15 MHz, with an occupied bandwidth of 3.2 MHz.

3. An analog video return signal from the local high school, with a picture carrier at 31 MHz. Its amplitude is set to yield 50 dB C/N from the laser path (noise in other portions of the path will reduce the C/N). Remember that if you are going to handle an analog return signal, the transmitter must be specified to have adequate linearity to keep distortion products out of the analog signal.

4. A 64-QAM DOCSIS 3.0 signal centered at 19 MHz with a bandwidth of 3.2 MHz.

5. A 64-QAM DOCSIS 3.0 signal centered at 23 MHz with a bandwidth of 3.2 MHz.

The digital signals get their allocation of power from the power left over after the analog signal receives enough power allocation to yield the desired C/N.

Figure 8.25 summarizes the level of all signals, using the procedure already outlined. The DOCSIS 2.0 and 3.0 signals have the same bandwidth, but we have assumed that the DOCSIS 2.0 signal is 16-QAM modulation and that the two DOCSIS 3.0 bonded carriers are 64-QAM modulation. Since the 64-QAM signal is about 4.6 dB more sensitive to noise than is the 16-QAM signal, the level is increased by this amount. The spreadsheet on the website is set up with this example.

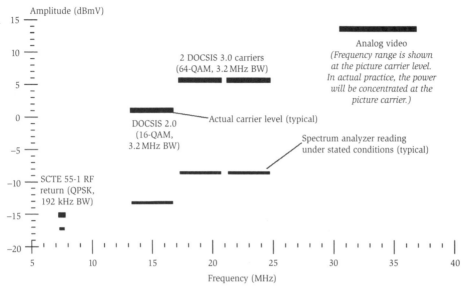

FIGURE 8.25

Signal apportionment, DFB laser, and more services.

8.16 **PRACTICAL LEVEL SETTING**

This is probably the most important part of the chapter and so should be read carefully. All the things we have talked about with respect to levels of return signals will go for naught if you do not pay close attention to this section.

Setting up return levels is not a simple matter of adjusting a level control until you get the right reading on a spectrum analyzer. (In fact, absent specialized techniques, a spectrum analyzer will not do you much good in the upstream direction. But fortunately there are valid ways to set upstream levels.) For this section, please refer all the way back to the discussion about Figure 8.6 early in this chapter. We have reproduced it with some example levels in Figure 8.26. The "design" signal levels and C/N are what are intended by the system design. The italicized *After "fix"* numbers illustrate a "fix" that goes wrong because of the long-loop ALC (discussed in the following paragraphs).

For instance, we assume a 16-QAM upstream carrier similar to that of the previous example. A 16-QAM signal needs an Eb/No of about 15 dB in order to produce a very low bit error rate. (Eb/No is a way of expressing C/N in terms of unit bandwidth, so that you take out the effect of RF bandwidth and bit rate. This is explained in Chapter 4 of our previous book, *Modern Cable Television Technology: Voice, Video and Data Communications*, 2nd edition (Morgan Kaufmann,

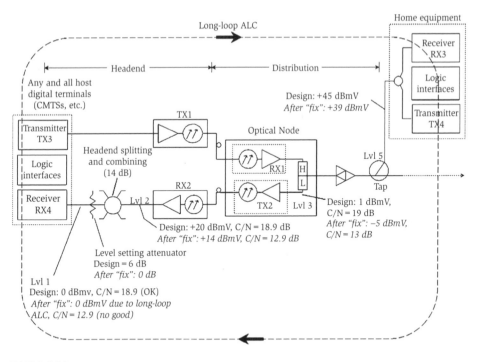

FIGURE 8.26

Example of the effect of long-loop ALC control.

2004.) Assuming DOCSIS 2.0 upstream at a baud rate of 5120 kbaud (the fastest DOCSIS 2.0 upstream speed), this converts to a required

$$C/N = 15 + 10\log(5120) - 10\log(3200) = 17 \text{ dB}$$

where

5120 = baud rate of data (kbaud)
3200 = receiver noise bandwidth (KHz)

We must achieve a C/N of 17 dB at the input of the upstream receiver in order to achieve a good bit error rate (without error correction).

8.16.1 Signal Level Issues

The signal levels computed in Sections 8.2 and 8.3 apply at the point where the NPR of the upstream optical transmitter, TX2, is measured. Usually this is the input to the upstream transmitter, Lvl 3 in Figures 8.6 and 8.26. However, it may be that a manufacturer will report NPR based on output power. Check the *x*-axis label of the published NPR curves. It will tell you where the NPR is measured. You may also see the input power listed as the total power rather than the power density (NPR). If total input power is listed, the units will be in dBmV rather than in dBmV per Hertz. The spreadsheet on the website will do the conversion for you: put in the power density in dBmV per Hertz, and read the corresponding total power. Be sure to change the measurement bandwidth if it is not 35 MHz.

For purposes of this example, we started with levels similar to those in Section 15.3, and we will concentrate on the DOCSIS 2.0 16-QAM signal, which should be at a level of +1 dBmV (rounded) into the upstream RF transmitter, TX2. We assume for the present illustration that the loss from the output of the house to the input of TX2 is such that we need a level of +45 dBmV coming out of the home. Furthermore, to make the example interesting, we assume that the C/N of the RF portion of the return is 19 dB. Where did we get this? We got it because it makes for an interesting example. You will need to fill in your own numbers, hopefully determined more objectively than what we did in this case.

Source Signal Level

Once you know the signal level into the upstream transmitter, Lvl 3 in Figure 8.6, you need to make sure this level works with the rest of the upstream system. The upstream system must be designed such that the level you choose for Lvl 3 allows all transmitters in homes to output enough level to produce Lvl 3 at the node. This part is pretty obvious, but the next part is not always obvious and is the source of a lot of problems with the upstream.

Signal Level at the Headend

So far, all we have talked about is the signal level at the upstream transmitter, Lvl 3, and that coming out of the home, Lvl 5. These levels are important in design of the system, but they cannot be conveniently observed. What we need to talk about really is the signal level at the headend. We have the signal level coming out of the upstream receiver, RX2. We call this signal level Lvl 2. It obviously depends on the level at the input to the transmitter TX2 at the node, and it also depends on the received optical level at the headend or hub. This level in turn is a function of the output level of transmitter TX2 and on the optical signal loss to the headend. The actual optical path is probably not as simple as we showed in Figure 8.6. There are optical connectors and splices that have loss, and of course the cable itself has loss. To an extent, the loss in the optical network is not completely known, and the headend signal level, Lvl 2, changes 2 dB for every 1 dB of optical signal level change due to the nature of optical transmission.

So what we are really interested in is the signal level at the headend, Lvl 2, even though our starting point in design of the return path was Lvl 3 at the optical node. We only know Lvl 2 with a lower level of accuracy due to ambiguities in the received optical level, combined with the ambiguity of the gain of RX3. But the problem gets worse in the next section.

Signal Level at the Headend Receiver

We showed a simple situation in Figure 8.6, with the output of upstream optical receiver RX2 being coupled to a single receiver RX4 in one host terminal such as a CMTS or a set-top control system. The real world is much more complex, though. You will have several receivers in the headend, maybe for several DOCSIS channels and for a set-top control system. The output of receiver RX2 must be split several ways to serve these receivers, and there may be some combining of the output of several nodes to service one set-top control receiver. All of these splits and combining steps have attenuation, represented in Figure 8.26 by an arbitrary 14-dB loss in the splitting and combining network at the output of RX2.

Now things start to get complicated. Recall the long-loop automatic level control (ALC) used by almost all return systems, and shown in Figures 8.6 and 8.26. Each receiver, RX4, has a target level at which it expects to receive its upstream signal. If this return level is not achieved, that host digital terminal will send a signal to the transmitter, TX4, at the home, adjusting its level until the headend receiver, RX4, gets the level it expects (its target level). Thus, all of the calculations we have done on return levels will go for naught if we do not make sure that the level we want at the optical node transmitter, Lvl 3, corresponds with the level receiver RX4 wants to see, Lvl 1. Achieving this for every return signal can be complex and becomes more so with every return service added. Getting these levels correct demands a good design of the headend network for every service from every node.

Furthermore, once you get everything at the right level, your problems are not over. For example, suppose you have a 16-QAM upstream channel that is experiencing $C/N = 18.6$ dB, roughly 1.5 dB better than you need for good data communications. Now suppose you decide you need a little more level on that return signal, possibly because you are experiencing a poor bit error rate. You have a 6-dB pad in front of receiver RX4, so it seems easy to take out that 6-dB pad and get more level at the receiver. Unfortunately, this is going to have the opposite effect of what you want. Taking out that 6-dB pad initiates the *After "fix"* situation in Figure 8.26.

When you try to send a 6-dB higher level to the receiver, that host digital terminal is going to send a signal to each in-home transmitter, TX4, telling it to turn down its level by 6 dB. So now the C/N drops 6 dB because we reduced the signal level on the return path by 6 dB, and suddenly a return path that was sort of working is not working at all. When we tried to increase the signal level at the headend receiver by removing an attenuator, we actually kept the signal level at the receiver constant but we decreased the C/N enough to cause the data communications path to fail. This happened because we triggered the long-loop ALC to reduce the carrier level in the return path, but the noise did not change. So the carrier-to-noise ratio, which we expected to improve, actually got worse.

Getting into Trouble the Other Way

We showed just before that you can get into trouble when you remove attenuation in order to get higher signal level (which would probably not have solved your problem anyway). You can also get into trouble the other way, by adding attenuation and driving signal levels up. Over time, you may add more upstream signals, which means possibly adding more upstream signal splitting. This will have the opposite effect on the system, of driving up the return signal levels. You might get away with this for a while, depending on the original system design, but sooner or later one of two things is going to happen.

You will drive upstream signal levels high enough that the upstream transmitters in some homes, TX4, cannot put out the required signal level. With luck, you will get an alarm when this happens.

You will drive the total signal power into the optical transmitter, TX2, over the peak of the noise power ratio (see Figure 8.11) and into the clipping region. When the return laser starts clipping too badly, your distortion goes up quickly and your upstream bit error rates go up very, very fast. There may be no alarm generated in this case, but you will know quickly that something is wrong.

The bottom line is that the upstream plant needs to be designed just as does the downstream plant, and once that happens, you need to stick within the design. The upstream design starts by determining signal levels at the input to the upstream transmitter at the optical node, and this signal level in turn drives a lot of other calculations. You have to make sure that the signal level you require at the input to the upstream transmitter is compatible with levels coming out of the home and through the RF portion of the plant. Then, at the headend, you have to know what signal level you are going to get out of the upstream receiver, you have to know the net loss between there and each receiver using the signals, and you have to make sure the signal level reaching the receiver RX4 equals the target level that the receiver is looking for. Each time you change the splitting and combining in the headend, you have to look at this issue again for every upstream service you operate. To paraphrase a scuba-diving expression, "Plan your build and build your plan."

8.17 SUMMARY

This chapter focused on a number of items of interest in operating the return HFC plant. It began with a description of the components unique to a two-way plant. We showed key characteristics of those components. Level setting in the return plant received a lot of attention because it is crucial to the operation of reliable return plant, just as it is to proper operation of the downstream plant. We examined lasers used for return services and gave practical methods of evaluating them. We discussed important characteristics of return signals and their interaction with the laser transmitters.

Noise in the return plant is important and received considerable attention, along with proposed mitigation methods. Finally, we gave examples of ways to set up the levels of various return services and showed how to estimate key performance parameters.

Chapter 9 deals with system architecture. Methods of plant design are described that optimize performance using the principles shown in this chapter.

ENDNOTES

1. Data courtesy of H. Carnes, R. Oberloh, et al. ANTEC, Norcross, GA. (This division is now part of Cisco.)

2. National Cable Telecommunications Association, "Upstream Transport Issues," *NCTA Recommended Practices for Measurements on Cable Television Systems*. The "Upstream" portion was added to the *Recommended Practices* in late 1997. This document is available from the NCTA, Washington, DC. See *http://www.ncta.com* and search for *Recommended Practices*.

3. John Kenny, "Characterization of Return Path Optical Transmitters for Enhanced Digitally Modulated Carrier Transmission Performance," *Technical Papers of the NCTA Annual Convention*, National Cable & Telecommunications Association, Washington, DC, 1997.

4. Lamar West, "Analysis of Reverse Path Laser Loading in HFC Networks," *HFC '97 Conference*, Phoenix, AZ, September 1997. Society of Cable Telecommunications Engineers, Exton, PA.

5. H. Blauvelt, et al., "Return Path Lasers for High Capacity Hybrid Fiber Coax Networks," *1995 NCTA Technical Papers*. National Cable & Telecommunications Association, Washington, DC.

6. Donald Raskin and Dean Stoneback, *Broadband Return Systems for Hybrid Fiber/Coax Cable TV Networks*. Upper Saddle River, NJ: Prentice-Hall, 1998. See especially Chapter 9.

7. Data courtesy of D. Junghans, of Arris Interactive, and T. Mitchell, formerly of Arris Interactive. Private communication.

8. "Supplement on Upstream Transport Issues," *NCTA Recommended Practices for Measurements on Cable Television Systems*, 2nd ed. Washington, DC: National Cable & Telecommunications Association, October 1997, pp. 57–63.

9. D. Large and R. Bullinger, "A Proposed Method for Quantifying Upstream Ingressing Carriers," *1997 NCTA Technical Papers*. National Cable & Telecommunications Association, Washington, DC.

10. Richard S. Prodan, et al., "Results of Return Plant Testing," *1997 NCTA Technical Papers*. National Cable & Telecommunications Association, Washington, DC.

11. This section is adapted from the *NCTA Recommended Practices for Measurements on Cable Television Systems*.

12. Petr Beckmann, *Probability in Communication Engineering*. New York: Harcourt, Brace & World, 1967, p. 107.

13. National Cable & Telecommunications Association, "Upstream Transport Issues."

14. West, "Analysis of Reverse Path Laser Loading in HFC Networks."

15. The concept of required C/N for various modulation types is covered in Chapter 4 of Ciciora et al., *Modern Cable Television Technology: Video, Voice and Data Communications*. Specifically, Figure 4.17 of the second edition plots bit error rate versus normalized (for bandwidth) carrier-to-noise ratio.

Architectural Requirements and Techniques

9.1 INTRODUCTION

The architecture of a cable system is a description of how the major elements—signal acquisition, signal processing, signal transport, and subscriber terminal equipment—are interconnected. The first step in selecting or analyzing a specific network architecture is to analyze the services to be delivered and their requirements. In a dynamic telecommunications market, however, service penetration and customer usage will grow and new services will emerge. Therefore, the second requirement of the selected network configuration is that its initial cost be consistent with expected revenues but that it be capable of scaling economically to meet market opportunities and customer demands. It is these analyses that this chapter will cover.

Distribution system architecture, however, is but a part of a much larger overall architecture that can include multiple layers of national, regional, and local processing and must take into account processing that is distributed between headend and CPE processes. For a more detailed treatment of these larger architecture issues, the reader is referred to our previous book, *Modern Cable Television Technology* (Morgan Kaufmann, 2004).

We discuss first the categories of service-related parameters that are affected by architecture, then the requirements of various specific service types, and, finally, scalability and the interaction of bandwidth assigned to each service with the physical granularity of the network. The emphasis will be on the process for setting standards and on alternative means of meeting those standards, rather than on suggesting specific values.

Chapter 10 will deal with specific HFC architectures and how they differ relative to the parameters discussed here. Chapter 11 will cover the same issues for emerging fiber-deep architectures. Chapter 12 will cover the calculation of network reliability and availability, given a specific equipment configuration.

9.2 PERFORMANCE PARAMETERS

Network performance can be measured by many "yardsticks." Signal quality in the broadband distribution system, including noise, distortion, levels, frequency response, and other related parameters, is extensively discussed in Chapters 2 through 8. Other architecture-affected topics are discussed in this chapter.

9.2.1 Information Capacity

The information capacity of a network that includes an RF FDM layer is a composite of many factors, including the RF bandwidth, the efficiencies of the processes by which raw information is encoded for modulation onto RF carriers, spatial reuse of the network, and efficient sharing among users with varying needs for information transmittal rate. Networks with linear fiber-optic links include another layer, which measures how much modulated RF spectrum can be carried through the optical cables. Not all of these parameters are relevant to certain fiber-deep architectures.

Optical Link Capacity

In linear optical links, as discussed in Chapter 4, a composite RF spectrum is used to modulate the amplitude of an optical source at one end of a link with a matching demodulation at the other end used to recover the modulating spectrum. The maximum bandwidth of the modulating spectrum is limited by the bandwidth and linearity of the modulating devices, by the minimum acceptable C/N of the link, and by the interaction between the modulated optical signal and the fiber medium. The trade-off among bandwidth, signal loading, noise, and distortion is similar to that for coaxial links.

The capacity of an optical link can be increased simply by installing cables containing multiple fibers. For example, most fiber-optic links between hubs and nodes use separate fibers for upstream and downstream communications. So long as the cables are not bent sharply, the crosstalk between signals on adjacent fibers is extremely low, and cables of less than an inch in diameter can hold approximately 1000 fibers.

As discussed in Chapter 5, however, it is also possible to send multiple modulated light signals through a shared fiber with a low level of mutual interference, so long as they are on sufficiently separated optical frequencies and the optical power levels are not too high. This is a form of FDM, but since optical wavelengths, rather than frequencies, are usually specified, it is known as *wavelength division multiplexing* (WDM).

Downstream RF Bandwidth

One of the fundamental measures of the broadband, linear distribution network is the range of frequencies used to transport signals toward customers. In residential coaxial distribution networks, the lower limit of downstream frequency range is constrained by the fact that upstream signals are almost always carried below downstream signals in shared cables.* Furthermore, the bands must be separated sufficiently that reasonable-cost diplex filters can be deployed in amplifier stations to properly route the different spectra for processing without causing amplifier instability or excessive group delay at the band edges. Additionally, systems that deliver analog television programming to residential customers must include the lowest over-air television channel within the downstream spectrum, whereas those not carrying such programming are sometimes designed with different crossover points between the bands. It is not clear what the carriage requirements will be after analog over-air television ceases in February 2009.

In both North and South America, the lowest VHF television channel starts at about 53 or 54 MHz depending on channelization plan, with the result that the lower downstream frequency limit is typically near 50 MHz (see Chapter 2 for a discussion of amplifier station internal RF circuitry, and the Appendix for details of standardized channelization plans). These are called *low-split* networks. Lower downstream band limits for some nonresidential networks are 150 MHz and 234 MHz, commonly called *mid-split* and *high-split* networks, respectively. Proposals for a modified "next-generation" mid-split configuration have been put forth to change the downstream/upstream crossover frequency in residential networks in the future, in order to expand the upstream spectrum to 85 MHz and start the downstream spectrum at 105 MHz. This would result in a loss of only five downstream channels (including the offset channels 5 and 6, which are affected by low-side CSO products) while more than doubling the upstream bandwidth. All four of these spectrum plans are illustrated in Figure 9.1. For networks requiring more RF bidirectional bandwidth, separate cables and amplifying stations may be used for each direction of transmission with dual coaxial cables, thereby freeing constraints on bandwidth in both directions. In the 1980s, a few dual-cable, low-split residential networks were constructed as a means of increasing both downstream and upstream bandwidths while retaining conventional channel plans, but most have been converted to single cables of extended bandwidth.

At the top end of the spectrum, the bandwidth of coaxial networks is limited primarily by amplifier technology. Chapter 3 contains a discussion of how total RF bandwidth can be balanced against other broadband performance parameters, such as levels, noise, and distortion. The maximum downstream frequency has steadily increased as technology has improved, with 750-, 870- and 1000-MHz amplifiers commercially available.

Upstream RF Bandwidth

Before 1990, few all-coaxial cable television systems were used for two-way communication with subscribers, for the very practical reason that large, all-coaxial plants

---

*One experimental network, however, carried upstream signals in the 900- to 1,000-MHz band, while another vendor offers equipment with additional downstream and upstream spectrum enabled between 1.2 and 2.5 GHz.

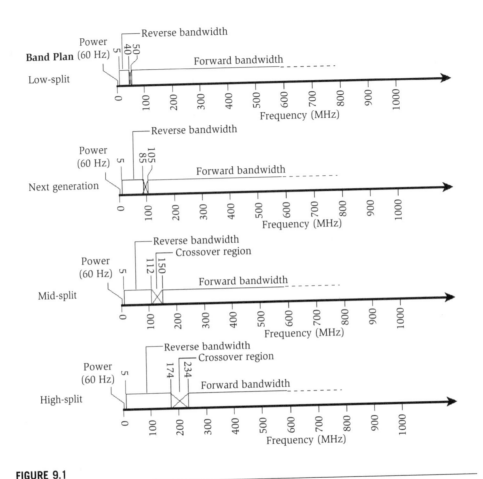

FIGURE 9.1

Common two-way spectrum plans.

contained so many amplifiers and branches that the combination of noise funneling and ingress made upstream communications problematic. Among those with two-way capabilities, some were used for point-to-point applications, in which the system had few, if any, upstream signal-combining points. Others were used to carry low-information-rate signals, such as data from two-way set-top converters or status monitoring, where only a single transmitter was activated at a time, upstream levels could be high, and rugged frequency shift keying (FSK) modulation was used. In the few systems that offered true subscriber interactivity (such as the pioneering Columbus, Ohio, "QUBE" system), electronic switches were employed at field branching points to dynamically reduce the effective upstream combining. Two-way operation is practical in modern HFC systems due primarily to the smaller, electrically separate, broadband distribution subnetworks. Chapter 8 discusses the unique problems with upstream communications.

The low end of the upstream spectrum is limited by the need to separate signals from the harmonics of the powering that is multiplexed with the RF signals. It is also effectively limited by the practical frequency range of the magnetic components used in amplifiers and passive elements, such as power inserters, taps, splitters, and directional couplers. The most common lower frequency limit is 5 MHz.

The upper end of the return spectrum is limited by the need to provide an adequate crossover band between upstream and downstream signals, and also by the need, in residential networks, to avoid feeding high-level signals into the input terminals of television receivers in the common intermediate frequency (IF) band, which is 41 to 47 MHz.

Typical upstream band limits in older amplifiers were 5 to 30 MHz, whereas modern designs are typically 5 to 40 MHz or a little higher. For nonsubscriber mid-split and high-split networks, the upper upstream frequency limits are typically 112 MHz and 174 MHz, respectively.

Bandwidth per Customer

The instantaneous RF bandwidth is one factor fundamentally limiting information capacity when a common set of signals is to be delivered to all customers, which was exclusively the case in the early history of cable television and true for much of the programming on most cable systems today. Increasingly, however, new services require communications paths to individual customers. To the extent that the network can be logically or physically divided into independent transmission systems, we can use the same frequencies to simultaneously deliver differentiated services to subscribers in different network sections. This is known generically as *space division multiplexing* (SDM).

A measure of the network's ability to deliver customized services is the *bandwidth per customer*. In the downstream direction this is simply equal to the instantaneous RF bandwidth devoted to some service divided by the number of homes in the smallest portion of the network that can be fed unique signals multiplied by the penetration of that service among homes passed. In the upstream direction, it is the bandwidth devoted to that service divided by the number of customers sharing that bandwidth at any point along the path. The upstream and downstream per-customer bandwidth requirements may be symmetrical (for instance, for telephone) or highly asymmetrical (for most interactive video services). Since service penetration changes with time, network capability is often measured in terms of achievable bandwidth per home passed rather than bandwidth per customer. Note also that the bandwidth per customer must be measured on a service-specific basis because different services will, in general, have different-sized service groups and communications symmetry requirements. While simply dividing the total system bandwidth by the smallest group of homes that can be fed independent signals may be useful as a measure of ultimately achievable throughput, it is of limited usefulness operationally.

The independence of upstream and downstream bandwidth in optical links has led to designs in which the upstream signals from each of several coaxial distribution legs emanating from a fiber node are frequency-translated to nonoverlapping bands and combined before feeding the upstream optical transmitter. Known as *block conversion*, this is discussed in Chapter 8 and illustrated in Figure 8.3. The major benefit is increased average upstream RF bandwidth per customer because signals can use the same upstream frequencies on different legs simultaneously without mutual interference. Although equipment is available commercially for this application, it has seldom been deployed. One factor may be that the phase noise requirements for both high-speed data and digital video are strict and the block conversion process inevitably eats into that aspect of the operating margin. In a more modern, but functionally equivalent version, each of several upstream legs is converted to a baseband digital signal, and the signals are then time-multiplexed and fed to a baseband transmitter. At the headend, the signals are demultiplexed and reconverted to the original RF spectra. All major manufacturers of optical nodes now offer this option.

It is usual in residential system planning to divide the available downstream bandwidth among common signals, those directed to large groups of customers, and those directed to individual customers. For example, it is efficient to distribute the most popular television channels systemwide, whereas local educational or government access channels may vary across a large system that covers several communities. Switched digital video service groups may serve areas of about 1000 homes, while individual cable modem data packets, on-demand movies, or digitized voice for telephony need to be directed to specific customers. Finally, revenue opportunities in targeted advertising will ultimately require sending ads to specific customers regardless of their viewing choices. Network architectures offering various levels of segmentation will be discussed in Chapter 10.

Figure 9.2 shows the elements in a simple HFC architecture that contribute to the determination of effective bandwidth per home passed for any given service. The effective downstream bandwidth per customer for any given service in that configuration is

$$B_c(\text{fwd}) = \frac{B_s(\text{fwd})}{P_s RHN} \qquad (9.1)$$

where

$B_c(\text{fwd})$ = the downstream bandwidth per subscriber to a specific service
$B_s(\text{fwd})$ = the total downstream bandwidth assigned to that service
P_s = the penetration of that service among homes passed
R = the number of nodes served from one downstream optical transmitter
H = the number of homes passed by the coaxial distribution lines extending from each node
N = the number of node transmitters fed from one service transmitter

In the reverse direction, the effective bandwidth per customer is given by

$$B_c(\text{rev}) = \frac{nB_s(\text{rev})}{mP_s H} \qquad (9.2)$$

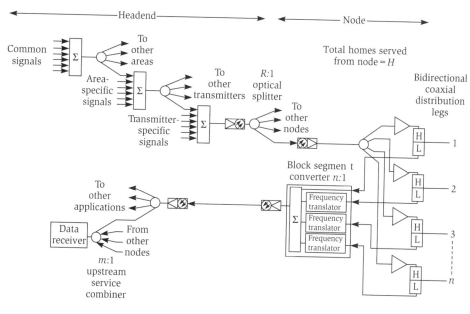

FIGURE 9.2

Factors controlling bandwidth per home.

where

$B_c(\text{rev})$ = the upstream bandwidth per subscriber to a specific service

$B_s(\text{rev})$ = the total upstream bandwidth assigned to that service

P_s = the penetration of that service among homes passed

H = the number of homes passed by the coaxial distribution lines extending from each node

m = the number of nodes whose signals are combined into each data receiver input

n = the number of independent (and equally sized) coaxial distribution lines emanating from each node whose signals are effectively isolated (using block converters, separate optical transmitters, separate data streams within shared digital transmitters, or other means) at nodes (Note that the upstream equation is valid only if the data receiver contains an independently functioning input module for each upstream frequency path created at the node.)

For example, a network consisting of multiple fiber nodes, each fed by an independent optical transmitter and each providing signals to a coaxial network passing 400 homes, can provide different programming to customers in those nodes than to those fed from other, similar nodes. If the downstream bandwidth allocated to wired telephone service is 6 MHz and the service penetration is 30% of homes passed, then the bandwidth per customer is 50 kHz. The bandwidth per customer can be converted to data throughput capability per customer by multiplying the bandwidth by the modulation efficiency in bits/second/Hz (b/s/Hz). 256 QAM has a bandwidth efficiency of 6.33 b/s/Hz, and so 50 kHz of per-customer bandwidth translates to 317 kb/s per customer on average, sufficient for five simultaneous uncompressed telephone calls.

If the upstream bandwidth was 2 MHz, multiple-input digital transmitters were used to isolate the signals from each of four coaxial 100-HP legs, and no node combining was used at the headend, then the return bandwidth per customer would be 66.7 kHz. If the upstream modulation had an efficiency of 3 Mb/s/MHz, the available throughput per customer would be 200 kb/s. Whether this is adequate depends on whether that bandwidth is all usable, how efficiently it is shared, and simultaneous usage rates among telephone subscribers. It can be increased, however, only by further subdividing the node, adopting a more aggressive modulation, or increasing the bandwidth assigned to telephony service. Such considerations have been a major factor in choosing node sizes where extensive subscriber-specific services have been contemplated.

Bandwidth Efficiency

The next important parameter is how much information can be carried in the available spectrum. This comprises two parts: information coding and, as already referred to, modulation efficiency.

Nonscrambled analog television signals are modulated in the same format as over-air broadcast signals to enable direct connection to subscribers' television receivers and/or connection to those receivers after processing through simple frequency conversion set-top boxes. In the United States and Canada, in fact, most cable systems are required to carry the programming making up their lowest level of service in this format, though it is not clear what the requirements will be after over-air analog broadcasting ceases. The required bandwidth for each analog television signal is 6 MHz for NTSC and PAL-M formats and 7 or 8 MHz for PAL-B/G formats.

When video signals are converted to digital form, the resultant data rate is a measure of the information required to adequately describe the pictures and sound for the specific application. For entertainment-quality television, the Moving Picture Experts Group (MPEG) has defined a number of levels of data compression. These cover resolution levels comparable to analog television as well as higher resolutions and different screen aspect ratios for high-definition television (HDTV). Since the information needed to describe a video program depends on the rate of change in the picture from frame to frame, the data rate can vary widely. While encoders continue to improve in encoding efficiency for a given picture quality, today approximately 4 Mb/s (peak) is required for NTSC-quality pictures using the MPEG-2 encoding and transmission formats, whereas 19 Mb/s is required for U.S. HDTV broadcasting. Other standards, such as MPEG-4, achieve even lower data rates.

Unfortunately, the advanced codecs are not compatible with existing MPEG-2 receivers and so their deployment must await the gradual introduction of dual-standard receivers. The ratio of the digitized-but-not-compressed video stream data rate to that at the output of the compressor is the *coding gain*, which can easily be 30 or more. For nonentertainment applications, such as video conferencing and surveillance cameras, standards are available that use much lower data rates and higher coding gains.

Nonvideo data signals include packetized data for cable modems, system monitoring signals, digitized telephony of several varieties, utility control and monitoring applications, digitized audio services, interactive games and video-related services, and so on. Some of these require permanent dedicated virtual channels, while others are "bursty," with peak rates far exceeding average rates. Average data rate requirements per customer for these may vary from tens of bits per second to millions of bits per second.

Once the data stream is defined, it must be prepared for transmission. Baseband optical digital modulation is the process whereby a single datastream (which may include the time-multiplexed content from more than one source) is used to turn the output of an optical transmitter on and off. This technique is used in such formats as Gigabit Ethernet (GbE), which is commonly used for transporting signals within headends and between headends and hubs. While such formats have the advantage that very high data rates can be supported (1 Gb/s is widely deployed, while prototypes of 100-Gb/s equipment are in development) and long transmission lines are possible, all signals must both be digital and able to time-share a common datastream.

Where digital signals are to be transmitted over a shared wideband analog network, they must first be modulated onto RF carriers. While simple on–off modulation of the RF carrier could be used, that would result in a very noise-tolerant signal but with a usable bandwidth efficiency of only about 0.6 b/s/Hz. Since cable networks must provide a very low noise signal path for analog television, more bandwidth-efficient modulation schemes are possible.

Over-the-air digital television broadcasting uses an 8-VSB format, while cable generally uses 64- or 256-QAM modulation for both data packets and digitized video. Because each transmitted symbol represents more than one bit of information, high-order modulation schemes have greater bandwidth efficiency. For instance, 64 QAM has a theoretical bandwidth efficiency of 6 b/s/Hz and a practical efficiency of about 5 b/s/Hz. Note that after modulation onto an RF carrier, we no longer have a digital signal, but rather a digitally modulated analog signal that will share the analog transmission network with other analog signals.

The more "aggressive" modulation methods offer greater bandwidth efficiency but are less tolerant of channel impairments. The DOCSIS version 1.1 high-speed modem standard provides for up to 256 QAM for downstream transport and up to 16 QAM for upstream modulation, depending on the service tolerance for errors and channel conditions. Some upstream technologies are able to adjust their modulation order to suit channel conditions. Several advanced standards, such as code division multiple access (CDMA) and orthogonal frequency division multiplexing (OFDM) allow a more efficient use of impaired upstream bandwidth. DOCSIS version 2.0 allows use of a version of CDMA known as synchronous CDMA (S-CDMA).

In summary, the instantaneous information capacity of any part of the broadband network is equal to the RF bandwidth multiplied by the bandwidth efficiency of the signals occupying it. To calculate its ultimate capacity, if a network with a downstream bandwidth extending from 54 to 860 MHz were entirely loaded with 256-QAM signals (net information rate of 38 Mb/s per 6-MHz channel), it could carry over 5 Gb/s of information.

The information capacity per customer is equal to the information capacity of each separate network segment divided by the number of subscribers served from that segment. In the special case of digital video, digital music, and certain voice signals, the effective instantaneous channel capacity is further related to the coding efficiency used to convert the analog signal to a bitstream. System operators will not realize all the theoretically available information capacity per customer to the extent that they use part of the bandwidth for systemwide or regional common signals.

Time Sharing

The third leg of network information capacity is how efficiently the available information capacity is shared among users and applications. As mentioned previously, early cable systems delivered all video channels simultaneously to all homes. In a system with many channels and small nodes, however, it is likely that some channels are not being watched in some nodes some of the time (in some small-node systems, in fact, there may be more viewing choices than customers per node). If less popular channels are delivered to nodes only when desired by a subscriber, it is possible to offer more program choice without increasing the total available information capacity. A network able to do this incorporates a form of time sharing known as *switched virtual circuit*, whereby a user is granted full-time use of a video stream for the duration of his or her use, after which the capacity is freed up for other users. The terms *switched broadcast* and *switched digital video* (SDV) describe the special case where the system delivers, to one or more viewers, program streams that operate on a regular schedule and are not under the control of viewers. The term *video on demand* (VOD) is generally limited to systems in which the content is streamed from a server under the interactive control of a specific viewer.

Providing a customer temporary use of a communications path is the same principle applied in the design of central office telephone switches, where use of a "path" through a switch is granted exclusively to someone making a call but then is freed up for the next caller. Depending on the statistical usage pattern, switched-channel time sharing can be a very inefficient use of available information capacity. Most telephone callers, for instance, spend roughly the same amount of time listening as talking and, even when talking, do not talk in a continuous stream but are silent for a surprising percentage of the time (although we all know exceptions!). Thus, they use only a fraction of the system resources dedicated to them during the call.

Sometimes time sharing is on a much smaller scale. For instance, a T1 telephony circuit at 1.544 Mb/s is made up of 24 digitized voice streams, each of which requires 64 kb/s (plus a total of 8 kb/s of "overhead"). Thus, 24 telephone calls are carried over one datastream, with the time slots of about 5 μs allotted to each call on a rotating basis. This is known as *time division multiplexing* (TDM); hierarchies are available up to multiple rates of gigabits per second. TDM methods that grant a fixed percentage of the total data rate to each user is known as the *constant bit rate* (CBR). In the T1 example, each voice channel is a 64-kb/s CBR virtual circuit.

Where user needs are variable, more efficient sharing of a data channel results when the capacity is divided among datastreams as needed, a method known as *statistical multiplexing*. For instance, where many telephone calls share a common circuit, it is possible to greatly increase the total call capacity simply by not transmitting any bits when a caller is silent and using that capacity for another conversation. Another example of statistical sharing is the Ethernet local area network, where computers send data packets to other computers on the network only as needed. A final, and very important, example is digital video, where the bit rate required for each video stream varies greatly, depending on the degree of change from frame to frame of a video source. It is possible to squeeze more video programs into a given datastream if we take advantage of the statistics of combining sources with varying data rates. In the case of MPEG-2 compressed, standard-resolution video, it is possible to combine as many as 12 to 15 *variable-bit-rate* (VBR) programs into a single 6-MHz RF channel, compared with 8 to 10 for CBR programs or a single analog program.

Where many nonsynchronized users must share a channel, a time-sharing scheme known as *time division multiple access* (TDMA) may be used. The upstream communications from cable modems are an example of such a situation.

A key advantage of statistically sharing a digital datastream is that each application can have access to peak data rates that are much greater than needed on average. This is particularly important in the case of highly bursty data services such as Internet access.

Time sharing can be used at various levels in the network. For instance, blocks of RF channels may be shared among analog video services, contribution streams in a multichannel digital video multiplex, or individual packets in an IP network.

Summary of Information Capacity

The concept of effective information capacity per customer needs to be expanded to include statistical sharing of available capacity on two levels: simultaneous service usage rates and the instantaneous data rate required to support simultaneous users. Predictions of *simultaneous service usage rates* are done to estimate how many subscribers to a given service will use it simultaneously. This is generally known as *traffic engineering* and is well known and documented with regard to voice telephony. Usage of switched video channels and packetized data channels is less well studied. *Instantaneous circuit data rate* is a measure of the average and peak data rates needed to support simultaneously active users of VBR services.

Thus, the total information capacity of a network can be seen to be a complex that includes

- Total RF bandwidth in each direction of the broadband distribution system
- Logical segmentation of the distribution network into subsections that can support independent signals (space division multiplexing)
- Division of available bandwidth in each subsection among various shared and user-specific services (frequency division multiplexing)
- Division of optical spectrum in each fiber among multiple lightwave signals, each on its own wavelength (wavelength division multiplexing)
- Coding efficiency with which signals are prepared for transmission
- Bandwidth efficiency with which signals are modulated onto RF carriers
- Statistical usage of services among subscribers
- Time-shared use of available information channels among active users (multiplexing efficiency)

Figure 9.3 shows the elements that determine effective information capacity. Not shown in this simplified diagram are such elements as forward error correction and network layer overhead, both of which detract from net capacity.

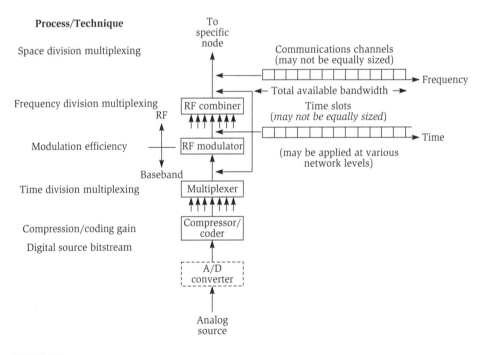

FIGURE 9.3

Elements that determine effective network information capacity.

Techniques to Increase Information Capacity

Both competitive responses and new revenue opportunities put pressure on the cable technical community to increase network information capacity. Each of these has capital and operating cost implications and may have regulatory issues as well. Some of the technologies considered follow:

Increased upper frequency limit. As discussed in Chapter 3, this requires a change-out of active (and sometimes passive) network elements, but may also require respacing of amplifiers, replacement of cable, and revision of network powering. It will almost certainly require replacement of optical transmitters. Depending on the frequency limit, it may also require replacement of terminal equipment; in particular, most deployed cable modems and digital video set-top boxes (some owned by customers) do not tune above 864 MHz, and thus any bandwidth increase to a greater frequency may require a substantial investment beyond the distribution network upgrade and, in the case of customer-owned equipment, may run into regulatory issues.

Switched digital video. As discussed above, SDV offers bandwidth usage efficiency. Where customers already have digital video STBs that accept downloads of new applications, deployment can be quite smooth. The available gain, however, is limited by two principal factors: no bandwidth gain results from switching the most popular channels, as it is likely that at least one subscriber in any service group will always want to view it, and FCC rules currently appear to forbid switching any channel designated as "one way," to ensure compatibility with "unidirectional digital cable products" (one-way cable-ready receivers), as defined in the rules.* Finally, the future ability to send personally targeted ads to customers accessing SDV channels demands dedicating streams to individual viewers (as opposed to groups of viewers requesting the same programming) and this reduces the effective throughput gain somewhat.

Node splitting. Splitting of existing nodes into smaller subnodes, each of which can receive independent signals, creates the potential to multiply both downstream and upstream capacity inversely to the ratio of homes in each subnode to those in the original node. The key word here is "potential," however, because it depends on how bandwidth is used by the operator. In most cable systems today, the majority of RF bandwidth is devoted to signals that are sent in common to all subscribers, or at least to groups of subscribers that are at least as big as the unsplit node and for which there is no benefit to a smaller service group. Only for services that can efficiently share bandwidth in smaller groups (e.g., Internet access) is there a gain through node splitting. For other shared-bandwidth services, there will be a throughput gain but at the expense of more total headend transponder equipment than before the split.

---

*CableLabs' "tuning resolver" initiative, announced in August 2007, is aimed at resolving this dilemma through an additional piece of hardware that works in conjunction with one-way receivers.

Recovery of spectrum used for analog video. The majority of bandwidth on most cable systems is used for the downstream nonswitched transmission of analog video signals, primarily those making up the "basic" service level. These services are also often "simulcast" in digital form on the same networks, primarily because it allows operators to purchase digital-only converters that are less expensive than hybrid analog/digital models. While it seems inevitable that the need for delivery of analog signals will eventually go away (as customers gradually replace their old analog receivers), there may be both legal and marketing reasons to continue to support older receivers for many years. Given that reality, there are two methods by which the distribution system spectrum devoted to analog signal transmission can be recovered: supplying digital converters for every analog television receiver still in use by customers or re-creating the analog spectrum at the side of each home (or, potentially, at each tap). The first is a straightforward cost issue: capital cost to purchase the converters plus ongoing operating cost to install and service them must be balanced against the value of the recovered spectrum. The trade-off of the second approach is similar, except that it requires fewer, but more expensive, new devices.

Expansion of the upstream band. So long as over-air broadcast stations were assigned low-VHF channels, together with the right to demand coverage on those channels through cable systems, the top end of the upstream band was effectively limited to 41 MHz. With the demise of over-air analog television transmission, there may be few stations assigned to channels 2 to 6. This would allow shifting the upstream/downstream frequency division, as discussed in Section 9.2.1. Although this looks simple on paper, in fact it requires changing every diplex filter in every amplifier and node and upgrading or replacing upstream amplifiers and many optical transmitters and headend receivers. As with downstream bandwidth expansion beyond 864 MHz, it requires deployment of new terminal equipment that can use the expanded frequency range.

Use of advanced digital video-encoding techniques. Standards for cable television use of more efficient digital video encoding formats have been approved and their usage will allow roughly twice as many digital video streams to share the same RF channel. As with several other initiatives, however, the problem is that most deployed terminal devices do not have the ability to decode this advanced format, nor can they be upgraded to that capability. This means that operators will be faced with the choice of an expensive accelerated terminal equipment replacement schedule or waiting for attrition to accomplish the same task much more slowly. Furthermore, FCC regulations (via SCTE 40) require one-way digital video services to be delivered in an MPEG-2 format.

In summary, there are several options available to operators to increase effective network throughput capability, but all have trade-offs that must be evaluated against a company's near- and long-term expansion plans.

9.2.2 Network Reliability and Availability

Network *availability*, in the most general sense, is a measure of the likelihood that it will be available for use by customers, while *reliability* is related to the rate at which failures occur. Some factors that affect availability and reliability are discussed here.

Equipment Reliability

The first requirement in building a reliable network, to state the obvious, is that its component parts be reliable. Although the discussion of internal equipment reliability is beyond the scope of this book, in general the overall reliability (usually expressed in terms of mean time between failures, MTBF, in hours) will be affected by such factors as operating temperatures, complexity of the unit, environmental protection, mechanical strength of interconnections, protection from powering transients, and long-term aging characteristics of materials and components. Typically, manufacturers provide MTBF data for their network components based on theoretical analyses and sometimes also based on test data obtained under controlled environmental conditions.

Experience has shown that classical failure analyses, based on internal electrical parts and how they are interconnected, typically yield reliability predictions that have a limited relationship to the performance of field-installed equipment. On the other hand, accurate field failure data are difficult to gather, given that field crews are often more focused on restoring service than on performing postevent failure analysis.

Network Failure Rate

The failure rate of the network is determined by the number of high-level devices (such as amplifiers), their individual failure rates, and how they are interconnected, as well as certain outside factors. Chapter 12 is devoted to the calculation of network failures rates and availability. In general, however, networks that have more components that can independently cause a signal transmission failure will be less reliable. Thus, a 40-amplifier cascade will be less reliable than a 4-amplifier cascade. Not only electronic components but the power to those components contribute to failures and must be considered in the analysis. Service-related reliability requirements are one factor leading to the choice of serving area size.

Network reliability can be improved by architectures in which the failure of some network elements does not lead to a communications outage. A simple example is the provision of two diversely routed fiber cables between the headend and a node, with separate optical transmitters and receivers on each link and the node configured to automatically select the alternate path if the primary path fails. The probability of failing to get signals from the headend to that node then becomes the product of the probabilities of failure of each of the redundant links taken independently. For example, if each of the links has a probability of failure in some time period of 1%, then the probability of failure of the redundant network is only 0.01% in the same time period. The gain from redundancy, however, is reduced by the failure rate of the added equipment that must decide which of two redundant paths to use and then switch between them. Redundant structures are part of many high-reliability architectures.

In most existing cable television networks, service outages are more likely to be due to commercial electric power interruption than due to actual equipment failures. Thus an important factor in distribution system design is the degree and type of backup powering provided and the placement of field power supplies at points in the utility's power grid that are less likely to fail.

Network Availability—Failure Related

Given a network failure rate, whether due to component failure or powering failure, the next important parameter is the percentage of time that the network (or a specific service) is available for use. This is treated in detail in Chapter 12, but the general equation for availability is

$$availability(A) = \frac{1}{1 + \frac{MTTR}{MTBF}} \tag{9.3}$$

where MTBF is the mean time between failures and MTTR is the mean time to restore service when failures occur. MTBF is governed by the reliability of network elements and how they are interconnected, as discussed earlier; however MTTR is both an operational practices and a network design issue. Such issues as field response time and field crew training are operational issues. System-monitoring capabilities, however, are part of network design and control how soon an outage is known to repair crews. Finally, more subtle design issues, such as the number of fibers in shared cables, may affect the time required to repair a cut.

Service Availability—Signal Quality Related

Even when the physical network is operating properly, individual services may experience outages due to temporarily degraded transmission conditions. For example, an ingressing signal may interfere with an upstream data transmission. If the terminal equipment operates on a fixed frequency, the service will be lost until the signal stops transmitting or the point of ingress is located and repaired. If, on the other hand, the headend equipment is able to sense such interference and the upstream transmitters are frequency agile, the service can be restored by merely shifting the frequency of operation. While such considerations are not affected by distribution system physical architecture (except, of course, that smaller node-serving areas are less likely to be affected by the interference in the first place), they are affected by the selection of terminal equipment and the allocation of available operating spectrum—in other words, the architecture of the specific service.

Several means of quantifying data circuit availability include signal quality issues. Bit error rate (BER) is a measure of the percentage of individual bits of information that are lost, whereas packet error rate, errored seconds, severely errored seconds, and errored minutes all measure lost information on related but different scales.

Service Availability—Traffic Loading Related

Where transmission paths are statistically shared among users, there is always the possibility that demand will sometimes exceed available capacity. Thus, even if the network is working properly and the transmission channels are unimpaired, the service may sometimes be unavailable to a specific user. This happens at places in the U.S. telephone network every Mother's Day, for instance, when, at some hours of the day, more people attempt to call their families than there are available long-distance circuits. It also frequently happens after any major disaster, when high numbers of incoming and outgoing calls exceed call capacities.

As with signal quality issues, capacity-limited blockages are affected not by the reliability or architecture of the transmission network, but rather by the architecture of the individual service. In essence, they are designed as an economic choice, since providing sufficient capacity for the largest possible traffic load would not be economically justifiable if that load level occurs only rarely.

The design of an appropriate load capability for a given service is known as *traffic engineering*. This is a mature art in the case of voice telephony networks and a less well-developed art in the case of such services as cable modems and video on demand.

In summary, overall service unavailability is approximately the sum of unavailabilities due to network failures, signal degradation, and capacity-related blocking (the approximation is due to the possibility of simultaneously occurring unavailabilities in two categories).

Single Points of Failure

A final topic related to network reliability and its consequences is the management of single points of failure. Failures of components at various points in the network will affect different portions of the service and differing numbers of customers. For instance, the failure of a terminating tap will, at most, affect only the customers directly connected to it, whereas failure of the optical receiver at the node may affect hundreds of customers. Failure of a single headend channel processor may affect one channel throughout the network, whereas failure of the satellite antenna low-noise converter may take out well over 100 digital video channels.

One measure of the quality of an architecture is how immune the system is to single points of failure that affect many customers and how quickly such failures can be detected and repaired. Note that this is not necessarily the same as providing high reliability and availability. For instance, a single headend outage that takes out all services for several minutes will not greatly affect overall yearly availability, but will likely overload the customer service telephone lines with complaints, something that will not happen with a random distribution of small outages. For this reason, if for no other, systems are designed to eliminate as many large single points of

The advantages to using an NID include:

- Isolation of the network from the effects of in-building wiring, both losses and signal ingress
- Simplified network powering, particularly for wired telephony services
- Cost savings in multiservice installations through sharing of common equipment
- Sharing of a single upstream transmitter at the NID by all upstream signals

Balanced against these advantages are the generally higher costs of the first installed service due to the flexibility required in the NID to support incremental features or services. Also, the use of a common NID implies, in most cases, that all two-way services must be interoperable. Often in the cable industry, this means a common and sole source for equipment.

In summary, network architecture includes not only the physical network topology but also the distribution of signal-processing equipment for various services. Network information capacity can vary by service and includes the RF bandwidth, how efficiently that bandwidth is used and shared, and the effects of equipment distribution on the information required to support the service. On an operational level, architecture has an effect on the reliability and availability of services, on the size and frequency of outages, and on how difficult it is to recover from those outages.

9.3 REQUIREMENTS BY SERVICE TYPE

A key factor in designing a network architecture is a clear understanding of the services that will be offered, because each has unique requirements. The signal quality requirements for various analog and digital services are well covered elsewhere and will only be summarized here. Additionally, specific services require different levels of reliability and availability, switching, per-customer data capacity, and links between network customers and networks that are external to the cable system. Although many service categories may not be covered in the following discussion, the general process of assessing requirements should be similar.

9.3.1 Broadcast Video Services

The U.S. cable television industry was founded on the retransmission of analog, NTSC, over-air broadcast service to improve reception for viewers as compared with what they could get with private antennas. In the late 1970s, those channels were supplemented by satellite-delivered networks. In the context of this chapter, *broadcast services* will refer to all programming delivered to all subscribers in common, regardless of the ultimate source of that programming. Today, most of the bandwidth of typical residential networks is still dominated by analog programming delivered in nonscrambled, broadcast analog format to subscribers. The requirements for such networks are that they have sufficient downstream bandwidth for all channels, coupled with quality and availability that are acceptable to subscribers (and that conforms to regulatory requirements, as outlined in Chapter 7).

With the practical implementation of digital video compression, the theoretical program capacity of such networks has been increased tenfold or more for standard-resolution programming and by two to three times for high-definition programming, compared with over-air broadcast formats. Digitally modulated video signals, whether in broadcast (VSB modulation) or cable (QAM) format, have a greater tolerance to noise and intermodulation distortion than analog video signals (the FCC requires 33-dB C/N for 256 QAM versus 43 dB for analog video), with the result that they can be run at lower power levels in the network and, therefore, provide less loading of the active devices.

As opposed to the lifeline telephony situation, where network reliability is related to emergency services access and is, therefore, a governmental and public concern, most video services consist of nonessential entertainment, and therefore network reliability is primarily a marketing issue. In other words, programming must be delivered with sufficient reliability so that customers do not prefer alternate service providers. It can be argued that the transmission of Emergency Alert System (EAS) warnings through cable networks creates an overriding public interest in their reliability, but no federal standards have been issued (although local governmental authorities sometimes negotiate customer service standards with franchised cable operators that include outage measurements).

CableLabs' Outage Reduction Task Force reported on industry research to determine customer tolerance of various outage rates and durations in their landmark 1992 publication *Outage Reduction.*[1] Based on its findings, the task force group proposed the following performance target:

> *No customer should experience more than two outages within a three-month period. While less accurate, because the cumulative effect of outages over time is lost, a secondary standard could be set at no more than 0.6 outages per customer per month.*[2]

This guideline is based on research that showed, when outage frequency exceeded the target rate, that it became a major factor in customers' perception of service quality, whereas below that rate the overall satisfaction rating was largely independent of outage frequency.

Another important result of the research showed that although there was a difference in perceived quality for outages of various lengths, the dissatisfaction level for 10-minute outages was nearly as high as for all-day outages, and the dissatisfaction with outages of one minute was about one-half the 10-minute rating. The task force, however, did not put forward a recommended standard for service restoration, or network availability percentage, though they state that "A[n availability] figure in a good month is 99.99% or greater. In a poor month, the figure might be as low as 99.95%."[3] If we use an average service restoration time of 4 hours for all outages, then 0.6 outages per month corresponds to a network availability rate of 99.7%, a frequently quoted cable industry availability goal.

In the same document, the task force proposed the following definition for an *outage*:

> An outage *is defined as any event in which two or more customers experience loss of reception on one or more channels arising from a common cause, regardless of the cause.* Loss *is defined as an interruption rather then degradation of signal. Loss of a single channel at the headend or hub site is included.*[4]

This is an interesting definition from a network design standpoint. For one thing, it includes only outages "experienced" by subscribers. Thus, outages that are detected and repaired before they are noticed by subscribers do not count. The relationship between actual failure rate and subscriber-experienced failure rate is discussed in Chapter 12.

Second, by excluding single-subscriber outages, the definition ignores all outages occurring because of faults in drop wiring or terminal equipment, whether furnished by either the network operator or the subscriber. Given that many, if not most, subscriber outages arise in either the drop or terminal equipment, this is an important exception.

By excluding single-subscriber outages, the definition also eliminates from consideration any single-channel outages that affect only single customers. Although this is not important for broadcast services, it is important in the case of interactive services such as video on demand, discussed later, where each video stream is used by only a single subscriber.

Clearly, the outage definition is not consistent with the research on subscriber tolerances. Subscribers are likely to be just as dissatisfied with an outage occurring because an individual set-top converter failed to descramble as with one occurring because a headend modulator failed. It would be prudent for those designing networks to include all elements involved in service delivery in setting acceptable outage rates. Given the relative independence of outage length on dissatisfaction rating, it would also be prudent to set separate goals for outage rate and network availability (or service restoration time).

A final parameter in determining reliability parameters for delivery of broadcast video services is outage size. When customers experience an outage, a certain percentage of them will attempt to contact the network operator to report the event. If the outage affects many customers, this can cause the telephone call volume to swamp the customer service department and its incoming telephone trunks. Since many franchises (as well as voluntary industry guidelines) contain requirements regarding telephone responsiveness, it is incumbent on operators to design networks that have as few common elements as possible and to tailor repair efforts to respond most quickly to those outages affecting the largest number of customers.

Although individual network operators must set their own service standards, they should consider defining outages to include single-subscriber outages and to define not only outage rate but response times and net availability of service. Furthermore, service restoration times should be managed so that they are inversely proportional to the number of customers affected.

9.3.2 **Narrowcast Video Services**

Narrowcast services are defined, for purposes of this discussion, as those that are not available to all subscribers but whose generation is not under direct control of viewers. Included in this category are the services known as pay, pay-per-view (PPV), and near video on demand (NVOD). In each case, the services are delivered, in accordance with a fixed transmission schedule, to a subset of the subscribers receiving the broadcast channels.

The three categories blend into each other. Pay services historically refers to services such as HBO that are subscribed to on the basis of monthly fees. PPV refers to a fixed schedule of movies and events that are sold on a per-event basis, with different orderable events transmitted sequentially on one or more channels. NVOD is a logical extension of PPV whereby movies are typically displayed with sufficient frequency that the average wait time for a particular movie is short enough to discourage subscribers from seeking other means to access the programming. As content available on various on-demand platforms grows, it is likely that both PPV and NVOD service categories will be dropped. It remains to be seen how various monthly-fee pay services will fare.

The parameters specifically related to narrowcast services include the means used to control access, ordering mechanisms, and the efficiency of network information capacity usage. Today, such services are almost always delivered in encrypted digital form and, with the exception of fixed-fee-per-month services, are ordered electronically through two-way digital converters.

As systems offer an increasing number of optional video services, the effective information of the capacity of the network devoted to those services must be increased. There are basically three ways to do that: increasing downstream bandwidth, providing greater information density (e.g., digital video compression), and/or implementing switched broadcast technology. The first two are obvious; the third is in the process of achieving widespread deployment.

Common versus Switched Information Capacity

Given a need to deliver a defined range of services to a group of customers, operators have the option of providing sufficient network-wide information capacity that all signals can be delivered throughout the network, or providing switching and multiplexing so that a reduced instantaneous information capacity, combined with a customized signal load for each network segment, accomplishes the same end. In multilevel architectures, this switching can take place at the headend or at some lower level or levels in the network.

In the special case of switched broadcast services using digital video, several questions need to be answered. How many program streams will be switched? What is their range of popularity? How many RF channels will be used? How many subscribers will share a set of switched broadcast signals? What is the cost to switch the input signals and to create and modulate each output multiplex? The optimal engineering solution will depend on the specific problem. Figure 9.4 illustrates the basic principles and headend signal-handling hardware involved.

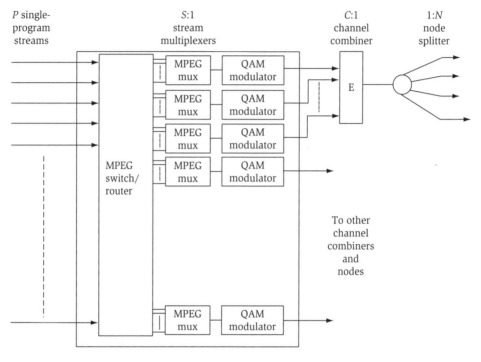

FIGURE 9.4

Switched broadcast parameters.

When considering required bandwidth for a switched broadcast service, a key issue is the degree to which it will be used to support more precise matching of ads to viewers' perceived interests. At one extreme, the system can be optimized to minimize required bandwidth, in which case all viewers in each service group who request the same program stream share access to a single stream. In this case, the only possible targeting is that which matches ads to people living in the particular neighborhoods included in a service group. At the other extreme, the system can maximize the opportunity to match ads to individual viewers' interests, in which case each viewer will require exclusive use of a dedicated stream in which the ads transmitted with the viewed program are targeted to that individual. An intermediate step is to group viewers into broad demographic categories and share streams among viewers in the same category.

The difference in the number of streams required is significant. According to a recent study,[5] when the system was optimized for bandwidth savings, a given number of program streams required only 29% as much bandwidth when switched as opposed to broadcast, while if an individual stream were provided to each viewer, 62% as much bandwidth was needed—in other words, over twice as many streams were required to enable individual-viewer ad targeting. While the economics of targeted advertising versus the cost of bandwidth are still being studied, one cost optimization proposal is to use individual targeting when usage is light but to scale back to broader demographic targeting as usage increases, and then only to area targeting at peak demand periods.

Neither the U.S. cable industry nor federal regulators have suggested reliability standards for optional video services as opposed to broadcast services. The rather outdated research done by CableLabs, discussed earlier, did not distinguish among service levels or consider the relative expectations of subscribers to premium services. Since customers pay more per channel for some such services, it is logical to predict that they expect a higher reliability.

9.3.3 On-Demand and Interactive Video Services

On-demand video services are defined as those delivered to specific subscribers, generally in response to real-time requests. Such programming might include more than entertainment categories. Generally this implies a degree of real-time interaction between the subscriber and the program generation and control system through a two-way cable system. As an example, a subscriber might use a multilevel menu system to select from among audio, video, and print material, or might search a database of articles in a research project. Alternatively, the subscriber might select a movie and start time from an available library and then be granted VCR-like control over its playback (known as *video on demand*, VOD).

From an architectural requirements standpoint, on-demand services will differ primarily in the acceptable latency times and in the nature of the information source. In the case of video games, for instance, acceptable latency times may be on the order of a few milliseconds, whereas database searches may tolerate several seconds depending on the application.

Whatever the nature of the information being transmitted, the downstream requirement is to provide exclusive use of a communications channel for each simultaneous user. As with narrowcast services, required bandwidth is affected by service penetration rate, simultaneous usage rates, and node size. The upstream requirement is for a channel with appropriate bandwidth and latency. Generally, the upstream bandwidth per user, even for the extreme case of interactive games, is relatively modest, although latency requirements may be strict.

With respect to reliability of service delivery, it can be assumed (because of its publication date) that the CableLabs' research on subscriber tolerance of outages was based largely on broadcast and monthly pay services. As with narrowcast services, it is reasonable to assume that subscribers who are the sole users of channels and who may be paying far higher per-channel costs for that exclusivity will be more demanding of service reliability. On the other hand, narrowcast services are viewed for a shorter time than, say, broadcast services, so the statistical probability of failure will be lower—a balancing factor. To the extent that these narrowcast, on-demand services share the same physical cables as the broadcast video channels but also use relatively complex server devices, their inclusion in a network operator's offerings may place a more stringent reliability requirement on the broadband delivery system.

9.3.4 Packet Data Services—Internet Access

For purposes of this discussion, *packet data services* are defined as nonvideo digital transport in which data are packaged in short bursts and sent through a time-shared channel on a demand basis. The most common noncable example of such a network is an Ethernet, in which variable-length packets are sent between any two terminals on the network. Included within this broad definition are both TCP/IP and ATM.

Packet data services are commonly provided through two-way cable networks in accordance with the international DOCSIS standard. The network quality requirements are those that will result in an acceptable service quality. This means that the net loss of packets (after any provided forward error correction) must be low enough that the net throughput does not materially suffer. Typical, well-maintained HFC networks will provide uncorrected bit error rates in the range of 10^{-9} to 10^{-10} in the downstream direction with 256 QAM and 10^{-5} to 10^{-7} in the upstream direction with QPSK modulation.

In the downstream direction, a 6-MHz RF channel containing a 64-QAM signal will provide a data rate of about 30 Mb/s; 256 QAM will carry 38 Mb/s. The total number of such required channels will be a function of service penetration, simultaneous usage among subscribers, average data rate per simultaneous user, acceptable blocking rates, and the number of homes that share common data signals.

In the upstream direction, the requirements are slightly more complex. In addition to the preceding factors, the upstream capacity includes the efficiency with which users are controlled so as to share each RF channel. Under DOCSIS, modems request use of the channel and then are allotted time slots on a specific upstream RF channel. In order for the system to accommodate subscribers who might be located at different distances (and therefore different transmission times) from the headend and at different tap ports, upstream transmitters must be level-agile and able to synchronize their transmissions in time.

Although average data rates will change as usage patterns and applications develop, a typical cable modem traffic analysis (for a user using a search engine or doing email) might go as shown in Table 9.1.

If we assume that the dominant use of modems is file downloading, then the upstream traffic will consist primarily of 64-byte acknowledgments of the 1600-byte downstream packets—a 1:25 ratio. Thus, the upstream data rate to support the given downstream rate is 128 kb/s ÷ 25 = 5.12 kb/s.

In recent years, however, Internet usage has included an increasing percentage of long-term streaming of high-bit-rate communications, such as real-time gaming, short-form video, and music, that will increase downstream average rates by an order of magnitude or more above those calculated previously. To the extent that

Table 9.1 Elements in Each Simultaneously Active User's Session

	6	downstream messages/minute
each consisting of	100	packets
with an average length of	1600	bytes/packet
multiplied by	8	bits/byte
divided by	60	seconds/minute
equals	128	kb/s *average* data rate per active session

these include peer-to-peer communications, upstream and downstream rates will also become more symmetrical.

Marketing data services based on peak gross downstream user rate is common, with the upstream limit being set to a fraction of that—typically 20 to 25%. What the user experiences, however, may have little relation to what is marketed, based on the following factors (among others):

- The user experience data rate will always be lower than the peak rate, due to DOCSIS IP overhead.
- The peak rate may exceed the advertised rate unless the network operator programmatically sets the maximum rate.
- The peak rate may be less than that advertised when usage of the network is heaviest and there is contention for resources, both on the RF and network sides of the CMTS.
- The measured rate to any Internet site will be limited by the capacity available on every intervening link in the path.
- The rate will be limited by the remote server and contention among simultaneous users there.

The relationship among node size, number of nodes sharing a datastream, usable downstream data rate, service penetration (measured against homes passed), and simultaneous usage rate is given by the following:

$$\frac{\text{usable data rate}}{\text{average data rate per active session}} = \text{HP/node} \times \text{nodes} \times \text{penetration} \times \text{simultaneous usage}$$

where the usable data rate is the net available user data rate in the data stream, average data rate per active session is as calculated earlier, HP/node is the number of homes served from each node, nodes is the number of nodes that share a downstream data stream, penetration is the percentage of homes in each node that subscribe to cable modem service, and simultaneous usage is the number of data subscribers using the service simultaneously.

For example, if we assume that the net usable data rate from a 256-QAM, 6-MHz-bandwidth signal is 38 Mb/s, and that the average downstream data rate per active user is 128 kb/s, then each channel will support 297 simultaneous users. If two 500-home nodes share a common downstream signal and we allow for up to 35% simultaneous usage among data subscribers, then the system will support an 85% penetration among homes passed.

In the upstream direction, total usable data rates, data rates per session, and circuit sharing will differ; otherwise, the calculation is similar. Since the upstream spectrum is subject to ingressing signals (and also malfunctioning modems that transmit continuously), modems are frequency-agile upstream so that the system can "side-step" a degraded frequency provided that the CMTS has the feature enabled. Providing such capability, however, requires that additional bandwidth be allocated.

Network reliability/availability standards have not been set for packetized data services. To the extent that such services compete with those delivered by DSL modems, the local public-switched telephone distribution network arguably will meet the 0.9999 availability recommendation for local telephone service but with an overall reduced availability due to the failure rate of the digital subscriber line access multiplexer (DSLAM)—the equivalent of cable's CMTS for DSL service. Balancing the possibly higher cable network failure rate, however, is the ability of cable modem equipment to "ping" (test) each modem on an ongoing basis and thus to quickly determine if there is a communications or equipment problem. Even a relatively low penetration of such devices will ensure that virtually the entire cable network can be continuously monitored for integrity, which allows proactive service restoration and thus better subscriber-experienced availability.

For another competitive comparison, AT&T's Digital Data System (DDS), which offers duplex data channels to users at speeds ranging from 2.4 kb/s to 1.544 Mb/s, guarantees a BER of at least 10^{-7} and an availability of 0.9996, with the local circuits on each end of the network (T1 carrier plus baseband loop) assumed to have an availability of 0.9999.[6]

9.3.5 Voice-Grade Telephony Services

Voice-grade telephony comes in several forms, including conventional wired telephony, PCS telephony, cellular telephony, and IP telephony, also known as *voice over IP* (VoIP). Wired telephony requires a physical connection between the user's terminal equipment and the distribution system, whereas PCS and cellular systems use bidirectional radio transmission. VoIP can be supported over any IP network with sufficient transmission fidelity and latency properties. As implemented in cable, VoIP typically shares DOCSIS headend equipment with high-speed data service.

Although there are distinct legal and frequency usage differences between cellular and PCS telephony, from a network perspective there is almost a continuum in terms of cell sizes, cell interconnection requirements, and available services. Generally, cellular base stations and telephones both use higher power than PCS and correspondingly greater spacing between base stations. Also, PCS is a purely digital service, whereas cellular can be either analog or digital in the air link.

Wired telephony is now commonly transported through HFC networks, as could be the interconnection between cellular (including PCS) transceiver antenna locations, though the network requirements are considerably different. Despite promising early engineering work, PCS station interconnect has never been widely deployed. However, the interested reader is encouraged to consult the notes at the end of the chapter for further information.[7]

Switched-Circuit, Constant-Bit-Rate Telephony

By definition, wired telephony requires that cable systems support two-way communication to and from every home. Since the greatest percentage of upstream ingress problems occur in the drop system and internal building wiring, the communications equipment used must be designed to work in relatively "dirty" channels. One architectural choice that eliminates many in-home problems is the use of an external NID on each home that contains the data receivers and transmitters for telephony, with standard twisted-pair copper used to transport baseband analog telephony within the building. By using a NID, the network is protected from in-home ingress (see Section 9.2.3 for a general discussion of the advantages and disadvantages of using NIDs). NIDs may be telephone-only or, with VoIP, may terminate both voice and data services.

The requirement to have the service survive localized power outages also favors the use of a NID, which can be directly powered from the coaxial plant, which in turn can be equipped with standby power. In other cases, operators may choose to equip each NID with batteries and a local charger. Either choice involves compromises. Network powering, unless the NID has very low power consumption, can significantly increase the total power consumed by the network and for that reason make the design of reliable standby power more difficult. The use of a home-powered charger and batteries creates the need to maintain that equipment and to dispose of worn-out batteries on a regular basis. Also, power for the charger within the home is likely to be less reliable than distribution plant power and also may have a shorter battery-mode standby time.

Telephony signals are sent to and from individual subscribers. Thus, the RF bandwidth used will be related directly to node size, number of nodes sharing common telephone signals, modulation efficiency, service penetration, and simultaneous usage among subscribers. As an example, assume that a system is built with 500-home nodes, with pairs of nodes sharing telephone signals. If the network operator is a local exchange carrier (LEC) and expects to serve virtually all residences with at least a primary telephone and a 50% chance of a second phone, then it must plan on a capacity of 1500 lines per service group. Assuming the company's traffic engineering studies predict 20% maximum simultaneous usage (known as *line concentration* in the telephone industry), then the network must be able to handle 300 simultaneous telephone calls per node. At 64 kb/s per voice stream, the network must be able to transmit 19.2 Mb/s per node. Finally, if QPSK modulation is used on the RF carriers (with a bandwidth efficiency of 1.5 b/s/Hz), the theoretical required bandwidth will be 12.8 MHz in each direction. Commercially available equipment is not that bandwidth efficient, however, and is typically limited to 24 simultaneous calls per 2 MHz, so a total of 24 MHz would be required, equivalent to four standard 6-MHz downstream television channels and a significant percentage of the usable upstream bandwidth of most standard low-split systems.

As the primary communications link into homes, the local telephone service is expected to provide very high reliability and availability and to work when the power is out. All of these are greater than the demands required to deliver nonessential entertainment video services. Bellcore, the research consortium of the former Bell operating companies, has established availability objectives for the telephone industry. Those relating to the subscriber loop are contained in TR-NWT-000418.[8] The basic criterion is that "the two-way service availability objective of a narrowband transmission channel should be a minimum of 99.99% (0.9999 probability) for the subscriber loop." This corresponds to an average yearly unavailability of 53 minutes. *Narrowband transmission channel* is further defined to mean services, including voice, that are transmitted at speeds lower than DS-1 (1.544 Mb/s).

It is important to understand what the Bellcore criterion includes and what it does not. In terms of applicability, everything in the central office on the subscriber side of the switch (or remote terminal) is included. For HFC systems, the equivalent headend components would include the RF modulators, for instance, but not the shared HDT. Bellcore's definition includes the distribution network and, if used, the NID. The subscriber-provided, in-building wiring or telephone instrument is not included.

Equipment failures and the time to repair them are included in the calculation. Not included, however, are service outages due to both primary and backup powering. Since the majority of outages in HFC networks are power related, actual subscriber unavailability may far exceed 53 minutes per year and yet meet the Bellcore criterion. By comparison, the CableLabs' guideline quoted earlier includes power outages. In addition, Bellcore's definition defines the restoration time as beginning when the operator becomes aware of the outage, which may be long after it actually starts in the case of an outage affecting a single customer. Finally, the unavailability experienced by individual customers is further affected by their usage patterns and by failures of their own terminal equipment. Despite its limitations, the Bellcore criterion is accepted for measuring availability of residential lifeline telephone service.

The relationship of subscriber-perceived outage rate and unavailability to network reliability and availability is complex and involves usage patterns as well as the depth of network monitoring. This subject is discussed further in Chapter 12. It is interesting that although the added complexity of HFC networks using NIDs may *increase* the actual hardware failure rate, the addition of automatic subscriber line monitoring may allow a *decrease* in customer-perceived outages relative to lower-failure-rate, but unmonitored, networks.

VoIP

IP telephony began as a means of bypassing the long-distance carriers. Computers at each end of an IP telephone link were equipped with microphones, speakers, and audio coders/decoders (codecs) and could use voice communications provided the two-way data rate was sufficient to support the digitized voice.

Although the initial results were crude in comparison to the normal public-switched telephone network, hardware improved to the point that major carriers are now taking an interest in it. One development has been the emergence of facilities in numerous cities that serve as gateways between the Internet and local exchange carriers (LECs). This allows calls between standard phones and IP phones. Both the legal and technical frameworks for this service are still under development.

IP telephone service using extensions to the DOCSIS standard is now rapidly replacing CBR telephony for cable operators. Modems equipped with an embedded multimedia terminal adapter (eMTA) provide the interface between the RF domain and existing telephone wiring within subscribers' homes. DOCSIS 1.1 (and later) and PacketCable standards provide the necessary definitions and ensure interoperability of various manufacturers' equipment. Home powering of terminal equipment has also become the de facto standard, partially because the power consumption of DOCSIS modems is higher than that for CBR NIDs.

9.3.6 Utility Monitoring and Control Services

A final example of services that can use the broadband infrastructure are various low-average-data-rate monitoring and control functions. Examples are electric utility customer load control and meter reading; burglar, fire, and medical alarm monitoring; and traffic light monitoring and control.[9] These services can be characterized generally as relatively low-speed data circuits with varying latency and transmission reliability requirements. Most require highly accurate end-to-end data integrity.

The two applications with the greatest apparent hope of commercial success are electric meter reading and demand-side management (DSM). Since electric power companies must provide capacity based on peak, rather than average, demand, DSM offers them a means of trimming peak electric loads by selectively turning off high-powered appliances, such as water heaters and air conditioners, during the hottest hours of the day. By turning off rotating groups of such appliances for a short time, they can materially reduce peak load while minimizing inconvenience to users.

Although the data rates are not high, the overall reliability by which the DSM process functions must be exceptional because the result of failure could be a widespread power outage. On the other hand, only the common equipment must meet this high standard because the failure of a single node or of the equipment in a single home will not have a material effect on overall load management. Nevertheless, it has been suggested that network availabilities in excess of 0.99997 might be required by some utilities.[10] By contrast, the requirements for meter reading are less stringent since timing is not critical and data can be retransmitted if necessary to ensure accuracy.

A similar situation exists for medical, burglar, and fire alarm monitoring. The average data rates are quite small, and transmission delays of a few seconds are tolerable. Still, network availability is crucial, as is transmission accuracy, since lives could be lost if alarms are not promptly and accurately reported.

9.4 SCALABILITY

Engineering has, somewhat simplistically, been defined as finding the lowest-cost solution to a technical problem given a complete definition of that problem, including performance, operational parameters, and reliability. Unfortunately, in broadband network engineering, the requirements are usually ill defined.

The network's owners (be they stockholders, partners, or investors) want a network that provides an initial set of services to customers with adequate quality and reliability and at the lowest cost. However, they also expect the network to be able to provide undefined future services when and where required and to be able to provide services to whatever penetrations of homes marketing is able to sell—all this, if possible, without abandoning any of the original capital.

Thus, scalability has become an important element of network architecture. It can be measured by the following parameters:

- The ability to increase the bandwidth per subscriber for any given service without increasing the cost of providing other services (service-specific scalability)

- The ability to increase the bandwidth per subscriber in a given geographic area without increasing the network or service provision cost elsewhere (area-specific scalability)

- The ability to increase the bandwidth per subscriber for any given service in a given geographic area without increasing the cost of providing other services or the same services to other areas (service- and area-specific scalability)

Chapter 10 presents a detailed example of a specific architecture that will illustrate the trade-offs required to achieve scalability in each of these parameters.

9.5 SUMMARY

Networks can be described by a number of parameters, including the following:

- Noise, distortion, and other signal degradation measures
- Instantaneous RF bandwidth
- Various means, such as segmentation and switching, to increase the effective bandwidth per user

- Reliability and availability
- Service-specific and geography-specific scalability

Services that may be delivered over those networks place varying demands on the distribution system:

- Quality of the RF channel occupied by its signals
- Occupied bandwidth, both forward and reverse
- Availability of the network to carry signals
- Network powering for unique service-related processing equipment

The network architecture must support adequate performance and effective bandwidth for all contemplated services. Chapters 10 and 11 will discuss various architectural examples and how they meet the needs of certain services; Chapter 12 will deal with reliability and availability modeling.

ENDNOTES

1. Cable Television Laboratories, "Outage Reduction," CableLabs, Louisville, CO, September 1992.
2. Ibid., p. I-18.
3. Ibid., p. V-10.
4. Ibid., p. I-8.
5. Jim Nguyen, "Evolving Switched Broadcast Beyond First Generation Deployments," in *Proceedings Manual*, Society of Cable Telecommunications Engineers, Cable-Tec Expo 2006.
6. Bernhard E. Reiser, *Broadband Coding, Modulation, and Transmission Engineering*. Washington, DC: CEEPress Books, 1994, pp. 96–97.
7. George Hart, "Cost-Effective Cable Television Transport for PCN," *1992 NCTA Technical Papers*. Washington, DC: National Cable & Telecommunications Association, May 1992, pp. 148–156; Douglas E. Holulin and Robert W. Hammond, "Integrated Wireless PCS—Hybrid Fiber Coax Network Architecture," *1996 NCTA Technical Papers*, National Cable & Telecommunications Association, Washington, DC, April 1996, pp. 10–18.
8. Bell Communications Research, "Reliability Assurance for Fiber-Optic System Reliability and Service Availability," *TR-NWT-000418*, Issue 2, December 1992.
9. Rainer Kochan, "Value-Added Services and Functions for MATV and CATV Systems," *Symposium Record, CATV Sessions, 16th International TV Symposium*, Montreux, Switzerland, June 1989, pp. 524–535.
10. Dean Ericson and Dan Carter, "Demand-Side Management Considerations in Advanced Network Deployment," *1994 NCTA Technical Papers*, National Cable & Telecommunications Association, Washington, DC, May 1994, pp. 8–14.

Architectural Elements and Examples

10.1 INTRODUCTION

Network architecture is the logical and physical interconnection of all elements between a signal's generation and its termination. Chapter 9 dealt with ways of measuring architecture-related parameters and the needs of various types of services. This chapter will first delineate each of the elements from which an architecture is constructed and then present some examples of high-level HFC distribution networks that have been proposed or built. Fiber-deep architectures will be covered in Chapter 11; the relationship between network architecture and service reliability and availability will be dealt with in Chapter 12.

10.2 ARCHITECTURAL ELEMENTS

Although network architecture is often thought of in terms of physical distribution topology, everything from the internal headend (and pre-headend) processing through network termination equipment affects how services are delivered. It is important, therefore, to understand the implications of available options at all levels of the network. This broader context is discussed in our earlier book, *Modern Cable Television Technology* (Morgan Kaufmann, 2004). In this volume, we will discuss only the linear HFC network that receives a fully multiplexed FDM spectrum of modulated RF signals at the headend or hub and delivers it intact to subscriber outlets served by the system.

10.2.1 Terminal Equipment

Terminal equipment is relevant to this discussion to the extent that it affects the design and operation of the HFC network. Most customer terminal equipment is connected to outlets within the customer's premises. In Section 3.8, we discussed **299** typical characteristics of internal drop wiring. Since customers are allowed to modify their own internal wiring using cable and devices of uncontrolled performance, the characteristics of in-home coaxial networks can vary widely, however. *Point-of-entry* (POE) equipment is located where the drop enters the customer premises, before any splitting. Examples include telephone *network interface devices* (NIDs) and devices that might be used to re-create the analog video spectrum for each customer from incoming digital video signals in order to free spectrum formerly used for analog video transport.

By nature of its location, a POE device that incorporates an RF transceiver can tolerate a lower receive level at the tap, and it will not require as high an upstream transmit level as a device connected to an in-home outlet since it avoids the losses due to internal customer splitters and outlet wiring. By avoiding the variation in internal wiring losses, POE devices can also tolerate a wider variation in levels at the tap and will have a more consistent transmit level.

Another category of POE device is the drop amplifier. By adding gain (sometimes bi-directional), this device reduces the required tap level, and overcomes high internal splitting and cable losses, but also adds distortion and noise that must be factored into the overall system performance budget since cable operators are responsible for the signal performance as measured at the input port of customers' television receivers and modems.

If network powered, POE devices affect the overall powering design of the coaxial distribution system and also require that all taps be capable of extracting power from the network. Finally, POE devices may include full or partial filtering of the upstream spectrum, and thus offer some protection for the network against signals that ingress into, or are generated within, customers' premises. Figure 10.1 summarizes the advantages of POE versus in-home terminal equipment placement.

10.2.2 Coaxial Distribution Network

The generic design of coaxial distribution systems was covered in Chapter 3. Within the general framework of amplified, split, and tapped networks, however, there are many architectural variables.

RF Bandwidth

The most basic parameter of any coaxial network is the forward and return bandwidth. Since these are determined primarily by the amplification equipment, some operators are proposing the use of coaxial distribution networks small enough that they can be totally passive between the output of the fiber node and the user. Such networks have the advantage that the division between upstream and downstream bandwidth can be altered at will, as can the upper frequency limit. As a practical matter, however, these freedoms are restricted by regulations covering carriage of over-air broadcast signals (even after the cessation of analog broadcasting in February 2009), regulations about signal delivery to customer-owned devices, and the tuning range of deployed cable-supplied devices. Also, the upper frequency will

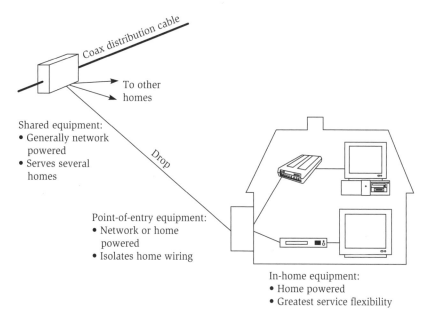

Coax distribution cable

To other homes

Shared equipment:
• Generally network powered
• Serves several homes

Drop

Point-of-entry equipment:
• Network or home powered
• Isolates home wiring

In-home equipment:
• Home powered
• Greatest service flexibility

FIGURE 10.1

Choices for locating network termination equipment.

be constrained by the characteristics of the passive devices used, by the increasing loss of the cables, and by the practical limits on signal levels in the network, as discussed in Chapter 2.

Coaxial Serving Area Size

The next most basic decision in the design of an HFC network is the size of the area (measured in number of homes passed) to be served by each physically separate coaxial subnetwork that can transport a unique set of signals. Since the use of the RF bandwidth is shared among all the users in the serving area, this determines the upper limit on bandwidth per home passed.

Since reliability is inversely proportional to the number of series-connected critical components, the required network availability and failure rate for the services to be offered should also be a factor in determining serving area size. The calculation of network reliability and availability will be discussed in detail in Chapter 12.

Typically, three to four separate coaxial distribution legs will be served from each fiber-optic node, offering opportunities for subsequent node size reductions. Some operators, in fact, design nodes for subsequent subdivision.

Coaxial Powering

The average reliability of commercial power is often lower than the total end-to-end required network performance. Thus, systems usually employ a powering strategy that minimizes the effects of power interruptions. Conventional cable television "standby" power supplies typically provide 1 to 2 hours of operation from self-contained batteries. While this is sufficient for short interruptions, some percentage of interruptions will exceed this length. In systems where customers are affected by more than one such power supply, reliability will further decrease due to the typically noncorrelated nature of those interruptions.

Where the individual coaxial distribution legs are limited to approximately 150 homes passed (assuming typical suburban, single-family home densities), it is practical to power the entire coaxial subnetwork from a single location, even when network-powered POE interface devices are used. This is, in fact, the strategy typically used by U.S. telephone companies that have constructed HFC networks. Single-point powering of this size network, however, generally requires using 90 volts, with maximum currents on the order of 15 amperes. Voltage limitations as well as electrical safety issues are controlled in the United States by the National Electrical Safety Code or local codes, at the option of each community.[1]

In order to achieve telephone-grade reliability, operators offering primary-line telephone service and high-availability data services have sometimes equipped these common power supplies with 8-hour battery capacity and/or backup generators. The generators, in turn, can be powered by self-contained fuel supplies or tied to available natural gas mains. Whether these steps are justified is, in part, related to the reliability of local utility power.

Where the current-handling capabilities of components or the voltage drop through distribution cables might otherwise limit application of single-point powering, the output from one power supply is sometimes divided among several power distribution cables whose resistance per unit length is less than the RF distribution cables. These power bypass cables may be routed alongside the signal cables past the first split point, where lower currents can be inserted into each of several network legs. This is illustrated in Figure 10.2. Since these power distribution cables do not carry RF, lower impedances and nonstandard construction are sometimes used to reduce power loss.[2]

When battery backup supplies are used, major improvements in outage rate and availability can occur if the supplies are equipped with monitoring systems that alert network operators to commercial power outages so that crews with portable generators can provide interim power before the batteries expire.

10.2.3 Fiber Node

Individual fiber nodes provide the interface between the linear fiber trunking system and coaxial distribution legs. At the simplest level, such a node may consist of a single optical receiver whose output is amplified to feed the downstream amplifiers and an upstream optical transmitter whose input is driven by the output of a combiner whose inputs are the upstream signals from all connected coaxial distribution legs. There are, however, many architectural variations.

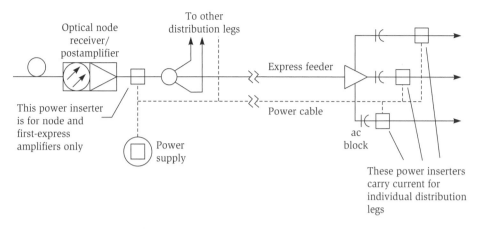

FIGURE 10.2

Bypass powering to increase the reach of a node-located power supply.

Split-Band Multiple Fiber Inputs

Some nodes provide the option for multiple downstream input fibers that are fed to separate optical receivers whose outputs are then combined in a diplex filter. This results in improved signal quality because, with a lower signal load, the optical modulation index per signal can be higher (leading to improved C/N) while the lower number of signals results in fewer second- and third-order distortion products and thus improved C/CTB and C/CSO. Additionally, the diplex filter eliminates distortion products at each receiver output that would affect the (nonoverlapping) RF output spectrum from the other receiver. The relative gains in C/N and distortion can be exchanged, within a limited range, by adjusting the optical modulation depth.

A more common reason to use split-band optical inputs is to allow signals that are common to multiple nodes to be carried on a single optical carrier and those that are node-specific to be carried separately. As will be seen later in the chapter, this can result in overall bandwidth scalability per customer and cost savings, but it restricts future ability to reallocate bandwidth between common and narrowcast signals (because the diplex filters in every node will have to be changed).

Redundant Multiple Fiber Inputs

An alternate use for multiple downstream input fibers is redundancy of the fiber-optic trunking network. In nodes equipped with redundant inputs, each fiber is routed to its own full-bandwidth receiver. A switch at the output of the receivers selects the better (or surviving) signal in the case of failure or degradation of one path. If the fibers feeding the node are diversely routed (so that the probability of simultaneous cut is low), significant gains in reliability can result. As a practical matter, the gain in reliability is limited by the reliability of the switch (and its control

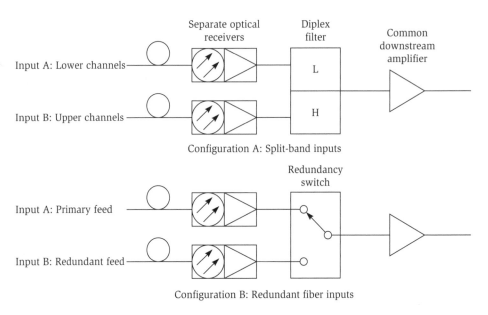

FIGURE 10.3

Fiber node multiple input options.

circuit), which is an added critical element in the signal path. As Figure 10.3 shows, the configurations are very similar; in fact, some manufacturers offer either one as an option in the same node platform.

Redundant Signal Processing

For applications where availability is critical, nodes are available with additional redundant elements. Power supplies, downstream and upstream amplifier modules, and upstream optical transmitters are all available in dual configurations. In the last-mentioned case, dual upstream optical outputs are provided, enabling diversely routed external cables.

Handling of Multiple Coaxial Distribution Legs

Generally, optical nodes are used to feed more than one coaxial distribution leg. Although this is a design convenience that allows for shorter coaxial cascades by placing the feed point near the logical center of the node-serving area, electrically separating the coaxial legs also offers opportunities for effective bandwidth expansion and improved upstream performance. One option, described in Chapter 8, is block segment conversion, whereby the upstream signals from different legs are converted to nonoverlapping frequency ranges. Thus, the bandwidth per home passed is limited by the coax-serving area rather than by the larger node-serving area. Offsetting the per-subscriber bandwidth gain is the increased performance required of the upstream optical transmitter, which must handle more signals and increased RF bandwidth. In some cases, this will require upgrading from FP to DFB transmitters, at a considerable increase in cost. In addition, each frequency conversion step generally involves phase-locked loops tied to some sort of pilot (to ensure that the conversion and reconversion do not create any net frequency offsets), and that, in turn, adds an irreducible amount of phase noise to the converted signals, which must not cause the total upstream phase noise to exceed allowable standards.

An alternate way of achieving the same upstream bandwidth expansion is to use separate upstream transmitters and fibers for each distribution leg. A third alternative is to use separate (and more expensive) upstream transmitters operating on different optical wavelengths and to combine their outputs using a wavelength division multiplexer (WDM). Whether the separate fibers or WDM option is less expensive will depend on the length of the fiber transmission path and the relative cost of the transmitters and multiplexers.

A final option is to first process the entire upstream spectrum from each coaxial leg by converting it to a high-speed baseband digital signal, to time-multiplex these signals, and to then feed them to a high-speed baseband digital optical transmitter. Several manufacturers offer versions of this technique, with either two or four inputs multiplexed to create a single baseband datastream of about 2 Gb/s. These transmitters are also available in ITU-grid DWDM wavelengths so that they can be further multiplexed at the hub before transmission to the headend.

These four options are illustrated in Figure 10.4. Note that optical splitting or use of additional laser transmitters can, in theory, be used with any option to create dual outputs for feeding diversely routed fibers for higher upstream reliability, though the incremental cost is least for single-fiber configurations.

10.2.4 Fiber Interconnects

Linear fiber-optic links provide the connectivity between the point where the FDM spectrum is created and its delivery to coaxial distribution legs. Fiber links are also used at higher levels in the network to distribute selected signals of all types, often in digital form. Although fiber-optic links are used among headends and between headends and outside information sources (such as broadcasters and Internet service providers), this section will discuss only those links that form part of the linear network extending from headends to and from end customers. Fiber architecture will form the largest part of this chapter, beginning with basic network options and proceeding to specific examples.

Star

The simplest optical architecture, and the one most commonly deployed for transmitting analog FDM signals from headends or hubs to and from nodes, is the *star*, defined as separate paths from a common point to multiple termination points. When constructed with dedicated optical fibers, driven by separate transmitters, the star architecture allows complete independence in the signals delivered to each

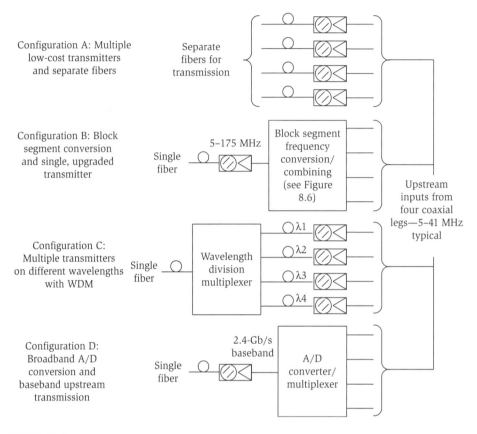

FIGURE 10.4

Options for segmentation of upstream coaxial inputs.

node (as opposed to the most common type of microwave broadband star network, which splits the output of a common transmitter to feed multiple antennas and paths). In fact, many cable systems optically split fiber transmitter outputs to feed two to three nodes, but do that splitting in the headend so as to allow easy separation of nodes in the future when greater network segmentation is appropriate.

Though the failure of an individual fiber feeding a receiving point affects only the subscribers on that node, practical cable routing often results in one cable sheath holding the fibers for many nodes and thus creates a possible single point of failure that is much larger (see Figure 10.5).

Sheath Ring

The exposure to outages caused by fiber cuts or failures can be reduced significantly by sending the signals between the common point and each termination via physically diverse routes. When multiple termination points can be arranged in a ring

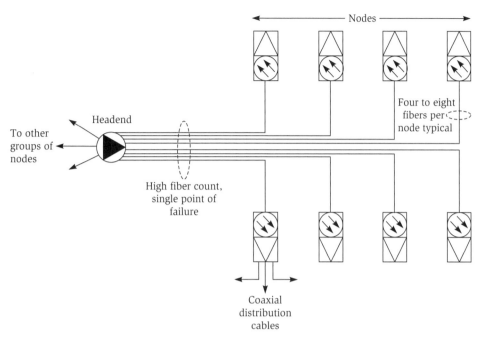

FIGURE 10.5

Star architecture.

configuration, considerable savings result from the sharing of common construction costs, as shown in Figure 10.6. This architecture is known as a *sheath ring*. Note that the diagram shows only a single line in each direction around the loop from the common point to each node, whereas in fact there may be several (at least one upstream and one downstream). Analysis of the figure will show that the cable can be cut at any point without destroying continuity from the common point to each node.

Although the sheath ring architecture preserves the signal independence of the star and adds a considerable degree of protection against fiber cuts, it does so at the expense of a considerable increase in total *fiber* footage. Depending on the physical layout of the ring, however, the total *cable* footage may be only slightly greater than for a simple star. Since construction costs typically are much greater than fiber costs, the incremental cost of the installation may be only moderately higher.

Sheath rings are a common architecture among competitive access providers (CAPs) who offer highly reliable data transport to commercial customers. They are also commonly provided between headends and hubs in multiple-level architectures, to protect against potentially very large outages should a major optical trunk cable be cut; one major U.S. multiple system operator (MSO) pioneered its use between hubs and nodes.

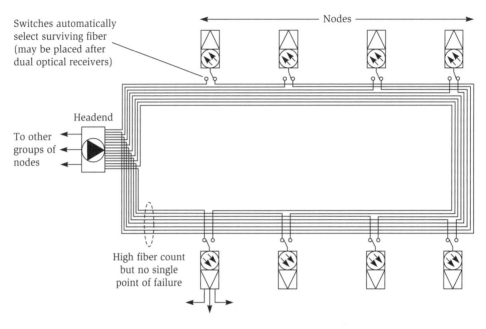

FIGURE 10.6

Sheath ring architecture.

Analog Shared Ring

Where a common set of signals must be sent to multiple nodes, an economical structure is the shared ring, illustrated in Figure 10.7. The common signal spectrum is transmitted both clockwise and counterclockwise from the common point using separate fibers (and often separate transmitters to increase the degree of redundancy). At each node, a portion of the signal is coupled from both rings and fed to separate optical receivers. A redundancy switch, as described in the optical node options section, selects the surviving path in the event of a cable cut or transmitter failure. Alternatively, the optical switch can be placed ahead of a single receiver.

Though shared rings can be constructed at 1310-nm wavelength, the maximum available optical budget of approximately 17 dB (see Chapter 4) limits the number of receiving nodes. At 1550 nm, however, fiber losses are lower, and optical amplifiers are available that can considerably increase the available loss budget.

A major advantage of the shared ring is obviously a considerable savings in optical fiber usage and number of transmitters, as compared with either a simple star or a sheath ring, while preserving the protection against fiber cuts and transmitter failures. Although its application is limited to distribution of a common signal spectrum, analog shared rings are effective when combined with other structures.

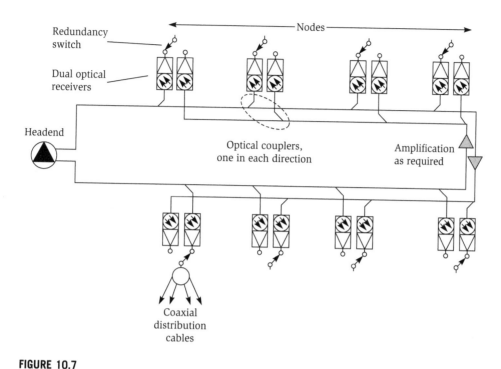

FIGURE 10.7

Analog shared ring architecture.

Passive Optical Networks

Another optical distribution architecture is known as the passive optical network (PON), in which common signals are split optically (usually at multiple levels) to feed multiple endpoints from a common hub. Since no active equipment is required between the hub and the end customer, powering is simplified and reliability is determined by the physical fiber and the passive optical devices. PONs are discussed in Chapter 11.

10.3 ARCHITECTURAL EXAMPLES

Engineering is the art of solving a technical problem for the lowest cost, given a well-defined set of requirements for performance, reliability, scalability, and other factors. Unfortunately for the engineer, the problem is not always well defined, although the budget for a given project may be. In that case, the task is to find innovative ways of meeting the short-term essential goals while planning for an ill-defined future expansion. Such is almost always the case when designing the architecture for a cable television system. The many variants now deployed are testimony to the ingenuity of different designers. Thus, this section will concentrate more on the trade-offs among options than on comparing complete architectures.

The following basic requirements are the same for any architecture:

- The end-of-line technical quality must meet corporate standards. At the least, it must meet FCC-defined performance levels with a sufficient margin to cover normal operating variations.

- The reliability and availability must be adequate for the services to be offered.

- The bandwidth must be sufficient to deliver all services to all customers. As a practical matter, the available bandwidth will be divided among commonly delivered signals and those delivered to specific customers on a demand basis.

- The number of potential customers affected by any single network element failure must be limited to those who can be reasonably responded to by the customer service organization.

- The initial capital investment must be as small as possible, consistent with delivering the initial slate of services to the existing, or anticipated, initial number of customers.

- The network must be capable of cost-effective expansion to deliver additional services, to respond to higher utilization of initially defined services, and to respond to greater penetration among homes passed. This requirement is known as *scalability*, and the best designs allow scalability that is specific to individual services and specific geographic areas.

10.3.1 Historical Development and Small-System Architectures

One of the earliest HFC architectures to develop was the cable area network (CAN), conceived as a rebuild strategy for older coaxial networks. The principal is illustrated in Figure 10.8. Fiber-optic links from the headend were used to transmit the common spectrum to selected nodes inserted at regular intervals in a former all-coaxial distribution network. This effectively shortened the cascades, which allowed the system to be upgraded to a greater RF bandwidth. Reliability, which was improved by shortening the cascade, was further enhanced by leaving the coaxial network between the nodes in place as a backup in case a fiber strand or transmitter failed.

Although a number of systems were upgraded using the CAN architecture, they were limited by being constrained to a common channel lineup. In fact, the architecture was useful primarily as a mechanism for minimum-cost bandwidth expansion and reliability improvement.

The first step toward truly innovative fiber architectures was similar to the CAN architecture, except that instead of just inserting nodes into an existing amplifier cascade, greater cascade reduction was realized by feeding both directions from the nodes. This was originally known as a *fiber backbone* and, like CAN, was proposed as a cost-effective system upgrade strategy. It became favored over CAN

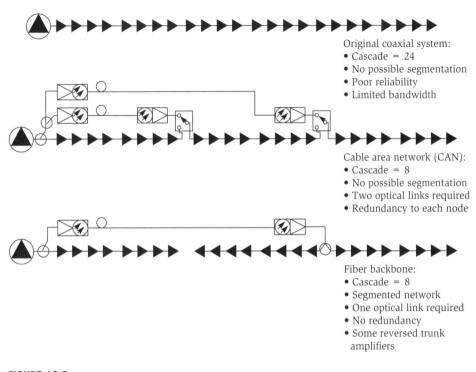

Original coaxial system:
- Cascade = 24
- No possible segmentation
- Poor reliability
- Limited bandwidth

Cable area network (CAN):
- Cascade = 8
- No possible segmentation
- Two optical links required
- Redundancy to each node

Fiber backbone:
- Cascade = 8
- Segmented network
- One optical link required
- No redundancy
- Some reversed trunk amplifiers

FIGURE 10.8

Principles of CAN and fiber backbone architectures.

because, although it lost the redundancy feature, far fewer fiber links were needed for a given cascade reduction and fiber links were perceived to be highly reliable. The critical difference, however, was that the fiber backbone architecture had created the ability to independently program nodes, thus creating a simple star network.

10.3.2 Node Size and Architecture

A basic building block in any HFC architecture is the node, where optical signals are detected and launched into coaxial distribution cables and into the coaxial distribution subnetwork extending from there to customers. An important decision that fundamentally limits per-customer effective bandwidth is the number of potential customers served by each node.

As the cost of fiber cables, transmitters, and receivers has dropped and performance has improved, the smallest economic node sizes have dropped continuously. With sufficiently small nodes, it has become practical to offer bandwidth-intensive subscriber-specific services such as telephony, high-speed modems, and video on demand. RF bandwidths of 870 to 1000 MHz combined with 500-home nodes are common for new construction, but many designs call for much smaller nodes, with a continuum from there down to fiber-to-the-curb (FTTC) designs that use individual cables to customers. Also common are designs in which multiple coaxial distribution legs are fed from a common node housing configured so that it can be divided electrically into separate logical nodes, one for each leg.

Figure 10.9 shows one example of a three-step, serving-area division plan that uses evolutionary capabilities built into some manufacturers' nodes. As initially installed, one optical receiver detects commonly delivered analog signals and the other detects node-specific signals. After RF combining, output is split to feed all four coaxial output legs, each designed to deliver signals to approximately 125 homes. Each leg consists of an express feeder followed by an amplifier that drives tapped distribution cables. In the upstream direction, all four legs are combined at RF and fed to one input of a shared A/D converter, followed by an upstream transmitter. Thus, node size is 500 homes in both directions. Three active fibers are required.

At the first level of scaling, a second node-specific downstream receiver is added and the downstream configuration changed to create two 250-home downstream virtual nodes, and a second two-input upstream converter/transmitter module is

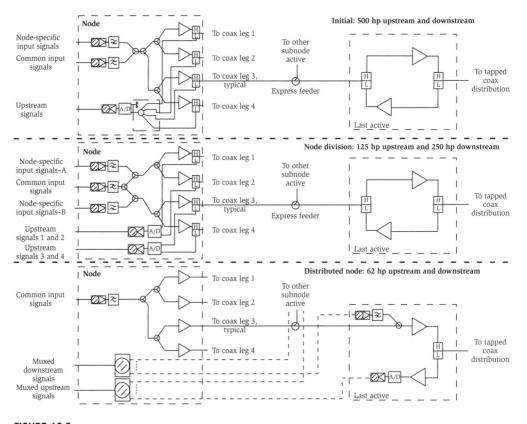

FIGURE 10.9

A typical node-scaling strategy.

added (or a four-input A/D used—both are commercially available) to create four 125-home upstream virtual nodes. This asymmetry is consistent with predictions that upstream bandwidth will be saturated before downstream bandwidth. Five fibers are required to support this configuration, unless WDM is used. This is a very cost-effective upgrade, since only modules in the node, and the matching headend equipment, need be changed.

At the third level of evolution, fibers (dashed lines in the figure) are lashed over the express feeder to selected amplifier locations. Optical receivers are added there for only the node-specific programming, with the power and common signals traveling over the coaxial link. There are several options for upstream node division. In this example, CWDM transmitters are added at each amplifier location and a CWDM multiplexer at the original node location. On the assumption that eight amplifiers are ultimately required to serve the 500-home serving area, the final virtual node size has been reduced to approximately 62 homes. With downstream and upstream CWDM devices at the original node location, as few as three fibers from the hub are sufficient to support this level of division.

10.3.3 Multilayer Networks

As pointed out earlier, pure star networks require a lot of glass and typically have single points of failure affecting many subscribers because the fibers feeding multiple nodes share the few available physical paths leading away from the headends. These problems are proportionately worse as systems get bigger and as nodes get smaller. Given the trend toward regional consolidation and deeper fiber penetration, different architectures are required.

These larger networks include intermediate processing points called *hubs*. Depending on the specifics of the design, more than one intermediate layer may be specified. The addition of hubs offers some or all of the following advantages, depending on design:

- Shared use of fibers in the headend-to-hub link, thereby reducing the number of fibers required
- Provision of redundant transport between headend and hub, thereby improving reliability and reducing the possibility of outages affecting many subscribers simultaneously
- Use of intermediate signal processing at each hub to realize a net improvement in end-of-line quality
- Distribution of switched-service processing equipment to reduce instantaneous demand on headend-to-hub circuit capacity

There are two divergent opinions on how best to use hubs. One camp prefers to push as much signal-processing equipment out to the hubs as possible. This reduces the bandwidth requirement between headend and hub because many signals are locally generated at the hub and only the multiplexed network-side signals need be transported back to the headend. For instance, VOD movies may be stored at hubs and streamed from there to specific customers on demand; only the occasional content updates need be sent down from the headend to hub-based servers. Similarly, CMTSs at hubs can terminate both telephone and data signals with only the multiplexed signals transported over baseband optical links back to the headend.

A second advantage is potentially improved analog video quality. If such signals are digitized, transported in that form to the hub, and reconverted to analog for transmission over the relatively short distance to customers, a higher end-to-end quality may be realized, especially where the total distance from headend to customer is at the outer limits of analog transport links. If the signals transported from headend to hub are all digital, the distance between them can be virtually unlimited, allowing arbitrarily large networks.

Offsetting these advantages, it is almost always more costly to divide processing among several locations than to do it all in the headend. Second, the more complex the signal processing at each hub, the greater the likelihood that failures will occur there. Then system operators are faced with a choice between a longer time to restore service outages and the higher staffing costs required to station personnel at each hub. Finally, the larger and more complex the hub, the higher will be the associated costs for real estate, emergency powering systems, air conditioning, and so on.

The alternative multilayer philosophy centralizes as much signal processing as possible at the headend. Hubs are then used primarily or exclusively for optical processing and redundancy switching. For instance, DWDM transport may be used in a redundant sheath ring between headend and hub, with redundancy switching and DWDM demultiplexing there to separate the signals for each served node. Thus, the operator is able to realize reduced fiber usage and redundancy over the greater part of the path between the headend and the subscriber while utilizing a very compact and inexpensive hub. With 16-wavelength multiplexing, it is entirely possible to build a hub serving more than 100 nodes in a half-dozen standard equipment racks, with similarly modest requirements for power and air conditioning.

Offsetting these advantages, purely optical nodes, although more efficient than pure star networks, typically require more fibers in the headend-to-hub link than hubs that include more local processing functions. In addition, the use of linear optical transport puts an upper limit on headend-to-hub distance and thus on system size. Although optical amplification is possible, each stage of amplification adds noise, and fiber-related cross-modulation and second-order distortion increase with distance, as discussed in Chapter 5. Depending on the specific design, a typical upper limit is about 30 to 40 miles.

These architectural philosophies are not necessarily exclusive. A large system might well have several interconnected major hubs containing much of the signal generation and service support equipment, each connected through linear optical links to smaller optical hubs that support clusters of nodes. The impact of multilayer networks on HFC distribution network design is that not all modulated RF signals may originate at the same location, creating a need for downstream combining of some sort, as seen in the following examples.

10.3.4 **Centralized Architecture Example**

Figure 10.10 is an example of the optical distribution network in a centralized architecture. As can be seen, it is characterized by

- Separate processing of commonly distributed downstream signals (or, more accurately, area-specific since some metropolitan area channels generally vary from city to city), node-specific downstream and upstream signals, with the downstream split-band scheme maintained all the way through node receivers
- Generation of node-specific signals at the headend level
- Redundant transport of node-specific QAM signals from headend to optical hub using DWDM to reduce the number of fibers required
- Star distribution from the hub to individual nodes
- Redundant transport of digitized upstream signals from hub to headend using DWDM
- An all-optical hub, with no RF or baseband signals except for status monitoring
- Flexibility in scaling each interactive service within the headend

Analyzing this network in sections is easiest.

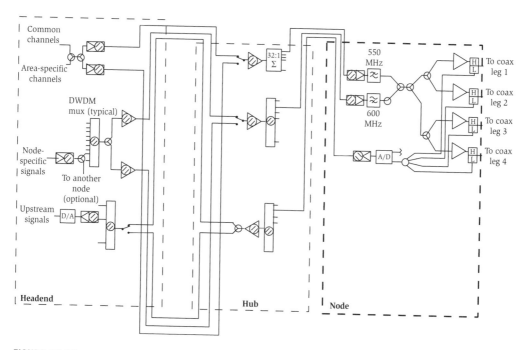

FIGURE 10.10

Optical transport portion of a centralized headend-hub-node architecture.

Optical Transport Options

The optical transport architecture uses an externally modulated transmitter and a dedicated fiber for the analog-modulated video signals. At the hub, the signal is optically amplified and split 32 times, with one leg feeding each node on a dedicated fiber. Two headend transmitters drive separate fibers in the sheath ring configuration to provide redundancy against both transmitter and optical cable failure. DWDM is not an option for this link because the crosstalk mechanisms would result in interference below system specifications. Directly modulated transmitters are similarly not an option, because more than an octave is carried and transmitter chirp and self-phase modulation interacting with the fiber dispersion would result in serious CSO distortion.

The QAM signals directly modulate DFB transmitters that are combined using 16-wavelength DWDM between headend and hub. There, the combined signal is amplified and then the wavelengths separated, with a second dedicated fiber feeding a separate receiver in each node. Since less than an octave is carried and the output of the QAM detector is filtered before combining with the analog video spectrum, the second-order distortion is not a problem. Crosstalk mechanisms are a factor in determining the end-of-line C/N, but it is possible to achieve a 40-dB end-to-end system specification, which is adequate for 256 QAM signals.

There are other options that a system engineer should consider in deciding on an architecture for the downstream signals. Some examples follow:

- Common and node-specific signals could have been combined at the headend and used to modulate an externally modulated transmitter for each node. This would require fewer node receivers but more expensive transmitters as well as a dedicated fiber for each node.

- The common signals and node-specific signals could have been detected at the hub, filtered and combined, and then used to modulate a 1310-nm DFB transmitter for transmission to the node, as shown in Figure 10.11. This would trade the cost of the optical amplifiers at the hub, the second downstream receiver at each node, and one downstream fiber for the cost of one DFB transmitter at the hub and the additional noise penalty from two series-connected transmitter–receiver pairs. It would also allow city-specific channels to be mixed at the hub level.

- The common and node-specific optical signals could have been combined optically at the hub and then transmitted over a single fiber to a single receiver at the node, as shown in Figure 10.12. One U.S. MSO uses a version of this architecture extensively. As discussed in Chapter 5, however, it
  - Restricts the hub-to-node distance to minimize the level of second-order products, or
  - Requires the use of dispersion-shifted fiber and very flat DWDM demuxes to reduce the amplitude of second-order products, or
  - Restricts the node-specific bandwidth to less than 50 MHz to keep those products below channel 2.

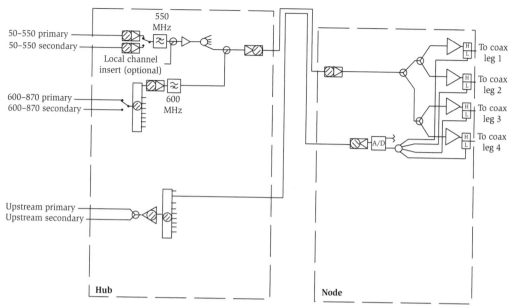

FIGURE 10.11

Optional repeating at the hub.

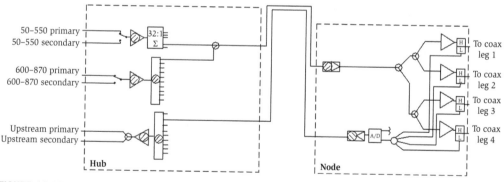

FIGURE 10.12

Optical combining at the hub.

- Although the upstream signals in the example were generated by converting the entire 5- to 41-MHz return band to a digital stream and transmitting as a high-speed baseband signal, the architecture would be similar if they were transmitted as analog signals. The trade-off is cost versus upstream optical budget and signal "durability" relative to degradation in the optical link.

There is no right answer here, only options that should be considered and evaluated against required performance, cost, scalability, and maintainability.

Optical Redundancy Options

Other choices determine the degree of redundancy. Figure 10.13, for instance, shows some alternatives for the analog common signal spectrum that could also be applied to the other signals:

- The *expanded-redundancy option* shows that placing two optical amplifiers ahead of the redundancy switch would protect against failure of any active hub device for the cost of one high-power amplifier for every set of nodes.

- As the *highly redundant option* shows, using two optical amplifiers in the hub driving separate, diversely routed fibers to each node, with a redundancy switch after the detectors there, would protect against amplifier failure, cable cuts between hub and node, and node receiver failure. For the highest redundancy, the two sets of hub equipment could be in separate facilities, offering added protection against a major facility failure (such as a fire). The use of redundant rings between hub and nodes is a feature of the Cox Communications "ring-in-ring" architecture.[3]

- Rather than two separate headend transmitters, a single transmitter can be used to drive both directions around the headend-to-hub ring, at a considerable savings in cost and some reduction in reliability, as shown in the *reduced-redundancy option*. In the case of externally modulated transmitters, this is particularly easy since a second, isolated output is "free" because of the way Mach-Zehnder modulators work.

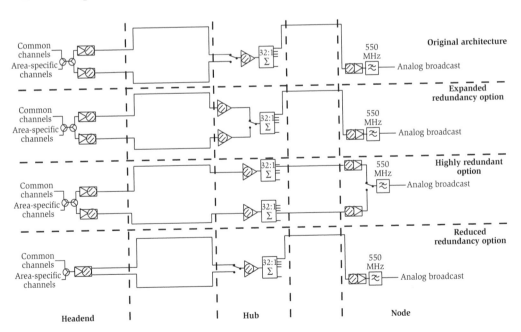

FIGURE 10.13

Examples of redundancy options for analog broadcast spectrum transport.

Scalability

Scalability is simply a way of expressing the ability of a system to meet growing demand for existing services or to deliver new services. What that means, on a technical level, is the ability to grow the service- and area-specific ratio of bandwidth to homes. Section 10.3.2 covered options for scaling the node and its serving area. Such scaling can obviously be applied on a node-by-node basis, as required, but it affects all services. Additionally, the downstream virtual node can initially be made larger by splitting the downstream QAM transmitters in the headend to feed multiple nodes.

Services can be scaled independent of the distribution plant scaling in a properly designed headend, however. The size of the *service group* of customers sharing signals devoted to some given service can initially be made up of as many nodes as desired, with the number of nodes decreasing as penetration increases. As penetration and use increase further, additional bandwidth can be devoted to the services, further increasing the service-specific bandwidth per customer. All of this scaling is independent of plant-dependent techniques such as increasing RF bandwidth and splitting nodes.

10.4 SUMMARY

The architecture of a system determines the services it can deliver. It controls effective bandwidth, reliability, flexibility, and distribution of signal processing. This chapter has described some of the architectural elements and how each is related to essential network characteristics. The examples given illustrate choices made or proposed to meet specific service requirements in specific service areas.

The most common small-system architecture in use today is the single star, with nodes connected directly to a single headend. In large regional systems, formerly independent headends are often linked by either digital or 1550-nm analog, fiber-optic links to a large master headend and become hubs. Single coaxial cable low-split-band plans are used in the vast majority of systems, with individual nodes serving 400 to 1000 homes. Coaxial amplifier cascades vary from 1 to 6 in typical new upgrades.

It is possible to "push" much signal processing out to hubs in order to increase the efficiency of the headend-to-hub links, or to centralize the processing for easier management at the expense of needing more fiber capacity. In the largest systems, both structures may be used in multitiered architectures.

In considering an architecture, initial cost is certainly a factor. But just as important is the ability to scale to meet market demand and opportunities without "stranding" capital and without causing excessive service interruptions to existing customers because of required reconfiguration.

The relationship between architecture, network reliability, and network availability is a major topic in itself. This chapter has been limited to options within conventional HFC networks. Chapter 11 discusses FTTC and FTTH networks. The methodology for estimating reliability-related parameters is given in Chapter 12.

ENDNOTES

1. *National Electrical Safety Code.* Published by the Institute of Electrical and Electronics Engineers, New York, and approved by the American National Standards Institute as C2-1997.

2. Dan Kerr, "Power Distribution in a Lifeline Network," *Communications Technology,* May 1997, pp. 64-70.

3. Cox Communications Corporate Engineering Staff, "Rings, Clamshells and Spurs," *CED Magazine*, February 1995, pp. 24-34.

Emerging Architectures

11.1 INTRODUCTION

This chapter covers binary (digital) modulation of a fiber-optic cable as well as deep-fiber architectures. The two are covered together because binary optical transmission is frequently used in last-mile (to the home and/or business) applications. In addition, binary optical transmission is used extensively in metropolitan loops and in intercity trunks. An advantage of digital modulation is that it can operate with much lower signal-to-noise ratio than can analog modulation, as shown in Figure 4.13. Also, output level is not dependent on optical level, and there is no degradation of signals through the system (to the point that they go away, of course). We compare digital optical transmission with analog optical transmission normally practiced in cable television, and then we show popular architectures for bringing fiber to or near the home.

11.2 ANALOG AND DIGITAL OPTICAL MODULATION

Figure 11.1 illustrates the difference between digital and analog optical modulation. Figure 11.1a represents digital modulation of the optical transmitter. The data are not modulated onto an RF carrier. Rather, they directly modulate the laser, turning it on and off. If more than one datastream is provided, they are *time division multiplexed* (TDM) by switching first to one and then to another until all have been sampled. Since no data can be lost during the multiplexing process, the output data rate must be the sum of all input data rates, usually with more bits added to synchronize data recovery, and to make sure the message gets to the right place. The data rate actually carried by the laser is called the *wire rate*.

Contrast this to the common cable television technique of broadcast (RF-based) optical transmission, as covered in Chapter 4 and shown in Figure 11.1b. In this system, we often transmit digital signals, which may be TDM'd and then modulated onto RF carriers, normally using either 64- or 256-QAM modulation. These digitally modulated carriers are combined with analog-modulated carriers, and the sum of all signals modulates an analog laser, which operates in its linear range, where **321**

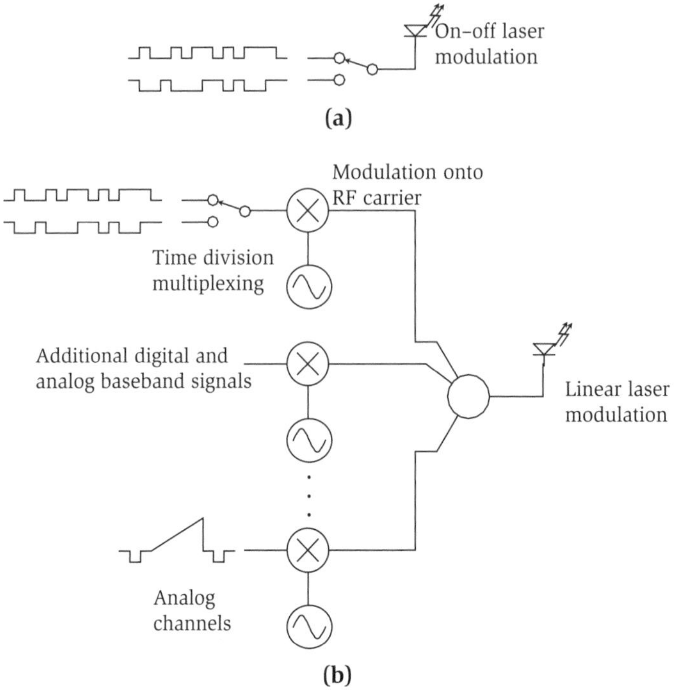

On-off laser modulation

(a)

Modulation onto RF carrier

Time division multiplexing

Additional digital and analog baseband signals

Linear laser modulation

Analog channels

(b)

FIGURE 11.1

Difference between digital and analog optical modulation.

output power is proportional to input current. The use of multiple carriers to transmit different signals is called *frequency division multiplexing*, or FDM.

The term *analog* is applied to the optical transmitter in Figure 11.1b. It is true that this must be an analog transmitter, since a digital transmitter would never be able to carry the multiple frequencies without creating intolerable intermodulation distortion. However, the information carried as modulated signals on the analog transmitter may be either analog or digital.

11.2.1 The Difference between Analog and Digital Optical Modulation

Figure 11.2 illustrates the difference between analog and digital optical modulation of a laser. Compare with Figure 4.14, which covers analog modulation only. The analog signal occupies a range of diode currents in a more nearly linear range of laser operation. Note that the real analog waveform is not a sine wave; rather, it exhibits quite high peaks, as shown in Figure 4.21. Because of this, the carriers actually exceed the range shown, with resulting clipping distortion, as described in Section 4.10.3. The levels must be managed so that the clipping distortion is not excessive.

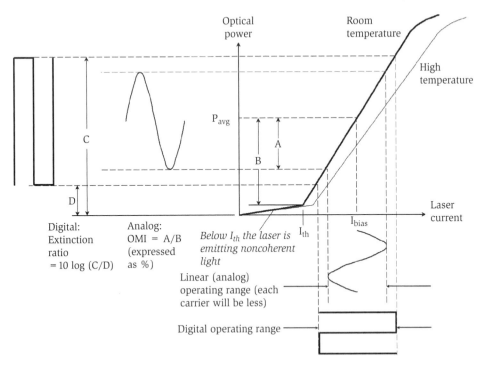

FIGURE 11.2

Modulation transfer functions for analog and digital optical modulators.

The digital signal is ideally a rectangular waveform occupying only two levels, with fast transition between them.

Both analog and digital optical transmitters are rated by their output power, which is the average power the transmitter puts out, P_{avg}, as defined in Figure 11.2. Analog transmitters are characterized by the optical modulation index, or OMI, as explained by Figure 4.14. By contrast, digital modulation is characterized by the *extinction ratio*, defined as the ratio between the light output in one binary state to the light output in the other binary state. Extinction ratio is expressed in dB, as shown in Figure 11.2. The laser is biased so as not to extinguish the lasing process at any time, because restarting the lasing process causes problems in transmission. A high extinction ratio is desirable in order to maximize the ability to discern between the two states. However, over temperature and the life of the laser, the laser must never turn off during either of the two states. A typical minimum extinction ratio is about 9 dB.

11.2.2 Digital and Analog Transmitters

Figure 11.3 illustrates a block diagram of a digital transmitter in part (a) and an externally modulated analog transmitter in part (b). Data is supplied to the input of the

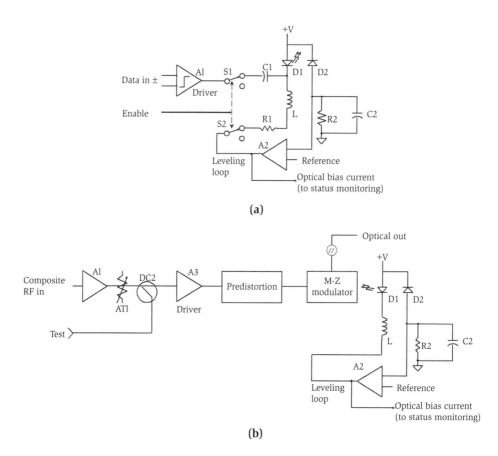

FIGURE 11.3

Optical transmitter block diagrams. (a) Digital. (b) Analog externally modulated.

digital transmitter, usually balanced to minimize signal radiation and noise pickup. The driver amplifier Al is a limiting amplifier, meaning that its output takes on only two states corresponding to the maximum and minimum laser output (C and D, respectively, in Figure 11.2). The drive signal to laser diode Dl is coupled through switch S1 and coupling capacitor C1.

Monitor photodiode D2 samples the light output from Dl. The light is converted to a current in D2, and the current to a voltage in R2. Capacitor C2 averages the voltage so that it is proportional to the average light output from D1. The voltage appears on the inverting input of leveling loop amplifier A2, which compares the voltage with a reference. If the two differ, then the output of A2 changes, thus changing the bias in Dl and hence changing its optical output power. The output of the leveling loop amplifier A2 is often supplied to a status-monitoring (or as element management) system, which monitors the current. The sensitivity of the laser diode decreases as it ages, resulting in more bias current needed to keep the light output constant. As the bias current approaches a specified threshold, it is time to replace the laser. This threshold may be monitored in the element management system, and/or a comparator (not shown) may be added to the transmitter to generate a binary alarm signal.

Switches S1 and S2 are used when the transmitter must be switched off and on, as when it is used for time division multiple access (TDMA) applications. TDMA is used in upstream transmissions, where many transmitters must "talk" to the head-end, each in its turn. When the laser is switched off, both the modulating signal from A1 and the bias from A2 must be removed to make sure the laser is extinguished.

Digital transmitters can use F-P lasers for short distances at 1310 nm and DFB lasers for longer distances and other wavelengths. Because of their simpler circuitry and because the laser does not have to operate linearly, digital laser transmitters are significantly lower in cost than are analog transmitters.

Contrast this to the externally modulated analog transmitter of Figure 11.3b. For fiber-deep applications, externally modulated transmitters are usually used because of their superior characteristics. Composite RF is applied to amplifier A1. In a typical cable television architecture, the composite input is the frequency-division-multiplexed set of signals that define the broadcast service. Attenuator AT1 sets the drive level. After driver amplifier A3, the signals are usually sent to a predistortion circuit, which compensates for distortion in the optical transmitter and signal path. Finally, signals are coupled to an external modulator, such as the Mach–Zender (M-Z) modulator described in Section 4.6.4. Monitor photodiode D2 serves to keep the output light level constant, as in the digital transmitter.

11.2.3 Digital and Analog Receivers

Figure 11.4 illustrates digital and analog receivers. In the digital receiver of Figure 11.4a, detector diode D1 receives the light and converts it to a current. The average current is filtered in L1 and converted to a voltage in resistor R1. Signal output is developed across L1, and AC-coupled through capacitor C1 to a *transimpedance amplifier* (TIA). The TIA has a high input impedance and a controlled output impedance, such as 50 ohms. It is a linear amplifier, so the output waveform is an accurate representation of the input light power. Automatic gain control (AGC) may or may not be used. The output of the TIA is filtered in low-pass filter FL1 to remove out-of-band noise and improve the waveform. Finally, the signal is shaped in limiter A3, which converts the analog levels to logic 1 and logic 0. Typically the output of A3 is balanced, again to keep switching currents out of the ground system. An activity detector detects the loss of either the optical signal or the digital modulation on the signal and can report this fact to a status-monitoring system.

Contrast the digital receiver just described with the analog receiver shown in Figure 11.4b. Light is again converted to a current in Dl, and the signal portion of the current is impedance-transformed in T1 before being applied to preamplifier Al. The gain is adjusted in attenuator R2 under control of either an AGC feedback loop or a feed-forward gain control circuit. A conventional feedback AGC circuit is often used in optical nodes, but for other applications the feed-forward gain control

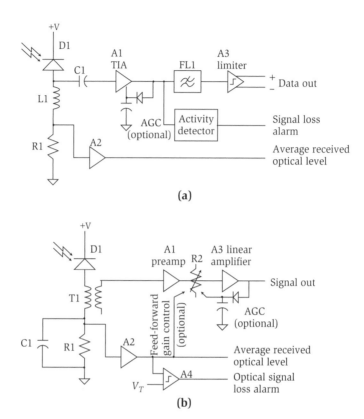

FIGURE 11.4

Optical receiver block diagrams. (a) Digital. (b) Analog.

may be used. The feed-forward circuit measures changes in the average optical level received, and corrects the gain for the RF level changes produced by changes in optical level. The average received signal level is derived as in the digital receiver, and a threshold detector, A4, may be used to generate a *loss-of-input* alarm.

11.3 COMBINING ANALOG AND DIGITAL TRANSMISSION ON THE SAME FIBER

It is quite possible to combine analog and digital transmission on the same fiber by using wavelength division multiplexing (WDM). Figure 11.5 illustrates a fiber-to-the-home (FTTH) system that uses WDM in accordance with the standards described later. One downstream transmitter (the digital transmitter) operates at 1490 nm, while the other (analog) operates in the 1550-nm region. The upstream digital transmitter operates at 1310 nm. Current standards (discussed later) use the wavelengths shown. Two or more wavelengths may be combined using a WDM, which is the

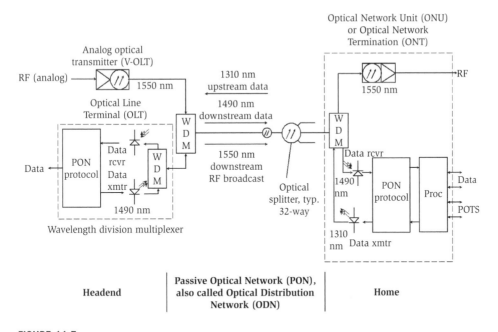

FIGURE 11.5

Wavelength standards for PONs. (Proc—processor; rcvr—receiver; xmtr—transmitter).

optical equivalent of a diplex filter. Each wavelength passes from its port to a common port with little attenuation.

Wavelengths closer to each other, such as multiple wavelengths in the 1550-nm region, may be multiplexed. The International Telecommunications Union (ITU) has specified standard wavelengths in this band. The technique of multiplexing closely spaced wavelengths is referred to as *dense wavelength division multiplexing* (DWDM) and is discussed in Chapter 5.

11.4 BIDIRECTIONAL TRANSMISSION

Almost all digital networks are bidirectional full-duplex links, in which transmission takes place simultaneously in both directions. Full-duplex transmission is accomplished differently in different situations. For long-distance transmission using either ATM or Ethernet, it is common to use different fibers for transmission in the two directions. Because of the high volume of transceivers for the these applications, it is possible to buy low-cost, very small transmitters specified for the different distances to be covered.

In the fiber-deep networks described in this chapter, a single fiber usually carries all transmissions. This reduces the cost of the fiber because less is used. More important, it reduces the number of splitters needed and reduces the number of splices and connectors required. Full-duplex transmission is still practiced.

11.5 FIBER-DEEP ARCHITECTURES

Several architectures are being used to drive fiber deep into the network, even as far as the home. These architectures are driven by the improved quality of signals delivered over fiber-optic plant as compared to those delivered over coaxial plant, by improved reliability due to fewer devices in the network, and by improved bandwidth. The lack of amplifiers means lower maintenance costs due to the lack of a need to sweep and balance amplifiers. In fiber-to-the-home systems (FTTH), the RF signal level never approaches 10^{-4} W (+38.75 dBmV), the level above which composite leakage index (CLI) measurements must be made. HFC networks routinely deal with higher signal levels, necessitating measurement of CLI.

11.5.1 Fiber-to-the-Home

Fiber-to-the-home systems have been built in several configurations. They can be subdivided into various types, but all have in common that they usually extend the fiber to the side of the home but sometimes into the home.

Passive Optical Networks—GPON and GE-PON

Figure 11.6 illustrates a basic FTTH system using a *passive optical network* (PON). Terminology from the telephone industry defines the endpoints. The headend (or hub or central office) side includes equipment known as *optical line termination* (OLT). The OLT is analogous to a CMTS in a cable TV HFC system in that it conditions all data (including telephony) for transport on the fiber-optic plant. Also included, when used, is broadcast transmission equipment, essentially identical to that used in HFC. Some people call this portion a *video OLT*. The subscriber-side circuitry, which frequently goes on the outside of the home, is called *optical network termination* (ONT). Sometimes the ONT is placed inside the home, or in new construction a niche may be provided for it at the utility entry point. Usually the subscriber-side interfaces at the ONT include a broadcast coaxial connection (when broadcast service is supported), one or more Ethernet connections, and one or more analog telephone interfaces.

One point of passive optical splitting is shown in the figure, but in practice two cascaded optical splitting points may be used. Tapped architectures are used occasionally. One advantage of a PON over the active architectures described next is that there is no active equipment in the field between the hub and the subscriber. No power is required in the field.

Figure 11.7 illustrates a fully featured ONT designed for mounting on the side of a home. A WDM in the front end separates the 1550-nm downstream broadcast wavelength from the 1490/1310-nm data wavelengths (downstream and upstream, respectively). The broadcast wavelength is supplied to a broadcast optical receiver that is not unlike those found in HFC nodes. Frequently a service disconnect switch will be provided at the broadcast receiver output in order to allow remote service removal and restoration through the *element management system* (EMS).

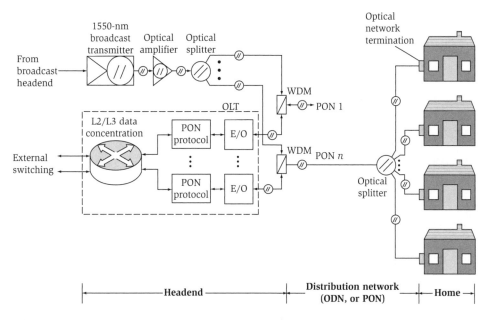

FIGURE 11.6

Typical passive optical network.

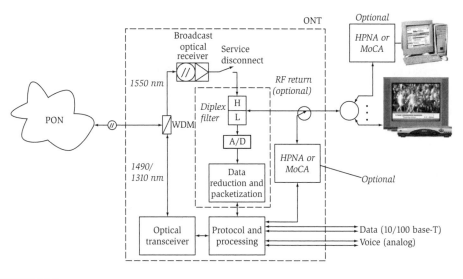

FIGURE 11.7

Fully featured ONT for use in a PON.

As shown in Figure 11.7, the ONT supports RF return from set-top boxes in the home, although this is an optional feature. The diplex filter routes the downstream signals to the RF output, where they are supplied to set tops and TVs in the usual way. It routes upstream signals to the analog-to-digital converter (A/D), and from there to signal processing, which inserts the upstream signal into an IP packet for transport to the headend. At the headend it is reconverted to RF and supplied to the control system for the set tops. Other systems modulate the upstream RF onto a separate upstream laser, as is described in the RFoG section, or RF return may not be provided. It is possible to provide complete service using only the data portion (video is provided as IPTV in that case). When this is the service configuration, the entire RF portion of the ONT may be eliminated.

The data path is through the lower portion of the WDM, to an optical transceiver that converts between optical and electrical data, with the electrical interface being supplied to the protocol and processing function. The first step in this function is the PON protocol conversion, complementary to the PON protocol processing in the OLT of Figure 11.6. The remaining portion of the protocol and processing block handles conversion of the data to standard formats, usually 10/100Base-T Ethernet, and conversion to voice lines (POTS, or plain old telephone service—the analog phone lines in nearly universal use).

An optional feature shown is for so-called data over coax, whereby data may be placed on the inside coaxial wiring to avoid having to install new data wiring inside the home. While many homes built since about the turn of the century have included data wiring, older homes do not have it. Rather than having to add wiring at significant labor cost, two standards have been developed for putting data over coax and, in one case, over phone wiring. The same standards may be used for delivering IPTV service in addition to providing data to computers or home networks. Two systems are in use today:

1. *MoCA—Multimedia over Coax Alliance*. This standard modulates data in each direction onto a carrier above 860 MHz (a number of channels are available). More information is available at *http://www.mocalliance.org/en/index.asp*.

2. *HPNA* started as *Home Phone Networking Alliance*, but later when people started using the standard over coax, the name was changed to HomePNA Alliance. It uses RF frequencies below 50 MHz to transmit two-way data over both coax and phone lines. More information is available at *http://www.homepna.org/en/index.asp*.

RFoG and GPON/GE-PON

PONs are differentiated by the underlying layer-2 transport protocol used. The classifications will be discussed later. Figure 11.8a illustrates the GE-PON/GPON architecture, and Figure 11.8b illustrates a possible RFoG architecture. (RFoG is an emerging standard developed by the SCTE specifically for its compatibility with HFC plant.) In each case, the headend comprises what headends usually comprise in the way of video,

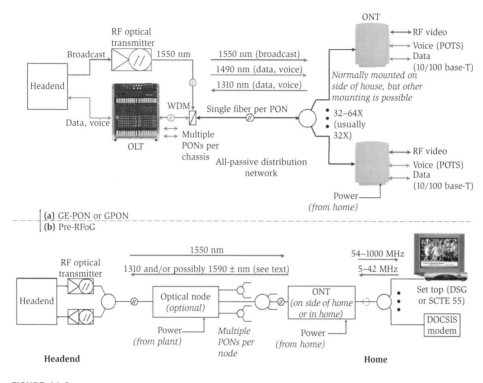

FIGURE 11.8

Comparison between GE-PON or GPON architectures with RFoG.

voice, and data equipment, except that in the PONs of Figure 11.8a, there is no CMTS, as it was replaced by the OLT shown. Downstream RF signals are supplied to a downstream optical transmitter, usually an externally modulated transmitter and always at 1550 nm because amplification of the optical signal is needed.

A possible RFoG system is shown in Figure 11.8b. (As of this writing the RFoG standard has not been completed, so we cannot say with certainty what it looks like.) The headend is identical to that of an HFC system because RFoG is really an HFC node serving a single subscriber. The downstream is again a 1550-nm transmitter, because you will need to amplify the optical signal. The upstream transmitter at the home is a little different from that used in upstream paths today. Because many upstream transmitters will be combined to feed one upstream receiver, it is necessary that each transmitter be turned off until an upstream RF signal is detected coming out of that home. Then the optical transmitter must turn on quickly to transmit the upstream data. It must turn off quickly at the end of a transmission in order not to interfere with the next transmission from another home.

An optical node in the field is shown as optional. Of course, if the optical node is used, the network is no longer completely passive. If used, the optical node will likely contain optical amplification in the downstream direction, and combining (in the optical and/or RF domains) in the upstream direction. It may digitize the upstream signal.

Active FTTH

Figure 11.9 illustrates an active FTTH system. It is differentiated from a PON by the addition of active processing equipment in the network in the form of the remote Ethernet switch. Power is required at that remote location. In known systems, there is only one active component between the hub and the subscriber. Beyond the processing point, fiber is home-run. The active processing equipment may be installed in a roadside cabinet, a controlled environmental vault (CEV), or may be strand- or pedestal-mounted, as an optical node or an amplifier is mounted in an HFC network.

A disadvantage of an active fiber system is that power must be provided for the active point, though the system may consume less power per home than do HFC networks. An advantage frequently claimed for active Ethernet systems is greater bandwidth to the home. It is true that the dedicated bandwidth between the active processing equipment might be as high as 1 Gb/s (but more likely 100 Mb/s for economy), but the bandwidth sharing to the left of the active processing equipment

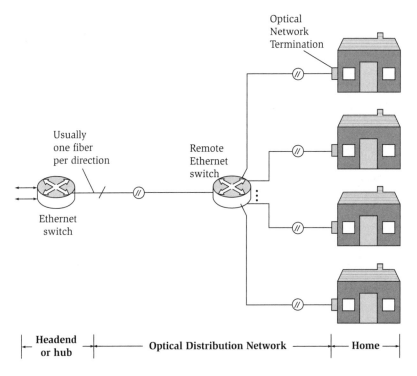

FIGURE 11.9

Active Ethernet system.

limits the bandwidth per home to whatever that total bandwidth is. In general, active systems don't have more bandwidth than do PONs. Broadcast video is rarely used with active Ethernet because the broadcast wavelength would have to be individually WDM'd into each fiber after the remote Ethernet switch. Usually when active Ethernet is used, then, video is only provided through IPTV, although there have been a few systems built with a separate fiber for video.

11.5.2 Fiber-to-the-Curb

In *fiber-to-the-curb* (FTTC) architectures, fiber-optic cable brings signals to a termination point, where they are converted to electrical form for distribution to a small number of subscribers located within a few thousand feet of the fiber termination. This is generally the architecture that AT&T installs in non-greenfield areas. From the termination point, coaxial cable may be used for broadcast video services (although many FTTC architectures, including AT&T's, do not use broadcast video). Twisted pair is used for voice and data, the data usually being delivered over one of the many types of DSL (digital subscriber line) technology.

FTTC systems usually use the Internet Protocol to deliver video (IPTV). This allows use of the data infrastructure to deliver video service. Limitations in data speed limit the number of video signals that can be delivered simultaneously to a subscriber, though with advances in video compression, this problem is easing somewhat. The short copper loop lengths of FTTC deployments improve the data rate that can be delivered.

Figure 11.10 illustrates a typical FTTC system. One or more optical fibers extend from the headend to an optical termination point. The optical termination includes a bidirectional digital optical transceiver and interfaces for data (including video). The connection from the central office (CO) or headend is by any convenient protocol, usually Ethernet or ATM. The DSLAM is a *digital subscriber, line access multiplexer*, which is analogous to a CMTS in an HFC system in that it converts data into the appropriate transmission format, in this case some form of DSL. Normally the DSLAM is located close to a cluster of homes in order to minimize the length of twisted pair that must carry high-speed data. The twisted pair is limited in the distance over which it can carry high-speed data. In the home, the twisted pair is terminated in a DSL modem and can also be terminated with conventional analog telephones.

11.6 CLASSIFYING FIBER-TO-THE-HOME SYSTEMS

We have talked about the physical architectures of PONs. Now we need to make some sense of the various types of PONs, organizing them so we can understand what each does and where they fit with each other. Figure 11.11 diagrams the options under discussion.

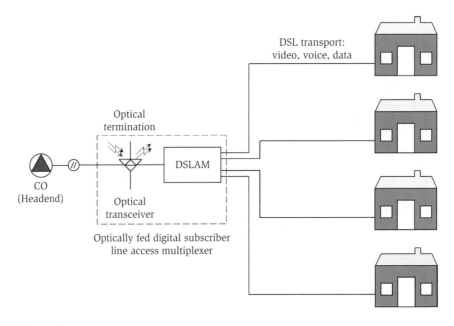

FIGURE 11.10

Typical fiber-to-the-curb architecture.

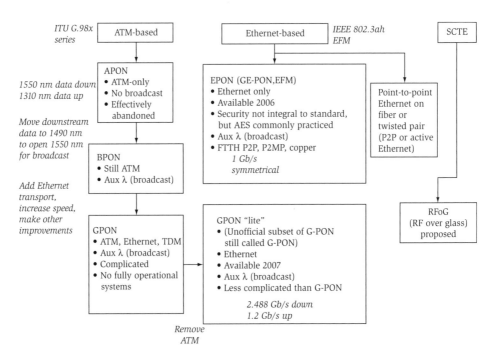

FIGURE 11.11

Classification of FTTH PON systems.

11.6.1 **RFoG**

Starting on the right of Figure 11.11, we have the ongoing development of RFoG (RF over glass). This standardization effort is ongoing within the SCTE, in the Fiber Optics Working Group of the Interface Practices Subcommittee. It is an option for cable operators to consider when installing FTTH.

11.6.2 **GE-PON**

In the center of the figure is the IEEE effort, which has been incorporated into the Ethernet specification, which is managed by the IEEE 802.3 Committee. The standard is referred to in this chapter as GE-PON, but it is also known as EPON (*Ethernet passive optical network*), 802.3ah (after the IEEE designation of the working group that developed it), or EFM (*Ethernet in the first mile*—to emphasize that this applied close to the subscriber and so was considered to be the first, rather than the last, mile). Although not PONs, the active Ethernet architecture of Figure 11.10 is a part of this standard, as is a version operating on twisted pair, at much lower data rates.

The specification was approved in 2004, and volume quantities of ASICs became available in about 2006. GE-PON is very popular in Asia, which is currently leading the world in FTTH deployment, so most of the PONs in the world are GE-PON. It is also being used in North America and in Europe.

Currently GE-PON operates at 1 Gb/s in both directions. The wire speed, or speed on the fiber, is actually 1.25 Gb/s, but 8b/10b coding[1] is used in order to ensure frequent transitions for clock recovery and other purposes. Thus, the net speed is 1 Gb/s. The IEEE is currently working on a new version of the standard that will operate at 10 Gb/s downstream and either 1 Gb/s or 10 Gb/s upstream.

11.6.3 **GPON**

To the left in Figure 11.11 are the ITU standards. The first standard, circa 1995, was called APON for *ATM passive optical network*. It used 1550 nm for downstream data and 1310 nm for upstream. It was soon replaced by BPON (*broadband PON*), which moved the downstream data to 1490 nm to make room for a broadcast overlay at 1550 nm. This is the version of PON that Verizon is currently deploying, though they have announced an eventual switch to the next standard in the ITU series, GPON (*gigabit PON*). APON and BPON operate at 622 Mb/s downstream and 155 Mb/s upstream.

GPON, ITU's G.984 series, was approved, in parts, in 2003 and 2004. It started as a combined standard that would encompass ATM, Ethernet, and TDM (*time division multiplexing*, in this context referring to DS-1 or E-1 transmissions). The standard is written to encompass all three layer-2 technologies. The problem was that implementing the complete standard was exceedingly complex. By the time that people started considering implementing G.984, it had become clear that Ethernet was the choice of technology for the last mile (or first mile if you use IEEE-speak).

Thus, the real implementation of GPON is based on the Ethernet portion of the standard, with the ATM portion not implemented. The author has called this "GPON lite," but this is not an official designation—it is still known as GPON. The currently favored version of GPON has a downstream wire speed of 2.488 Gb/s and an upstream speed of 1.2 Gb/s. It is specified to work with splits as high as 128-way, but current optics don't support this many splits. The ITU's announced plan for future enhancement has been to use wavelength division multiplexing, where either each subscriber or a group of subscribers gets a different wavelength. However, this tends to be expensive, and there is some talk in the industry about revisiting the strategy.

11.7 DISTANCE LIMITATIONS

In this section we examine the distance limitations of PON systems. We use numbers for GE-PON, but the numbers for GPON are nearly identical. We first look at the distance limitations for the digital link, including the loss that results from adding broadcast video. Then we look at the reach of the broadcast tier. We see that, while the two are balanced fairly well, the limitation tends to be on the digital side. Be careful using these numbers for anything except examples. A number of things can affect range which are not explicitly stated herein. We have used commercial specifications in some cases when they are better than the specifications in the standards. But there is no guarantee that some manufacturer will not use lower-performance components if they meet the specification. Consult your manufacturer on exact reach numbers.

Fiber-deep architectures must trade off distance and the number of times the signal can be split. Each time the signal is split, loss is introduced. Both GE-PON and GPON specify multiple levels of optical performance, which some people tend to equate with distance for a given split ratio. GE-PON specifies two levels of optical performance, PX-10 and PX-20. These were conceived originally as implying a distance, but the correct way to look at them is that PX-10 is designed for shorter distances and smaller loss budgets. GPON defines a lot of different classes of optics, designated classes A, B, B plus, and C. At the OLT side, only PX-20 and class B plus optics are manufactured because the cost savings of lower-performance optics would not justify the increased inventory. On the ONT end, you can get both PX-10 and PX-20 optics in GE-PON, and classes B and B plus in GPON. There is a cost difference.

11.7.1 PX-20/PX-20

Figure 11.12 illustrates the reach of a GE-PON system using PX-20 optics on each end, following the model of Figure 11.5. Distance is plotted on the x-axis and loss on the y-axis. The nearly horizontal lines at the top of the graph represent the available loss budget, essentially the difference between output power at the transmitter and minimum received power at the receiver. A few other assumptions, such as extinction ratio, are built into the numbers. The reason the lines slope slightly from

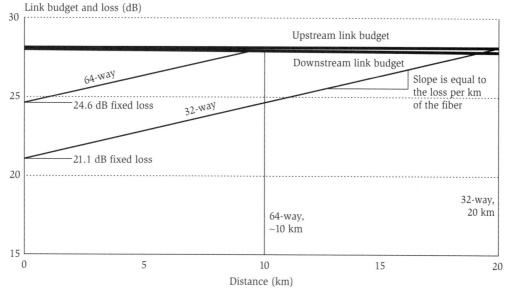

FIGURE 11.12

Reach of a GE-PON system with PX-20 optics at both the OLT and the ONT.

left to right is that dispersion is at work on the transmission. In PX-20 systems, transmitters are assumed to use DFB lasers, which have relatively (compared with F-P lasers) low spectral spreading. However, the spectral spreading is not zero, and since the downstream transmitter is operating at 1490 nm, well away from the zero-dispersion wavelength of the fiber (typically about 1311 nm), there are some slight effects due to dispersion. This tends to reduce the link budget as you go farther from the transmitter.

The upstream transmitter operates at about 1310 nm, close to the zero-dispersion wavelength of the fiber. However, we assume the ONT to be outside, so the laser is subject to a wider temperature variation and thus to more wavelength drift. Therefore, its link budget tends to drop with distance. We will see more drop in the next example.

We must test both the downstream and upstream directions to see which limits us, but in these cases the upstream direction limits us, so we have omitted some of the lines we have to add when we examine both directions. We have shown the actual loss for both 32-way (most common today) and 64-way splits. We assume 21.1 dB of fixed loss for a 32-way split and 24.6 dB of fixed loss for a 64-way split. These numbers tend to be a little conservative and consist of the usual splitter loss plus an allocation for connector and splice loss. The upward slope of the two "upstream" curves represents the loss per kilometer of the fiber itself. When the "upstream" curves meet the "upstream link budget" line, we have used up all of our loss budget, and this is as far as we can extend the reach of the PON. Note that for 64-way splits, the maximum length is about 10 km. For the 32-way split, the curves intersect right at 20 km.

In some cases, the curves will intersect beyond 20 km, but we stop at 20 km anyway because there is yet another consideration in setting maximum distance. The PON must conduct *ranging* between the OLT and the ONT, just as a DOCSIS modem must range. Ranging means that the round-trip time between a signal being sent from the OLT to the ONT and returned to the OLT is measured, and a timing offset is added for transmissions from the ONT, such that return signals arrive at the OLT at the proper time regardless of the propagation delay. The GE-PON specification requires ranging to work up to 20 km, but does not require it any further. The GPON specification allows for ranging to 60 km, with the restriction that the difference between the nearest and farthest ONTs is still no more than 20 km (today's optics will not support these longer distances). Thus, while the optics may support a slightly longer distance, the ranging may not have the capability to compensate for that longer distance.

11.7.2 **PX-20/PX-10**

Compare Figure 11.12 with Figure 11.13. The only difference is that in Figure 11.13 the ONT is equipped with PX-10 optics for the sake of economy. Note that the *upstream link budget* curve drops precipitously as the distance exceeds about 12 km. The reason is that PX-10 optics employ an F-P laser for the sake of economy.

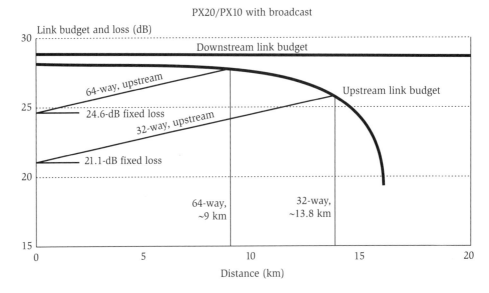

FIGURE 11.13

Reach of a GE-PON system with PX-20 optics at the OLT and PX-10 at the ONT.

The F-P laser has a much wider spectrum, so dispersion in the fiber is much greater. This is true even though the wavelength in question, 1310 nm, is close to the zero-dispersion wavelength of the fiber. The dispersion limits the reach with PX-10 optics, particularly in a 32-way PON. The distance has dropped from over 20 km to about 14 km.

Design data are frequently presented in tabulated form, with a loss budget and a loss penalty (reduction in loss budget) at certain distances. This loss penalty is a result of the link budget dropping, as shown particularly in Figure 11.13, due to dispersion. The loss penalty is a measure of how much the *link budget* curve has dropped at the specified distance.

11.8 LIMITATIONS ON ANALOG TRANSMISSION DISTANCE

Analog transmission on any fiber, be it in FTTH or normal HFC applications, is limited by several things. The most important in FTTH systems are the maximum power level that can be launched into the fiber and the minimum signal level at the optical detector required to deliver an acceptable carrier-to-noise ratio.

11.8.1 Stimulated Brillouin Scattering

Stimulated Brillouin scattering (SBS) limits the maximum power that can be injected into the fiber. When the power level of monochromatic light injected into a long fiber strand is increased, the output power increases proportionately until a threshold is reached. Beyond that level, the received power stays relatively constant, and light scattered back toward the source increases dramatically. The carrier-to-noise and signal-to-distortion ratios of the received signals both degrade. (For more information, see Section 4.4.6.)

As the state of the art in optical components has improved, the maximum injection level has increased. The current state of the art for externally modulated video transmitters is about +20 dBm of optical power injection into a 50-km fiber. This high power is achieved by applying any of several techniques to spread the optical spectrum of the emitted light. The reason that spreading the spectrum works is that SBS is a function of light energy at a single wavelength. Transmitting at multiple wavelengths partially mitigates the effect of SBS, but introduces dispersion issues.

For shorter distances, the SBS limit increases, so you can inject more optical power. Optical transmitter manufacturers give the maximum SBS threshold, either for a given length of fiber or for an infinite length. From this information, the SBS limit at other fiber lengths may be computed. Figure 11.14 shows the SBS limitation for various fiber lengths for a particular transmitter. Note that the fiber distance at work here is only to the point where the fibers are split and not to the ONT. After splitting the signal, level will usually be low enough that SBS is not an issue.

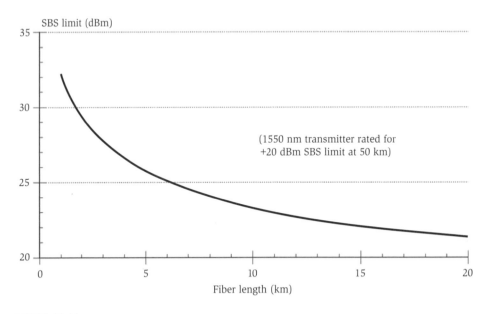

SBS limit (dBm)

(1550 nm transmitter rated for
+20 dBm SBS limit at 50 km)

Fiber length (km)

FIGURE 11.14

SBS limit for optical launch power.

Thus, SBS determines the maximum power we can inject into the fiber. Now we must decide on the minimum signal level we can detect. There are a number of considerations that go into coming up with this number.

11.8.2 Shot Noise

Review Figure 11.4b for the schematic of the RF receiver at the ONT. A significant limitation in the performance of analog optical receivers is shot noise. Shot noise is generated in the receiver photodiode, caused by the statistical variation in the arriving photon distribution. The subject is covered in Section 4.8. As the modulation of the light source (the OMI) increases, C/N_{SHOT} improves.

Higher receiver diode responsivity also improves the carrier-to-shot-noise ratio. When shot noise is a significant contributor to total optical link noise, the total C/N (carrier-to-noise ratio) will change less as a function of optical receive level than would be the case based on just thermal noise considerations.

11.8.3 Thermal Noise in a Fiber-Optic Receiver

The heart of an optical receiver is the photodiode, which has an output current proportional to the light power impinging on the diode. The photodiode is coupled to an amplifier, which amplifies the current and converts the signal to a standard impedance, usually either 50 or 75 ohms. The C/N of the output signal is dependent on the shot noise current in the diode, as shown earlier, and by thermal noise in the amplifier(s) following the photodiode.

As a practical matter, most optical receivers designed to receive analog carriers are limited to a minimum light input level of about −5 dBm for a C/N of 48 dB. There is work today on more sensitive receivers. For node operation in HFC plants, the minimum level is somewhat higher. This is because a large portion of the noise budget must be reserved for coaxial amplifiers following the node in HFC networks, whereas in most fiber-deep systems there is no amplification following the receiver.

11.8.4 Optical Amplifier Noise Contribution

Section 4.7 describes the most common type of optical amplifier, an EDFA. Its noise contribution is the final significant contribution to the noise performance of an analog link. The noise added depends on the input signal level and on the amplifier's noise figure. When several amplifiers are used in cascade, their noise contributions add up, just as with RF amplifiers.

11.8.5 Other Noise Contributions

There are a few other noise contributors besides the ones just described, which as a practical matter tend to be of a less limiting nature. These include laser relative intensity noise, which is defined in Section 4.6.

11.8.6 Analog Transmission Distance Limitation

We have established that the maximum optical signal level into the fiber is a function of fiber distance, limited by SBS, and that the minimum level at the optical receiver is −5 dBm. We can construct curves similar to those of Figures 11.12 and 11.13 for RF transmission.

Figure 11.15 illustrates that as the fiber distance gets longer, the maximum power that can be injected is reduced (downward-sloping curves) whereas the fiber loss increases (upward-sloping straight lines). Where the curves intersect is the maximum distance we can achieve. Note that this maximum distance is really to the first point where the fiber is split—fiber beyond that distance does not contribute to the SBS because the optical level is lower, so if the first split in the PON is significantly before the first home, we may be able to inject more power and achieve longer distance. On the other hand, we have not allowed for noise contribution from EDFAs in this figure, so that will reduce the distance. You can see that the distance you can go with RF is about the same to slightly farther than the distance limitation imposed by the PX-20 digital tier (see Figure 11.12). Thus, we have a pretty good balance between the distances we can achieve, as limited by either the RF or digital tiers.

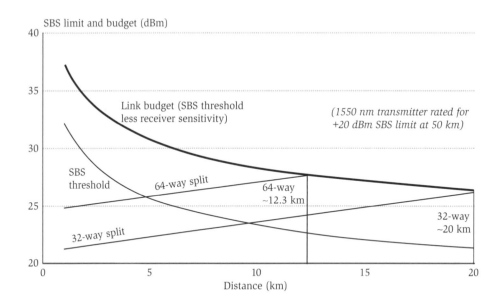

FIGURE 11.15

Distance limitation for RF transmission (C/N = 48 dB, no EDFA contribution).

11.9 LIMITATIONS ON DIGITAL TRANSMISSION DISTANCE

The distance limitations of the digital wavelengths (1490 nm downstream and 1310 nm upstream) are set by receiver sensitivity and transmitted power, both of which are set by the standards. Several other things can limit the distance, including but not limited to dispersion in the fiber when F-P lasers are used and the extinction ratio of the transmitter. We show an example of the distance limitations for the digital tier; however, you should consult the manufacturer of your equipment for more details.

11.9.1 Signal-to-Noise Ratio

As a practical matter, digital transmission, where the laser is turned on and off (*amplitude shift keying,* ASK), is limited by thermal noise, mode partition noise, and crosstalk. The receiver (Figure 11.4a) includes a low-pass filter, FL1, that limits the noise bandwidth. When the bandwidth of the transmission is doubled, the low-pass filter cutoff frequency must also double, meaning that the noise power reaching the detector doubles. Thus, every time the data rate doubles, the received signal power must also double. You can double the received power by halving the number of times that the signal is split, which is done by reducing the distance drastically or doubling the transmitted power.

11.9.2 **Mode Partition Noise**

Low-cost lasers are needed for FTTH applications. The lowest cost in common use today over single-mode fiber are Fabry–Perot (F-P) lasers. F-P lasers are multi-mode lasers, which produce light over a band of wavelengths. The amount of power at each wavelength tends to vary randomly due to the reflective structure in the laser. Without modulation, the total power is reasonably constant, but the wavelength at which that power is emitted changes. This phenomenon is known as *mode instability*. By itself, mode instability is harmless, but when it exists *and* the light passes through a fiber-optic cable having dispersion, the result is *mode partition noise* (MPN), a limiting factor in transmission distance. Dispersion is discussed in Section 4.2.5. MPN in this context refers to noise that develops as a result of differences in the propagation speed of different wavelengths put out by the F-P laser, as well as polarization of that light. Dispersion is the characteristic of optical fiber by which the velocity of propagation is a function of the wavelength of the light.

As light output from the laser shifts between wavelengths, the velocity at which the pulses propagate changes due to *chromatic dispersion* in the fiber. This means that pulses recovered at the receiver will be "smeared" in time. If the smearing becomes excessive, the pulse cannot be recovered and the bit error rate (BER) increases. A frequent measure of the effect is to determine the amount by which received power must be increased in order to get back to the same BER as would obtain without MPN. A useful relationship is the inequality

$$\sigma GBLD = \sigma \times \text{bit rate} \times \text{distance} \times \text{dispersion} < 0.15 \qquad (11.1)$$

where $\sigma GBLD$ is an abbreviation for *b*it rate (in Gb/s), fiber *l*ength (units of km), and *d*ispersion (units of ps/nm-km). The laser RMS line width is σ (units of nm). Dispersion versus wavelength—chromatic dispersion—is described in Section 4.4.3. The inequality is dimensionless when compatible units are used for all parameters. This relation ensures that the power penalty is low. In order to achieve longer distance, you can reduce the bit rate (this is going in the wrong direction—we want faster transmission, not slower), or you can decrease the line width of the laser (i.e., the spectrum over which the laser spreads its energy due to MPN) by choosing a suitable (more expensive) laser. Reducing the dispersion in the fiber is rarely practical. The dispersion issue involves the uncertainty of fiber zero-dispersion wavelength (1300 to 1324 nm) and the laser wavelength (including unit-to-unit variation and variation over temperature). Finally, you could shorten the distance (contrary to the idea of extending the fiber farther into the system).

11.9.3 **Chirp**

The term *chirp* comes from the way many birds make their chirps: over the period of one chirp, the frequency of the pitch changes, going either up or down. In fiber optics, chirp is a change in the wavelength of the light. A directly modulated laser will change its output wavelength with changes in the laser current. This change in wavelength interacts with the chromatic dispersion characteristic of the fiber to produce deleterious effects, noted shortly.

11.9.4 SRS

SRS, or *stimulated Raman scattering*, is a nonlinearity in fiber-optic transmission whereby a signal at a shorter wavelength can have some of its power transferred to a signal copropagating (i.e., in the same direction) at a longer wavelength. The primary way in which this affects current FTTH systems is crosstalk from the digital downstream signal on 1490 nm to the broadcast signal on 1550 nm. The effect when random data are being transmitted is decreased carrier-to-noise ratio for the recovered RF signals. Because of the way that power levels have been selected, the effect is worse with GE-PON than with GPON class B plus. However, if someone ever builds a GPON class-C OLT, watch out!

Figure 11.16 illustrates the effect of SRS, under worst-case conditions, in a GE-PON system. The operative transmission is downstream transmission of data on 1490 nm along with transmission of RF video on 1550 nm. The graph shows the worst-case C/N of the system for channels 2 to 4, the most affected channels (the effect decreases as RF frequency increases). The lowest set of curves applies to the maximum optical level being transmitted on the downstream data (1490 nm)

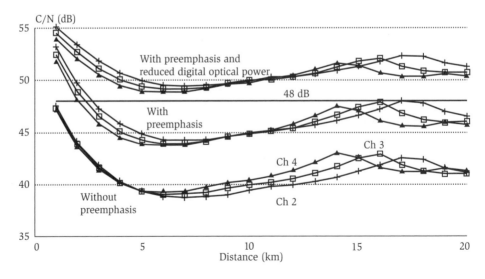

FIGURE 11.16

Effect of SRS on C/N, GE-PON PX-20, maximum amplitude.

for the three channels indicated. Note that, due to the way SRS works, the optical level of the 1550-nm broadcast carrier is not a factor. The second set of curves from the bottom shows what can be done by preemphasizing the lower channels; that is, those lower channels are transmitted at a slightly higher optical modulation index (OMI) (see Section 4.6.3 and Figure 11.2) than they normally would be. This gets close to the common C/N target of 48 dB, but in order to deliver signals with C/N over 48 dB, we must control the output level of the 1490-nm optical carrier, keeping it a few decibels below the specification maximum. The top graph shows what we can do using this technique while staying within the distance limitations shown before.

There are a few additional things that can be done to mitigate the effects of SRS on C/N. Since the effect is very nonlinear with optical power level, it is best to consult with your equipment supplier to optimize the design.

There is yet another effect of SRS that can be more damaging than the C/N effect shown earlier. With both GE-PON and GPON, when no information is being transmitted on the downstream data carrier, a short idle code sequence is transmitted. This is a repetitive code sequence, which means that the signal power, rather than being spread over a wide band as it is during normal data transmission, is concentrated in a few frequencies, looking more like a CW interference than random noise. This will, of course, produce a beat in the picture. Channel 3 is the most affected channel, with lesser effects at harmonics. There are countermeasures for eliminating the effects of idle codes.

11.10 LOW-FREQUENCY CONTENT REMOVAL IN DIGITAL TRANSMISSION

As with most communications systems, a digital optical system is not able to transmit frequencies down to dc, so there must be some method of low frequency (sometimes called DC) removal. Note that the transmitters and receivers are both AC-coupled. There must be a way of ensuring that the data do not contain energy below the cutoff frequency of the system. Besides causing problems with the ac coupling in the transmitter and receiver, content approaching dc implies that you can have a long time between state (1 or 0) changes. Clock signals are recovered by locking a local clock to state changes in the incoming data, so that an excessively long time without a state change will allow the recovered clock to wander out of phase, damaging data recovery.

Removal of dc may be accomplished in a number of ways. One method is to establish rules limiting the number of like symbols (1 or 0) that can be transmitted in a row. Another method, used in GPON, is to scramble the data by exclusive-ORing it with a pseudorandom data sequence before transmission, and repeating the process at the receiver. One can show that this effectively randomizes the data, effectively limiting any run of consecutive like bits.

Another common method is to use a substitution set of symbols for each byte of data to be transmitted. This technique is used in gigabit Ethernet transmission.[2] The substitution method used in gigabit Ethernet and in certain other applications is called 8b/10b encoding. For every 8 bits (1 byte), a 10-bit symbol is substituted— hence the name. The substituted 10-bit symbol is chosen to have very close to an equal number of 1s and 0s and three to eight transitions per symbol. The codes satisfy the requirement of no DC component in the signal, and the large numbers of transitions ensure clock synchronization. Furthermore, since a limited number of the available codes are used, the encoding provides another way to detect transmission errors. The penalty is that, since 10 bits must be transmitted to represent 8 bits, the bandwidth required is increased by 25%. For instance, in a gigabit Ethernet system, the desired data are transmitted at 1 Gb/s, but because of 8b/10b encoding the data rate on the fiber (the so-called wire rate) is 1.25 Gb/s.

Other substitutions besides 8b/10b are possible. Sometimes 34b/36b is used, resulting in 36 bits being transmitted to represent 34 bits. This has the same effect with less overhead.

11.11 SUMMARY

Besides using frequency division multiplexed (FDM) analog transmission of multiple carriers, it is possible to use digital (binary or on/off) modulation of lasers, modulating them with a time division multiplexed baseband digital signal. Both forms of optical modulation may be used on the same fiber if different wavelengths are multiplexed. One application of such digital systems is intercity and metro data transmission, but it is becoming more common to use it, often in conjunction with analog FDM modulation, to deliver signals via fiber directly to homes and businesses. This is known as fiber-to-the-home (FTTH) and fiber-to-the-business (FTTB). Some systems deliver fiber signals to the curb (FTTC). Collectively, these are known as fiber-deep systems.

Fiber-deep systems can be differentiated by the layer-2 technology used for data transmission: ATM or Ethernet, with Ethernet almost completely taking over the market. Typically, such systems deliver baseband data and modulated video signals to a box on the side of the home, which converts signals back to their more familiar electronic form. The data interface is Ethernet, whereas telephone interfaces are predominately analog, and broadcast television is delivered as in conventional cable plant or as Internet Protocol television.

ENDNOTES

1. Walter Ciciora, et al., *Modern Cable Television Technology: Video, Voice, and Data Communications*, 2nd ed. Morgan Kaufmann, 2004, chapter 19.
2. Institute of Electrical and Electronics Engineers, *Standard 802.3, 2005 Edition*.

Network Reliability and Availability

12

12.1 INTRODUCTION

Chapter 9 described the network requirements of certain service classifications that can be offered over broadband FDM distribution networks. Among those are transmission quality, effective bandwidth, *reliability* (the probability that a system will survive without interruption for a defined period), *outage rate* (the average rate at which service interruptions occur), and *availability* (the percentage of time that service is available). Transmission quality was treated in detail in Chapters 2 through 8, and effective bandwidth was covered in Chapter 10. This chapter will deal with the calculation of network reliability and service availability. It will also discuss how those parameters vary as a function of the topology of the distribution system, among other factors. Finally, it will explore the difference between true availability and that experienced by users of a particular service.

Service interruptions can result from a variety of causes, including equipment failure, commercial power problems, interfering signals, and blocking due to inadequate circuit capacity, as discussed in Chapter 9, or upstream interference issues, as discussed in Chapter 8. This chapter will deal with outages caused by either equipment or powering.

While the mathematics of reliability and availability calculations are straightforward, the task of organizing and entering the information required to calculate performance of a network of even moderate complexity is daunting. To simplify the process, an Excel workbook, *SOAR.xls,* and its companion instruction book, *Soar Manual.doc,* are available for download from the book's website—*www. elsevierdirect.com/companions/9780123744012*. Using this tool, engineers can enter a "catalog" of network components with assumed failure rates, and then build a simple model that interconnects them appropriately for calculating their effect on end-to-end reliability. Entering repair times then allows the workbook to calculate net availability on both an absolute and a customer-experienced basis.

12.2 HISTORY AND BENCHMARKING

Logically, service availability should be just that—the net availability to the end user, irrespective of the cause of any interruptions. Historically, however, different industries have used different measures of their own service integrity.

12.2.1 Telephony

As we discussed in Chapter 9, the most widely quoted service availability requirement is 99.99% for local, wired, voice telephony service. It is important to review, however, how the exchange carriers define this parameter.

The service availability objective for the subscriber loop is 99.99%, which corresponds to 0.01% unavailability or 53 minutes/year maximum downtime. This objective, incorporating all network equipment between the local switch and the network interface (excluding the local switch and customer premises equipment), refers to the long-term average for service to a typical customer.[1]

This is not the same as end-user service availability. It excludes, for instance, availability of dial tone from the switch, for whatever reason, and availability of inter-switch or long-distance circuits. It also excludes any wiring within the home and terminal equipment problems. Though this may be understandable from a local network operator's point of view, the history of the cable television industry has been that in-home problems are the largest single cause of service outages.[2]

Second, this is a goal for performance that is averaged over the entire customer base and over time. Thus, a significant minority of customers may have consistently unreliable service, yet the carrier meets the service goal if the majority of customers have few problems.

Third, carriers do not count "unavailability due to the loss of both primary and back-up powering"[3] in cases where there is powered equipment between the central office and the home, such as in some fiber-in-the-loop (FITL) configurations. The importance of this exception depends, obviously, on the integrity of the field powering systems. It has been the experience of cable television network operators, however, that utility power interruptions cause more outages than all equipment failure classifications combined.

Finally, availability includes not only failure rates but also the time required to restore service. The problem is that, though a cut telephone drop wire (as an example) causes service to be unavailable, the network operator will typically not be aware of the outage until the customer tries to use the telephone and discovers the line is dead, then reports the outage to the phone company. The phone company calculates the length of the outage, for purposes of measuring compliance with the availability goal, from when it is *reported*, not from when it actually begins.[4] Arguably, therefore, the actual outage times may far exceed the reported times. As the traditional telephone network evolves by deploying fiber and performance-monitoring equipment closer to homes, this disparity will presumably decrease.

12.2.2 **Cable Television**

Although the cable television industry has not historically had formal goals covering availability or outage rates, CableLabs undertook a study of field reliability and subscriber tolerance of outages under the auspices of its Outage Reduction Task Force. Its report, published in 1992,[5] is discussed in detail in Chapter 9. In summary, the report set as a failure rate target that no customer should experience more than 2 outages in any 3-month period, with a secondary standard of no more than a 0.6 outage per month per customer.

As with the telephony goal, it is important to review what is included in the definition of an outage:

- Only multicustomer outages are included, thereby excluding all drop, NID, set-top terminal, and in-house wiring problems.

- Single-channel outages are included, thereby including headend processing equipment.

- Only signal outages, not degraded reception, are included.

- All elements of signal distribution between headend and tap are included, including the effects of commercial power availability.

- Although the language refers only to outages that are "experienced by customers," the software distributed with the report calculates all outages, and therefore it can be assumed that customer awareness of outages is not important to the definition, even though the goal was based on customer experience.

- The "no customer shall experience" clause in the goal clearly indicates that a worst-case, not average, analysis is called for.

Based on an estimated mean time of 4 hours to restore service, CableLabs translated a 0.6 outage per month into a minimum acceptable availability of 99.7%. Clearly, this standard (which dates from a time when cable's business was exclusively delivering analog video) is outdated in a world where cable is a major provider of both primary telephone and high-speed data services.

The equivalence between customer-perceived individual outages and distribution system outages is tenuous at best. On the one hand, some outages may be detected and repaired without some subscribers being aware of the outage; on the other hand, individual subscribers may have in-home problems that will not be included in the preceding definition. Nevertheless, CableLabs chose a 0.6 multicustomer outage per month as its benchmark for distribution system outage modeling.[6]

In the field measurements portion of its study, the task force gathered actual field failure analysis reports from some of its members and used those to predict failure rates of certain classifications of components (discussed later) and to develop models that could be used to predict the failure rates of arbitrary network architectures. The accuracy of the raw data used in this type of analysis is limited by the analytic skills of the field technician and by its completeness. For instance,

Table 12.1 Comparison of Bellcore and CableLabs Outage Definitions

Outage definition	Factors included in definition of outage						
	Centralized processing/ switching	Distribution network	Distribution power	Drop	Network terminal equipment	In-home wiring	Analysis
Bellcore		X		X	X		Average customer
CableLabs	X	X	X				Worst-case customer
Customers' experience	X	X	X	X	X	X	

it is not obvious that a technician would think to report a brief outage caused by a routine maintenance procedure or by a brief power outage that did not cause a formal trouble call to be entered into the dispatch system. Second, the gathered data, necessarily representative of typical cable systems of that time, did not include modern HFC systems. Finally, cable systems (at least in 1992) routinely reported only *distribution system outages*, not *individual customer outages*, in their reports.

12.2.3 Cable Television versus Telephony Reliability and Availability Definitions

Clearly, the CableLabs and Bellcore definitions of reliability and availability are not equivalent, and the numbers should be not compared directly. Table 12.1 illustrates the approximate inclusion of each industry's outage definition compared with those elements that actually affect customer service.

As a final note, *availability* is traditionally the most important parameter applied to telephone services though CableLabs found that the *rate at which outages occur* was most important to television viewers, with the length of the outage (and thus availability) of only secondary importance.[7]

12.3 DEFINITIONS AND BASIC CALCULATIONS

It is important to have a clear understanding of the terminology used in calculating reliability-related parameters. Thus, the following definitions will be used throughout this chapter.

Component Failure Rate The failure rate of a component or system is defined as the statistical probability of failure of any one of a similar group of components in a given time interval. The measured period should be contained within the normal service life of the device—that is, failure rate is not intended to measure time to wear out, but rather "midlife" random failures. For the purposes of this chapter, we will generally express failure rates on a yearly basis.

Failure rates of individual electronic components (capacitors, resistors, semiconductors, and so on) are generally determined by their manufacturers using carefully designed tests that are conducted on a sample of products selected at random from the production line.

Failure rates of system-level components such as amplifiers, taps, connectors, and set-top terminals can be determined theoretically based on the failure rates of their internal electronic parts and the way in which they are interconnected, or they can be determined based on actual failure data from field-installed units. We have a strong preference for the latter since the installed failure rate is influenced not only by design but also by craft issues, environmental conditions, and how the unit is powered.

When field observations are used to determine failure rate, the appropriate formula is

$$\lambda = \frac{k}{nt} \tag{12.1}$$

where

λ = the annual failure rate
k = the number of observed failures
n = the number of items in the test sample
t = the observation time in years

The failure rate can be converted to other units as required. For instance, the failure rate per hour is the annual failure rate divided by 8760.

System Failure Rate—Simple Nonredundant Connection Where n components are connected in such a way that the failure of any one of them will lead to a failure of some defined system or function (such as a subscriber service outage or a single-channel failure), and the failures do not have a common cause, the resultant failure rate of the system is given by

$$\lambda_{\text{system}} = \sum_{i=1}^{n} \lambda_i \tag{12.2}$$

where

λ_{system} = the net system failure rate
λ_i = the failure rate of component i
n = the number of components, any of whose failure will cause a system failure

Note that this formula is not exact since it assumes that none of the failures over-lap in time. Thus, it is accurate only when the failure rates and repair times are such that multiple, independent, simultaneously occurring outages are statistically insignificant. Generally, this is a good assumption for well-designed and managed cable systems.

System Reliability—Simple Nonredundant Connection   System reliability is the probability that the system will not fail during some specific period. In general, reliability can be calculated once the failure rate is known using

$$R(t) = e^{-\lambda t} \qquad (12.3)$$

where λ and t are in consistent units (i.e., failure rate per year and years or failure rate per hour and hours).

The result of this calculation may be less than intuitive. For instance, if the annual failure rate of a given system were 1 (meaning that if we measured a large number of similar systems, we would detect a number of failures per year equal to the number of systems), the probability of any single system surviving one year without a failure is $e^{-1} = 0.37$.

When components or subsystems of known reliability are connected in a configuration where the failure of any component leads to a system failure, the net system reliability can be calculated using

$$R_S(t) = R_1(t)R_2(t)\dots R_n(t) \qquad (12.4)$$

where

$$R_S\ (t) = \text{the net system reliability over period } t$$
$$R_1, R_2\ , \dots,\ R_n = \text{the reliabilities of the individual components, measured over the same period}$$

Mean Time between Failure   The predicted time between failures is simply the inverse of the failure rate, or

$$MTBF = \frac{1}{\lambda} \qquad (12.5)$$

where *MTBF* and λ are in consistent units.

Generally, this chapter will express MTBF values in hours. When manufacturers provide predicted MTBF data, it is also generally given in those units. As with failure rate, MTBF is not a measure of useful service life. In fact, many components have an MTBF that exceeds their wear-out time.

Mean Time to Restore (MTTR)   When a failure does occur, the mean time between failure and restoration of the defined function is the MTTR. For the purposes of this chapter, MTTR values will usually be expressed in hours.

Note that MTTR is sometimes used to express mean time to *repair* rather than mean time to *restore*. We use the latter definition here to distinguish between when service is restored and when the failed component is actually repaired.

Since it is more common in cable television to restore service after a failure by swapping a good for a failed network component, this is more accurate when our goal is to determine service reliability.

Availability (*A*) The ratio of time that a service is available for use to total time is known as availability. It can be calculated from MTBF and MTTR (expressed in consistent units) using

$$A = \frac{MTBF}{MTBF + MTTR} \qquad (12.6)$$

Unavailability (*U*) Unavailability is the ratio of time that a service is unavailable to total time and is, by definition, equal to $1 - A$.

Outage Time (T_U) Outage time is the amount of time that the network is unavailable during a defined period. In general, the outage time during some period t is equal to the unavailability multiplied by t. It is common to express outage time in minutes per year, which can be calculated as follows:

$$T_U(\text{min/yr}) = (\text{minutes/year})(1 - A) = 525{,}600(1 - A) \qquad (12.7)$$

12.4 EFFECTS OF REDUNDANT NETWORK CONNECTIONS

The preceding simple calculations apply to situations in which the failure of any single component leads to the failure of the defined system or function. In a redundant connection, either of two (or more) components can provide a function should the other(s) fail. Thus, the system user experiences a failure only if the redundantly connected components simultaneously fail. As discussed in Chapter 10, a common example in fiber architectures is a ring configuration, where signals can travel by either of two cable routes between headend and hubs.

Unavailability When two network sections are connected in a redundant configuration, the equivalent unavailability is the product of the unavailabilities of the two individual sections. Since, for each section, the unavailability is simply the number of outage minutes per year divided by the total minutes in a year, the equivalent unavailability is

$$U_R = \frac{(T_{U1})(T_{U2})}{(525{,}600)^2} \qquad (12.8)$$

where

$$U_R = \text{the net unavailability}$$
$$T_{U1} \text{ and } T_{U2} = \text{the yearly outage times (in minutes) of the redundantly connected sections}$$

Converting this back into equivalent yearly outage minutes for the combined section:

$$T_{UR} = 525{,}600 U_R = \frac{(T_{U1})(T_{U2})}{525{,}600} \qquad (12.9)$$

Failure Rate The equivalent failure rate is the sum of the failure rate of the first segment multiplied by the probability of the second section failing before the first can be restored, plus the failure rate of the second section multiplied by the probability of the first section failing during an outage in the second section.

The probability of section 1 failing during an outage in the redundantly connected section 2 is

$$P_{F1} = 1 - e^{\frac{-(\lambda_1)(MTTR_2)}{8,760}}$$
(12.10)

where

P_{F1} = the probability of failure of section 1
λ_1 = the failure rate of section 1 per year
$MTTR_2$ = the period (in hours) over which the probability of failure is to be measured, namely, the MTTR for a failure in network section 2

Thus, the net failure rate when two sections join in a redundant feed is

$$\lambda_R = \lambda_1 \left[1 - e^{\frac{-(\lambda_2)(MTTR_1)}{8,760}} \right] + \lambda_2 \left[1 - e^{\frac{-(\lambda_1)(MTTR_2)}{8,760}} \right]$$
(12.11)

12.5 ABSOLUTE VERSUS USER-PERCEIVED PARAMETERS

The preceding equations yield reliability-related performance parameters for the network, independent of usage. For applications that require continuous use of the network, the calculated failure rates and network availability are the same as those experienced by a user. For most services, however, usage of the network by individuals is only partial. For instance, most families watch television about 4 hours per day, whereas telephone users may access the public-switched telephone network for a half hour daily, at most.

The importance of partial usage is that some outages will occur and service restored before all potential users are affected. Thus, the average network reliability, as experienced by occasional users will be higher than for full-time users. However, the relationship between the network outage rate and availability and that experienced by occasional users is complex and affected not only by average aggregate usage time but also by the pattern of usage.

As an example, if a television subscriber watches 4 straight hours of television every evening, but at no other time, and the network MTTR is 1 hour, the probability is that he or she will experience slightly more than one-sixth of all outages. On the other hand, a person who uses the same network to make a 1-minute phone call every 6 minutes (say, a 24-hour business using a telephone modem to do credit card verifications) will experience every outage (and, in fact, will perceive a greater outage *rate*, since the restoration time for each outage will affect 10 attempted phone calls) even though his or her total daily usage time is the same.

A further complication is in the user's response to a failure and how we quantify the modified usage pattern. For example, assume that a user normally averages one phone call every 4 hours. If the user attempts to make a call and finds the phone not working, he or she may try again every few minutes until successful. If the outage lasts an hour, the user will have experienced many more failures than during his or her normal usage pattern. At the other extreme, a television viewer who would normally watch an evening's programming may, upon discovering an outage, abandon viewing for the entire evening and thus not be aware that the outage lasted only a few minutes. Again, the viewer's perception of the network's availability is affected by his or her changed usage pattern. A legitimate question for reliability modeling is whether these failure-induced retries are counted as independent failures.

For a hypothetical fiber-to-the-curb, fully status-monitored network, one researcher has calculated that a telephone user making 10-minute calls spaced 100 minutes apart (roughly a 9% utilization factor of the network) will experience 30.2 of the network's 53 minutes of unavailability every year.[8] If any portion of the network is unmonitored, the outage time experienced by the customer will increase and could, in fact, exceed the Bellcore-defined outage time for the network!

For cases where usage patterns are not modified as a direct result of outages, we can estimate perceived outage rates and service availability as follows.[9]

First, define the usage pattern for a service consisting of an average *call length* as T_C, and an average *call cycle* time (from the start of one call to the start of the next) as T_S. To keep things simple, all times will be expressed in hours.

The probability of a service failure during a call period T_S can be calculated from Equation 12.3 (the probability of failure is 1 minus the reliability):

$$P_f = 1 - e^{-\lambda T_S} \tag{12.12}$$

where T_S is in hours and λ = the service failure rate per hour.

If we multiply the probability of failure per call cycle by a scaling factor that takes into account both call length and service restoration time, we can calculate the probability of failure per attempted usage of the network:

$$P_c = \left(1 - e^{-\lambda T_s}\right)\left(\frac{T_c + \text{MTTR}}{T_S}\right) \tag{12.13}$$

where T_C and MTTR are both in hours.

The total number of attempts to use the service per year can be calculated using

$$B = \frac{8{,}760}{T_s} \tag{12.14}$$

from which we can calculate the user-experienced yearly failure rate:

$$\lambda_{\text{EXP}} = P_C B \tag{12.15}$$

The average length of experienced outages is

$$T_O = \frac{(T_c)(\text{MTTR})}{T_c + \text{MTTR}} \tag{12.16}$$

so that the total experienced outage time per year is

$$T_{\text{EXP}} = 1 - (P_C)(B)(T_O) \tag{12.17}$$

Finally, the experienced availability (i.e., 1 minus the ratio of outage time to attempted usage time) can be calculated using

$$A_{\text{EXP}} = 1 - \left[\frac{(P_c)(T_o)}{T_c} \right] \tag{12.18}$$

As an example, assume that a network fails once every 3 months (MTBF = 2,190 hours, $\lambda = 0.000457$ per hour) and that the MTTR is 2 hours. Based on these data, an application that used the network continuously would experience an outage rate of 4 per year, a yearly outage time of 8 hours, and an availability of 0.999088.

A television viewer using the network 4 hours per day ($T_C = 4$, $T_S = 24$) would experience a yearly outage rate of 0.9953, a yearly outage time of 1.327 hours, and an effective availability of 0.999091. Thus, although using the network only one-sixth of the time, the viewer experiences roughly one-fourth the outage rate but nearly the same effective availability as a 24-hour user.

A telephony user who makes a 10-minute call every 4 hours ($T_C = 0.16667$, $T_S = 4$) would experience a yearly outage rate of 2.1665, a yearly outage time of 0.333 hour, and an effective availability of 0.999087. Thus, even though the telephone user makes use of the network for a lower percentage of the time, he or she experiences about the same effective availability but a higher failure rate than the television viewer because of his or her more frequent attempts at access.

As can be seen, network effective availability—the probability that service is available—is quite insensitive to usage patterns, whereas experienced outage rate is closely tied to both call length and call rate.

12.6 NETWORK ANALYSIS

Once the basics of reliability are understood, they can be applied to the analysis of actual and proposed networks. The steps in this analysis include breaking the network into manageable sections, properly assigning the components to the sections, determining the failure rates of individual network components, estimating the service restoration times for failures at various network levels, and calculating the various reliability parameters. Although the principles of the process will be described here, in practice, the calculations are much more easily performed using a computer, which also allows the engineer to assess the effects of changes in topology, operating practices and component reliability. The downloadable *system outage and reliability* (SOAR) calculator tool referenced earlier is invaluable for this purpose.

12.6.1 Logical Subdivision of the Network for Analysis

The first step is subdividing the network into segments. The degree to which this is required depends on the required level of analysis. For instance, if the only parameter of interest is failure rate and availability as experienced by the most distant subscriber, then the many branches in the coaxial distribution system can be ignored and only the longest cascade analyzed in a single calculation.[10] As a minimum, however, any network branches that form redundant structures must be separated, analyzed separately, and then used as variables in the equations in Section 12.3 to determine the effective performance of the redundant structure.

For those desiring a more thorough analysis, a separate analysis of each physically separate branch and calculation of reliability data at every customer port will allow additional data such as total failures and performance as experienced by the average as well as by the most disadvantaged customers. It also allows analysis of the contributions of various network sections to overall failure rate and unavailability. The analysis given at the end of this chapter was done using a large spreadsheet that allowed a very detailed analysis.

To limit the amount of data to be analyzed, it is common to analyze only a typical subsection of a large network. In the case of an all-coaxial network, this might be a single trunk, whereas in the case of an HFC network, it is likely to consist of a single fiber-fed node, along with the fiber trunking structure feeding that node.

Figure 12.1 shows a typical example. In this case, a sheath ring fiber structure is used between the headend and the node receiver, while coax cascades of up to five amplifiers are used beyond the node. Should only the performance to the last user be required, then analysis of all but the longest cascade can be omitted. Only the downstream optical structure is shown in the figure. See Section 12.6.6 for a discussion of the calculation of two-way structures.

Figure 12.2 shows the logical division of this network into segments for analysis. Note that the number assigned to each section identifies a unique structure, whereas the letter denotes the instance of that structure. Thus, all four of the segments numbered 5 are similar, and only a single analysis of that structure is required. Since a single headend optical transmitter feeds both downstream fibers between the headend and node, it is part of segment 1A. Separate optical receivers are used in the node, however, so each of the segments numbered 2 includes both the fiber and the connected node receiver.

12.6.2 Assigning Network Components to Subdivisions

Sometimes, network components' effect on transmission integrity may be determined by other than their physical placement in the network. Power supply 1 in Figure 12.2 is physically located in section 5A, but it powers the node and the first amplifier in sections 5A and 5B. Therefore, for purposes of calculating reliability parameters, it should be included in section 3A. Similarly, power supply 2 is physically located in section 6A, but must be included in section 4A since it powers the amplifier that feeds sections 7A and 6A, and its failure would affect the signals in all the downstream branches.

With the components properly assigned to network segments, based on their effect on operation, the components in each section should then be listed in a column as a first step to segment analysis.

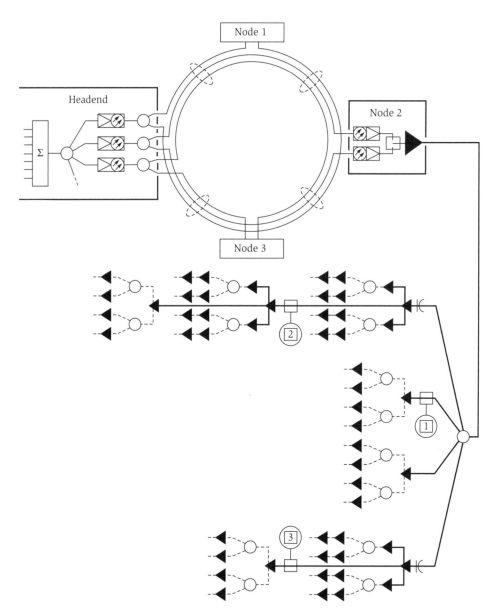

Note: Only downstream F/O network shown for simplicity. Taps omitted for clarity, untapped cable shown solid, tapped cable shown dashed.

FIGURE 12.1

Topology of a typical HFC node and sheath ring trunk.

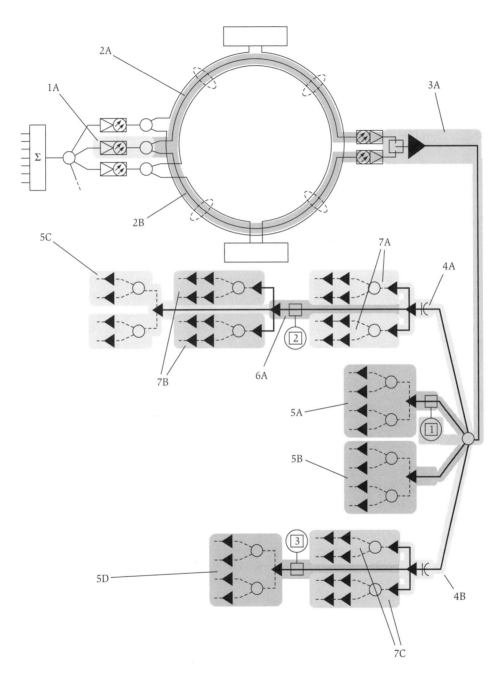

FIGURE 12.2

Division of a network into segments for analysis.

12.6.3 **Determining Component Failure Rates**

To estimate the performance of the defined sections, the field failure rate of each network component type must be determined. Manufacturers' design analyses, based on the MTBF of the individual subcomponents used and their temperature/voltage stress levels, often have limited relationship to failures of field-installed equipment where such factors as voltage transients and the skill levels of field personnel may dominate inherent failure rates. Also, a failure of a series-connected component may or may not cause a loss of service to all downstream subscribers. For instance, a tap port may fail, causing a loss of service to one customer but not disrupting the through signal to subsequent taps.

With those caveats, it is instructive to examine the failure rates of a few key components.

Commercial Power

CableLabs' task force recorded average commercial power failure rates of 30% (all failure rates are on a yearly basis unless otherwise noted), meaning that the probability of a commercial power interruption at any given power supply is 0.3 each year. Since these data are based on outages caused by power failures, it is to be presumed that this rate relates to *unprotected* commercial power outages rather than all power outages. Also, given that their data were derived from reported system outages, it can be presumed that many short interruptions were not included in the data.

By contrast, the Network Reliability Council report quotes from a study showing an average commercial power *unavailability* of 370.2 minutes per year.[11] They did not report on the rate at which outages occurred, however. The net unavailability with varying durations of standby power capacity is shown in Table 12.2.

From these data, it is readily apparent that even standby battery capacity of several times the 2 hours normally designed into cable television standby power supplies will result in unprotected outages well in excess of Bellcore's 53-minute availability guideline. Thus, normal standby powering will need to be supplemented by other means (such as built-in generators or status monitoring combined with deployable mobile generators) for high-availability services.

It is the experience of one of the authors, however, that the reliability of commercial power varies widely from location to location, so that Table 12.2 can be taken only as a measure of average conditions. Accurate network reliability predictions must depend on locally viable commercial power data unless networks are so hardened against commercial power outages as to make the issue irrelevant.

Table 12.2 Average Commercial Power Unavailability in the United States*

Zero backup	4-hour backup	8-hour backup	12-hour backup
370.2	192.4	153	128.5

*In minutes per year.

Power Supplies

Independent of the availability of commercial power is the reliability of the power supplies themselves. CableLabs' data has suggested a failure rate of only 3%. Although such a rate may be achievable by a nonstandby power supply, it is the industry's common experience that standby power supplies are often much less reliable (although the overall reliability of commercial power plus standby power supply will exceed that of a nonstandby supply by itself). Standby supply reliability will be dramatically affected by the age and condition of the batteries as well as by the level of routine maintenance in the system.

Amplifiers

CableLabs found field failures occurring in trunk amplifiers at the rate of 10%, whereas failures in the simpler line extenders occurred at a 2% annualized rate. "Distribution" amplifiers used in modern HFC networks have a complexity somewhere between these extremes, and 5% is often used in modeling HFC networks, although upgraded designs may justify lower values. Werner has quoted "empirically derived" failure rates for distribution amplifiers as low as 1.75%.[12] Merk has suggested that operators use failure rates of 0.5% for trunk amplifiers and 0.15% for line extenders, based solely on warranty repair data.[13] This range of values illustrates how difficult it is to be confident of failure rates and how competent engineers can arrive at rates that vary by more than 10:1.

Optical Transmitters

Werner and Merk are consistent in reporting 2.3% downstream transmitter failure rates. If CableLabs' failure rates for other headend equipment of 20 to 30% are to be believed, then these values are suspiciously low. On the other hand, the base of equipment that went into the latter study varied in age, whereas optical transmitters are likely to be much newer given the relatively recent widespread rollout of HFC systems.

Werner rates upstream transmitters identically to downstream, whereas Merk suggests that upstream transmitters experience a failure rate of only 0.9%. Given that most upstream transmitters operate at much lower powers, do not require a thermoelectric cooler, and do not require a high-power driver, there is some logic to believing a lower upstream value.

Optical Receivers

When evaluating optical receivers, it is important to distinguish between the receiver itself and the entire optical node. Since nodes often include all the essential components of normal trunk amplifier stations, in addition to optical components, it is advisable to rate the receiver independently of its host station unless it is a stand-alone unit. Werner's value here is 1.7%, whereas Merk uses 0.7%, with both authors rating upstream and downstream receivers as essentially identical.

Passive Devices

MTBF data supplied to CableLabs by manufacturers suggests that passive device (taps, power inserters, splitters, directional couplers) failure rates should be on the order of 1%. CableLabs' field data suggest that actual numbers are closer to 0.1%—a rare case where actual experience is superior to predicted. Werner's data are even more optimistic at 0.04%. Merk suggests the use of values between 0.07% and 0.26%, depending on the device.

Coaxial Connectors

Neither CableLabs nor Merk suggests failure rates for coaxial connectors, though CableLabs' "cable-span" failure rate may be a composite of the actual cable and the attached connectors. Werner suggests a failure rate of 0.01%. Although this may seem insignificant, it must be remembered that the signal must pass through at least two connectors for every series-connected device in the system, so that a cascade of 5 amplifiers, 1 power inserter, 2 splitters, and 25 taps will include 66 connectors.

The preceding values are for the connectors used for solid-sheathed aluminum cable. From experience, the failure rate (as measured by outages and associated trouble calls) for drop connectors is much higher. Based on actual experience operating numerous systems, it is suggested that 0.25% be used pending better industry statistics. As with distribution connectors, a typical drop system will include several series-connected F connectors. Among all the components considered, the greatest actual field variation may be in the performance of drop connectors owing to both craft sensitivity and the wide range of available connector quality choices.

Fiber-Optic Cable

The modeling program provided with CableLabs's report suggests the use of 3% failure rates for fiber-cable spans (regardless of length). Merk suggests the use of Bellcore's data of 0.44% per mile, whereas Werner suggests the use of 0.44% (presumably per span). Hamilton-Piercy suggests that Bellcore's data on fiber failures is equivalent to 0.3% per span per year but uses his company's experiential value of 1.5% per span.[14] Clearly, these are widely varying numbers that reflect several variables.

For one thing, the Bellcore data were based on analysis of "FCC-reportable" outages only, meaning those that affect at least 30,000 customers.[15] Thus, most instances of fiber damage on the subscriber side of switches went unreported, whereas the failures occurred in telephone interoffice cables that are placed in well-protected trenches because of the high volumes of traffic being carried. Fiber serving small pockets of customers is more economically installed and more likely to be damaged as a result. For example, most of the damaged cables reported by telephone companies were located 4 to 5 feet underground, well below the depths used in most cable television construction.

Second, the lengths of the spans considered vary from 5 miles or less for typical suburban HFC architectures to 50 miles or more for long-distance telephone links. Finally, available failure data may have been difficult to coordinate to the total length of the failed cable.

Given that most fiber cable failures are due to dig-ups and should increase proportionally with distance, a value of 0.1% per mile is suggested pending better data. This is roughly equivalent to Hamilton-Piercy's value if 15-mile average link distances are assumed, or Werner's value if 4.4-mile spans are assumed.

Coaxial Cable

Coaxial distribution cable might be thought to suffer similar failure rates. CableLabs' field data, however, suggests 3% annual failures. Even if it is assumed that spans are a half-mile long (about the longest expected between trunk amplifiers), this would be the equivalent of 6% per year per mile, or 40 times the optical cable failure rate. Werner's 1996 data suggest the use of 0.23%—less than one-tenth the failure rate. Based on the fact that fiber cable is generally armored and therefore both stronger and not as subject to rodent damage, it seems reasonable to use a value of 0.2% per mile for distribution coaxial cable or double the risk factor for fiber cable.

Drop cable is not as well protected, nor is it made to the same quality standards as distribution cable. Analysis of trouble call rates and causes suggests that annual failure rates of drop cables may be in the 1 to 2% region.

Set-Top Terminals and Other Operator-Supplied Terminal Equipment

The failure rates of terminal devices will obviously vary considerably with complexity and age. New, digital terminals will have very low failure rates, whereas first-generation addressable products often failed at several percent per month. Few authors who have modeled cable television failure rates have included terminal data since CableLabs' definition excludes individual subscriber outages. Based on field failure data from several systems over a number of years, we suggest that a default value of 7% be used, lacking more device-specific data. For purposes of analysis, this failure rate is taken to include non-hardware failures such as the failure of a terminal to receive necessary enabling data, data entry errors that result in unintended deauthorizations, and power failures that cause the terminal to lose its authorization status for some time after power restoration. From the subscribers' viewpoint, these are still service outages.

Active Network Interface Devices

Where services terminate at the outside wall of residences, the equipment is subjected to greater weather exposure but may be rigidly mounted and so not subject to handling damage. Bellcore suggests network interface devices (NIDs) containing active termination equipment, whether for video or telephony service, have a net unavailability of about 26 minutes per year.[16] If it is assumed that individual customer outages are restored in a mean time of 8 hours, this is equivalent to a 5.4% yearly failure rate.

Headend/Rack-Mounted Equipment

CableLabs' initial data indicated very high (20 to 30%) failure rates among headend equipment. In general, however, a failure rate of 5%, averaged over all classifications of headend equipment, is more in line with operators' experience and will be used in our example calculations.

In the case of telephony, headend units are required to interface between the ports on the switch and the HFC distribution system. Although the term often has a more precise meaning in different contexts, *host digital terminal* (HDT) will be used to refer to all the headend equipment between the switch and the broadband distribution system, considered as a subsystem. Although Bellcore did not predict the failure rate of HDTs, they assigned 10 minutes of annual unavailability to this subsystem. On the basis of an assumed 0.5-hour MTTR, the HDT is assigned an annual failure rate of 33%.

In summary, there is reasonable industry agreement on some average failure rates but widely diverging data on others. As the cable industry gains more experience with reliability as an essential element of network design, better data will likely become available for predicting performance. We have a bias toward carefully collected field data derived from systems operating in conditions similar to the system to be analyzed (regional differences in such factors as lightning strikes and the availability of laws requiring utility locations before commencing underground construction can have a major effect on outages). For the purposes of the example discussed later in this chapter, the annual failure rates shown in Table 12.3 will be used.

Table 12.3 Typical Individual Network Component Annual Failure Rates

Component	Failure rate (%)	Component	Failure rate (%)
Commercial power (unprotected)	300	Optical receivers	1
Power supplies (nonstandby)	3	Passive devices	0.1
Power supplies (standby)	6	Coaxial connectors (distribution)	0.01
Amplifiers (trunk or distribution)	4	Coaxial connectors (drop)	0.25
Amplifiers (bridger modules or line extenders)	3	Fiber-optic cable	0.1/mile*
Optical transmitters (downstream)	3	Coaxial cable (distribution)	0.2/mile
Optical transmitters (upstream)	1.5	Drop cable (length-independent)	1.5
Redundancy switches	0.5	Set-top terminals/modems	7
NIDs	5.4	Headend equipment	5
HDTs	33		

Because the major cause of failure is dig-ups and cuts, the failure rate applies to the entire cable and all the fibers within it. Therefore, no redundancy gain is realized by using separate fibers to deliver signals to a node, for instance, if they share a common cable sheath.

12.6.4 **Estimating MTTR**

Although the elapsed time between failures is a function of network architecture and the quality of the components used, the time required to restore service after an outage occurs is almost entirely within the operator's control and is a function of staffing levels and training in addition to performance-monitoring systems.

Total time to restore service consists of four time segments[17]: (1) the time between the start of the outage and when the operator is aware of it; (2) the time for crews to respond to the outage location; (3) the time for the technician to identify the cause of the outage; and (4) the time to repair or replace the failed item and restore service.

Werner quotes average MTTR values varying from 66 to 243 minutes, depending on the diligence of the system operator. Although CableLabs did not put forth an industry goal, they did quote from a Warner Cable guideline calling for 2-hour maximum MTTR for damaged fiber-optic cables.[18] Data provided by the telephone industry to the FCC on fiber repairs showed that, in most cases, service was restored within a 2- to 4-hour or 4- to 6-hour window.[19]

Historically, many cable systems used manual trouble call routing, staffed during business hours only (except for major outages, storms, and so on), and operated many headends without any regularly present technicians. As larger, regional systems offering a wide variety of services have evolved, 24-hour, 7-day staffing of headends is no longer uncommon, and field service staffs often work two shifts, with on-call technicians for late-night situations.

As an economic choice, the response to outages is proportional to the number of customers affected. Large outages inevitably clog the customer service telephone lines and may lead to bad publicity since customers already affected by loss of service are doubly inconvenienced by being unable to report the situation.

Based on experience from a number of systems, the MTTR values in Table 12.4 will be used in the example discussed later in the chapter. To the extent that operators do better or worse than these values (which may be overly pessimistic for a

Table 12.4 Typical Cable System MTTR Values

Failure level	MTTR
Headend (24-hour, 7-day staffing)	0.5 hour
Fiber trunk cables	2 hours
Optical node components	1 hour
Distribution system coaxial components	4 hours
Individual customer drop or components	8 hours with remote monitoring
	12 hours without remote monitoring (customer call-in delay)

well-organized system), the availability will vary from that calculated.[20] Factors such as traffic conditions, dispersal of personnel, training, availability of repair materials, and communications systems and utilization will have a major impact on MTTR.

12.6.5 Special Considerations for Headends and Hubs

When Bellcore set up the availability standards for telephony, they specifically excluded the switch and everything on the network (nonsubscriber) side of the switch. CableLabs, on the other hand, specifically included headends to the extent that a single-channel outage is counted the same as a total system outage.

Those wishing to model cable system reliability factors may want to consider some interim approach that accounts for all critical common equipment (such as combining amplifiers and headend power) but only some percentage of individual channel-processing equipment. Without such an approach, it can readily be shown that the failure rate of a modern 750-MHz, fully loaded headend will be theoretically very high, yet the average viewer will be unaware of those failures if they happen to occur in channels he or she is not watching.

In previously published studies, one of the authors has proposed that viewers, in a typical viewing session, are exposed significantly to 10 channels (that is, they access and view programming on 10 channels in an evening of typical viewing); he therefore modeled headend reliability based on the sum of the critical common equipment, plus all the equipment required to create 10 channels (satellite antennas, receivers, modulators, and so forth).[21] In the example discussed later, it has been assumed that the viewer is exposed to the potential failure of the approximately 30 channel-specific pieces of equipment needed to process the 10 channels viewed, plus 3 common combining amplifiers. For other services, different calculations of headend equipment reliability might be appropriate. As with equipment failure rates, there is little statistically valid field information on the number of channels viewed by typical subscribers.

A complete analysis of video headend–caused subscriber outages should include not only signal-processing equipment but control equipment—for instance, the telemetry generators that send enabling signals to terminals, addressability control computers, and (for two-way terminals) upstream data receivers.

12.6.6 Special Considerations for Upstream Communications

Most of the distribution system is shared between upstream and downstream signals, including amplifier stations (though a detailed analysis might assign different failure rates to upstream and downstream modules within the station), power supplies, passive devices, and the cable itself. The optical portion of the plant, however, almost always uses separate fibers for upstream and downstream communications, and always uses separate upstream and downstream optical transmitters and receivers.

When modeling the optical trunking segments, therefore, both upstream and downstream transmitters and receivers are critical to two-way applications and must be included. Assuming the fibers share a common cable, however, the reliability of a pair of fibers will not differ significantly from a single fiber, and so the number will be the same as for one-way transmission. When calculating the failure rate of the headend for a two-way application, it is also necessary to include equipment that processes both incoming and outgoing communications.

12.6.7 Calculation of Failure Rates and Availability

Once the structure of the network is defined and the field failure rates and repair times of the equipment used are known, the next step is to calculate the total failure rate of each segment. This is simply the sum of the failure rates of each of the elements in the segment (Equation 12.2). Next, using Equations 12.6 and 12.7, it is possible to calculate the availability of each section and the total yearly minutes of outage.

If the only result desired is total system failure rate and availability to the most affected subscriber, failure rates and outage minutes of each of the critical series-connected sections can be added. The net availability can then be calculated using Equation 12.7. Additional data can be derived from the analysis, if desired, by, for instance, calculating the number of subscribers affected by each outage, calculating the outage rate and availability to each subscriber, and/or calculating the cost of repair for each class of failure. Although this level of analysis is much more complex, it yields a significant amount of additional information about the performance of the network, including

- Reliability and availability to the average, as well as the most affected, customer
- The total number of outages and the total number of customer outages (the summation of each outage multiplied by the number of customers affected)
- The total cost of outage repair
- The distribution of outages by size

This additional information is very helpful in making design trade-offs that include not only the cost of construction but also the required customer service staffing levels and predicted repair costs.[22]

12.7 ANALYSIS OF A TYPICAL HFC NETWORK

There have been many published analyses of the reliability and availability of specific network configurations. One of the most comprehensive compared 13 different architectures and found availability values ranging from 99.7 to 99.99% based on 0.3% fiber link failure rates and 10% amplifier failure rates (failure rates for other components were not given). Using 1.5% fiber link failures and 5% amplifier failures, two architectures were found to exceed 99.98% availability: a ring/ring/star and a double star.[23]

As an illustration of attainable reliability factors, as well as of the degree of information available from a comprehensive analysis of failure rate data, we give a complete analysis of a typical HFC cable system.

12.7.1 Architecture

The analyzed system is typical of an early 1990s upgrade; a more recent upgrade would most certainly have fewer amplifiers, a shorter cascade, no cascaded strings of taps, and a single power supply. Thus, this example is given because it serves to illustrate several analysis features, but its performance should not be taken as typical of a more modern system.

Although the example system is logically a simple single-star network, several nodes are served from each large fiber-optic cable leaving the headend, and the analysis accounts for this shared risk. Figure 12.3 is a simplified diagram of a typical node. As with Figure 12.1, the tap configuration is not shown though each of the dashed lines contains taps (and sometimes splitters and/or directional couplers). Even though not shown in the figure, the taps and branching are included in the analysis. The distribution system extending from each node passes approximately 2000 homes, with a basic penetration rate of 70%. The total number of homes served from the headend is 150,000, split among 75 similar nodes.

The coaxial amplifier cascade beyond the node is limited to four, and the entire node distribution system contains 53 amplifiers. Three power supplies are required to power all the active devices, with a maximum power supply cascade of two. The total number of series-connected taps in any one distribution leg is about 20.

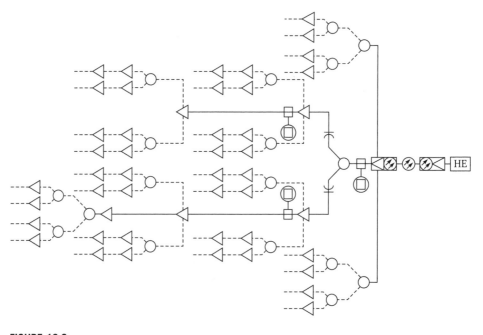

FIGURE 12.3

Simplified schematic diagram of an analyzed system.

The initial analysis is based on the use of a generator, but no uninterruptible power supply (UPS), at the headend and field standby power supplies with 2-hour battery capacity. It is assumed that this results in a 30-second headend outage every time the commercial power fails (three times per year) until the generator "kicks in," and that the field standby power supplies have the effect of reducing the power failure rates to 50% per year in each location, with 1 hour of unprotected outage when the batteries do run down (based on dispatching a crew with portable generators as a result of customer-reported outages). It is assumed that there is no status monitoring of power supplies that would have allowed crews with portable generators to back-power supplies before the batteries expire. Again, this is not typical of recently upgraded systems, but serves to illustrate reliability trade-offs in system design. The Excel application entitled *SOAR*, available for downloading from *www.elsevierdirect. com/companions/9780123744012*, includes a parameterized spreadsheet that can be configured for any architecture and loaded with any component reliability assumptions. It will calculate each of the factors discussed later. The associated instruction manual, *SOAR-Manual.doc*, is essential for correctly using the calculation tool.

12.7.2 Video Services Performance

The network was analyzed for delivery of conventional cable television video services. It was assumed that the viewer was "exposed" to the reliability of 30 pieces of headend channel-processing equipment plus three headend combining amplifiers during a typical viewing session, as discussed in Section 12.6.5.

A typical home drop system was assumed, including a digital converter. No monitoring of the home equipment was assumed so that subscribers were exposed to all failures occurring beyond the tap (since they would not be known to the network operator until reported by the user), but to only a portion of the failures earlier in the network, as discussed earlier in the section an user-perceived reliability factors.

The outage rate per year for the most affected customer is 6.11. Although there are no specific standards for telephony service, this is close to CableLabs' suggested maximum of 0.6 per month for video service. (Even though the CableLabs' guideline did not include drop and premises elements, this analysis does since subscriber satisfaction was measured on overall outage rate independent of cause.) Figure 12.4 shows the relative contribution of various network sections to this rate. As can be seen, powering is by far the largest contributor, although headend outages also make a major contribution to unavailability. The large power contribution reflects the use of a generator, but no UPS at the headend, so that customers experience a short outage each time the power fails at the headend.

The network availability to the most affected customer was calculated to be 0.99951, equivalent to yearly service outage time of about 4.3 hours. The unavailability is one-sixth of that suggested by CableLabs for cable television service.

As Figure 12.5 shows, the largest contributor to unavailability is also powering, followed by the drop, headend, coaxial distribution network, and fiber trunking. The large contribution from powering reflects both the limitations of battery

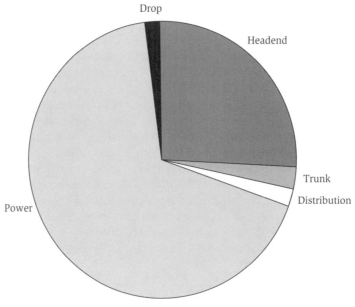

FIGURE 12.4

Relative network section contributions to outage rate.

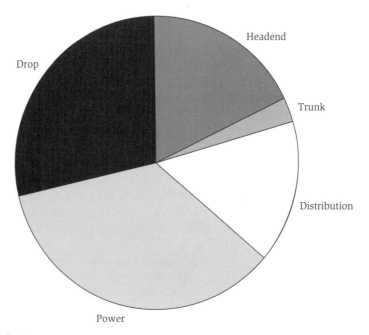

FIGURE 12.5

Relative network section contributions to outage hours.

capacity and the lack of status monitoring. (In Section 12.7.4, we will see the effect of adding power supply status monitoring.) Although the drop hardware is reasonably reliable, its contribution to total outage time is disproportionately large since the MTTR is much higher than for outages affecting multiple customers. The size of the headend contribution is affected primarily by the large number of moderately reliable units involved in producing a multichannel video lineup. Nevertheless, the headend contribution is proportionately less than that of outage rate since the MTTR is much less.

A third useful result of the failure analysis is the distribution of multisubscriber outages on the basis of the number of customers affected. This analysis is important because it allows the network operator to size his or her customer service operation knowing the expected volume of outage-related customer calls. Figure 12.6 shows the outage size distribution for the network analyzed.

12.7.3 Wired Telephony Services Performance

The network was also analyzed as a delivery means for wired telephony. In that case, there was no exposure to headend video equipment, and in accordance with Bellcore methodology, the switch reliability was not included though the interface between switch and distribution system (the host digital terminal) was. In the case of telephony, the drop system included only the drop itself plus a system-powered

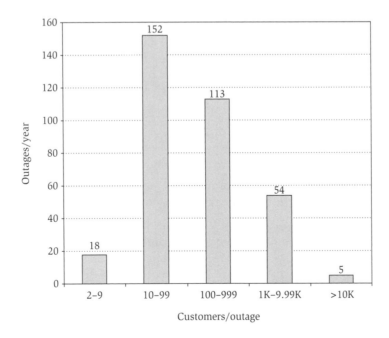

FIGURE 12.6

Outage distribution by number of affected customers.

network interface device, or NID (if telephony is provided through an in-house eMTA, reliability will be slightly lower, since additional wiring is involved and because the ability of the eMTA to withstand an extended power outage may be more limited), on the assumption that the in-house wiring and analog instruments should not be included in accordance with Bellcore practice. The failure rates assigned to the HDT and NID resulted in 10 and 26 minutes per year of downtime in accordance with Bellcore's allocations in TR-NWT-000418.[24]

When analyzed in this telephony configuration, the outage time is 26% less than for video services, resulting in an availability of 0.999636, whereas the number of outages is 27% less (4.82 per year). Analysis of the causes of the remaining outages shows that power-related issues dominate all others. Although the unavailability is about 3.6 times worse than Bellcore standards for wired telephone service, they are not comparable because of the factors not included in the Bellcore outage definition (this analysis, for instance, includes powering and measures outages from actual occurrence, not from when they are reported).

12.7.4 Effect of Improved Powering on Telephony Performance

If a UPS is added to the headend and status monitoring to the field supplies (so that crews can deliver temporary generators before the batteries lose their charge), then all power-related outages can be eliminated except those due to the reliability of the powering equipment itself. In that case, telephone service availability improves to 0.99976 and the outage rate declines dramatically to 0.82 per year.[25]

As Figure 12.7 shows, powering is still a significant contributor to network unavailability but is less important relative to the drop (dominated by the NID failure rate and slow repair time) and the distribution network. Figure 12.8 shows that the number of large outages drops dramatically as a result of improved powering.

It is clear from this analysis that true 0.9999 availability for the consumer can easily be achieved in modern systems whose enhancements, relative to our example, include

- Improved HDT and eMTA reliability—in our example the Bellcore-assigned outage time allocations consume 68% of the 53-minute total allowed.

- Hardened, status-monitored, and more reliable powering, allowing repair crews to reach areas with localized power outages within the running time of internal batteries.

- Shorter cascades of both coaxial equipment and power supplies. HFC networks serving 500 or fewer homes are usually powered by a single power supply located at the node and have active equipment cascades beyond the node of only two to three.

- Reliable status monitoring throughout the network. Since the time required to become aware of a failure and then to analyze its cause, is a material part of total MTTR, extensive status monitoring plays an essential part in reducing repair times.

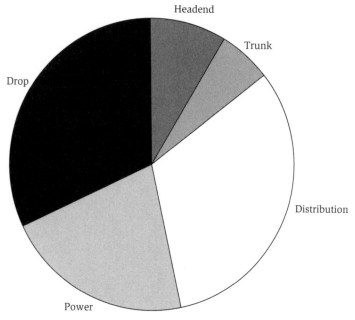

FIGURE 12.7

Reduced effect on unavailability of powering with headend UPS and status monitoring.

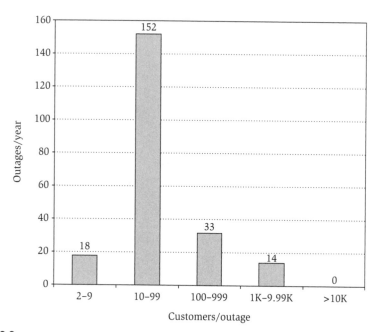

FIGURE 12.8

Reduction in number of large outages with improved powering.

Note that the fiber-trunking portion of the network is a minor contributor to unavailability in all cases, even in this simple star network. Thus, use of various ring topologies will reduce the instance of large outages (an important consideration), but will not significantly reduce network unavailability in this network. As other factors are brought under control, the fiber contribution will become more important.

12.8 SUMMARY

The estimation of network availability, failure rate, and other reliability-related factors is very straightforward, if somewhat tedious, given a particular topology, known component failure rates, and repair times. Unfortunately, a great deal of the effort needed to produce accurate reliability predictions is involved in developing believable component and commercial power failure rates. Once a logical model of a proposed network is constructed and entered into a spreadsheet for analysis, it is simple to test the effect of various component choices and operating practices.

The preliminary analysis done in this chapter illustrates that modern HFC networks are easily capable of achieving low customer-experienced outage rates and unavailability for video services.

HFC networks that are properly designed for wired telephone services are capable of achieving the required availability, whereas lower-cost networks may be entirely adequate for various levels of video and data services. It is the function of the network engineer to design the most cost-effective network to carry the desired services.

ENDNOTES

1. Bell Communications Research, *Generic Requirements for FITL Systems Availability and Reliability Requirements*, Bellcore TA-NWT-00909, Issue 2, Bell Communications Research, Piscataway, NJ, December 1993, p. 13–1.

2. Brian Bauer, "In-Home Cabling for Digital Services: Future-Proofing Signal Quality and Minimizing Signal Outages," *1995 SCTE Conference on Emerging Technologies*, Orlando, FL, Society of Cable & Telecommunications Engineers, Exton, PA, pp. 95–100.

3. Bell Communications Research, *Reliability Assurance for Fiber Optic Systems System Reliability and Service Availability*, Bellcore TR-NWT-000418, Issue 2, Bell Communications Research, Piscataway, NJ, December 1992, p. 31.

4. Network Reliability Council, *Final Report to the Federal Communications Commission, Reliability Issues—Changing Technologies Working Group, New Wireline Access Technologies Subteam Final Report*, Reston, VA, February 1996, p. 13.

5. CableLabs, *Outage Reduction*, September 1992. CableLabs, Louisville, CO.

6. Ibid., p. II-5.

7. Ibid., p. V-10.

8. Network Reliability Council, *Final Report*, p. 15.

9. Private communication from Andrew Large. The formulas are valid for cases where $TC + MTTR < TS$.

10. This statement is not true when considering *signal* as opposed to *hardware* reliability in the upstream direction since ingress and noise from all branches will affect the reliability of communications on any given branch. Also, as will be seen, we are talking about logical, not physical, cascade here, and the powering configuration may require modification of what we would normally consider the cascade order. Finally, electrical short circuits in network branches that are not part of the signal cascade can nevertheless affect communications.

11. Network Reliability Council, *Final Report*, p. 16. The figures are from Allen L. Black and James L. Spencer, "An Assessment of Commercial AC Power Quality: A Fiber-in-the-Loop Perspective," International Telecommunications Energy Conference, in *Intelec '93 Proceedings*, IEEE.

12. Tony Werner and Pete Gatseos, "Network Availability Consumer Expectations, Plant Requirements and Capabilities of HFC Networks," *1996 NCTA Technical Papers*, National Cable & Telecommunications Association, Washington, DC, pp. 313–324.

13. Chuck Merk and Walt Srode, "Reliability of CATV Broadband Distribution Networks for Telephony Applications—Is It Good Enough?," *1995 NCTA Technical Papers*, National Cable & Telecommunications Association, Washington, DC, pp. 93–107.

14. Nick Hamilton-Piercy and Robb Balsdon, "Network Availability and Reliability," *Communications Technology*, July 1994, pp. 42–47.

15. Network Reliability Council, *Network Reliability: A Report to the Nation, Compendium of Technical Papers*, National Engineering Consortium, Chicago, June 1993, pp. 1–32.

16. Bell Communications Research, *Generic Requirements for FITL Systems Availability and Reliability Requirements*, Bellcore TA-NWT-00909, Issue 2, Bell Communications Research, Piscataway, NJ, December 1993, p. 13-5–13-6.

17. Tony Werner and Pete Gatseos, "Network Availability Consumer Expectations, Plant Requirements and Capabilities of HFC Networks," p. 318.

18. CableLabs, *Outage Reduction*, p. V-16.

19. Network Reliability Council, *Network Reliability: A Report to the Nation, Compendium of Technical Papers*, National Engineering Consortium, Chicago, June 1993, p. 22.

20. One large multiple system operator reports systemwide MTTRs ranging from 1.64 to 2.39 hours for multiple customer outages. The measured systems are all HFC with various sizes of nodes and wide deployment of both fiber node and coaxial amplifier status monitoring. All headends have UPS plus generator backup. Private correspondence from Nick Hamilton-Piercy.

21. David Large, "User-Perceived Availability of Hybrid Fiber-Coax Networks," *1995 NCTA Technical Papers*, National Cable & Telecommunications Association, Washington, DC, pp. 61–71.

22. David Large, "Reliability Model for Hybrid Fiber-Coax Systems," *Symposium Record, 19th International Television Symposium and Exhibition*, Montreux, Switzerland, June 1995, pp. 860–875.

23. Hamilton-Piercy and Balsdon, "Network Availability and Reliability."

24. Bell Communications Research, *Loop Downtime Allocations—FITL Systems*, Table 4, Bellcore TR-NWT-000418, Piscataway, NJ, December 1992, p. 37.

25. The average monthly video availability among cable systems comprising one large MSO (that has widely deployed status monitoring) varied from 0.9992 to 0.9996 over a 10-month period. Private correspondence from Nick Hamilton-Piercy.

Channel Allocation

The channel allocation shown here conforms to the requirements of CEA/ANSI 542-B, which specifies the correspondence between channel number and frequency for North America. This standard was developed by the joint EIA (now CEA)/NCTA Engineering Committee, and the original version has been adopted by the FCC as the standard for channel allocations in the United States. (As of this writing, FCC rules refer to the standard by its old working designation, IS-132.) Picture carrier frequencies are shown, even for QAM signals that have but do not transmit a carrier.

The channel extends from 1.25 MHz below the analog picture carrier, to 4.75 MHz above. For QAM signals, the carrier is in the center of the channel. For 8-VSB signals, the carrier is 310 kHz above the low band edge. For all digital modulation, there is a single carrier, not separate carriers, for picture and sound. Three channelization plans are shown.

The complete standard is available from the Consumer Electronics Association's duplication contractor, Global Engineering, at 877-413-5184, *http://global.ihs.com/*. (Content in this appendix is reprinted with permission of the Consumer Electronics Association.)

Channel	Channel Edge Low (MHz) (Standard and IRC)	High (MHz)	Note	Analog Picture Carrier STD (MHz)	IRC (MHz)	HRC (MHz)	Digital Carrier STD 8/16VSB (MHz)	STD QAM (MHz)	IRC 8/16VSB (MHz)	IRC QAM (MHz)	HRC 8/16VSB (MHz)	HRC QAM
1	72.0000	76.0000	+++			72.0036	72.3100		72.3100	75.0000	71.0600	73.7500
2	54.0000	60.0000		55.2500	55.2625	54.0027	54.3100	57.0000	54.3100	57.0000	53.0600	55.7500
3	60.0000	66.0000		61.2500	61.2625	60.0030	60.3100	63.0000	60.3100	63.0000	59.0600	61.7500
4	66.0000	72.0000		67.2500	67.2625	66.0033	66.3100	69.0000	66.3100	69.0000	65.0600	67.7500
5	76.0000	82.0000		77.2500	79.2625	78.0039	76.3100	79.0000	78.3100	81.0000	77.0600	79.7500
6	82.0000	88.0000		83.2500	85.2625	84.0042	82.3100	85.0000	84.3100	87.0000	83.0600	85.7500
7	174.0000	180.0000		175.2500	175.2625	174.0087	174.3100	177.0000	174.3100	177.0000	173.0600	175.7500
8	180.0000	186.0000		181.2500	181.2625	180.0090	180.3100	183.0000	180.3100	183.0000	179.0600	181.7500
9	186.0000	192.0000		187.2500	187.2625	186.0093	186.3100	189.0000	186.3100	189.0000	185.0600	187.7500
10	192.0000	198.0000		193.2500	193.2625	192.0096	192.3100	195.0000	192.3100	195.0000	191.0600	193.7500
11	198.0000	204.0000		199.2500	199.2625	198.0099	198.3100	201.0000	198.3100	201.0000	197.0600	199.7500
12	204.0000	210.0000		205.2500	205.2625	204.0102	204.3100	207.0000	204.3100	207.0000	203.0600	205.7500
13	210.0000	216.0000		211.2500	211.2625	210.0105	210.3100	213.0000	210.3100	213.0000	209.0600	211.7500
14	120.0000	126.0000		121.2625	121.2625	120.0060	120.3100	123.0000	120.3100	123.0000	119.0600	121.7500
15	126.0000	132.0000		127.2625	127.2625	126.0063	126.3100	129.0000	126.3100	129.0000	125.0600	127.7500
16	132.0000	138.0000		133.2625	133.2625	132.0066	132.3100	135.0000	132.3100	135.0000	131.0600	133.7500
17	138.0000	144.0000		139.2500	139.2625	138.0069	138.3100	141.0000	138.3100	141.0000	137.0600	139.7500
18	144.0000	150.0000		145.2500	145.2625	144.0072	144.3100	147.0000	144.3100	147.0000	143.0600	145.7500
19	150.0000	156.0000		151.2500	151.2625	150.0075	150.3100	153.0000	150.3100	153.0000	149.0600	151.7500
20	156.0000	162.0000		157.2500	157.2625	156.0078	156.3100	159.0000	156.3100	159.0000	155.0600	157.7500
21	162.0000	168.0000		163.2500	163.2625	162.0081	162.3100	165.0000	162.3100	165.0000	161.0600	163.7500
22	168.0000	174.0000		169.2500	169.2625	168.0084	168.3100	171.0000	168.3100	171.0000	167.0600	169.7500
23	216.0000	222.0000		217.2500	217.2625	216.0108	216.3100	219.0000	216.3100	219.0000	215.0600	217.7500
24	222.0000	228.0000		223.2500	223.2625	222.0111	222.3100	225.0000	222.3100	225.0000	221.0600	223.7500
25	228.0000	234.0000		229.2625	229.2625	228.0114	228.3100	231.0000	228.3100	231.0000	227.0600	229.7500

26	234.0000	240.0000	235.2625	235.2625	234.0117	234.3100	237.0000	234.3100	237.0000	234.3100	233.0600	235.7500
27	240.0000	246.0000	241.2625	241.2625	240.0120	240.3100	243.0000	240.3100	243.0000	240.3100	239.0600	241.7500
28	246.0000	252.0000	247.2625	247.2625	246.0123	246.3100	249.0000	246.3100	249.0000	246.3100	245.0600	247.7500
29	252.0000	258.0000	253.2625	253.2625	252.0126	252.3100	255.0000	252.3100	255.0000	252.3100	251.0600	253.7500
30	258.0000	264.0000	259.2625	259.2625	258.0129	258.3100	261.0000	258.3100	261.0000	258.3100	257.0600	259.7500
31	264.0000	270.0000	265.2625	265.2625	264.0132	264.3100	267.0000	264.3100	267.0000	264.3100	263.0600	265.7500
32	270.0000	276.0000	271.2625	271.2625	270.0135	270.3100	273.0000	270.3100	273.0000	270.3100	269.0600	271.7500
33	276.0000	282.0000	277.2625	277.2625	276.0138	276.3100	279.0000	276.3100	279.0000	276.3100	275.0600	277.7500
34	282.0000	288.0000	283.2625	283.2625	282.0141	282.3100	285.0000	282.3100	285.0000	282.3100	281.0600	283.7500
35	288.0000	294.0000	289.2625	289.2625	288.0144	288.3100	291.0000	288.3100	291.0000	288.3100	287.0600	289.7500
36	294.0000	300.0000	295.2625	295.2625	294.0147	294.3100	297.0000	294.3100	297.0000	294.3100	293.0600	295.7500
37	300.0000	306.0000	301.2625	301.2625	300.0150	300.3100	303.0000	300.3100	303.0000	300.3100	299.0600	301.7500
38	306.0000	312.0000	307.2625	307.2625	306.0153	306.3100	309.0000	306.3100	309.0000	306.3100	305.0600	307.7500
39	312.0000	318.0000	313.2625	313.2625	312.0156	312.3100	315.0000	312.3100	315.0000	312.3100	311.0600	313.7500
40	318.0000	324.0000	319.2625	319.2625	318.0159	318.3100	321.0000	318.3100	321.0000	318.3100	317.0600	319.7500
41	324.0000	330.0000	325.2625	325.2625	324.0162	324.3100	327.0000	324.3100	327.0000	324.3100	323.0600	325.7500
42	330.0000	336.0000*	331.2750	331.2750	330.0165	330.3100	333.0000	330.3100	333.0000	330.3100	329.0600	331.7500
43	336.0000	342.0000	337.2625	337.2625	336.0168	336.3100	339.0000	336.3100	339.0000	336.3100	335.0600	337.7500
44	342.0000	348.0000	343.2625	343.2625	342.0171	342.3100	345.0000	342.3100	345.0000	342.3100	341.0600	343.7500
45	348.0000	354.0000	349.2625	349.2625	348.0174	348.3100	351.0000	348.3100	351.0000	348.3100	347.0600	349.7500
46	354.0000	360.0000	355.2625	355.2625	354.0177	354.3100	357.0000	354.3100	357.0000	354.3100	353.0600	355.7500
47	360.0000	366.0000	361.2625	361.2625	360.0180	360.3100	363.0000	360.3100	363.0000	360.3100	359.0600	361.7500
48	366.0000	372.0000	367.2625	367.2625	366.0183	366.3100	369.0000	366.3100	369.0000	366.3100	365.0600	367.7500
49	372.0000	378.0000	373.2625	373.2625	372.0186	372.3100	375.0000	372.3100	375.0000	372.3100	371.0600	373.7500
50	378.0000	384.0000	379.2625	379.2625	378.0189	378.3100	381.0000	378.3100	381.0000	378.3100	377.0600	379.7500
51	384.0000	390.0000	385.2625	385.2625	384.0192	384.3100	387.0000	384.3100	387.0000	384.3100	383.0600	385.7500
52	390.0000	396.0000	391.2625	391.2625	390.0195	390.3100	393.0000	390.3100	393.0000	390.3100	389.0600	391.7500
53	396.0000	402.0000	397.2625	397.2625	396.0198	396.3100	399.0000	396.3100	399.0000	396.3100	395.0600	397.7500
54	402.0000	408.0000	403.2500	403.2625	402.0201	402.3100	405.0000	402.3100	405.0000	402.3100	401.0600	403.7500
55	408.0000	414.0000	409.2500	409.2625	408.0204	408.3100	411.0000	408.3100	411.0000	408.3100	407.0600	409.7500

(continued)

Channel	Channel Edge Low (MHz) (Standard and IRC)	High (MHz)	Note	Analog Picture Carrier STD (MHz)	IRC (MHz)	HRC (MHz)	Digital Carrier STD 8/16VSB (MHz)	STD QAM (MHz)	IRC 8/16VSB (MHz)	IRC QAM (MHz)	HRC 8/16VSB (MHz)	HRC QAM
56	414.0000	420.0000		415.2500	415.2625	414.0207	414.3100	417.0000	414.3100	417.0000	413.0600	415.7500
57	420.0000	426.0000		421.2500	421.2625	420.0210	420.3100	423.0000	420.3100	423.0000	419.0600	421.7500
58	426.0000	432.0000		427.2500	427.2625	426.0213	426.3100	429.0000	426.3100	429.0000	425.0600	427.7500
59	432.0000	438.0000		433.2500	433.2625	432.0216	432.3100	435.0000	432.3100	435.0000	431.0600	433.7500
60	438.0000	444.0000		439.2500	439.2625	438.0219	438.3100	441.0000	438.3100	441.0000	437.0600	439.7500
61	444.0000	450.0000		445.2500	445.2625	444.0222	444.3100	447.0000	444.3100	447.0000	443.0600	445.7500
62	450.0000	456.0000		451.2500	451.2625	450.0225	450.3100	453.0000	450.3100	453.0000	449.0600	451.7500
63	456.0000	462.0000		457.2500	457.2625	456.0228	456.3100	459.0000	456.3100	459.0000	455.0600	457.7500
64	462.0000	468.0000		463.2500	463.2625	462.0231	462.3100	465.0000	462.3100	465.0000	461.0600	463.7500
65	468.0000	474.0000		469.2500	469.2625	468.0234	468.3100	471.0000	468.3100	471.0000	467.0600	469.7500
66	474.0000	480.0000		475.2500	475.2625	474.0237	474.3100	477.0000	474.3100	477.0000	473.0600	475.7500
67	480.0000	486.0000		481.2500	481.2625	480.0240	480.3100	483.0000	480.3100	483.0000	479.0600	481.7500
68	486.0000	492.0000		487.2500	487.2625	486.0243	486.3100	489.0000	486.3100	489.0000	485.0600	487.7500
69	492.0000	498.0000		493.2500	493.2625	492.0246	492.3100	495.0000	492.3100	495.0000	491.0600	493.7500
70	498.0000	504.0000		499.2500	499.2625	498.0249	498.3100	501.0000	498.3100	501.0000	497.0600	499.7500
71	504.0000	510.0000		505.2500	505.2625	504.0252	504.3100	507.0000	504.3100	507.0000	503.0600	505.7500
72	510.0000	516.0000		511.2500	511.2625	510.0255	510.3100	513.0000	510.3100	513.0000	509.0600	511.7500
73	516.0000	522.0000		517.2500	517.2625	516.0258	516.3100	519.0000	516.3100	519.0000	515.0600	517.7500
74	522.0000	528.0000		523.2500	523.2625	522.0261	522.3100	525.0000	522.3100	525.0000	521.0600	523.7500
75	528.0000	534.0000		529.2500	529.2625	528.0264	528.3100	531.0000	528.3100	531.0000	527.0600	529.7500
76	534.0000	540.0000		535.2500	535.2625	534.0267	534.3100	537.0000	534.3100	537.0000	533.0600	535.7500
77	540.0000	546.0000		541.2500	541.2625	540.0270	540.3100	543.0000	540.3100	543.0000	539.0600	541.7500
78	546.0000	552.0000		547.2500	547.2625	546.0273	546.3100	549.0000	546.3100	549.0000	545.0600	547.7500
79	552.0000	558.0000		553.2500	553.2625	552.0276	552.3100	555.0000	552.3100	555.0000	551.0600	553.7500

80	559.7500	557.0600	561.0000	558.3100	561.0000	558.3100	558.0279	559.2625	559.2500	564.0000	558.0000
81	565.7500	563.0600	567.0000	564.3100	567.0000	564.3100	564.0282	565.2625	565.2500	570.0000	564.0000
82	571.7500	569.0600	573.0000	570.3100	573.0000	570.3100	570.0285	571.2625	571.2500	576.0000	570.0000
83	577.7500	575.0600	579.0000	576.3100	579.0000	576.3100	576.0288	577.2625	577.2500	582.0000	576.0000
84	583.7500	581.0600	585.0000	582.3100	585.0000	582.3100	582.0291	583.2625	583.2500	588.0000	582.0000
85	589.7500	587.0600	591.0000	588.3100	591.0000	588.3100	588.0294	589.2625	589.2500	594.0000	588.0000
86	595.7500	593.0600	597.0000	594.3100	597.0000	594.3100	594.0297	595.2625	595.2500	600.0000	594.0000
87	601.7500	599.0600	603.0000	600.3100	603.0000	600.3100	600.0300	601.2625	601.2500	606.0000	600.0000
88	607.7500	605.0600	609.0000	606.3100	609.0000	606.3100	606.0303	607.2625	607.2500	612.0000	606.0000
89	613.7500	611.0600	615.0000	612.3100	615.0000	612.3100	612.0306	613.2625	613.2500	618.0000	612.0000
90	619.7500	617.0600	621.0000	618.3100	621.0000	618.3100	618.0309	619.2625	619.2500	624.0000	618.0000
91	625.7500	623.0600	627.0000	624.3100	627.0000	624.3100	624.0312	625.2625	625.2500	630.0000	624.0000
92	631.7500	629.0600	633.0000	630.3100	633.0000	630.3100	630.0315	631.2625	631.2500	636.0000	630.0000
93	637.7500	635.0600	639.0000	636.3100	639.0000	636.3100	636.0318	637.2625	637.2500	642.0000	636.0000
94	643.7500	641.0600	645.0000	642.3100	645.0000	642.3100	642.0321	643.2625	643.2500	648.0000	642.0000
95	91.7500	89.0600	93.0000	90.3100	93.0000	90.3100	90.0045	91.2625	91.2500	96.0000	90.0000
96	97.7500	95.0600	99.0000	96.3100	99.0000	96.3100	96.0048	97.2625	97.2500	102.0000	96.0000
97	103.7500	101.0600	105.0000	102.3100	105.0000	102.3100	102.0051	103.2625	103.2500	108.0000	102.0000
98	109.7500	107.0600	111.0000	108.3100	111.0000	108.3100	108.0250	109.2750	109.2750	114.0000*	108.0000
99	115.7500	113.0600	117.0000	114.3100	117.0000	114.3100	114.0250	115.2750	115.2750	120.0000*	114.0000
100	649.7500	647.0600	651.0000	648.3100	651.0000	648.3100	648.0324	649.2625	649.2500	654.0000	648.0000
101	655.7500	653.0600	657.0000	654.3100	657.0000	654.3100	654.0327	655.2625	655.2500	660.0000	654.0000
102	661.7500	659.0600	663.0000	660.3100	663.0000	660.3100	660.0330	661.2625	661.2500	666.0000	660.0000
103	667.7500	665.0600	669.0000	666.3100	669.0000	666.3100	666.0333	667.2625	667.2500	672.0000	666.0000
104	673.7500	671.0600	675.0000	672.3100	675.0000	672.3100	672.0336	673.2625	673.2500	678.0000	672.0000
105	679.7500	677.0600	681.0000	678.3100	681.0000	678.3100	678.0339	679.2625	679.2500	684.0000	678.0000
106	685.7500	683.0600	687.0000	684.3100	687.0000	684.3100	684.0342	685.2625	685.2500	690.0000	684.0000
107	691.7500	689.0600	693.0000	690.3100	693.0000	690.3100	690.0345	691.2625	691.2500	696.0000	690.0000
108	697.7500	695.0600	699.0000	696.3100	699.0000	696.3100	696.0348	697.2625	697.2500	702.0000	696.0000

(continued)

Channel	Channel Edge Low (MHz) (Standard and IRC)	Channel Edge High (MHz)	Analog Picture Carrier Note	STD (MHz)	IRC (MHz)	HRC (MHz)	Digital Carrier STD 8/16VSB (MHz)	STD QAM (MHz)	IRC 8/16VSB (MHz)	IRC QAM (MHz)	HRC 8/16VSB (MHz)	HRC QAM (MHz)
109	702.0000	708.0000		703.2500	703.2625	702.0351	702.3100	705.0000	702.3100	705.0000	701.0600	703.7500
110	708.0000	714.0000		709.2500	709.2625	708.0354	708.3100	711.0000	708.3100	711.0000	707.0600	709.7500
111	714.0000	720.0000		715.2500	715.2625	714.0357	714.3100	717.0000	714.3100	717.0000	713.0600	715.7500
112	720.0000	726.0000		721.2500	721.2625	720.0360	720.3100	723.0000	720.3100	723.0000	719.0600	721.7500
113	726.0000	732.0000		727.2500	727.2625	726.0363	726.3100	729.0000	726.3100	729.0000	725.0600	727.7500
114	732.0000	738.0000		733.2500	733.2625	732.0366	732.3100	735.0000	732.3100	735.0000	731.0600	733.7500
115	738.0000	744.0000		739.2500	739.2625	738.0369	738.3100	741.0000	738.3100	741.0000	737.0600	739.7500
116	744.0000	750.0000		745.2500	745.2625	744.0372	744.3100	747.0000	744.3100	747.0000	743.0600	745.7500
117	750.0000	756.0000		751.2500	751.2625	750.0375	750.3100	753.0000	750.3100	753.0000	749.0600	751.7500
118	756.0000	762.0000		757.2500	757.2625	756.0378	756.3100	759.0000	756.3100	759.0000	755.0600	757.7500
119	762.0000	768.0000		763.2500	763.2625	762.0381	762.3100	765.0000	762.3100	765.0000	761.0600	763.7500
120	768.0000	774.0000		769.2500	769.2625	768.0384	768.3100	771.0000	768.3100	771.0000	767.0600	769.7500
121	774.0000	780.0000		775.2500	775.2625	774.0387	774.3100	777.0000	774.3100	777.0000	773.0600	775.7500
122	780.0000	786.0000		781.2500	781.2625	780.0390	780.3100	783.0000	780.3100	783.0000	779.0600	781.7500
123	786.0000	792.0000		787.2500	787.2625	786.0393	786.3100	789.0000	786.3100	789.0000	785.0600	787.7500
124	792.0000	798.0000		793.2500	793.2625	792.0396	792.3100	795.0000	792.3100	795.0000	791.0600	793.7500
125	798.0000	804.0000		799.2500	799.2625	798.0399	798.3100	801.0000	798.3100	801.0000	797.0600	799.7500
126	804.0000	810.0000		805.2500	805.2625	804.0402	804.3100	807.0000	804.3100	807.0000	803.0600	805.7500
127	810.0000	816.0000		811.2500	811.2625	810.0405	810.3100	813.0000	810.3100	813.0000	809.0600	811.7500
128	816.0000	822.0000		817.2500	817.2625	816.0408	816.3100	819.0000	816.3100	819.0000	815.0600	817.7500
129	822.0000	828.0000		823.2500	823.2625	822.0411	822.3100	825.0000	822.3100	825.0000	821.0600	823.7500
130	828.0000	834.0000		829.2500	829.2625	828.0414	828.3100	831.0000	828.3100	831.0000	827.0600	829.7500
131	834.0000	840.0000		835.2500	835.2625	834.0417	834.3100	837.0000	834.3100	837.0000	833.0600	835.7500

Ch												
132	846.0000	840.0000		841.2500	841.2625	840.0420	840.3100	843.0000	840.3100	843.0000	839.0600	841.7500
133	852.0000	846.0000		847.2500	847.2625	846.0423	846.3100	849.0000	846.3100	849.0000	845.0600	847.7500
134	858.0000	852.0000		853.2500	853.2625	852.0426	852.3100	855.0000	852.3100	855.0000	851.0600	853.7500
135	864.0000	858.0000		859.2500	859.2625	858.0429	858.3100	861.0000	858.3100	861.0000	857.0600	859.7500
136	870.0000	864.0000		865.2500	865.2625	864.0432	864.3100	867.0000	864.3100	867.0000	863.0600	865.7500
137	876.0000	870.0000		871.2500	871.2625	870.0435	870.3100	873.0000	870.3100	873.0000	869.0600	871.7500
138	882.0000	876.0000		877.2500	877.2625	876.0438	876.3100	879.0000	876.3100	879.0000	875.0600	877.7500
139	888.0000	882.0000		883.2500	883.2625	882.0441	882.3100	885.0000	882.3100	885.0000	881.0600	883.7500
140	894.0000	888.0000		889.2500	889.2625	888.0444	888.3100	891.0000	888.3100	891.0000	887.0600	889.7500
141	900.0000	894.0000		895.2500	895.2625	894.0447	894.3100	897.0000	894.3100	897.0000	893.0600	895.7500
142	906.0000	900.0000		901.2500	901.2625	900.0450	900.3100	903.0000	900.3100	903.0000	899.0600	901.7500
143	912.0000	906.0000		907.2500	907.2625	906.0453	906.3100	909.0000	906.3100	909.0000	905.0600	907.7500
144	918.0000	912.0000		913.2500	913.2625	912.0456	912.3100	915.0000	912.3100	915.0000	911.0600	913.7500
145	924.0000	918.0000		919.2500	919.2625	918.0459	918.3100	921.0000	918.3100	921.0000	917.0600	919.7500
146	930.0000	924.0000		925.2500	925.2625	924.0462	924.3100	927.0000	924.3100	927.0000	923.0600	925.7500
147	936.0000	930.0000		931.2500	931.2625	930.0465	930.3100	933.0000	930.3100	933.0000	929.0600	931.7500
148	942.0000	936.0000		937.2500	937.2625	936.0468	936.3100	939.0000	936.3100	939.0000	935.0600	937.7500
149	948.0000	942.0000		943.2500	943.2625	942.0471	942.3100	945.0000	942.3100	945.0000	941.0600	943.7500
150	954.0000	948.0000		949.2500	949.2625	948.0474	948.3100	951.0000	948.3100	951.0000	947.0600	949.7500
151	960.0000	954.0000	++	955.2500	955.2625	954.0477	954.3100	957.0000	954.3100	957.0000	953.0600	955.7500
152	966.0000	960.0000	++	961.2500	961.2625	960.0480	960.3100	963.0000	960.3100	963.0000	959.0600	961.7500
153	972.0000	966.0000	++	967.2500	967.2625	966.0483	966.3100	969.0000	966.3100	969.0000	965.0600	967.7500
154	978.0000	972.0000		973.2500	973.2625	972.0486	972.3100	975.0000	972.3100	975.0000	971.0600	973.7500
155	984.0000	978.0000		979.2500	979.2625	978.0489	978.3100	981.0000	978.3100	981.0000	977.0600	979.7500
156	990.0000	984.0000		985.2500	985.2625	984.0492	984.3100	987.0000	984.3100	987.0000	983.0600	985.7500
157	996.0000	990.0000		991.2500	991.2625	990.0495	990.3100	993.0000	990.3100	993.0000	989.0600	991.7500
158	1002.0000	996.0000		997.2500	997.2625	996.0498	996.3100	999.0000	996.3100	999.0000	995.0600	997.7500

++ These channels have been used as the 1ST IF in a few TVs. The use of these frequencies may result in interference on these TVs.

+++ Channel 1 is the gap between channels 4 and 5. It is only 4 MHz wide in the standard plan and is not used for television signals. In the HRC and IRC plants it opens to 6 MHz and may be used for television transmissions.

* Excluded from comb due to FCC offset in analog HRC.

10/100Base-T Two common forms of Ethernet transmission that transmit data at 10 or 100 Mb/s, respectively.

8b/10b encoding An encoding method used in gigabit Ethernet, ASI video interconnections, and other applications, in which each 8-bit binary word is replaced by 10 bits such that a minimum number of data transitions per symbol is enforced.

Absorption (optical) Attenuation of optical signals due to conversion of optical energy into heat energy.

Active Ethernet A FTTH technology different from **PON**, in which an Ethernet switch is used in the field to switch data to each home, with a dedicated fiber cable running from the switch to each home.

Actives Components that handle signals and require power; examples are line amplifiers and nodes.

Adaptive equalizer A circuit (or software) that compensates for signal degradation in a path by adjusting taps in a delay circuit until the recovered waveform is as good as it can get.

AGC Automatic gain control. Circuitry in an amplifier that senses the level of a signal at the output and adjusts the gain such that the signal level is constant regardless of input level.

AGL Above ground level. Used in microwave systems to designate the elevation of various antennas relative to the ground level at the foot of the tower.

AML Amplitude modulated link. A microwave technology in which the cable television spectrum is up-converted to a microwave band for transmission, then down-converted at the receiver for transmission through a cable distribution system.

AMSL Above mean sea level. The official designation of elevation used in microwave systems.

Analog television Television transmission in which picture levels are represented by a continuously varying amplitude level.

ANSI American National Standards Institute. An umbrella standards organization for the United States.

APC Angle polished connector. A fiber-optic connector that exhibits reduced reflections due to an angled fiber end.

ASC Automatic slope control, also known as dual-pilot **AGC**. A system in which one low frequency carrier and one high-frequency carrier are both monitored for AGC purposes. By monitoring two carrier levels in different parts of the spectrum, the system can compensate for changes in gain over the entire spectrum. ASC systems tend not to be used in newer designs due to cost and the reduced need due to the relatively short cascades used with HFC architectures.

Attenuation A measure of the RF or optical signal loss (generally in dB) of a component, circuit, or cable.

Aural An adjective implying an RF or IF carrier that is modulated with an audio signal.

Availability A measure of the fraction of time that a circuit or system is available to carry signals.

Azimuth The compass heading of an antenna, measured in degrees clockwise from North.

Backbone Point-to-point or ring connections between headends or linking headends and major hubs in a cable system. Often signals traveling in the backbone are not in the same format used to deliver services to homes (e.g., digital baseband).

Balun Balanced-to-unbalanced. A device that converts a transmission between balanced and unbalanced media.

Bandpass filter A filter than passes only the frequencies within some band

Bandstop filter A filter that passes all frequencies except those within some band.

Bandwidth efficiency The ratio of bits per second transmitted through a communications channel to the channel bandwidth in Hz. The units are b/s/Hz.

Baseband A signal not modulated onto an RF carrier. In video, refers to the visual signal as it is handled before being modulated onto an RF carrier.

BellCore Bell Communications Research. The Research and Development arm of the Bell Telephone companies. Now known as Telcordia, it is no longer owned by the telephone companies.

BER Bit error rate. A measure of the proportion of the bits in a datastream that are corrupted in transmission.

Binary Representation of a number by a series of elements (usually called "bits") that can take on only one of two values. Contrast binary representation with our normal base 10 representation of numbers, where each element representing the number can take on any of ten values.

Bit A single binary data element having a value of either 1 or 0, usually represented by two different voltage levels.

Bit rate The number of bits of data transmitted per second.

Bit stuffing The process of adding extra data bits to a bit stream to get the data rate up to the transmission data rate. Bit stuffing is practiced when the incoming datastreams have a total bit rate less than that demanded by the channel.

Block conversion A technique for putting more signals on a return optical path by converting some incoming signals to alternate frequency bands.

BPON Broadband passive optical network. A protocol for FTTH developed by the ITU. It is being replaced by GPON. The downstream wire rate is 622 Mb/s, and the upstream wire rate is 155 Mb/s.

BPSK Bi-phase shift keying. A digital modulation method in which the phase of a carrier is changed by 180 degrees to represent transmission of a 1 or a 0.

Bridger An amplifier (or module within a larger amplifier station) that is fed a sample of the trunk input signal and is used to create a distribution leg.

Broadband   As used in the cable industry, refers to the ability to frequency division multiplex many signals in a wide bandwidth of RF frequencies, using an HFC network.

CableLabs Cable Television Laboratories.   The research consortium of the cable television operating companies.

Carrier, or RF carrier.   A signal on which another, lower-frequency signal is modulated in order to transport the lower-frequency signal to another location.

Carrier-to-noise (C/N) ratio   In analog visual transmission, the ratio, usually expressed in dB, between the RMS power present in the visual carrier during sync tips, to the RMS noise power in 4 MHz. In cable television work, the term implies a measurement made at radio frequencies. Contrast with S/N, measured at baseband. In digital transmission, the "carrier" level is the average power of the signal, as opposed to the maximum (sync tip) power used as the reference in analog transmission. **Noise** is measured in the noise bandwidth of the receiver, about 6 MHz for 256 QAM. For digital transmission, C/N is often expressed normalized to 1 b/s, and abbreviated E_b/N_0.

CARS Cable antenna relay service.   The official FCC designation for a set of microwave frequencies and service category reserved for the use of cable television companies.

Cascade   A configuration in which a signal passes through more than one stage or system. In cable usage, it usually refers to the system of line amplifiers through which the RF signals pass between the optical node and the subscriber. It can also refer to multiple stages of amplification or filtering through which a signal passes.

Cat 5 Category 5 cable.   A data and voice transmission cable consisting of four pairs of twisted cables having a characteristic impedance of 100 Ω.

CEA Consumer Electronics Association.   A trade and promotion organization representing the needs of consumer electronics manufacturers and dealers. It is no longer associated with the EIA.

Channel   A range of frequencies assigned to a signal in an FDM transmission system. In North America, analog video and most other downstream channels are 6 MHz wide and correspond to one of the allocation forms defined in the CEA-542-B standard.

Characteristic impedance   The impedance of a transmission line such that, if terminated in a pure resistance of the same value, the return loss would be infinite. That is, the cable would "look" to a driving circuit, as a resistor of the characteristic impedance.

Chirp   A property of directly modulated optical transmitters whereby the normal amplitude modulation of the optical level is accompanied by an incidental wavelength modulation.

Chroma, or chrominance.   Refers to the color information in a television signal, as opposed to the luminance (black and white) and aural (sound) portions.

Chroma-luma delay   A form of distortion of analog video signals in which the time of arrivals of the luma (black and white) and chroma (color) signals are offset, resulting in color information being shifted with respect to the black and white outline. Also called chrominance delay.

CIN Composite intermodulation noise. Noise-like distortion products resulting from even- or odd-order mixing among RF signals, at least one of which is digitally modulated.

Clipping A phenomenon where signal voltage or current peak is sharply limited at some value (e.g., in directly modulated DFB laser diode transmitters).

Coax, short name for coaxial cable. Used extensively for transmission of RF and baseband signals. The cable consists of an inner conductor on which signal voltage is impressed with respect to the shield. The center conductor is surrounded by a dielectric, then a shield. Frequently an insulation layer surrounds the shield.

Coaxial distribution The portion of the broadband cable television distribution network that starts at the node and terminates at the tap. Sometimes the drop system is included in the definition.

Color subcarrier A signal in an analog TV signal that carries color information.

Combiner A frequency-independent device comprising three or more ports used to combine two or more signals. It is identical to a splitter, except for the direction of use.

Compression A number of techniques for reducing the bandwidth needed to transmit a signal, by removing unnecessary or redundant information from the signal.

Crosstalk In either coaxial FDM or optical WDM systems, a situation in which information on one carrier is present in the demodulated signal from another carrier. In coaxial systems, cross-modulation is a form of crosstalk.

CSO Composite second order. A form of distortion generated by amplifiers and other devices handling multiple RF signals. It is second-order distortion that combines signals at frequencies A and B, to create new signal components as frequencies A $\pm$ B. Sometimes expressed numerically as the ratio of carrier to distortion product, or C/CSO.

CTB Composite triple beat. A form of distortion generated by amplifiers and other devices handling multiple RF signals. It is a third-order distortion product that combines signals at frequencies A, B, and C to create new signal components at frequencies A $\pm$ B $\pm$ C and 2A $\pm$ B. Sometimes expressed numerically as the ratio of carrier to distortion product, or C/CTB.

CWDM Wavelength division multiplexing in which the optical carriers are spaced 20 nm apart.

dB Decibel—a measure of the relative strength of two signals. Defined as 10 times the logarithm (to base 10) of the ratio of the two power levels in any consistent units, such as watts, or 20 times the logarithm of the ratio of the voltage or current levels, when measured in circuits of the same characteristic impedance.

dBm Decibels with respect to 1 milliwatt. A unit of RF signal strength used in satellite work and other communications applications.

dBmV Decibels with respect to one millivolt in a 75-ohm system. The unit of RF power used in cable television work in North America. In a 75-ohm system, 0 dBmV = −48.75 dBm.

Decibel See **dB**.

Demodulation The complementary process to modulation. Recovery of information modulated onto a carrier.

Demodulator A device used by cable television systems to convert an RF modulated video and/or audio signal to baseband.

DFB laser Distributed feedback. A laser technology in which the wavelength of the laser is set by the distance between reflecting surfaces at each end of the laser cavity, augmented by a grating running the length of the cavity.

Digital return A return path from a node to a headend, whereby the return signals are digitized and the digital signal is transmitted to the headend, where it is converted back to analog/RF form.

Digital television Television signals transmitted using digital techniques in which video levels are converted to digital states that approximate the original signal's analog level. As used in the consumer world, it also implies compressing the signal to minimize the transmission bandwidth required.

Digital video Representation of video signals in digital format. It does not necessarily imply a compressed video signal.

Diplex filter A filter used to separate RF signals into one of two paths, based on the frequency of the signals. Can also be used to combine signals that exist in different frequency bands.

Direct pick-up, or DPU. The characteristic of a TV or VCR that a signal is picked up off-the-air in the device, creating interference with the signal being received via cable.

Directional coupler A three-port device for unequally dividing signal between two paths. Can also be used to combine signals with more loss in one input than in the other, with the signal from the high-loss port being routed to only one of the other two ports.

Directivity In a tap or directional coupler, the difference in sensitivity to upstream and downstream signals, as measured at the side port.

Dispersion The variation of transmission velocity due to some controlling parameter; most commonly in optical transmission, as a function of wavelength (chromatic dispersion).

Distribution The broadband portion of a cable television network extending from the point where the broadband spectrum is created in the same format as it will be received by subscribers (e.g., in a simple star HFC network, the distribution system starts at the input to the linear optical transmitter).

DOCSIS Data-Over-Cable Service Interface Specification. The formal name of the cable modem specification produced by a consortium led by **CableLabs**.

Downstream Signal flow from a headend toward subscribers.

DPU See **direct pick-up**.

Drop The portion of the distribution plant between the tap and the individual subscriber's home.

DWDM Wavelength division multiplexing in which the optical carriers are spaced 50 to 200 GHz apart (about 0.4 to 1.6 nm).

EDFA Erbium-doped fiber amplifier. The most common technology used to construct optical amplifiers for cable systems.

Egress A measure of the degree to which signals from the nominally closed coaxial cable system are transmitted through the air. Also known as signal leakage.

EIA Electronic Industries Alliance. A trade organization in Washington that represents companies that manufacture electronic equipment.

EIRP Effective isotropic radiated power. The total power supplied to an antenna, multiplied by the gain of the antenna in a certain direction.

Elevation (A) The number of feet that a location is above mean sea level (AMSL). (B) The number of degrees by which an antenna is tilted upwards from a horizontal plane.

Error correction In data transmission, the technique of adding extra bits to a transmitted signal, with the extra bits being used to detect and correct errors in the transmission.

Ethernet A popular layer-2 protocol used for interconnecting data equipment.

Express feeder An untapped coaxial line between two amplifiers in the coaxial portion of an HFC distribution system.

External modulation A method of modulating a fiber-optic transmitter by operating the laser at a constant output level, and sending the output through an external modulator.

Extinction ratio In a binary laser transmitter, the ratio between the maximum light output in one binary state, to the minimum light output on the other binary state.

Fabry–Perot laser A laser technology in which the wavelength of the laser is set by the distance between reflecting surfaces at each end of the laser cavity.

Failure rate The per-unit average rate at which a group of similar devices will randomly fail during their normal service life. Usually expressed in fraction, percentage per year, or parts per million (PPM).

FCC Federal Communications Commission. The governmental body in the United States that oversees telecommunications. In other countries, the corresponding body may be called the Department of Communications or may be part of a Ministry of Posts, Telegraph and Telecommunications.

F-Connector The RF connector commonly used to attach drop cables to taps and other devices.

FDM Frequency division multiplexing. The process of combining signals modulated on carriers of differing frequencies to create a signal spectrum for transmission or optical modulation.

Feeder The portion of the coaxial subnetworks that starts at an amplifier fed by an express feeder or trunk and supplies signals directly to subscriber taps.

Filtering   In communications, usually refers to the transmission of power in some frequency range(s) combined with the nontransmission of power in other frequency range(s). In computer use, may also refer to the elimination of certain types of information, with passage of other types.

Flat loss   The loss in a cable plant that is not a function of frequency. Typically, taps and attenuators have flat loss, as contrasted to coaxial cable, whose loss is approximated as being proportional to the square root of frequency.

FM/AM conversion FM to AM conversion.   A type of distortion to a modulated signal, in which frequency modulation is translated into amplitude modulation.

Forward   Downstream transmission of cable signals.

Forward error correction (FEC)   In data transmission, a process by which additional data are added; that is, are derived from the payload by an assigned algorithm. It allows the receiver to determine whether certain classes of errors have occurred in transmission, and in some cases, allows other classes of errors to be corrected.

Fourier series   A mathematical expression relating the time domain representation of a periodic waveform with the frequency domain representation. It shows that any periodic waveform may be expressed as a series of harmonically related sine and cosine waves. (Sine and cosine waves have the same shape, but are shifted in phase by 90°.)

Frequency agile   The ability to operate on more than one frequency (but not simultaneously).

Frequency response   The gain as a function of frequency through a system or device, relative to the defined ideal. In the case of a cable distribution system, this is also known as peak-to-valley response or **P/V**.

Fresnel zone   In a microwave path, this describes a hypothetical ring centered on the path such that the distance from transmitter to ring to receiver is one-half wavelength longer than the distance from transmitter to receiver.

FSAN Full service access network.   A standard for passive optical networks based on ATM.

FTF Fiber-to-the-feeder.   A distribution architecture in which fiber nodes feed coaxial feeder lines without any intervening coaxial trunk links.

FTTC Fiber-to-the-curb.   A distribution architecture in which directly fiber-fed termination units are shared by a number of dwellings. FTTC implies fiber to within a few thousand feet of the home, with DSL being used to carry data from there to the home.

FTTH Fiber-to-the-home.   A delivery technology in which signals are delivered from the headend to the home completely in the optical domain.

GE-PON Gigabit Ethernet passive optical network.   Also known as EPON (Ethernet passive optical network) or EFM (Ethernet in the first mile). A protocol for FTTH developed by the IEEE. It is used extensively in Asia and in other parts of the world. It features symmetrical wire rates of 1.25 Gb/s.

GPON Gigabit passive optical network.   A protocol for FTTH developed by the ITU and the announced next generation of technology to be deployed by Verizon.

Features a downstream wire speed of 2.488 Gb/s and an upstream wire rate of 1.244 Gb/s.

Group delay   Generally, the deviation from linear phase shift versus frequency through a circuit or network. This can occur due to reflections in a network. It is also a property of many practical filters that signal power near the edge of the passband are delayed in traversing the filter, with respect to signals away from the edge. This gives rise to waveform distortion, which can damage both analog and digital signals.

Hard cable, sometimes called hard line. An informal term applied to the solid-jacketed coaxial cable used in the coaxial distribution portion of a cable system ahead of the subscriber tap. Also applied as an adjective to that portion of the distribution system.

HDTV High-definition television.   Television with significantly more picture information (resolution) than that provided by a good NTSC or PAL television signal. While the definition of HDTV is nonspecific, it usually implies about twice the resolution in both the horizontal and vertical direction, and wide aspect ratio.

Headend   The point at which all programming is collected and formatted for placement on the cable system.

HFC Hybrid fiber-coax.   A network for transmitting signals modulated onto RF carriers, which consists of RF carriers modulated onto optical carriers and transmitted on fiber-optic cable, followed by transmission of the RF carriers on coaxial cable medium. The majority of cable plants built since the early 1990s use this architecture.

High pass filter   A filter that passes all frequencies above its cutoff frequency, but not below.

HRC Harmonically related coherent.   A method of establishing picture carriers on a cable plant, such that all carriers are harmonics of a single fundamental frequency close to 6 MHz.

Hub   A point in a distribution system where signals are converted to the form used to transmit them to subscribers. If a hub system is used, typically each hub will supply signals to a number of nodes.

IEEE Institute of Electrical and Electronics Engineers.   A professional organization of technologists interested in all aspects of electrical engineering.

IIN Interferometric intensity noise.   Noise in an optical link caused by the mixing of direct and doubly reflected signals in the optical detector diode.

Image response   The response of a tuner to signals in a portion of the spectrum separated from the IF by the local oscillator frequency, but on the wrong side of the local oscillator.

Index of refraction   The ratio of the speed at which light is transmitted in a vacuum to its speed in a material. It is a property of any material that can transmit light.

Ingress   Over-air signals that are inadvertently coupled into the nominally closed coaxial cable distribution system.

Internal modulation A method of modulating a fiber-optic transmitter by directly varying the bias current on the laser diode with the modulating information.

IRC Incrementally related coherent. A method of establishing picture carriers on a cable plant such that all carriers are spaced 6 MHz apart based on a master oscillator, but the carrier frequencies are offset 1.25 MHz from harmonics of 6 MHz.

Isolation In a tap or directional coupler, the difference between the amount of signal coupled to the side port and the directivity.

JEC Joint Engineering Committee. A joint committee (no longer active) of the EIA-CEMA and the NCTA that developed several standards in use by the two industries, such as the ANSI/EIA-542 band plan.

Laser In the context of cable systems, the device used to convert electrical signals to optical signals.

LE Line extender. A single-input, single-output amplifier used to boost signals in a coaxial distribution plant.

Long loop ALC Long loop automatic level control. A technique practiced in most systems using upstream RF transmission. The headend measures the RF level from each upstream transmitter and signals the upstream transmitter at the home to increase or decrease its power output until the correct level is received at the headend.

Low pass filter A filter that passes all frequencies below its cutoff frequency but none above.

Luminance, or luma. Referring to the black and white portion of the television signal, as opposed to the chrominance (color) and aural (sound) portions.

MER Modulation error ratio. A measurement of the quality of a digital modulated signal, which defines the average error between the proper location of all points in the constellation and their actual location.

Microreflections Small reflections occurring within both the coaxial distribution and drop portions of a cable plant. They can lead to impaired analog reception, group delay, and errors in digital signals.

Modal dispersion In a multimode fiber, the variation of transmission time among the various possible paths for the light.

Modulation The process of imposing information on an RF carrier by varying some parameter of the carrier. The parameters that can be varied are amplitude, frequency, or phase.

Modulator A device used by cable television systems to convert a baseband video and/or audio signal from baseband to the RF channel on which it is to be transmitted.

MPEG Motion Picture Experts Group. A group that developed standards for digital decompression of television pictures. The second generation of this standard, MPEG-2 is used for transmission of digital television in all parts of the world that have introduced such transmission. MPEG-4 is a newer standard being deployed in certain applications.

MPEG-2 The set of digital video decoding rules that form the basis of off-air and cable TV digital video transmission.

MPEG-4 An advanced set of digital video decoding rules. The basic MPEG-4 is intended to provide for very low data rate transmission of less than entertainment-grade video. MPEG-4 level 10 (also known as AVC, advanced video coding) is intended for entertainment-grade video. Compare with **MPEG-2**.

MSO Multiple system operator. A company that owns more than one separate cable system.

MTBF Mean time between failure. A measure of the average time interval between circuit restoration from a previous failure and the onset of the next failure in a network.

MTTR Mean time to restore. A measure of the average time required to restore proper network/circuit operation after a failure.

Multimode An optical fiber that supports more than one transmission path and thus has a transmission delay whose uncertainty increases with length, thereby limiting bandwidth.

Multipath A condition in which an over-the-air signal may reach a receiver via more than one path from a transmitter, leading to degraded reception. Applies to all transmission systems and frequencies.

Multiplex Use of a single data path for more than one set of data.

Multiplexing The combining of multiple independent signals into one signal path for transmission. Cable systems operate in a *frequency* multiplexing mode, in which signals at different frequencies are combined in one signal path. Another example is *time division* multiplexing, where multiple signals share the same path but are segregated in terms of time. A third example is *wavelength division multiplexing* in which signals modulated on different optical wavelengths share use of a single fiber.

Mux See **multiplex**.

NCTA National Cable & Telecommunications Association. A trade organization that represents companies in the cable television industry.

NID Network interface device. One of many names for a box on the side of the house that contains any required interfaces between a telephone line, FTTH, or cable plant, and inside wiring.

Node (A) The portion of a coaxial cable plant served from one optical receiver. (B) The equipment that receives the linearly modulated FDM spectrum, converts it back to RF form, and transmits it into one or more of the coaxial distribution legs.

Noise Generally defined as undesired signals in a transmission channel. In television, the term is commonly applied to broadband thermal noise excluding discrete carriers and distortion products.

Noise figure The ratio, expressed in dB, of the noise produced by a device over and above the thermal noise produced in a matched resistor at the input to that device. Higher noise figure devices require a higher signal level to deliver a given signal-to-noise ratio.

NPR Noise power ratio.   A method of specifying the quality of a transmission path by loading it with noise, eliminating the noise in a narrow band, and measuring the amount of noise filled in by the transmission path.

NTSC National Television Systems Committee.   An entity that developed the analog TV system used in North America and elsewhere. There were actually two NTSCs: the first developed the monochrome transmission system and the second added color.

OpenCable   A set of industry standards intended to define the next-generation digital consumer devices used by the cable TV industry, encourage supplier competition, and create a retail hardware platform. OpenCable has now been rebranded as tru2way.

OMI Optical modulation index.   A measure of how much optical modulation is applied to a laser. It is usually stated in terms of how much of the range from the laser's quiescent bias point to cutoff is taken up by the signal. The OMI may be expressed in terms of per channel or composite signal.

P/V Peak-to-valley.   The peak-to-peak variation in the frequency response of a cable distribution network relative to the ideal response curve.

PacketCable   A set of interoperable interface specifications for delivering advanced, real-time multimedia services over two-way cable plant. PacketCable is built on top of DOCSIS.

Passband   The frequency or wavelength region passed by a filter.

Passive   A component that handles signals, but which requires no power of its own. Examples are taps and power inserters.

Peak-to-average ratio   In data transmission, the ratio, usually expressed in dB, between the peak power of a signal and the average power.

Phase noise   A distortion in which a carrier signal is subjected to random variations in phase.

Pilot   A signal on the distribution plant that is used either as a level or as a frequency reference. In some cases, the pilot is one of the normal analog picture carriers that has been so designated.

PMD Polarization mode dispersion.   In an optical fiber, a measure of the transmission time as a function of the orientation of the E-field of the light relative to the fiber.

POE Point-of-entry.   Equipment that is placed between the drop and inside wiring of a dwelling and which processes some or all of the signals for specific services. One application is cable telephony where the POE device interfaces standard analog in-home wiring to the RF distribution system. See **NID**.

Polarization   An expression of the orientation of the electric field in a radiated RF signal or an optical signal in single mode fiber.

PON Passive optical network.   An all-optical network that consists of nothing more than fiber-optic cable and splitters.

Port   A logical construct through which data are transferred from one process to another.

Power inserter A passive device used to add ac power to the center conductor of a coaxial cable for the purpose of powering active devices.

Power pack In a cable system, the module within an amplifier station (or other active equipment) that receives the power multiplexed with the RF signals on the distribution system and creates the voltages required by the station's internal circuits.

Power supply In a cable system, the device that receives power from the utility, processes it for use in the cable system, and inserts it into the coaxial plant through a power inserter.

Predistortion A technique for reducing distortion in a linear transmission system by intentionally generating distortion at the transmit end; this distortion will be canceled by the real distortion of the network.

PSK Phase shift keying. In data transmission, a modulation format that depends solely on differences in phase of a modulated signal to convey information.

QAM Quadrature amplitude modulation. A digital modulation method in which the value of a symbol consisting of multiple bits is represented by amplitude and phase states of a carrier. Typical types of QAM include 16 QAM (4 bits per symbol), 32 QAM (5 bits), 64 QAM (6 bits) and 256 QAM (8 bits).

QoS Quality of service. Techniques for ensuring the delivery of data in a reliable and timely manner.

QPSK Quadrature phase shift keying. A digital modulation method in which the state of a 2-bit symbol is represented by one of four possible phase states.

Quadrature At right angles. In transmission, often used to express independence between two signals.

Rain fade In a terrestrial or satellite microwave link, signal loss due to absorption and reflections caused by rain drops within the signal path.

Reflectometer A device used to determine the location of a fault in a cable by propagating a signal down the cable and reading any signal reflected. May be used for RF or optical transmission.

Refraction The process by which optical signals are transmitted through the interface between two dissimilar materials. See **index of refraction**.

Reliability The probability that a component or network will survive for some interval of time, therefore is inversely proportional to its failure rate.

Return loss A measure of the amount of incident power that is reflected back toward the opposite end of a cable from a termination or other discontinuity in the characteristic impedance of the cable.

Reverse See **upstream**.

RFoG Radio frequency over glass. A form of FTTH being developed within the SCTE that features RF modulation only of optical carriers in both directions, to and from the home.

RIN Relative intensity noise. A measure of the residual internal noise modulation of an optical transmitter. RIN often limits the attainable C/N of RF signals transmitted through an optical link.

Ring network   An architecture in which terminal points are connected in a continuous ring and each terminal is connected to both of its neighbors.

SBS Stimulated Brillouin scattering.   A mechanism that limits the amount of optical power at a single wavelength that can be transmitted through an optical fiber.

Scattering   In an optical network, scattering is any process by which light is briefly delayed, and then retransmitted. Forward scattering causes an overall slowing of the signal (see **index of refraction**), while scattering in other directions leads to signal loss and, sometimes, distortion.

SCTE Society of Cable Telecommunications Engineers.   A professional organization of technologists interested in cable telecommunications technology.

SDM Space division multiplexing.   The simultaneous use of the different physical portions of a network (e.g., nodes) to carry different signals at the same frequencies.

SDV Switched digital video.   A method of delivering video programming whereby a given program stream is only delivered to any given service group when at least one member of the group requests it.

Set-top converter   Also known as a set-top terminal. A device used with a subscriber's TV to allow reception of programs. It may tune channels the TV does not tune and may include descrambling circuitry. It also may include a digital decoder and auxiliary functions such as an electronic program guide.

Shot noise   In an optical link, noise at the optical receiver that is caused by the statistical variation in the arrival of photons.

Signal level   In analog television work, the RMS level of the picture carrier measured over the occupied bandwidth of the signal, during sync tips. In digital communications as practiced by the cable industry, it is the average level of the modulated signal or the level that would be read on a thermocouple-type RF power meter.

Signal-to-noise (S/N) ratio   In video work, the ratio between the video signal amplitude and the noise power measured in a reference bandwidth. Many variations in the definition of "signal" and "noise" exist, and the reader must exercise care that the definitions in use are accurately conveyed.

Single mode fiber   Optical fiber that supports only a single transmission path and thus offers a better-defined transmission delay.

Skin effect   The tendency of RF signals to travel near the surface of conductors.

Spectrum analyzer   A piece of test equipment used to plot amplitude versus frequency.

Splitter   A device having three or more ports, used to divide RF signal equally between two paths, without regard for the frequency of the signal. Can also be used to combine two signals.

SPM Self-phase modulation.   In an optical fiber, incidental phase modulation at high optical levels caused by variation of the index of refraction with the instantaneous power level of the optical signal.

SRL Structural return loss.   A measure of the degree to which signals are reflected from a length of cable as a function of frequency.

SRS Stimulated Ramon scattering.   A mechanism in fiber cable that caused transfer of power from a shorter wavelength to a longer wavelength if the wavelength separation is within a certain range.

Standard definition   Loosely defined, the picture definition associated with analog NTSC video or with digital video formats that yield roughly equivalent resolution.

Stopband   The frequency or wavelength region rejected by a filter.

Supertrunk   In a cable system, the signal transportation link used to connect the point where the FDM signal complex is created to local coaxial distribution networks. In an HFC network, linearly modulated optical links are used, but other systems use AML microwave or coaxial supertrunks.

Tap   The component installed in the distribution cable that diverts a portion of the downstream distribution signal and splits it to feed two to eight individual subscribers. In the reverse direction, it combines the signals from subscribers and inserts them into the upstream direction of the distribution cable.

TCP Transmission control protocol.   A connection-oriented, layer-4 protocol often used with IP to transmit data. Includes various mechanisms to enhance the probability that a packet will arrive.

TDM Time division multiplex.   A data transmission method in which a number of individual digital datastreams share a transmission channel, each occupying the channel for a portion of the total time.

TDMA Time division multiple access.   A data transmission method in which a number of individual transmitters in different locations share a transmission channel, each occupying the channel for a portion of the total time.

TDR Time domain reflectometer.   A device that measures the quality of a transmission line by transmitting a pulse, then measuring signals reflected as a function of time. The reflections indicate the distance to the point of reflection. TDRs can operate in either the electrical RF domain or in the optical domain.

Telcordia   The current name of what was formerly known as BellCore, now a privately owned body that sets standards used in the telephone industry.

TEM Transverse electric and magnetic.   A description of the normal field configuration for signals transmitted through coaxial cables.

Transition region   The frequency or wavelength region(s) of a filter that are between the passband and the stopband.

Trap   A passive coaxial component inserted in series with a drop line that blocks transmission of a specific frequency or range of frequencies. Used to block or enable specific channels or to tailor the services available in homes.

Trunk   (A) The untapped portion of a coaxial distribution network. Trunk links are typically operated at lower levels than distribution links to minimize distortions. (B) An amplifier module used in the trunk portion of a coaxial distribution system. (C) An amplifier station that contains a trunk module. It may also contain a bridger module if creating a distribution leg at that location is desired.

Unavailability   The fraction of time that a network or channel is unavailable for use. See **availability**.

UPC Ultra-polished connector.   An optical connector that minimizes loss and reflections by careful preparation and polishing of the fiber end, and alignment with the mating fiber.

Upstream   Signal flow from subscribers toward a headend.

UTP Unshielded twisted pair.   A data cable consisting of one or more twisted pairs without shielding. See **Cat 5**.

Video   In television work, this term is reserved to mean a baseband electrical signal that conveys information regarding picture content.

Visual   An adjective implying an RF or IF carrier that is modulated with a video signal.

VOD Video-on-demand.   A video service that allows users to select the program and exact start time interactively. In some embodiments, it allows VCR-like control of the playback (e.g., pause, rewind, fast-forward).

Wavelength   The distance traveled through a transmission medium by an RF or optical signal in a time equal to the inverse of the frequency (e.g., for a 1-GHz signal, the distance traveled in 1 ns). It is equal to the speed of propagation in the medium divided by the frequency.

Wavelength dispersion   In an optical fiber, the variation in transmission time as a function of the wavelength of the light.

W-curve   The variation of subscriber perceptibility of interfering signals in an analog television channel as a function of frequency within the channel boundaries. So called because of the shape of the curve, caused by extreme sensitivity to interfering signals occurring near the visual and chrominance carriers.

WDM Wavelength division multiplexing.   The use of an optical fiber to simultaneously carry signals at different wavelengths. Can also refer to a wavelength-sensitive device used to combine and separate optical signals at different wavelengths.

Wire rate   The actual data rate at which a signal is transferred on an interface, including all overhead.

XMOD Cross-modulation.   A type of distortion in which the amplitude modulation of one signal causes incidental amplitude modulation to another signal. XMOD is an odd-order distortion.